WRITTEN ON THE BODY

Written on the Body

The Tattoo in European and American History

Edited by
JANE CAPLAN

PRINCETON UNIVERSITY PRESS

PRINCETON, NEW JERSEY

Published in the United States, its dependencies, and Canada by
Princeton University Press, 41 William Street, Princeton, New Jersey, 08540

In the United Kingdom,
published by Reaktion Books Ltd
79 Farringdon Road
London EC1M 3JU, UK

www.reaktionbooks.co.uk

First published 2000

Designed by Philip Lewis

Printed and bound in Great Britain by
Biddles Limited, Guildford and King's Lynn

Library of Congress Catalog Card Number 99–069245

ISBN 0–691–05722–2
       0–691–05723–0 (pbk.)

http://pup.princeton.edu

Contents

Notes on the Editor and Contributors

CLARE ANDERSON is a lecturer in the Department of Economic and Social History, University of Leicester. Her research interests include crime and punishment in colonial Mauritius and the transportation of Indian convicts overseas, on which she has published a number of articles. She has recently published *Convicts in the Indian Ocean: Transportation from South Asia to Mauritius, 1815–52*.

SUSAN BENSON is a Fellow of New Hall, Cambridge University and an affiliated lecturer in the Department of Social Anthropology, Cambridge University. She has worked on issues of race and ethnicity in Britain and is the author of *Ambiguous Ethnicity: Interracial Families in London* (1981). She has also worked on gender, Islam and colonial history in northern Nigeria. Increasingly, these and other interests have led her to focus upon issues of power, corporeality and personhood, of which her current interest in bodily inscription is one aspect.

JAMES BRADLEY is a Research Fellow at the Wellcome Unit for the History of Medicine at the University of Glasgow. His main areas of historical research are spa treatment, alternative medicine, the body, criminal identities and sport. He co-edited *Representing Convicts: New Perspectives on Convict Forced Labour Immigration* (1997) with Dr Ian Duffield. He has been a co-editor of the journal *Australian Studies* since 1996.

JANE CAPLAN is Marjorie Walter Goodhart Professor of European History at Bryn Mawr College, Pennsylvania. Her publications include *Government Without Admin-istration: State and Civil Service in Weimar and Nazi Germany* (1988), and she has edited *Nazism, Fascism and the Working Class: Essays by Tim Mason* (1995) and *Reevaluating the Third Reich* (1993). She is currently writing a book on the history of individual identity documentation in nineteenth-century Europe, and has co-edited a volume of essays *Documenting Individual Identity. The Development of State Practices since the French Revolution* (forthcoming).

IAN DUFFIELD is a Senior Lecturer in the Department of History, University of Edinburgh, and has published extensively on convict transportation and on African Diaspora History. His major publication to date in the former field is co-edited with James Bradley, *Representing Convicts: New Perspectives on Convict Forced Labour Immigration* (1997).

JULIET FLEMING is a lecturer in the Faculty of English at Cambridge University and a Fellow of Trinity Hall, Cambridge. Her essay in this volume is taken from her current book project, which investigates writing in early modern England.

ALAN GOVENAR is a writer, folklorist, photographer and film-maker. He is President of Documentary Arts, a non-profit organization to broaden public knowledge and appreciation of the arts of different cultures in all media. Dr Govenar is the author of twelve books including *Stoney Knows How: Life as a Tattoo Artist*; *American Tattoo*; *Flash from the Past: Classic American Tattoo Designs 1890–1965*; *The Early Years of Rhythm and Blues*; and *Portraits of Community: African-American Photography in Texas*. He has produced and directed numerous television documentaries, including two films on tattooing: *Stoney Knows How* and *The Human Volcano*.

HARRIET GUEST is co-director of the Centre for Eighteenth Century Studies at the University of York. She has published several essays on Cook's voyages and edited, with Nicholas Thomas and Michael Dettelbach, Johann Reinhold Forster's *Observations Made During a Voyage Round the World* (1996). Her most recent publication is *Small Change: Women, Learning, Patriotism, 1760–1810* (2000).

MARK GUSTAFSON is an Associate Professor of Classics at Calvin College in Grand Rapids, Michigan, where he teaches Greek, Latin and Ancient History. His main area of interest is the later Roman Empire. Current projects include a monograph on the conflict between Lucifer of Cagliari and Constantius II, various articles on Roman tattooing (which may be collected into a longer work) and a literary history of Robert Bly's Sixties Press.

C. P. JONES is George Martin Lane Professor of Classics and History at Harvard University. His books include *Philostratus: Life of Apollonius of Tyana* (1971); *Plutarch and Rome* (1971); *The Roman World of Dio Chrysostom* (1978); *Culture and Society in Lucian* (1986); and *Kinship Diplomacy in the Ancient World* (1999).

CHARLES W. MACQUARRIE is an Associate Professor of English at Antelope Valley College in Lancaster, California. He was the 1996–7 Washington Fellow at Pembroke College Cambridge and visiting scholar in the department of Anglo-Saxon, Norse and Celtic. He was recently elected to the Society of Antiquaries of Scotland.

HAMISH MAXWELL-STEWART has a Ph.D from the University of Edinburgh. Since completing his doctorate he has worked in the Wellcome Unit for the History of Medicine, University of Glasgow, and is currently the Port Arthur Fellow, School of History and Classics, University of Tasmania. He is the author of a number of articles on the nature of convict culture and resistance.

STEPHAN OETTERMANN (D.Phil., University of Marburg) is a freelance journalist and curator whose main research interest is the history of popular entertainments. He has curated exhibitions on Georg Büchner, Georg Christoph Lichtenberg and

Friedrich Nietzsche. His books include *Zeichen auf der Haut. Geschichte der Tätowierung in Europa* (1979, 1985 and 1994), *Das Panorama. Geschichte eines Massenmediums* (1980), *Die Schaulust an Elefanten* (1982) and *Läufer und Vorläufer. Zu einer Kulturgeschichte des Laufsports* (1984). He is currently preparing a historical encyclopedia of popular entertainment.

JENNIPHER A. ROSECRANS is an advanced doctoral student in the Department of History at the University of Michigan and is presently in the final stages of writing her dissertation, 'More Mutable than Proteus: A History of Body Alteration in Early Modern England', funded by a Mellon Doctoral Dissertation Fellowship.

ABBY M. SCHRADER is an Assistant Professor of History at Franklin and Marshall College in Lancaster, Pennsylvania. She is at work on a book-length manuscript titled *The Languages of the Lash: Corporal Punishment and the Construction of Identity in Imperial Russia.*

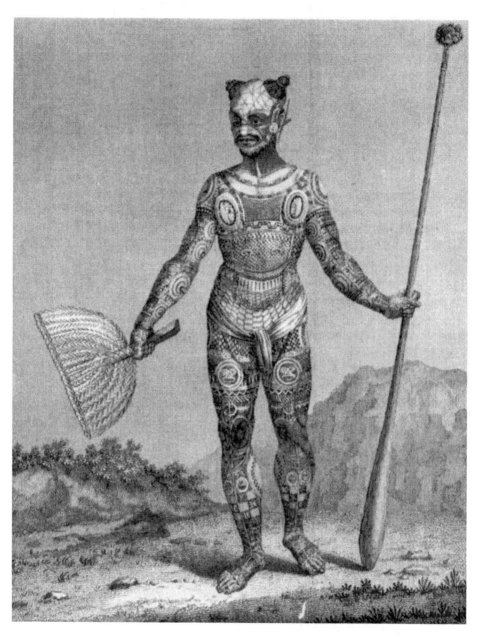

J. Storer, *An Inhabitant of the Island of Nukahiva*, 1813, engraving. British Library, London.

Introduction

JANE CAPLAN

Tattooing is one of many forms of irreversible body alteration, including scarification, cicatrization, piercing and branding, and it is the probably the oldest and most widespread of these. Physical evidence for the practice survives from the late fourth millennium BC in Europe and from about 2000 BC in Egypt, and tattooing can be found in virtually all parts of the world at some time.[1] The essays in this collection explore the history, representation and interpretation of the tattoo in Western culture – Europe and the USA – between antiquity and the present day. To invoke the 'Western' tattoo, as this book does, may therefore invite questions about the internal coherence of such a concept, about its demarcation from tattooing practices in other cultures and from comparable forms of body marking and modification. Does it make sense to distinguish it from similar practices, or to isolate the European tattoo and its American derivative from the rest of the world? The short answer is that tattooing alone has had an extended, if discontinuous history in Western culture. At the same time, it has occupied an uneasy and ambiguous status within a dominant culture in which body-marking was usually treated as punitive and stigmatic rather than honourable or decorative. Partly for this reason, there is a deficit of knowledge on the subject, compared with the societies where its status has been more secure or its aesthetics more complex, notably Polynesia and Japan.[2]

There is therefore no lack of literature on all forms of bodily decoration and alteration in cultural anthropology, but the kind of historical analysis of European tattooing offered in this book has a rather less solid foundation on which to build.[3] This history remains barely researched and widely misunderstood, and has achieved clearer definition only in the context of the new history and sociology of bodies and cultures. By addressing themselves to the details and complications of this little known history, the authors of these essays make their own contribution to the larger study of the inscriptions and instabilities of the human body across cultures and times. We do this in the knowledge of what is usually called the 'tattoo renaissance' that has swept through Europe and the USA in the past few years: that verb is not too strong to describe the centripetal force with which tattooing has recently emerged from the margins of Western culture. The new interest in the practice and history of tattooing generated by this movement has been met by a wave of new publications, and in its own way the present collection is also a response to the growth of interest in the subject.[4] But it differs from most of the existing work on the subject in its objectives and its scope.

Much of the recently published literature on tattooing is intended to illustrate the range and variety of tattooing in the past and the present, and to 'illustrate' it literally, for images tend to outweigh text in these publications. The photographic images are usually of extremely high quality and the work of contemporary tattooists figures prominently, presenting a new aesthetics of the decorated body and proclaiming the tattoo's arrival in commercial and popular culture. But the declared aim of this kind of publication is not the scholarly retrieval and evaluation of historical sources, nor the kind of precise textual and cultural analysis offered in the present collection of essays. Rather, the recent popular accounts of tattooing make a virtue of synthesizing a broad history of tattooing, as Susan Benson points out in this volume (Chapter 14). They forge a chain of fixed historical and cultural markers in order to anchor and legitimize the practice, with the reasonable hope of rescuing tattooing from its dishonourable and penal reputation in the modern West by associating it with the tribal cultures in which it has been socially integral, highly valued or aesthetically vital. Generalizing the tattoo as a meaningful historical and cultural performance is a way of reclaiming it for contemporary practice.

The popular synthetic histories therefore contain an important double implication – that tattooing *can* be culturally integral but that it has not enjoyed this status in modern Western culture. This suggests a cultural or historical rupture in the status of the European tattoo: once the tattoo was part of 'our' culture; then it was not. A concept of the tattoo's discontinuity or instability also suffuses the present essays, and I want to explore it further in this introduction. The point has been acutely captured by the anthropologist Alfred Gell, one of the most perceptive contemporary scholars of tattooing, whose work is repeatedly invoked in these essays. Gell distinguishes between the deeply embedded tattooing practices of the Polynesian cultures that are his principal object of study, and what he calls the 'unanchored' and historically contingent Western tattoo, which, by contrast with Polynesia, played no role in 'the fundamental mechanisms of social reproduction'. His principal hypothesis here is that in Polynesian societies tattooing 'played such an integral part in the organization and functioning of major institutions (politics, warfare, religion and so on) that the description of tattooing practices becomes, inevitably, a description of the wider institutional forms within which tattooing was embedded', and that it 'made

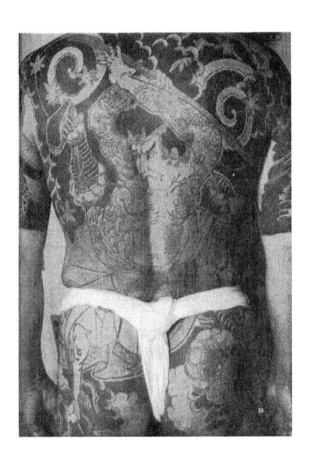

Contemporary Japanese tattoo of Kyumonryu Shishin, a hero of the classic epic *Suikoden*.

possible the realization of a distinctive type of social and political being'.[5] He then develops a complex schema of the functions of tattooed skin in both 'preliterate tribal societies [and] repressed or marginalized minorities within more complex state systems',[6] drawing on psychoanalytic interpretations of the skin's functions advanced by Jean-Thierry Maertens and Didier Anzieu. Gell seeks to do justice both to the specificity of these tattooing practices and to the invariant technical character of the tattoo as a particular elaboration of the skin's surface, an indelible insertion that is both visible and out of reach. This elaboration produces, in a kind of exchange between interiority and exteriority, 'a paradoxical double skin', which is thus made available to carry the culturally specific meanings assigned to the fundamental distinction between interior and exterior.

This theorization of the tattoo (which I have radically compressed here) is suggestive, because it captures a quality of ambiguity which the essays in this collection also examine. Gell's analysis turns on the idea that there is an

A Female British Pict,
engraving.

interaction or play between the 'interior' and 'exterior' aspects of the tattoo, an indelible mark that is simultaneously on and under the surface of the skin. This offers a fertile way of coming to grips with the multiple uses and meanings of the tattoo in Western history. The precise topology of the tattoo is developed most explicitly here by Juliet Fleming (Chapter 5) and Susan Benson (Chapter 14), but in different ways every essay in this collection addresses the question of how cultural meaning is derived from or attached to the tattoo's visible and indelible physical status on the body. The tattoo occupies a kind of boundary status on the skin, and this is paralleled by its cultural use as a marker of difference, an index of inclusion and exclusion. These projects of differentiation between insiders and outsiders can be found in all the periods and societies discussed in these essays. Thus the tattoo has been taken to mark off entire 'civilizations' from their 'barbarian' or 'savage' neighbours; to declare a convict's criminality, whether by branding him as a punishment or because he has inverted this penal practice by acquiring voluntary tattoos (thereby, ironically, marking himself); and more generally to inscribe various kinds of group membership, often in opposition to a dominant culture. Yet despite the fact that the tattoo is visible and indelible in a physical sense, the structures of exclusion and inclusion that it appears to support are also undermined by the conceptual instability inherent in a mark which is neither quite inside nor quite outside the skin. The tattoo's unfixity seems to be at its most blatant in Western society, as Gell notes, because it has not been fully integrated into Western culture, unlike the Polynesian societies that Gell discusses. Lacking any role in social reproduction, therefore, the European tattoo has been free to roam at will, so to speak, and opens itself to the variety of appropriations and inversions explored in this book.

A similar quality of mobility is reflected too in a dialectic of visibility and invisibility in the recorded history of tattooing in Europe. The tattoo is made apparent in the archaeological and written record between prehistoric times until some point in the early Middle Ages; it then becomes virtually invisible for several hundred years, before re-entering the field of vision in the eighteenth century. One should not read this long gap simply as a defect in the historical record, an empty space that can be made good or filled in by painstaking historical reparation, though that is certainly part of the project of this book. But it is also, I would argue, emblematic of the nomadic and contested status of the European tattoo itself, its character of always being in transit from or to the multiple horizons of a self-centred world, of circulating most actively on the margins where it is least visible. The tattoo has been a promiscuously travelling sign in Western culture, moving literally on the homeless bodies of the slaves, criminals, pilgrims, sailors, soldiers and transported convicts who populate these essays, and typically represented in official discourse as something that has arrived from somewhere else – from another culture, another country, another epoch.[7]

The most familiar account of the tattoo's travels accords great significance to the eighteenth-century European encounter with the tattooing cultures of the south Pacific. The status of this encounter, which apparently signals the crucial moment of rupture and departure in the history of tattooing in the West, is critical for any attempt to understand this history, and it deserves close attention here. Gell follows a well-trodden path in ascribing the status of modern Western tattooing to the European expansion into the Pacific. This gave Europe not only the word 'tattoo' (derived from the Polynesian root *tatu* or *tatau*, meaning to mark or strike), but also, he argues, a powerful impulse to ascribe tattooing to the 'ethnic Other' beyond Europe and hence, by a familiar dialectic of derivation and reascription, to the 'class Other' within this culture too.

That the Polynesian encounter was a critical event in the European imagination of its cultural identity and boundaries is undeniable, and the intricacies of that moment are subjected to subtle analysis in Harriet Guest's essay in this collection (Chapter 6). Nevertheless, it is also possible to embrace this without being persuaded by the further proposition that the Pacific encounter was the *origin* of the estranged status of tattooing in the West. For there is an alternative argument, which is developed in several of these essays, that this estrangement was already inscribed in the European tattoo well before the eighteenth century, because tattooing itself was already present. In this trajectory, the Pacific encounter is not originary, as we shall see. Moreover, it turns out to be a somewhat benign episode, by contrast with the more vicious reappropriations of the primitive that were responsible for relocating the tattoo on to the European social Other a century later. The scope and power of that process are attested by the large group of essays in this collection – by Clare Anderson (Chapter 7), Hamish Maxwell-Stuart and Ian Duffield (Chapter 8), James Bradley (Chapter 9), Jane Caplan (Chapter 10) and Abby Schrader (Chapter 11) – that describe in detail the nineteenth-century dynamics of criminal subjection and convict tattooing in Europe, its colonies and Russia. It was this process that captured the tattoo in the full glare of 'official' publicity and regulation, and also thrust it onto the margins of polite society where it lived the uneasily tolerated life described here by Stephan Oettermann (Chapter 12) and Alan Govenar (Chapter 13). I admit to some partiality in emphasizing these points, since my own interest is in the uneven conditions of this nineteenth-century reinscription.[8] But there is also more at stake here. The European practice of tattooing clearly did not originate in the Pacific, though it was heavily influenced by it: that much is difficult to dispute. But what we make of this is more debatable, and a pivotal theme of this collection.

The essays by C. P. Jones (Chapter 1) and Mark Gustafson (Chapter 2) demonstrate the entrenched use of tattooing by Greeks, Romans and Celts for penal and property purposes, to mark criminals and slaves. But they also show that this stigmatizing use was inverted when tattooing was appropriated by early Christians in Roman territories and, as Charles MacQuarrie argues in Chapter 3, by some Celtic Christians, as a voluntary and honourable token of their servitude to Christ. Apparently modelled on Christ's stigmata, the Christian inversion of tattooing and some other forms of physical chastisement complicated the status of bodily marking in European culture, or rather medieval Christendom.[9] It rescued and potentially preserved a tradition of honourable tattooing in a culture which otherwise deprecated bodily alteration and reserved gross physical marks like branding, mutilation and flogging for punitive purposes. Perhaps it was in recognition of the religious associations of tattooing that this form of bodily marking was apparently excluded from the otherwise versatile repertoire of corporal punishment in medieval Europe. But this can be no more than speculation. The hard evidence for the persistence of religious or other traditions of tattooing within medieval Christendom seems too tenuous at this point to support an unimpeachable case for survival.[10]

The case is much stronger, however, for a continuity of tattooing among Christian communities on the fringes of Christian Europe, and from this it may be legitimate to draw some inferences about the situation within Europe itself. The well-attested traditions of tattooing among Christians in the Holy Land, Egypt and the Balkans seem more securely to be survivals of early Christian practices.[11] And there is ample evidence, discussed in a number of the essays in this collection, that early modern European pilgrims to Palestine who were tattooed with the Christian symbols available in Jerusalem and elsewhere brought their own marked bodies back home. Pilgrimage forges another link too, for it appears that pilgrims to the shrine of Loreto in Italy were acquiring commemorative tattoos there as early as the sixteenth century; reliable later evidence shows imagery consisting of numerous Christian insignia, including symbols of the Virgin Mary and St Francis, who were specially associated with the shrine.[12] It is tempting to suppose that other Christian pilgrimage sites within Europe, with their repertoire of badges and commemorative symbols, may have generated similar body-marking practices, though there is no conclusive evidence for this. And one could plausibly speculate that other Europeans on the move, perhaps sailors in the Mediterranean trade, may have picked up tattooing with religious emblems from Holy Land practices at some point.[13]

The path is far from clear, but this and other evidence converges to suggest that the return of tattooing to European culture and/or the reinvigoration of indigenous European practices can be pushed back two centuries before the Pacific expeditions. Whether or not they still had an indigenous tradition of their own to draw on, European sailors had certainly already known and practised tattooing as a result of their relations with other cultures in the sixteenth and seventeenth centuries. They had met tattooed peoples in North America and the Philippines, brought 'specimens' of them back to Europe, and attempted to make sense of their markings, as the essays by Juliet Fleming (Chapter 5) and Stephan Oettermann (Chapter 12) amply demonstrate, and some other particles of information can be added to their evidence. Thus Bernal Díaz del Castillo's history of the Spanish conquest of New Spain in 1519 mentions the acculturated Spaniard Gonzalo Guerrero, living in Cape Catoche with his pierced ears and 'embroidered' face.[14] A century and a half later, Lionel Wafer's account of his voyages to Darien not only describes the inhabitants' painted bodies but also explains how finer Figures . . . are imprinted deeper, after this manner. They first with the Brush and Colour make a rough Draught of the Figure they design; and then they prick all over with a sharp Thorn till the Blood gushes out; then they rub the place with their Hands, first dipp'd in the Colour they design; and the Picture so made is indelible.[15]

Wafer also makes it clear that Europeans were acquiring tattoos from the natives of the region:

One of my companions desired me once to get out of his Cheek one of these imprinted Pictures, which was made by the Negroes, his name was Bullman; which yet I could not effectually do, after much scarifying and fetching off a great part of the Skin.

Such descriptions exactly parallel the Jerusalem pilgrim accounts, and Wafer may also be the first European to have described the almost always ineffective attempts to remove a tattoo.

Historians who have studied tattoos on American sailors from the 1790s argue that tattooing must have been a well-established practice among

Pilgrim tattoos from the shrine of Loreto, Italy, from Catherine Pigorini-Beri, 'Le Tatouage religieux et amoureux au pèlerinage de N.D. de Lorette', *Archives de l'anthropologie criminelle et des sciences pénales*, XVI (1891).

eighteenth-century seafarers, predating the Pacific encounter. Although they do not cite the evidence described above, they argue on common-sense grounds that the tattoo is unlikely to have diffused into the American seafaring population from small expeditions made less than 30 years earlier, and that the images favoured by American sailors were firmly rooted in their own rather than Polynesian iconic traditions.[16] A tattooed eighteenth-century sailor or soldier would be marked not by the abstract patterns that decorated the face or covered the entire torso or limbs of a native American, a Marquesan or a Hawaiian, but by one or two small images – initials, hearts, a crucifix, a patriotic emblem, maritime or military insignia and so on – placed almost always on his hand or arm. Tattoo iconography, as Alan Govenar explains in his essay (Chapter 13), continued to exhibit the typical patterns of folk art. It conserved a formulary of relatively stable designs across the centuries, but also responded to changes in the surrounding culture by absorbing new images from printed sources and later from films.[17]

The same inference could be drawn from the French and Prussian soldiers for whom we have evidence of tattooing at least as far back as the Napoleonic Wars, and from the penal tattooing practised by English authorities around the same time, which is described by Clare Anderson (Chapter 7).[18] Something similar was also implied by Hester Lynch Piozzi in her account of her voyage to Italy in 1785–86, when she observed that

> one need not . . . wander round the world with Banks and Solander, or stare so at the accounts given us in Cook's Voyages of *tattowed Indians*, when Naples will shew one the effects of a like operation . . . on the broad shoulders of numberless Lazaroni.[19]

Piozzi described the Neapolitans'

> half-Indian custom of burning figures upon their skins with gunpowder . . . The man who rows you about this lovely bay, has perhaps the angel Raphael, or the blessed Virgin Mary, delineated on one brawny sunburnt leg, the saint of the town upon the other: his arms represent the Glory, or the seven spirits of God . . .

Despite this obviously Christian imagery, Piozzi associated these markings with a locally unique combination of pagan superstition, fixed on the figure of Janus/St Januarius, with what she saw as alien 'Mahometan' influences.

Such evidence may strengthen the claims for a pre-existing practice of tattooing, but Piozzi's diary exemplifies the complexities of this late eighteenth-century moment. Here is an English traveller who, not twenty years after Cook's first expedition, is perfectly *au fait* with the concept of

Scrimshaw sperm-whale tooth decorated with an image identified as an ancient Pict, 19th century, from E. N. Flayderman, *Scrimshaw and Scrimshanders. Whalers and Whalemen* (New Milford, CT, 1972).

Polynesian tattooing, but is describing Neapolitan tattoos that appear to be quite independent of this source. The circulation of literate knowledge about Polynesian tattooing was extremely rapid in Europe, so how do we know that the practice itself did not diffuse with comparable velocity and lodge itself into wholly new regions and population groups? It is impossible to answer this question definitively.

Still, the evidence supports neither continuity nor importation alone, but rather a process of convergence and reinforcement. It would be rash to dispute the mountain of evidence that shows the tattoo being propelled into a new quality of visibility from the end of the eighteenth century, through which it occupied new positions in European and US popular culture and official discourse. But it also seems clear that Europeans learned neither the technique nor the imagery of tattooing from Polynesian societies, but drew on local practices that existed well before the eighteenth century, whether these were indigenous or imported. And although a vocabulary derived from the Polynesian word *tatu* quickly made its way into European languages

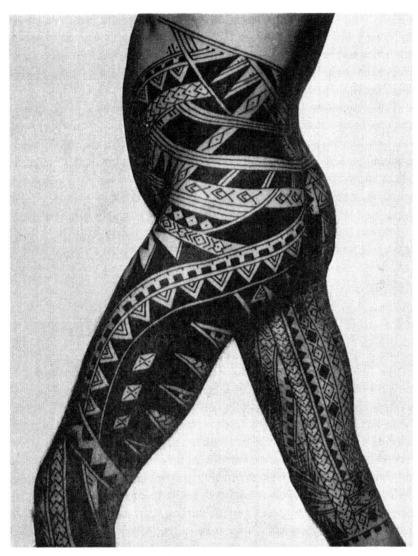

Tattoo by Alex Binnie, Into You, London, 1998.

from the 1790s, it was preceded and accompanied by an etymologically unrelated terminology that it did not entirely displace. This lexicon may also provide some cues for the location of tattooing in early modern European culture. Most terms carried connotations of pricking, piercing or stamping – for example, the English words 'pounce' and 'pink', the French *piqûre*, Dutch *prickschilderen* and *stechmalen*, German *stupfen* and *stempeln*, Italian *marco, nzito, segno* and also, tellingly, *devozione*.[20] In English, the term 'carve' is sometimes found (cf. the Spanish *labrar*, mentioned above); 'mark' and 'print' continued to be used well into the nineteenth century, and a certain amount of public confusion had to be sorted out in the 1860s and 1870s when the British army was called upon to defend what was popularly miscalled its 'branding' of deserters and 'bad characters'.[21]

These terminologies call attention to other practices of pricking and stamping that resemble the precise technique of European tattooing, and that may have smoothed the path of acceptance at different times. In Chapter 4, Jennipher Rosecrans discusses early modern inking practices in England which drew on the power of the embodied image and offer suggestive affinities with contemporary pilgrim tattooing. As far as techniques are concerned, there are some similarities between tattooing and the production of frescoes and Dutch tiles in medieval and early modern Europe. Both these processes involved a paper pattern – the cartoon and the spons respectively – that was pricked or pounced along the outline of the image and then rubbed with pigment in order to transfer it to the surface being decorated.[22] A more trivial and much later example is the pricking or scratching and inking of pupils' initials into school desks by pen-nib or compass point, which was perhaps what prompted nineteenth-century English schoolboys to apply the same technique to their own arms and hands.

The case of scrimshaw is also instructive. Scrimshaw – decorated and carved objects made with whale teeth, tusks and bones – was a sailors' pastime that can be dated back to the mid-eighteenth century, though it flourished most richly during the nineteenth-century heyday of the American whaling industry. Worked up by whaling seamen as a defence against the tedium of long voyages, scrimshaw articles were given away as tokens of absence, or sold as commodities: there are striking parallels and ironies in the comparison with tattoos here, which can be pursued in the essays by James Bradley (Chapter 9) on Victorian Britain (where tattooing was uniquely accepted) and by Stephan Oettermann (Chapter 12) and Alan Govenar (Chapter 13) on popular entertainers.[23] Scrimshaw employed a technique of pricking and inking (sometimes using illustrations cut from books or magazines as patterns), that was very close to tattooing:

> The design was transferred from the original by positioning it over the tooth and pushing pins through it following the basic lines ... Another method was to poke pin holes through the drawing and *then* transfer the design to the tooth or tusk by applying a pencil or other marker through the holes ... Black ... was the most common pigment used by scrimshanders. This was prepared from lamp black or from other

forms of carbon, from charcoal, or from bottled or solid pigments brought along on the voyage . . . After the pigment had been rubbed into the engraved lines, excess pigment was removed with a cloth.[24]

This description of scrimshaw work could just as well be a description of nineteenth-century tattooing techniques, not to mention the overlapping maritime environment: the scrimshander's techniques, tools and pigments were equally serviceable for tattooing, and no doubt were used for exactly that purpose too. The use of printed images as patterns also parallels the promiscuous absorption of popular print imagery into tattooing. Indeed, in what seems to be a remarkable testimony to the mobility and versatility of images, two nineteenth-century scrimshaw teeth, 'carved after popular prints of the era [and] probably the work of Scotish whalemen from the whaling ports of Dundee or Perth', depict a Pictish man and woman posed and decorated in the fashion of de Bry's sixteenth-century representation of 'Ancient Britons', discussed by Juliet Fleming (Chapter 5).[25]

My point in marshalling these analogies is not to force the tattoo into better company in order to salvage its reputation. But I want to urge that the tattoo needs to be located not only in a linear series that strings together chronologically dispersed evidence (in which the eighteenth century is ascribed its familiar role as a crucial dividing-line in European history), but also laterally, in the density of its immediate cultural milieu. Only a rigorous, multidimensional location of tattooing in these specific environments can rescue its history from the synthetic and reifying linearity I have already mentioned, and recover its full heterogeneity and instability. And one can achieve these purposes only through the meticulous tracing and evaluation of sources carried out by the authors of these essays. These sources are maddeningly sparse and deficient; they are often furtive and partial (in both senses of the word), and yet at the same time – if one pursues and interrogates them with enough enterprise – richly varied. The strength of the present collection of essays is that their authors have brought fresh eyes to this quest: they have re-evaluated the known sources on tattooing, and identified materials that have been undiscovered or incompletely exploited in the past. Between them, they bring to bear a range of specialist knowledge and linguistic skills that could not be wielded by any single scholar. The 'situated tattoo' of these essays reveals to us the full complexity of a mark whose status and meaning in the history of Western culture have been a metaphor for ambiguity.

1 Stigma and Tattoo[1]

C. P. JONES

> Both sexes paint their Bodys, *Tattow*, as it is called in their Language. This is done by inlaying the Colour of Black under their skins, in such a manner as to be indelible. Some have ill-design'd figures of men, birds, or dogs; the women generally have this figure Z simply on every joint of their fingers and Toes; the men have it likewise, and both have other differant [sic] figures, such as Circles, Crescents, etc., which they have on their Arms and Legs . . . Their method of Tattowing I shall now describe. The colour they use is lamp black, prepar'd from the Smoak of a Kind of Oily nut, used by them instead of Candles. The instrument for pricking it under the Skin is made of very thin flatt pieces of bone or Shell, from a quarter of an inch to an inch and a half broad, according to the purpose it is to be used for, and about an inch and a half long. One end is cut into sharp teeth, and the other fastened to a handle. The teeth are dipped into black Liquor, and then drove, by quick, sharp blows struck upon the handle with a Stick for that purpose, into the skin so deep that every stroke is followed with a small quantity of Blood. The part so marked remains sore for some days before it heals. As this is a painful operation, especially the Tattowing their Buttocks, it is perform'd but once in their Life times; it is never done until they are 12 or 14 years of Age.[2]

Thus Captain James Cook observed the practice of 'tattowing' on Tahiti in July 1769, and his description, though not published until 1893, is the first appearance of the word in the English language. His contemporaries (and this is the age of Winckelmann and Lessing) would have been shocked at the notion that the Greeks and Romans followed so barbarous a custom, and even now such an idea may come as a surprise. This essay is mainly concerned with two problems: how much did these two peoples practise either tattoooing or branding, and what terms did they use to describe them?

Greek and Roman texts referring to body-marking often use the term *stigma*, or cognate words like the verb *stizo*, and 'stigma' has passed into our own language with the sense of 'mark of infamy', 'moral blot'. In part because of the medieval phenomenon of 'stigmatization', the appearance of markings on the hands and feet of mystics like St Francis of Assisi, ancient references to *stigmata* have often been taken to denote some kind of branding or burning, as in *The New Catholic Encylopaedia*:[3]

> Term derived from the Greek root stigma, meaning mark and in particular, a brand impressed by iron. It was used in antiquity to refer to marks branded on cattle, on all slaves in the Orient, and on fugitive slaves in Greece and Rome. Soldiers also, of some Eastern countries, wore stigmata.

The present essay will argue that this view does not withstand analysis. 'Stigmata' among the Greeks and Romans are almost always tattoo- and not brand-marks. The branding of humans was almost unknown to the Greeks, and even among the more brutal Romans was comparatively rare, and was denoted by the word *stigma* only sporadically and at a comparatively late date. By contrast, animal-branding was universal, and is virtually never designated by the word *stigma* but by a word denoting a burn or a stamp.

Tattooing had certainly existed long before the dawn of Greek culture, even if we place that dawn in the mid-second millennium. The so-called 'Ice Man' discovered in the Alto Adige in September 1991 was tattooed; this extraordinary find is dated between 3300 and 3200 BC.[4] Among peoples who were later in contact with the Greeks, the Egyptians are the first to provide evidence for tattooing. Here it is first found on mummies of the Eleventh Dynasty, about 2100 BC; the colour used was a 'dark, blackish-blue pigment applied with a pricking instrument, perhaps consisting of one or more fish bones set into a wooden handle'.[5] (There is an obvious similarity with Cook's 'lamp black, prepar'd from the Smoak of a Kind of Oily nut' and with his 'instrument . . . made of very thin flatt pieces of bone or Shell'.) The practice is also found among the early Israelites, since the 'Holiness Code' of *Leviticus* contains the injunction, 'You shall not gash yourselves in mourning for the dead: you shall not tattoo yourselves.' The so-called Deutero-Isaiah, writing in the sixth century BC, predicts that the Jews too will adopt the practice after their redemption: 'This man will say, "I am the Lord's man" . . . another shall write the Lord's name on his hand.'[6]

About the time of Deutero-Isaiah, the Greeks began to notice that certain of their northern neighbours marked their skins with decorative patterns which are almost certainly tattoos rather than body-paint. They associated this practice above all with the Thracians, the 'barbarian' people living in what is now southern Bulgaria and European Turkey. Many Greek vase paintings, most of them of Athenian manufacture, show Thracian women with

Crater showing a woman (a mother or nurse) carrying the murdered son of King Lycurgus, *c.* 350 BC. British Museum, London.

Red-figure *lekythos* showing a tattooed Maenad slaying Orpheus, *c.* 460 BC. Museum of Fine Arts, Boston (Francis Bartlett Fund).

marks; these are usually placed on the leg or the arm, and consist of abstract designs or of simple figures such as deer. The women are often portrayed as 'Maenads', the 'mad women' who were believed to have murdered the poet Orpheus. Thus a *lekythos* (oil-vase) of *c.* 460 BC, now in Boston, shows a Maenad with a little rosette on her right elbow and left ankle, and V-shaped marks down her right forearm; it is unclear whether the three parallel lines round her wrists and ankles are tattoos or jewellery. A *crater* (wine-mixing vessel) of about 350 from Apulia, now in the British Museum, illustrates another myth, that of the Thracian king Lycurgus who murdered his wife and children in a fit of madness. One figure on it is a woman, who is either the nurse or the mother of one of the murdered sons. She has an elaborate display of alternating zigzags and double lines on her arms and legs. In literature, these markings are sometimes said to have been inflicted on the Thracian women by their menfolk as a punishment for their killing of Orpheus, or alternatively to be a sign of mourning for him. But this is probably an interpretation concocted by the Greeks, since in real life Thracian males were also tattooed, just as Captain Cook found 'tattowing' among both sexes in Tahiti.[7]

Clearly such designs are far too elaborate to be branded. The vases alone do not prove that they are tattooed rather than painted, but it is here that the evidence of literature enters. When referring to Thracian body-marking, the Greeks consistently use words of a single etymological family, all having the root *stig-*. The first to do so is Herodotus, the 'Father of History', writing *c.* 430, who makes a point often repeated by others, that for the Thracians 'to be marked [*estichthai*] is considered a sign of high birth, whereas to be unmarked [*astikton*] is considered one of low birth'.[8] The same point is made by the author of an anonymous work written in the fourth century, the *Double Arguments*: 'For the Thracians it is an adornment for girls to be marked [*stizesthai*], but among other peoples it is a punishment for criminals.'[9]

The question thus becomes an etymological one: why do ancient authors resort to verbs deriving from the root *stig-* in order to refer to Thracian body-marking? The Greek verb *stizein*, which is directly formed from this root, means 'to prick', and is related to the English *sting*, *stitch*, to the German *stechen* ('prick'), *sticken* ('embroider'). The commonest of the nouns formed from the same root, *stigma*, first appears in Greek with reference to the spots of snakes, and later it often means 'dot' or 'mark'. Remembering that Captain Cook talked of 'pricking [tattoos] under the skin', we can infer that the verb *stizein* refers to what we call tattooing, and that the Greeks regarded the puncture of the skin as the essential part of the operation.

This inference is borne out by the clearest account that survives from antiquity for the methods of applying and removing *stigmata*, though our source is as late as the sixth century of the Christian era. The doctor Aetius practised in Alexandria and Constantinople in the reign of Justinian, and his extant encyclopaedia of medicine, the *Tetrabiblon*, contains the following entry for the word *stigmata*:

They call *stigmata* things inscribed on the face or some other part of the body, for example on the hands of soldiers, and they use the following ink. [The recipe follows.] Apply by pricking the places with needles, wiping away the blood, and rubbing in first juice of leek, and then the preparation . . . In cases where we wish to remove such *stigmata*, we must use the following preparations . . . When applying, first clean the *stigmata* with niter, smear them with resin of terebinth, and bandage for five days . . . The *stigmata* are removed in twenty days, without great ulceration and without a scar.[10]

We can therefore safely understand the word *stigma* to refer to what we call tattooing. From here we can go on to question the cultural significance of this kind of body-marking: what did it mean to the peoples among whom the Greeks first encountered it, such as the Thracians? And, since the Greeks from the fifth century on began to use tattooing among themselves, did they give it the same meaning as those from whom they imported it?

We have no verbal evidence from the Thracians to show the significance of their tattoos, whether decorative, religious, medicinal, or a combination of two or more of these. In a presumably male-dominated society, however, female tattooing is not likely to be simply decorative, and may well be connected with the status of the family or clan. Though the Persians and the Egyptians, both peoples with whom the Greeks had many contacts, also used tattoos, what we have of their literature is of no help either. With them, however, we can discern several functions which, though separate, blend into one another. One is connected with social status, as possibly with the Thracians. Closely akin, since social status often confers desirability, is decoration – drawing attention to the body by adorning it with pictures and patterns. To the extent that status may be religious rather than secular, another function may be to mark the body with signs or emblems which denote membership in a particular cult-group. Another usage is also connected with status, but in an inverted way: the penal use of *stigmata* as marks of degradation. This last use is not so far from the religious as might appear. In certain religions, including Christianity for much of its history, the divinity is thought of as a 'lord' or 'master', and his followers (since such divinities are usually male) as his 'slaves'. It is no great distance, therefore, to treating *stigmata* as the mark of human slavery, especially slavery of an extreme kind which will never be commuted to freedom.

To begin with tattooing as a status-marker or as decoration, we have seen that this is its likely function among the Thracians, even though our Greek sources, both verbal and visual, single out females as the main carriers of tattoos. The same function is implied by child-tattooing, though it is very rarely mentioned. The historian Xenophon in the early fourth century describes a tribe called 'Mossynoikoi', 'Tower-dwellers', which he encountered on the shores of the Black Sea. These showed their Greek visitors 'children of good families . . . entirely decorated on back and front, being tattooed [*estigmenous*] with flowers'.[11] There is also ample evidence for males being tattooed among other 'barbarian' nations, for example the unsubdued tribes of Scotland. According to the late historian Herodian, 'these people tattoo [*stizontai*] their bodies with various designs and animal-representations of every kind; and hence they do not wear clothing, so as not to cover up the designs on their bodies'.[12] This might be a transference from tribes living in warmer climes, since it is hard to imagine Scottish highlanders in habitual nudity. If Herodian is correct, however, his statement coincides remarkably with the observations of Captain Cook on Tahiti.

It is probably because tattooing served a religious function among neighbours of the Israelites that it was soon banned in Jewish law. That agrees with an observation of Greek writers, that religious tattooing was used in the Fertile Crescent and in Egypt. Herodotus, who was our first witness to Thracian tattooing, says the following about a temple at the easternmost or 'Canopic' mouth of the Nile: 'If a slave belonging to any human owner at all takes refuge here and assumes the sacred tattoos [*stigmata*], giving himself to the god, no-one may touch him'.[13] Among the Syrians, the practice of sacred tattooing, especially on the wrist, is attested in the Hellenistic period. A papyrus of the mid-second century BC contains a description of a runaway slave from the city Bambyke (Hierapolis) in Syria, the chief sanctuary of the 'Syrian goddess' *par excellence*, Atargatis. The papyrus describes the slave as 'tattooed [*estigmenos*] on the right wrist with two barbarian letters', and since Atargatis had a consort-divinity named Hadad, these 'barbarian' letters are likely to be the Syriac initials of the two gods.[14] The satirist Lucian, writing about three centuries later in the period of the Roman empire, and describing this same sanctuary, says of Atargatis' devotees, 'They are all tattooed [*stizontai*], some on the wrist, some on the neck, and as a result all the Assyrians [that is, Syrians] have tattoos [*stigmatophoreousin*].'[15] We shall return to the subject of tattooing in early Christian literature, and to the survival of the practice in the Holy Land until modern times.

Herodotus regards the tattoos voluntarily adopted by runaway slaves at Canopus as a mark of self-devotion to the local god. Such slaves were now transferred from their human owners to a divine one, and thus became inviolable. Hence there is an easy transition from religious tattooing to what may be called 'chattel-tattooing'. Though the evidence comes mainly from Greece itself, there is reason to think that it was particularly prevalent among another set of neighbours of the Greeks: the Persians, who in the early fifth century tried to conquer Greece, and whose empire extended as far as the Aegean until the time of Alexander the Great. Here again, our first and best witness is Herodotus. A famous story in his *Histories* concerns the Persian king Xerxes and his crossing of the Hellespont into Europe. When a storm came up and destroyed the bridge which he had just built,

> Xerxes . . . ordered that three hundred lashes of the whip be inflicted on the water and a pair of shackles be thrown into it. I have even heard that in addition he sent tattooers [*stigees*] to tattoo [*stixontes*] the Hellespont. In any case, he ordered his agents to say as they did their whipping, 'O cruel water, your master imposes this penalty upon you for doing him wrong when he had done no wrong to you; and King Xerxes will cross you, whether you like it or not.'

Some modern scholars have argued that Herodotus must mean branding, not tattooing; but his language is clear, and the point of the story is the king's manic arrogance.[16]

It is notable that Herodotus talks of Xerxes' treatment of the Hellespont in terms of slavery ('your master'), and yet implies that it was punitive. In other words, he seems to regard it as something inflicted by masters on slaves that had 'done wrong'. The same is implied when Xerxes uses tattoos on Greek prisoners of war. Herodotus relates, with a dash of irony, that 'the Thebans who deserted to the Persians did not entirely prosper, since the barbarians killed some of them, and marked most of them with the royal tattoos [*estixan stigmata basileia*]'. All subjects of the Persian king were regarded as his 'slaves', a usage from which the Greeks inferred that he exercised an uncontrolled despotism over servile minions. But Herodotus' comment on the fate of the Thebans suggests that, like any Persian grandee, the king usually marked his recalcitrant slaves with punitive tattoos, and on this occasion tattooed the Thebans because their Greek compatriots resisted his claim of sovereignty.

Tattooing was not an ancient or embedded practice among the Greeks, to judge by its absence from literature and art down to the end of the sixth century, roughly coinciding with what is called the 'archaic' period. When they did adopt it, the source seems to have been Persia, which included in its empire many Greek settlers in Asia and the Aegean islands. The form in which tattooing was adopted was also Persian, that is, punitive. The very first reference to it in literature is in the word *stigmatias*, a 'marked slave', which occurs in a fragment from the poet Asius of Samos, usually dated in the sixth century. Samos, the wealthy city on the island of the same name just off the Asian coast, could well have been one of the first to adopt this 'barbarian' custom.[17]

By a curious coincidence, the Samians themselves became the victims of the same punishment at the hands of their fellow-Ionians, the Athenians. In

440, Samos revolted from the Athenian empire, and was only reduced after a long campaign. The biographer Plutarch, writing many centuries later, relates that the Athenians tattooed their Samian prisoners-of-war on the forehead (*estizon eis to metopon*) with a representation of the Samian ship called a *samaina*, while the Samians tattooed their Athenian ones with an owl, the emblem of Athens; but it is odd that the two sides should use the other's emblem to mark such prisoners, and other authors referring to this incident more plausibly reverse the tattoos.[18] By another irony of history, 30 years later the Athenians in turn suffered the same form of degradation. Plutarch again is our source for the story that, after the failure of the Athenian expedition to Sicily in 413, many Sicilians sold their Athenian captives as slaves, 'marking them with a horse on the forehead [*stizontes hippon eis to metopon*]'.[19] These accounts of the later fifth century, if they are historically true and not retrojections from later practice, show that the double function of tattooing as practised by the Persians, punishment and irrevocable ownership, had become ingrained among the most civilized of their opponents. Casual allusions in Athenian comedy of the fifth and fourth centuries, in which slaves often play a large role, show that tattooing had become routine at Athens, and it is a fair inference that the same is true for Greek cities which have no literature.

An essential text for the study of tattooing among the Greeks was first published only in 1891. It is by a writer of the second century BC called Herodas, and comes from one of his *Mimes* preserved on the ancient form of paper called papyrus. These are in fact short sketches from life very similar to comedy, though without the restrictions of place and scenery which ancient dramaturgy often imposed. In the fifth mime, a lady called Bitinna falls into a jealous rage at her unfaithful lover Gastron, who happens also to be her slave. She has him stripped and bound in preparation for a whipping, and Gastron begs her to have him tattooed (*stixon*) if he is ever unfaithful again. The merciless Bitinna orders Gastron dragged off to the town jail for a lashing, but then relents, and instead sends for 'Kosis the tattooer [*stiktes*] with his needles and ink'. One of the women slaves tries to intercede for Gastron, but Bitinna swears that he will soon 'know himself [a reference to the famous Greek proverb, 'Know Thyself'] when he has this inscription on his forehead'. At the end of the sketch, Bitinna relents, and lets her faithless lover off unharmed.[20]

The reference to an 'inscription' on the victim's forehead points to a method of treating delinquent slaves which is found elsewhere. Instead of being merely imprinted with a design or an emblem, like the Thracian women already discussed, Bitinna clearly intends that Gastron will have one or more words inscribed on his forehead so that all may know his crime.

According to an ancient commentator on the orator Aeschines, runaway slaves were 'inscribed' on the forehead with the words, 'Stop me, I'm a runaway' (kateche me, pheugo), and similarly the Cynic philosopher Bion claimed that his father was a freed slave 'who instead of a face had a document [syngraphen] on his face, the mark of his master's harshness'. Presumably he had so many vices as a slave that the tattoo enumerating them covered his whole face, and not just his forehead, though if so it is surprising that he went on to receive his freedom. Perhaps he was just too troublesome to be worth retaining.[21]

Because the Greeks had taken over the practice of tattooing almost exclusively in its punitive and degrading aspects, it was inevitable that, being also skilled doctors, they should soon devise ways of removing tattoos (if indeed they did not learn this skill from others such as the Persians). One of the most curious references to the removal of tattoos is as old as the fourth century BC. It is preserved in an inscription from the sanctuary of Asclepius of Epidaurus, one of the first great medical centres of Greece, where the lucky patients often showed their gratitude to the god by leaving a written record of their cures. One such account concerns a certain Pandarus who had tattoos (stigmata) on his forehead, which evidently he wanted removed. In the customary way, he spent the night in the sanctuary, and while doing so dreamed that the god tied a bandage on his face and told him to remove it after leaving the next morning. When he did so, the tattooed letters had been miraculously transferred to the bandage, and this he dedicated as a thanks-offering to the god with the letters still on it. He then commissioned a certain Echedorus to make a further dedication to the god, probably something in precious metal, but Echedorus sequestered the money. Consequently, he too had a dream, in which the god appeared to him and wrapped Pandarus' bandage on his head. He awoke to find the bandage still in place, and when he removed it his forehead had Pandarus' tattoo on it as well as a previous one (it is perhaps implied that he was an unreliable slave).[22] Whatever the reality behind this account, the bandage recalls the Byzantine doctor Aetius and his method of removing tattoos. We can perhaps infer that the priests of Asclepius at Epidaurus performed an early version of this operation on Pandarus, and that his imagination turned the 'cure' into a miracle.

So widespread had the practice of tattooing already become in the fifth century that it could serve as a source of images, whether the fantastic exaggerations of comedy, or metaphors and similes in serious literature. A slave in Aristophanes' Wasps exclaims, 'I'm being tattooed [stizomenos] to death with a stick', where the joke seems to lie in the similarity of a tattoo to the black and blue marks left by a beating.[23] A Greek writer of the Roman period,

Aelius Aristides, attacks Plato for slandering heroes of Athenian history such as Pericles, saying, 'You never tattooed [estixas] any of your own slaves, but you have as good as tattooed the most honoured of the Greeks.'[24]

One such metaphorical use of the word *stigma* was to have a very profound effect. At the end of his *Letter to the Galatians*, the Christian missionary Paul says, 'Henceforth let nobody give me trouble, since I carry the *stigmata* of Lord Jesus on my body' (*Gal.* 6.17). The King James version translates the last clause non-committally, 'I bear in my body the marks of the Lord Jesus', but the Revised Version of 1881 gives, 'I have been *branded* on my body with the marks of Lord Jesus', and this or something like it is now the standard interpretation; in particular, it found its way into the article on stigmatization in the most authoritative edition of the *Encyclopaedia Britannica*.[25] But once it is established that *stigma* usually refers to tattooing in antiquity, then it becomes easier to see Paul's metaphor in its conceptual context. Perhaps referring to marks such as bruises and welts, the visible signs of the ill-treatment which he has received as a 'slave of Christ', he compares them to tattoos, using the same comparison as the bruised slave in Aristophanes' *Wasps*. Paul may also have been led to the metaphor by the practice of religious tattooing, of the sort found at the sanctuary of Atargatis in Syria. Whatever the underlying idea, this scriptural passage engendered the later conception of *stigmata* as marks received on the body by participation in Jesus' sufferings, either by mystic communion or by self-laceration.

There may be another allusion to tattooing in early Christian literature, even though the word *stigma* does not appear. The author of *Revelation* says of the Scarlet Woman, 'On her forehead was written a name of mystery, "Babylon the Great, Mother of harlots and of earth's abominations".' The Woman, who is usually understood to be Rome, is portrayed not merely as a procuress but as a slave of the lowest kind, one whose face is tattooed with the catalogue of her vices, like the father of Bion the philosopher.[26]

The practice of punitive tattooing continues into the Byzantine period, when the capital of the Roman world had moved to Constantinople. As late as the ninth century, the iconoclastic emperor Theophilus punished two brothers named Theodore and Theophanes, convicted as 'iconodules' or worshippers of icons. 'First', we are told by the historian Zonaras, 'he had them severely beaten, then he had their faces tattooed [katestixe], and poured ink into the tattoos, and the tattoos formed letters.' Zonaras proceeds to write out the twelve lines of execrable poetry printed on the offenders' faces. The brothers later became saints revered with the surname of *graptoi*, 'the Inscribed'.[27]

By contrast with the persistent Greek use of tattoos for punitive purposes, attested for well over a millennium, the evidence for other uses is comparatively slight. Religious tattooing – marking the wrist or some other part of the body with the emblem, the initial, or the full name of a god – is attested from Herodotus onwards as a practice in the eastern Mediterranean, from Egypt to Syria, but is not found in cults of the traditionally Greek lands. Decorative tattooing continues to be noticed by Greek observers among barbarian peoples such as the highlanders of Scotland, but never among those subjected to the civilizing influence of Greece and Rome.

From the time of the First Punic War in the mid-third century BC, Greece was more and more drawn into the orbit of the growing power of Rome, and Rome's domination of the entire Mediterranean basin was sealed with Augustus' defeat of Antony and Cleopatra at Actium in 31 BC. Rome is in a sense the last and most important of Greece's neighbours, and by its absorption of Greek culture created a kind of double civilization that lasted, in an attenuated form, down to the conquest of Constantinople in 1453. But Rome began as an 'other' people, originally regarded by the Greeks as barbarian, and even when no longer barbarian was often placed in a third category between the two established ones.

Tattooing does not seem to have been native to the Romans any more than to the Greeks, but in the Roman case it was the Greeks who formed the source of transmission. This is shown above all by the fact that the Romans took over the noun *stigma* to denote a tattoo, though not the verb *stizo*, for which they had to find substitutes such as *inscribo*, 'inscribe', *imprimo*, 'imprint', and *inuro*, 'brand'. The nineteenth-century British army similarly used the term 'branding' for the process of punitive tattooing.[28]

An episode from a famous Latin novel, the *Satyricon* of Petronius, perfectly illustrates the Roman adaptation of tattooing, though it must be remembered that the novel may well have one or more Greek models, and that its principal setting is the Hellenized region of southern Italy.[29] The narrator Encolpius, his male lover Giton, and the rogue-poet Eumolpus are all on board a ship owned by a certain Lichas, while another passenger is the flighty matron, Tryphaena. In an earlier episode of the novel, Lichas seems to have been the lover of Encolpius and Tryphaena of Giton, though both affairs ended in hostility. Learning of the presence of their ex-lovers, Encolpius and Giton begin a comic deliberation about ways of escape. One such involves the ink which Eumolpus, as a man of literature, has brought aboard. Encolpius suggests that he and Giton dye themselves with it from head to foot and pretend to be Eumolpus' Ethiopian (that is, African) slaves. Giton contemptuously dismisses the idea, and proposes suicide. Eumolpus intervenes with what he considers a better idea. His manservant, who is a barber, will shave the heads and eyebrows of Encolpius and Giton, and then he himself

> will mark your faces with an elaborate inscription to give the impression that you have been punished with a tattoo [*stigma*]. That way the letters will serve at the same time to divert the suspicions of your pursuers, and to hide your faces with mock punishment.

The plan is adopted, and 'Eumolpus filled the foreheads of us both with huge letters, and with generous hand covered our whole faces with the well-known inscription of runaway slaves.' However, the trick goes awry, and eventually Encolpius and Giton are brought before Lichas and Tryphaena.

> Tryphaena burst into tears, thinking that real tattoos had been imprinted on our captive foreheads . . . Unable to restrain his rage, Lichas jumped forward and said, 'You stupid female! As if these were wounds prepared with iron so as to absorb letters. If only they had defiled themselves with this inscription, we would have the best of satisfactions. As it is, they have played a stage-trick on us, and fooled us with mere shadow-writing.'

The reference to ink makes it almost certain that Petronius means a tattoo, and 'the well-known inscription of runaway slaves' must be something like the words which were tattooed on such slaves in Greece, 'Stop me, I'm a runaway.'

Other references show that the Romans adopted tattooing with little change from the Greeks. At the same time, in their hands the practice underwent adaptations connected with their position as rulers of a world empire. One such adaptation, the tattooing of persons indispensable to the state, is first attested when the empire had become Christian in the fourth century. The military writer Vegetius describes how recruits are 'inscribed with permanent dots in the skin', apparently the names or numbers of their units. An imperial decision of the year 398 extends this practice to arms-manufacturers (*fabricenses*). 'Tattoos [*stigmata*], that is, a public mark, must be made on the arms of *fabricenses* as they are on recruits, so that in this way at least they may be recognized if they go into hiding.'[30] Behind this evolution there seem to be two converging tendencies: the ever-growing reliance of the Byzantines on a large and permanent army, and a process whereby soldiers and arms-manufacturers are treated practically as indentured servants of the state.

Already, however, tattooing had begun to encounter a contrary, restrictive tendency. The reign of the first Christian emperor, Constantine, began the process whereby Christian codes of behaviour, very often derived from

Jewish law, seeped into Roman legislation. A passage of *Leviticus* forbade tattooing, as we have seen, or at least was interpreted as so doing. In addition, if the body was God's handiwork and made in His image, then tattooing might appear to be sacrilegious interference with the divine creation. This line of thought seems to be in Constantine's mind when he issues a judicial decision whereby hardened criminals should not be 'inscribed' on the face, but rather on the hands or the calves. 'This will ensure', observes the emperor, 'that the face, which has been formed in the image of the divine beauty, will be defiled as little as possible.'[31]

This and similar legislation may account for a curious series of objects which have recently received an excellent discussion from David Thurmond. They are metal collars inscribed with mottoes such as 'I'm a runaway, take me back to the house of His Excellency Potitus near the Decian Baths on the Aventine.' These have sometimes been interpreted as animal-collars, similar to those still placed round the necks of dogs and cats. Though some of them date from the time of paganism, the majority have Christian emblems, and it is therefore almost certain that they are for miscreant slaves. Once Christian emperors had begun to forbid tattooing of the forehead or the face, inscribed collars became indispensable as a substitute for tattoos (for ones placed on the arms or wrists could of course easily be covered).[32]

A recent investigation by Mark Gustafson, however, has shown that Late Antiquity and the Middle Ages used penal tattooing as much as the classical Greeks and Romans had ever done.[33] In addition, Christians orthodox and otherwise had themselves tattooed with emblems or the name of Jesus, a clear continuation of the religious tattooing observed by Herodotus in Egypt and by Lucian in Syria. In these regions there is no visible break in the practice, at least among Christians, up to modern times. Hence it is that travellers to the Holy Land, such as Jean de Thévenot in the seventeenth century, have continued to observe the practice of tattooing, though naturally not using that word for it, which was only imported from the Pacific in the eighteenth.[34]

Though the Romans both adopted and extended the use of tattooing, there is reason to think that, unlike the Greeks, they sometimes branded human beings. Since this has caused some confusion in the history of ancient body-marking, it is worth taking a brief look at the practice of branding.

Animal-branding is still familiar in many cultures, including our own. The first evidence for it in antiquity, as for tattooing, appears to be from Egypt, where it goes back to the Old Kingdom.[35] The Greeks and Romans used it, as we do, on bovines, but also on equines, and in eastern lands on camels. Greek words for the practice include *charagma* or *character*, properly 'stamp', or *kauterion*, 'brand'. That the difference between this process and tattooing was still felt as late as the second century of our era is shown by the Greek moralist, Dio Chrysostom. Arguing that the accepted tokens of kingship and slavery are merely conventional, Dio points to the lowest class of slaves, those in shackles, wearing tattoos (*stigmata*), or condemned to hard labour:

> in Thrace free women are full of tattoos, and the higher their rank the more they have. It follows that a queen may be tattooed, and therefore a king too. On the other hand, kings deck themselves with symbols such as crowns and sceptres in order to declare their status, just as owners put brands [*characteres*] on their cattle so as to be able to recognize them.[36]

As for the cauterization of humans, this too is very old, and like tattooing has several functions. It may be medicinal: the Greek doctor Hippocrates observed as early as the fifth century that the Scythians of what is now Ukraine were covered all over with marks of surgical cauterization.[37] Cauterization, though clearly not on the same scale, was an important aspect of Greek surgery. A primary function, however, is penal. Here the earliest evidence is the law code of the Babylonian king Hammarabi from the eighteenth century BC, and there is abundant evidence from Egypt, both under the Pharaohs and their Greek successors, the Ptolemies.[38] In classical Greece, however, provided that *stigma* is correctly taken to refer to tattooing and not branding, then there is almost no evidence for the penal branding of humans. In the Roman period, authors from the eastern Mediterranean refer to self-inflicted branding by religious fanatics; thus Lucian predicts that the followers of the Cynic philosopher Peregrinus will establish a cult in his honour, 'with whips, brands [*kauteria*], or other enormities'.[39] Self-flagellation is known as a practice of eastern cults, for example among the priests of the Syrian goddess Atargatis, just as it persists among certain Christians today, and there is no reason to doubt the correctness of such observations. But the sum of the evidence suggests that Greeks, even 'adopted' ones like the Syrian Lucian, continued to regard human branding as aberrant, an 'enormity'.

The penal branding of humans is attested not only in ancient cultures such as Egypt, but in many modern ones. For example, it was used for convicts in France up to 1832, for Siberian exiles of the czars until 1864. It would not therefore be surprising to find it employed by the Romans, but most of the evidence is at best ambiguous. To take only one instance, the poet Martial like other poets of antiquity exploits the concept of the *stigma* as a metaphor for the indelible infamy which satire can place on a person: 'Whatever the heat of my anger burns into you [*inusserit*] will remain for good and be read throughout the world, and Cinnamus with his cunning skill will not erase the tattoos [*stigmata*].'[40] The word 'burns' suggests a brand-mark, while the use of *stigma* and the reference to surgical removal point to a tattoo. Perhaps Martial is thinking of both processes, but more likely the tendency of Latin-speakers to use words like 'inscribe' and 'brand' for the imposition of tattoos gives his language an appearance of ambiguity, which would not have misled his Roman readers.

There seems in fact to be only one passage, or rather series of passages, which refers to Roman branding. They occur in a description by the Sicilian historian Diodorus of a slave rising that had erupted in Sicily in about 135 BC. The text of Diodorus, as transmitted by Byzantine excerptors, uses the word *stigmata* to refer to the marks placed on the rebellious slaves by their Italian masters, and seems to imply branding, not tattooing: but while this may have been the punishment used, it is also possible that our Byzantine sources substituted the word *stigmata* for some other one like *kauteria*, since there is other evidence to show that the Byzantines extended the meaning of *stigma* to cover branding.[41]

In conclusion, cultures which were familiar to the ancient Greeks prac-tised what we would call tattooing. To describe it, the Greeks applied a cluster of Greek words deriving from the root *stig-*, meaning to 'prick' and related to our word 'sting', and the modern *stigma* derives from Greek by way of Latin. Tattooing in its social aspect, whether as a mark of high status or as pure decoration, the Greeks associated with 'barbarians' of the uncivilized kind, and never adopted it. Religious tattooing continued to flourish in the Levant throughout antiquity, and has continued among eastern Christians to the present day. This persistence of tattooing in European consciousness also explains how a learned commentator on Petronius, the Dutchman Pieter Burman, was able to recognize the *stigmata* he encountered in his author as tattoos rather than brand-marks. His second edition appeared in 1743, about 25 years before Captain Cook observed the practice in Tahiti.[42]

By contrast with tattooing, known as a living tradition only to travellers in the orient or, from the late eighteenth century on, in the South Pacific, the branding of humans and animals continued to be familiar. It was therefore easy for medieval and later readers to interpret *stigma* as branding when they met it in ancient literature, and when it passed into the vernacular languages, it carried the same connotation. Dr Johnson's Dictionary, for instance, first published in 1755, defines *stigma* as 'a brand; a mark with a hot iron', or meta-phorically as 'a mark of infamy'. The second sense has prevailed since; thus the nineteenth-century criminologist Cesare Lombroso classified 'criminal types' on the basis of physical 'stigmas' such as backward-sloping brows.[43] If the present arguments are correct, however, the word stigma originally and for most of classical antiquity meant something much less drastic than branding, and disgrace was only one, though the most important one, of its functions.

2 The Tattoo in the Later Roman Empire and Beyond

MARK GUSTAFSON

As long as he lives, he will have a *stigma*.

PETRONIUS, *Satyricon* 45.9

We are witnesses to a tattoo revival. We see bodies emblazoned with them everywhere, it seems, in our media-saturated society. Tattoos are flaunted in public, exhibited proudly on television and the Internet, in magazines and films, and touted as body art in glossy books of photographs. Yet it is probably safe to say that many people still react to tattoos in the same way as they might to a poke in the eye with a sharp stick. There is for some a lingering sense that tattoos are signs of degradation, criminality and deviance, and thus their appearance is deemed an assault on the viewer. So tattoos have a strange double nature. At the same time that tattoos have this uncanny power to affront, they can also attract and exert an almost irresistible fascination, even on historians. As this collection of essays attests, only now are the historical accounts being pieced together that show that the practice was not imported to the West as the symptom of a colonial encounter with 'primitives', but has been a permanent cultural feature of the ancient Mediterranean and of Europe and North America. Tattooing is a universal and age-old phenomenon with many functions, including: decorative; religious; magical; punitive; and as an indication of identity, status, occupation, or ownership. Although the decorative function is by far the most prevalent, all the others still have their place.

This essay has as its focus one function, that of tattooing in punitive circumstances, and especially as it was practised in late antiquity (from *c.* AD 250) and into the Byzantine period. For this time and place, the evidence is literary, and most of it concerns Christians. The phenomenon of tattooing and its many uses in the ancient Mediterranean have been amply noted in Christopher Jones's essay. It is hoped and intended that the present essay may be read as a complement (and a compliment) to Jones's fundamental work.[1]

What he makes perfectly clear is that the Greeks had an aversion to decorative or voluntary tattooing, which they associated with 'barbarians'. But they were quite ready to use tattoos as a means of punishment (for slaves, prisoners of war, and criminals). The Greeks transmitted their views to the Romans, who adopted the word *stigma* and used others, as we shall see, to describe the process. The present discussion begins with an examination of literary accounts of tattooing, and then of the legal evidence, after which the precise function and form of the penal tattoo is considered. As should become plain, the tattoos applied as signs of degradation and punishment could be highly ambivalent. That is, there was a dissonance between the intent of the tattoo and the way in which it came to be understood in some circles. This, at least in part, gave rise to the adoption of another functional context for the tattoo, to the voluntary self-application of tattoos as a badge of honour.

During the persecution under the emperor Valerian in the late 250s, the African bishop Cyprian had written to some Christians who had been condemned to the mines in Numidia (in North Africa). Pontius, Cyprian's deacon and biographer, later asks, in regard to these condemned clerics: 'Who was there, in short, to enliven so many confessors sealed with a second inscription on their tattooed foreheads [*frontium notatarum secunda inscriptione signatos*]?'[2] The 'second inscription' seems in this situation to indicate a tattoo, an assertion strengthened by the great frequency with which the words *frons* ('forehead'), *noto* ('mark'), *inscriptio* ('inscription'), *signo* ('seal') and their relatives occur in other references to penal tattooing. The implied 'first inscription', it follows, must be the invisible mark conferred by baptism.[3]

A century later, in 360 (and in a significantly different situation), Hilary, the bishop of Poitiers, in reaction to the recent Council of Constantinople and its creed, wrote an angry piece of invective against the emperor Constantius II (Constantine's son). Constantius, in Hilary's view, was an Arian Christian who had run roughshod over his 'orthodox' opponents. Hilary writes:

> The complaint is well known: on your order, the bishops whom no one dared condemn have been deposed, and now they have been tattooed on their catholic foreheads [*in ecclesiasticis frontibus scriptos*] and are re-appraised with the words 'condemned to the mines' [*metallicae damnationis titulo*].[4]

That Constantine had earlier forbidden tattooing on the face (as we shall see below) has caused at least one recent commentator to doubt that this passage means what it says.[5] But it surely is not difficult to allow the possibility that a local official, or even Constantius himself, may have deviated from a legal precedent set by Constantine. Minor legal details were never an impediment to action deemed necessary in a new situation. Furthermore, the meaning of the Latin in this context, when examined in comparison to other references to tattooing, becomes unmistakable. For example, in Claudian's attack (399) on Eutropius, the eunuch and grand chamberlain of the emperor Arcadius, he says that some of Eutropius' advisors are former slaves, as is evident from their tattoos (among other things).

> Some from the lowly commoners are generals; some magistrates –
> though their calves and ankles are still marked, black and blue from
> the iron fetters, and though their tattooed faces [facies . . . inscripta]
> are inconsistent with their office and betray them by their inscription
> [suo . . . titulo].[6]

Hilary, it is apparent, was referring to a punitive practice that had a long history and was familiar to his readers, and he does not assume the need to explain further. He characterizes the complaint as 'notorious', or 'much talked-about' (famosa). Hilary's accusation – that Constantius actually did approve the resumption of this punishment – cannot be definitively proven. But it may be noted that this particular barb was not borrowed from the well-stocked arsenal of formulaic accusations which provided so much of the verbal weaponry directed against Constantius by other antagonistic bishops of the period (such as Athanasius of Alexandria and Lucifer of Cagliari). Although Constantius is accused of many coercive and punitive actions against his episcopal opponents, the charge of tattooing is unique in the controversial literature of this time. So the exceptional nature of this remark may be another indicator of its veracity.

The Arian controversy was still in play in 373, when the emperor Valens came down hard on 'orthodox' Christians in Alexandria. The ecclesiastical historian Theodoret, writing of this in the 440s, was, like Hilary, decidedly anti-Arian, and Valens, similar to Constantius II, was aligned with an Arian faction. A deacon of Damasus, bishop of Rome, who had been sent to Egypt during this time, had shown support to those hardy souls who persisted in the Nicene faith, and was – outrageously – condemned to hard labour in the copper mines in Palestine. The deacon was put on a ship, so says Theodoret (in Greek), 'with the sign of the sacred cross inscribed on his forehead [epi metopou characterisas]'.[7] A tattoo on the forehead, as starts to become clear, accompanied the punishment of condemnation to the mines. But a 'sacred cross' would be a most unlikely tattoo for one Christian to impose upon another as punishment, and therefore this description is best understood as metaphorical. That is, the deacon was tattooed with a more mundane mark, but Theodoret's figurative description of it as a cross points to a wilful transformation of the tattoo's meaning.

In 523, Boethius, having been charged with treason and imprisoned, was awaiting his own execution. From him we hear of two men who had been arrested for fraud and sentenced to exile by the Ostrogothic king Theoderic. They then sought asylum in a church, after which Theoderic gave them a regal ultimatum: 'He ordered that, if they did not leave the city of Ravenna by the prescribed date, they would be tattooed on their foreheads [*notas insignitii frontibus*] and driven out.'[8] The tattooing here has no explicit connection with religion or religious controversy. It merely, but remarkably, demonstrates the practice of penal tattooing on the forehead, in the West, in the early sixth century, and it similarly involves exile (and probably condemnation to the mines).

The two remaining examples are Byzantine. Much later, in 793, the emperor Constantine VI suppressed a revolt by rebels from the Armeniakon theme (an administrative division of the empire). So we are told by the contemporary chronicler Theophanes, an icon-revering monk writing in opposition to the iconoclast emperors. This Constantine had three of the rebel leaders killed, punished the living ones with fines and confiscations, and then staged a triumphal procession in which one thousand of the defeated insurgents, bound in chains, were paraded before him. Theophanes writes of their additional adornments: 'He tattooed on their foreheads [*epigrapsas ta prosopa melani kenteto*: literally, 'he wrote on their faces with black pricking'] "Armeniakon traitor".'[9] These thoroughly degraded plotters were then exiled to Sicily and other islands (their future occupations left unspecified, though again we may assume perpetual hard labour).

Finally, no fewer than six sources report that, during the second period of iconoclasm, the emperor Theophilus (829–842) ordered that two monks charged with idolatry, the Graptoi brothers, Theodorus and Theophanes, be beaten and then have twelve lines of iambic verse tattooed on their foreheads. The process is described in detail in an anonymous biography:

> Then the prefect ordered that their faces be inscribed ... The executioners came forward and, stretching each of the saints upon a bench, they started inscribing their faces. And pricking their faces for a long time [*kentountes ta prosopa*], they wrote [*egrapson*] the iambic verses on them.[10]

It is a wonderfully extravagant story, the truth of which – especially in the explicit details of the verses – may justifiably be questioned. The poem comprises a short and somewhat vague narrative of their crime and its punishment. In the aftermath, they were exiled to Bithynia. Fifty years later, in a marginal comment on Constantine's law forbidding this particular practice, a jurist wrote: 'Woe to you, tyrant, who has tattooed the faces of the saints Theodorus and Theophanes!'[11] (Here is an echo, however unintentional, of Hilary's indictment of Constantius.)

This brief survey of the explicit literary evidence for punitive tattooing in the later Roman Empire (and later), now ended, makes it clear that tattooing persons on the forehead, far from being obsolete (as some have thought), was in fact a practice that persisted throughout this period. The next step is to put this evidence into a legal perspective.

The *Theodosian Code* (a collection of imperial legislation published in 438) preserves an edict of the emperor Constantine from the year 316:

> If someone has been condemned to a gladiatorial school or to the mines/quarries [*metallum*] for the crimes he has been caught committing, let him not be marked on his face [*facie scribatur*], since the penalty of his condemnation can be expressed both on his hands and on his calves, and so that his face, which has been fashioned in the likeness of the divine beauty, may not be disgraced.[12]

The effects of this law may be measurable. David Thurmond has recently examined the corpus of 37 extant slave collars, most of which are later than 316 and can be shown to have a Christian connection. Quite possibly, many Christian slave owners may have heeded Constantine's directive and abandoned the practice of tattooing recalcitrant slaves (even though he had condemned criminals in mind).[13] Furthermore, while this message applied, in principle, to a large number of citizens, it has often been held up as an example of Constantine's 'Christianizing' legislation. The emperor's own justification for altering – but not abolishing – the practice of tattooing condemned persons may well reflect his own Christian sympathies, but it says nothing about partiality towards Christian criminals. Even if such partiality existed, it would make no sense here. The famous 'edict of toleration' of 311 had intended the release of all Christians in *metalla* (and in prisons); why should Constantine assume more condemned Christians? Furthermore, the legal record reveals an emperor who is anything but bashful about introducing new and harsher penalties.

So the practice of tattooing was assumed. What was its place in Roman law? For the Romans, as for the Greeks, tattooing usually signified degradation (that is, a lowering of status), as it was a treatment customarily reserved for slaves. The Augustan *lex Aelia Sentia* (AD 4), a law regulating manumission, is explicated as follows:

> slaves who have been chained by their masters on the grounds of punishment, or who have been tattooed [*quibusve stigmata inscripta sint*], or who have been tortured under interrogation on account of wrongdoing and have been found guilty of that wrongdoing, or who have been handed over to fight [in the arena] with a sword or with the beasts, or who have been dispatched to a gladiatorial school or to prison, and afterwards have been manumitted either by their master or by another, become free men of the same status as foreigners who have surrendered [*peregrini dediticii*].[14]

None of these slaves could become citizens, as was customary upon manumission, but rather they would belong to the lowest possible category of free non-citizens. The association of tattooing with degradation is thus made plain. Of course, the additional burden of a permanent stigma would further alienate the tattooed ex-slaves from the others affected by this law. And the assumption is, clearly, that slaves were always justifiably punished. In the case of those who had been tattooed, it was the permanent mark, not the crime, that was decisive.

As is well known, the Roman Empire saw the development of a system in which social status, not the crime committed, determined the nature of one's punishment (with some exceptions).[15] The penalty of hard labour was reserved (in principle) for slaves and lower-class persons, who also were liable to beatings and especially cruel forms of execution. As for the particular penalty of condemnation to *metalla*, persons of the various higher social strata were, strictly speaking, exempt. Those so condemned had their property confiscated, lost all testamentary rights, lost their standing as free citizens (if they were not slaves already), became 'slaves of the penalty' (*servi poenae*), were beaten with clubs, chained and, the evidence plainly suggests, tattooed. Finally, the *metallici* (as the tattooed ones were now called) were transported over some distance to their new commissions.

It is simply not possible to draw a direct connection between the penalties meted out to Christian confessors and their social classes. Nero, according to Tacitus, burned, crucified, and threw Christians to the dogs, all of which were drastic penalties reserved in extreme cases for slaves and the lowest of the free.[16] Even in cases involving non-Christians, mistakes were made, or an emperor or a governor simply exercised his personal prerogative. It was also due to the elasticity of the imperial legal procedure (*cognitio extra ordinem*) which left the judge free – unhindered by the law – to prescribe the penalty as he saw fit. The early martyr acts (and other sources) reveal the protocol and various consequences of the trials of Christians in the second and third centuries.[17] Cyprian, as mentioned earlier, who had been relegated in 257, wrote to nine other bishops who suffered a worse fate than he. They had been beaten with clubs, chained, with their heads half-shaven, tattooed, and sent to the mines.[18] Why the difference in treatment? There is and can be no fully satisfactory explanation. In the edict of Diocletian and Maximian against the Manichees (302), it is explicitly stated that all those so charged will be sent to *metalla*, regardless of status.[19]

As for the bulk of the primary evidence of this investigation, in which the 'persecutors' and the 'persecuted' are all Christians (though of different brands), there is no one legal explanation that fits every case. Hilary refers to bishops going to the mines (for their obstinacy and obstruction based on religious disagreement with the imperial administration); the deacon of Damasus in Theodoret's history is headed that way as well (apparently for intervening in a religious dispute); Boethius' criminals are destined for exile (having been accused of fraud) – they are threatened with tattooing only if they refuse to leave the church in which they have sought asylum; Theophanes' account is of a thousand rebels bound for exile, but first they appear in the celebration of a triumph (their crime was rebellion, with religious overtones); and, lastly, the Graptoi are icon-adoring monks who refuse to yield to the icon-deploring emperor, and they too are, apparently, exiled. The crimes differ, surely the statuses differ, but the sentence of exile and, most likely, hard labour in *metalla* are standard parts of the total package of which the penal tattoo is the sign.

Was the tattoo conceived of as a punishment in and of itself? There is, after all, the pain of its application, especially when received involuntarily. But despite the obvious health hazards of tattooing and, most likely, the carelessness of those who applied them, the process and the pain involved cannot be construed as torture in any useful sense, nor as a possible means to a slow death. The governing authorities in this time period had more than enough creative methods of inflicting pain and executing criminals. But what about the various experiences of disgrace, humiliation and exclusion that were the consequences of having one's criminal nature indelibly written on one's face, for all to see?

As indicated in the evidence collected here, the tattoo was merely one aspect, a kind of attestation, of a more comprehensive punishment. Still, those in power were well aware that the body can function as a permanently running advertisement of one's guilt and subjugation. Given the heavy yoke of a tattoo, those released from their sentences and allowed to return home (as sometimes happened, for various reasons, including old age and infirmity, or as the result of a general amnesty at the beginning of a new reign, or other imperial indulgences) could never completely resume normal life. Unless, of course, they could get rid of those 'indelible' marks. Among others, the sixth century doctor Aetius (as Jones discusses) gives directions for the removal of tattoos by means of some highly caustic substances, which more than likely signals a clientele of ex-convicts and ex-slaves who wanted to erase their past from public view.[20] We can imagine that this was never an easy, popular option, nor likely a very successful one (that is, it must have left scars which were almost equally incriminating). Yet it demonstrates that there were some exceptions (then, as now) to the rule of 'permanence'.

But tattoos are more than skin deep. Beyond the external, superficial level, what were the purposes of these 'permanent' marks? Claude Lévi-Strauss said that the purpose of tattooing among the Maori people (which was a decorative cultural characteristic) was 'to stamp onto the mind all the traditions and philosophy of the group'.[21] This purpose is transferable to tattooing as a punitive measure. And Michel Foucault's analysis of the body as a site for cultural and political manipulation and control is especially pertinent here.

> But the body is also directly involved in a political field; power relations
> have an immediate hold upon it; they invest it, mark it, train it, torture
> it, force it to carry out tasks, to perform ceremonies, to emit signs.

Marking the body with a permanent sign and in a compulsory situation is a clear means of exercising what he calls a 'micro-physics of power' over that individual.[22] That person is thus clearly subjected to the authority that imposed the mark, and the domination and institutional framework and hierarchy relations are clearly expressed in it. In the second mime of Herodas (third century BC), a slave is tattooed on the forehead with the proverbial words 'know yourself'. In this context, however, they seem to have the more particular meaning of 'know your place', or 'know your status'. Such writing on the body serves as a label indicating the contents of that body, which can in turn serve as a vehicle for the word of the master.[23]

Together with this advertisement of constraint and affirmation of control, there is the effort to alter an individual's mind-set, one's notion of selfhood and of personal empowerment. Externally the tattooed person is subject-ified, marginalized, degraded and stripped of self-esteem, reputation and standing in the community. But the subjection and discipline of the body is accompanied by the subjectification of the soul. The forcible imposition of the external mark, this disfigurement, serves also to make a lasting impression internally, which is difficult (though not impossible) to escape. The routes of communication run both ways, as Gell explains:

> The inside-facing and outside-facing skins are . . . one indivisible structure, and hence the skin continually communicates the external world to the internal one, and the internal world to the external one. This traffic, mediated by the skin, is the formative principle of the ego's basic sense of selfhood in the world.[24]

Furthermore, the placement of the mark is hardly random. Constantine's edict mentions tattooing on the hands or legs as an alternative to the face. It is uncertain whether this indicates that the face of a condemned person had been the exclusive site for a tattoo previously, but, in light of the evidence, it seems quite probable.[25] The face is, without a doubt, the worst place to receive a tattoo against one's wishes. Not only does it defy most attempts at concealment, but the face is also commonly viewed as the reflection of one's person, of the self, of the soul. One's own face is so deeply internalized and yet, at the same time, also dependent on mediation, either through a mirror or through the eyes of others. The gaze of the onlooker is virtually inescapable; there is little defence against it.[26] The ancient Mediterranean city was a face-to-face society, and the discipline of physiognomics – that is, the attempt to detect one's character, disposition, or destiny from external, especially facial, features – was more than an idle pastime.[27] Yet self-consciousness and concern with one's own face is so fundamental to being human that it seems to render unnecessary any other explanations particular to place, time, circumstances or cultural patterns: the effects of a penal tattoo forcibly applied to the face must be similar, deeply felt, devastating even, and long-lasting.

What was the design of these tattoos, or what message did they convey? Is a consistent pattern detectable? To answer these questions, it may help to consider comparative evidence for penal and other kinds of tattoos, both in antiquity and in more recent times. First, the available explicit evidence (gathered by Jones) indicates that the tattoos applied to criminals usually consisted of the name of the crime. Plato says that a temple robber, if a slave or an alien, should have his offence marked on his hands and forehead. Plautus makes reference to a man whose forehead is lettered (it seems) with the three-letter word *fur* ('thief'), clearly indicating his offence. In another of his plays, one slave is called *fugitivus* ('runaway') and then *hic litteratus* ('this lettered man'). Cicero indicates that the letter *K* was the mark put on the head of those convicted of making a false accusation (*kalumnia*). Elsewhere he suggests that 'on the forehead of each and every man should be tattooed what he feels about the republic', which may be suggestive of the name of the crime. And Petronius mentions foreheads inscribed with the inscription of runaway slaves. While this inscription seems to have been well-known to Petronius and his contemporaries, it is, unfortunately, not so to us. Conjectures begin, logically enough, with F or FUG for *fugitivus*. Another idea is that the tattoo was similar to the words often found on the iron collars placed on recaptured runaways: 'Stop me, because I'm a runaway, and return me to my master' (*tene me quia fugi, et revoca me domino meo*). Here is the name of the offence, and a little something extra: instructions for appropriate action to take. It should be noted that, among the references considered above, 'Armeniakon traitor' is the only tattoo with explicit reference to the crime.[28]

There are also many examples from recent centuries, in France, in England and in the United States, among other places, of the name of the offence being expressed in a punitive tattoo or other mark. (For example: V = vagabond; M = malefactor; F = fraymaker [church brawler]; B = burglar; SL = seditious libeller; D = drunkard; AD = adulterer; etc.)[29] In the twentieth century, the example of Nazi Germany is the most notorious, where a label placed on the clothing signified one's crime, which was tied to one's religion, nationality or sexual orientation. (For example: a red triangle for a political prisoner; pink for a homosexual; brown for a Gypsy; superimposed triangles – forming a Star of David – for Jews; etc. The actual tattooing of serial numbers on the left forearm, although permanent, is less meaningful in this context.)[30] This method is still employed in some parts of the world. Just a few years ago, a news service circulated a photograph of four Sikh women, their foreheads tattooed with the Punjabi word for 'pickpocket', who protested that they were innocent and had been maliciously stigmatized.[31] And the AIDS epidemic has given rise, from certain quarters, to suggestions of tattooing.[32] More and more judges around the United States are imposing stigmatizing punishments on drunk drivers, deadbeat dads, child molesters, and others – by publicizing their names or naming their crimes on licence plates, lawn signs and the like.[33]

A second category of penal tattoos are those that inscribe the name of the emperor. Herodotus informs us that the Persians tattooed slaves and prisoners of war. He states that they marked some Thebans with the name or sign of Xerxes. Other sources indicate that it was customary for prisoners of war to be marked with the sign of their captors; for example, Athenians would mark their prisoners with an owl. Suetonius, in what may be a typical bit of sensationalism, says that 'many men of honourable rank were first disfigured with tattoos and then condemned to the mines, to work at building roads, or to the beasts' by the emperor Caligula.[34] One can only imagine the tattoo (allowing for some megalomaniacal creativity): if not the name of some trumped-up charge or other, could it have denoted the name of the punisher, Caligula himself?

Much later, Ambrose, bishop of Milan in the later fourth century, says: 'Young slaves are inscribed [*inscribuntur*] with their master's mark [*charactere*], and soldiers are marked [*signantur*] with the emperor's name.' Such became the standard practice, apparently, in the later empire (as did the tattooing of workers in arms factories).[35] Is it possible that condemned Christians and others were marked with the name of the emperor, instead of with the name of their offence? Mines and quarries were, typically, imperial possessions, and thus those condemned to the unceasing toil of a life sentence conceivably may have borne the mark of their ultimate taskmaster and owner, the emperor. The apocalyptic vision of the 'mark of the beast' in *Revelation* 13.11–18 would have been represented by an unforeseen reality.

Penal tattoos that named the crime were the most prevalent. As Foucault says,

> It was the task of the guilty man to bear openly his condemnation and the truth of the crime that he had committed ... in him, on him, the sentence had to be legible for all ... It made the guilty man the herald of his own condemnation. He was given the task, in a sense, of proclaiming it and thus attesting to the truth of what he had been charged with ...[36]

But the name of the emperor is another common variant, which is also logical given the understanding that, as Foucault also says,

> the crime attacks the sovereign: it attacks him personally, since the law represents the will of the sovereign; it attacks him physically, since the force of the law is the force of the prince. [Therefore] by breaking the law, the offender has touched the very person of the prince; and it is the prince – or at least those to whom he has delegated his force – who seizes upon the body of the condemned man and displays it marked, beaten, broken.

In this way, to mark the body of the criminal makes everyone aware 'of the unrestrained presence of the sovereign'.[37] And so penal tattoos vary in content according to what message they are meant to convey.

The third possibility for the penal tattoo is the name of the punishment. This is exhibited in the fantastic tattoos inscribed on the Graptoi brothers, in which both crime and punishment (at least in its tattooing aspect) are spelled out. And this leads us to consider another possibility for the mark, which will bring us back to Hilary. In eighteenth- and nineteenth-century France, some criminals were marked with the abbreviated name of their punishment: GAL for those condemned to the galleys (*aux galères*), and TP for those condemned to perpetual hard labour (*aux travaux forcés à perpétuité*).[38] During the same period, Russians sentenced to hard labour (*katorga*) in Siberia were tattooed on their cheeks and forehead with an abbreviation of that punishment.[39] In the nineteenth century, some prisoners in Massachusetts were tattooed with 'Mass. S.P.' (for 'Massachusetts State Prison') and the date of their release.[40] Hilary's passage discussed above may indicate a somewhat similar practice in antiquity. He refers to the punishment of condemnation to the mines, *damnatio ad metallum*, in a slightly compressed and less common form, as *metallica damnatio*. This, says Hilary, is the inscription tattooed on the foreheads of those bishops whom he accuses Constantius of condemning. Thus it may be that the tattoo consisted simply of those very words, or of *metallica* or *metallum* alone, or, more simply yet, of an abbreviation (*MET*, or *MD*, or something to that effect), that is, the name of the punishment. Possible confirmation of this suggestion is found in a legal source which says that those who are condemned to *metalla* are considered *metallici* even before reaching their destination.[41] It may be that Hilary has led us to the discovery of an empire-wide standard for the form of the punitive tattoo. Evidence from Prudentius of Troyes lends credence to this finding. He attacks the ninth-century work on predestination by John Scotus Eriugena, and marks each excerpt targeted for refutation with the Greek letter *theta* (an abbreviation of *thanatos* ('death')), which, he adds, was a customary mark placed on those sentenced to death. This Byzantine usage, Chadwick suggests, harks back to a similar practice in the Western Mediterranean of late antiquity. Boethius, marked for death, may have borne a *theta* on his clothing.[42] Obviously this is not about tattoos *per se*, but the use of one letter as a mark of punishment is similar to practices mentioned above.

Thus there are at least three distinguishable variations in the mark applied to criminals in the Graeco-Roman world: the most well-attested drew attention to the crime that had been committed; a second represented the ruler, the one in power, who was offended by the crime; and a third named the punishment in store for or, in retrospect, the punishment suffered and survived by the tattooed one. In view of the developments observed in the nature of punishment in the later Roman Empire, it seems likely that those who were condemned to the mines were marked with some abbreviation of that punishment.

There is a fair amount of evidence for voluntary tattooing among the early Christians that overlaps with the evidence for punitive tattooing discussed here. In the book of *Revelation*, a work replete with mentions of marks and seals both positive and negative, John, writing near the end of the first century, describes a vision of a martial Christ as 'the Word of God', leading the armies of heaven: 'And he has on his cloak and on his thigh the name inscribed: "King of kings and Lord of lords".'[43] Although this is clearly not a mark inscribed by human hands, it may help to explain a couple of later references. For example, Victor of Vita, writing a history of the Vandal persecution in the 480s, describes the hunting out of Manichaeans in North Africa. One of these, a monk named Clementianus, was found 'having [the words] written on his thigh: "Mani, the disciple of Jesus Christ"'.[44] It is a striking echo. Procopius of Gaza, writing at the end of the fifth century, says that many Christians chose to be marked on their wrists or arms with the sign of the cross or the name of Christ.[45] Theophylact Simocatta, writing in the early seventh century about the reign of the emperor Maurice (582–602), records a curious anecdote. Apparently, some Christians had once advised the eastern Scythians who were victimized by the plague to tattoo their children on the forehead with the sign of the cross, and the mothers had complied.[46] And the 27th canon of Basil, from the mid-fourth century, forbids tattooing as the pagans do and declares it a contemptible practice of Satan's adherents.[47] (Prohibitions also suggest fairly open practice.) Thus it is apparent that religious tattoos – as decoration, as identification, as an indication of baptism or (eventually) of pilgrimage to Jerusalem, as an apotropaic device, as a mark of membership – were in use at the same time that institutions of political authority were using tattoos in a punitive sense.[48]

How had this happened? What had caused a practice, prohibited in *Leviticus* 19.28 and used as a sign of degradation by slavemasters and the Roman government, to become desirable? A radical transformation was occurring, the roots of which, it appears, can be found in the Apostle Paul's statement in *Galatians* 6.17: 'I carry the marks of Jesus tattooed [*stigmata*] on my body.' While Paul surely speaks metaphorically here, he is deliberately invoking the degrading practice of punitive tattooing. Throughout his letters, Paul embraces the role of slave of God and of Christ, and thus embraces humiliation, extreme obedience and bodily suffering.[49] The effect was deeply subversive of earthly authority, a kind of paradigm shift. This trend of reordering established beliefs is also visible in the second-century martyr acts, as Judith Perkins has explained:

> Enduring and dying in every case is interpreted as domination . . . Traditionally, injuring other people, killing them, provided a method of establishing dominance, of establishing in explicit terms a winner and a loser. Bruises, wounds, broken bodies, provided unassailable, palpable evidence of realized power. But Christian discourse reverses this equation and thus redefines some of the most basic signifiers in any culture – the body, pain, and death.[50]

The account of the tattooing of the Graptoi brothers, treated above, is an interesting example of a deliberate undercutting and reversal of the punisher's intent, and of the ambivalent nature of a tattoo:

> In commanding that their faces be inscribed . . . you involuntarily and unwillingly revealed them to be martyrs of Christ . . . The cherubim and flaming sword, beholding the countenance of these holy martyrs thus inscribed, will be overawed, will retreat and yield to them entrance to paradise.

The faces of these monks who venerated icons, defaced by an emperor who detested such veneration, had themselves, in defiance of earthly power, become venerable 'living icons'.[51]

There are similar examples of such a transformation in other places and at other times. In ancient Japanese society there was a change from punitive, non-representational tattooing to the non-punitive, elaborate representational tattooing called *irezumi*, due, in part, to the effort to mask criminal stigmata with attractive designs.[52] Some prisoners in the Soviet Gulag are reported to have tattooed their own foreheads with letters signifying 'prisoner of Brezhnev'.[53] This is a clear example of defiance, of taking a tool of totalitarian power – for in previous times, as mentioned above, exiles to Siberia had been forcibly tattooed – and negating it by turning the tables and assuming control. Nathaniel Hawthorne writes in *The Scarlet Letter* (which is not a tattoo, but a stigma, nonetheless):

> But, in the lapse of the toilsome, thoughtful, and self-devoted years that made up Hester's life, the scarlet letter ceased to be a stigma which attracted the world's scorn and bitterness, and became a type of something to be sorrowed over, and looked upon with awe, yet with reverence too.

The A stood for 'adultery', but, as the sexton says to Arthur Dimmesdale, 'did your reverence hear of the portent that was seen last night? A great red letter in the sky, – the letter A, – which we interpret to stand for Angel.' Public opinion of Hester had softened over the years.

> She was self-ordained a Sister of Mercy; or, we may rather say, the world's heavy hand had so ordained her, when neither the world nor she looked forward to this result. The letter was the symbol of her calling. Such helpfulness was found in her, – so much power to do, and power to sympathize, – that many people refused to interpret the scarlet A by its original signification. They said that it meant Able; so strong was Hester Prynne, with a woman's strength.[54]

Those Christians who died under sentence of the Roman government, some of whom had surely been tattooed on their foreheads, were witnesses to the power of faith and shining examples to those left behind. And those who had been so marked and then were able to return to their own communities were often treated as heroes, courageous models in the flesh. (The wish to emulate them may have led to some voluntary tattooing.) And thus, what had been a mark of crime and punishment, or ignominy and disgrace, of degradation and subjection to earthly power, was intentionally (or sometimes not so intentionally) transformed into a sign of glory and honour, of integrity, of holiness, of the victory of God's power and of brazen testimony to what may, in some cases, still have been a hazardous choice. Such marks were reminders of vows taken and blessings received, and, among those who shared them, signs of solidarity and of protection under God and Jesus Christ.

It is precisely this ambivalent nature of tattoos – first applied as punishment and intended to signify criminality and degradation, but then seen by those so marked and their comrades as positive group symbols – that brings us back to the present day where this discussion began. In modern Western society, the association of tattoos with defamation – the perpetual stigma – persists, in the eyes and minds of many if not most of those on the outside. For the insiders, the tattooed and their sympathizers (who have yet to submit to the needle), it is a mark worn with pride, a sign of belonging, the positive connotations of which are strengthened by the negative opinions of the majority. Whether the agents of and participants in the 'tattoo renaissance' can alter this situation and bridge the gap between these deep-seated cultural attitudes remains to be seen.

3 Insular Celtic Tattooing: History, Myth and Metaphor

CHARLES W. MACQUARRIE

In the early medieval *Vita Sanctae Brigitae* ('Life of Saint Brigit') there is a remarkable episode in which the renegade son of a king and his followers, all wearing 'evil marks' (*stigmatibus malignis*), approach Saint Brigit and seek her blessing for a raid they have planned against neighbouring 'enemies'.[1] Brigit refuses to sanction their raid, and instead informs the raiders that she intends to petition God that they may neither harm nor be harmed by anyone. She further hopes that God will make it possible for them to remove their 'diabolical signs' (*signa diabolica*). Brigit's petition is granted; she successfully redeems the bloody-minded gang and helps them to remove the marks. But what is the nature of these marks? The primary difficulty of this otherwise fairly straightforward episode is the proper translation and interpretation of the two collocations *signa diabolica* and *stigmatibus malignis*, which seem here to refer to the same phenomenon, and the crux of the difficulty is the meaning of the word *stigmata*. Sean Connolly in his translation of the *Vita Prima Sanctae Brigitae* puzzles over *stigmata* and petitions archaeologists or historians for help; he notes that:

> The word is rendered 'amulets' in our translation, *faute de mieux*. None of the standard dictionaries gives an English equivalent which suits the context quite as well. These trappings, whatever they consisted of, are clearly considered pagan by the author.[2]

One solution, proposed by Richard Sharpe, is that the *stigmata* referred to were temporary signs which signified a murderous vow, and which could only be removed after the vow had been fulfilled.[3] While the word *signa*, which has a more general application, might be used for 'temporary signs', the word *stigmata* is almost always used to describe permanent marks on human skin, and as C. P. Jones has demonstrated, the word usually refers to tattoos (rather than brands or wounds).[4] In fact, the word *stigmata* in the *Vita S. Brigitae* may very well be a reference to a tradition (both literary and probably to some extent actual) of insular Celtic tattooing.

It is curious that neither Sharpe nor Connolly even mention the possibility that 'tattoos' may be involved here. Although there is only tentative physical evidence for the practice, tattooing has long been associated with insular Celts (the Celtic speaking populations of Ireland and Great Britain) in the written record.[5] They are not as conspicuous in the corpus of classical and medieval European literature as in modern life and letters, but tattoos are detectable there. In fact, the source texts do not merely testify to the historical existence of insular Celtic tattooing – they help us to read the significance of these tattoos. In these texts, tattoos are associated with soldiers, slaves and criminals, with pagans, but also with holy men and women (soldiers/slaves of Christ). When associated with exotic cultures they indicate sometimes the rudeness and sometimes the nobility of the 'savages' who wear them, and when connected with groups within the civilized world they are usually signs of deviance or self-discipline. Furthermore, these various interpretations seem to have remained germane from the classical period into the early Middle Ages and beyond. While most of the references to Celtic tattooing are found in Classical and/or continental medieval texts, there are a few references to tattooing in medieval Irish and Hiberno-Latin literature as well; these references associate the practice with two very different sorts of community: the one characterized by illiteracy, paganism and outlaw status, and the other, conversely with extremes of literacy, Christianity and enculturation.

By tattoo, I mean, of course, an indelible mark made on the skin by inserting pigments into punctures. As C. P. Jones has demonstrated, the most common Latin and Greek words for the practice, the words that Strabo, Herodian and other classical authors use, are formed from the noun *stigma*.[6] Besides the *stigma* words, the noun *cicatrice* when used in combination with a word and the verbs *grajein* and *scribere* 'to draw or write' are also sometimes used to refer to tattooing. There are two words that seem to describe tattoos and/or tattooing in medieval Irish literature: the word *rind*, more commonly used to mean 'point', 'pupil' or 'star', but also 'cut' and 'a satirizing',[7] and the word *crechad*, which usually denotes 'raiding' or 'plundering'.[8] A third word, the noun *cruth* ('shape or form' as in the name *Cruithne*) may also convey tattoo, and though I have found no evidence of this use of the word in medieval Irish, there has been much discussion of the relationship between and meaning of the words *Cruithne* and *Picti* in the scholarship.[9]

Whatever the word for it, Celtic scholars from both this century and the last have been loath to credit the accounts of tattooing among the insular Celts which are found in classical sources. Heinrich Zimmer, for example, in his 1898 article 'Matriarchy among the Picts' argued, in contrast to the reports of the classical authors who make no such fine distinctions, that the practice of tattooing divided the Indo-European Celts from the non-Indo-European Picts.[10] He insisted that tattooing, like matrilineal descent, was a savage custom not properly associated with the Aryan community. Zimmer's denial of Celtic tattooing seems to owe more to his own preconceptions than it does to the evidence, and Nora K. Chadwick seems to have been influenced by a similar prejudice. She ends a section of her 1958 essay 'The Name Pict' with the claim that 'the picture of Pict and Briton punctured and scarred with cicatrices and stigmata and tattooed with zoomorphic designs' was among the marvels which 'the Romans and Alexandrians loved to record of the barbarians whom they conquered'.[11] Although Chadwick offers other possible explanations of the references to tattooing among Picts and Celts, she does her best to avoid the probable conclusion that tattooing was customary among some tribes of insular Celts.[12] She prefers to believe that the Romans simply made it up and/or got it wrong. Tattooing, however, is fundamentally unlike reports of two-headed men, or men with their faces in their chests. In fact, considering the prevalence of tattooing in human culture, it would be more remarkable if the Celts had not tattooed than the reverse.[13]

While Zimmer and Chadwick were reluctant to credit the proposition that the insular Celts tattooed themselves, Isabel Henderson in her 1967 study *The Picts* and Kenneth Jackson in his 1956 essay 'The Pictish Language' are considerably less doubtful.[14] Both of these authors also assume that the practice is foreign to Indo-European culture and must have been picked up by the Aryan Celts from the primitive pre-Celtic inhabitants of Britain, but they credit the classical accounts and admit that the insular Celts may have practised tattooing.

The discovery in the 1950s of the frozen body of an elaborately tattooed Scythian warrior in Siberia, which is dated to the fifth century BC, and more recently of a tattooed woman 'poet' from the same region, force us to admit that the classical accounts are perhaps, in this respect at least, not so fantastic after all.[15] We are also less sceptical of and less put off by the image of our Celtic ancestors wearing tattoos because of changes in our own culture. In fact, now that tattoos have become fashionable we are faced with a prejudice opposite to that of Zimmer; many people now seem to very much want the Celts to have been tattooed. The truth, as we shall see, is that both the incredulity of Chadwick and Zimmer, and the overly enthusiastic optimism of some of our contemporaries are off the mark. In contrast to the received wisdom of many moderns, post-moderns, and even modern primitives, no classical author makes the claim that the Celts, generally speaking, were tattooed; on the other hand there is evidence in both classical and medieval sources that tattooing was customary among at least some tribes of insular Celts.

There are a number of references to insular Celtic tattooing in the classical sources. In perhaps the most famous relevant account, *The Gallic Wars*, Caesar notes:

> Of all the inlanders most do not sow corn, but live on milk and flesh and clothe themselves in skins. All the Britanni paint themselves with woad, which produces a bluish colouring, and makes their appearance in battle more terrible.[16]

The verb he uses for the process is *inficere*, to stain or dye. Caesar's account, along with similar accounts of the custom of dyeing or staining among the Britons in Propertius, Ovid and Pomponius, gains credence from the recent discovery of dye in the skin of the Lindow man III.[17] As Pyatt points out, Caesar seems to be describing the stained interior dwellers second-hand, and it is curious, if body painting was prevalent in British culture, that he does not mention blue-painted warriors elsewhere. Other classical authors, however, such as Solinus, Herodian and Claudian all associate the practice of colouring the skin with the insular Celts, and they refer specifically to tattooing, puncturing as distinct from painting.[18] Isidore of Seville, writing in the early seventh century AD and possibly drawing on Claudian, associates tattooing with both Britons and Picts.[19] He claims not only that the Irish and the Picts (Scotti and Picti) tattooed, but also implies that tattoos were used to convey high social status.

While 'markings' of various sorts are mentioned in the Bible, from the mark God puts on Cain in *Exodus* to the mark which it is prophesied that the anti-Christ will put on his disciples in *Revelation*, there are only two uses of the word stigmata in the Latin Vulgate. The first of these occurs in the Old Testament, in *Leviticus* 19:28 and the second in the New Testament, in Paul's *Letter to the Galatians* 6:17.[20] There are Irish glosses to *Galatians* 6:17 in the *Codex Paulinus Wirziburgensis* (*c*. eighth century). The first glosses the word *stigmata* with the phrase: '[in marg.] indá érrad .i. turmenta flagillorum fuirib', which Stokes and Strachan translate as 'the stigmata', but which actually says 'the pricks/marks i.e. the torments of whips on you'. The second gloss reads: 'mind nabstalacte .i. conicimm dígail et cosc neich', which Stokes and Strachan translate more accurately as 'i.e. the mark of apostleship, that is, I am able to punish and to correct any one'. Although the marks referred to here must mean the marks made by the tortures that Paul suffered in the name of Christ that mark him out as Christ's disciple, nevertheless these identifying marks may also refer to the identifying 'stigmata' worn by the

Roman soldiers and slaves to indicate their allegiance.[21] It is not impossible that Paul is saying that he has marked himself with a sign (possibly a cross) of his devotion to Christ. The transcription *mind*, 'insignia or crown' looks to me, based on a copy prepared for me by University of Würzburg Library, to be a mistake. The word that glosses stigma here is actually *rind*.[22] The explanation which follows this gloss seems to be a scribal appropriation of Paul's voice, and relies on a secondary meaning of *mind/rind*, the former which can mean 'a blade or weapon' and the latter 'a spear point'. According to this gloss, Paul is saying that no one will assault him because he carries the weapons (rather than the marks) of Christ on his body.

There are not, as far as I know, any medieval Irish glosses to *Leviticus* 19:28. There are, however, a couple of informative glosses from the Germanic world. The first of these, from the 'Rand glossary' explains the practice being described by referring to the customs of the Scotti: 'Stigmata {stingmata F} id pictura in corpore sicut scotti faciunt . . .[23] Stigmata that is put pictures on the bodies as the Irish do'.[24] The second, however, *c.* 750, from the Biblical commentaries of the Canterbury school, is less specific about the ethnicity of the tattooers but more specific about the nature of the tattoos: 'Stigmata [XIX. 28]: .i. diuersas picturas in corporibus uestris draconum uel serpentium ut multi faciunt'. Michael Lapidge translates this gloss on stigmata as 'Marks: that is, put various tattooed pictures on your bodies of dragons or serpents, as many people do'.[25]

Whichever insular groups were doing it, it is clear from these insular glosses that these tattoos were more like the proscribed stigmata of *Leviticus* than those advertised in *Galatians*. It seems, nevertheless, that both the positive and the negative associations of tattooing were still pointed in eighth century insular culture. The Report of the Papal Legates in AD 786 to Pope Hadrian mentions both diabolical and Christian tattoos:

> For God made man fair in beauty and outward appearance, but the pagans by devilish prompting have superimposed most hideous cicatrices, as Prudentius says, 'He coloured the innocent earth with dirty spots.' For he clearly does injury to the Lord who defiles and disfigures his creature. Certainly, if anyone were to undergo this injury of staining for the sake of God, he would receive a great reward for it. But if anyone does it from the superstition of the pagans, it will not contribute to his salvation any more than does circumcision of the body to the Jews without belief of heart.[26]

Audrey L. Meaney in a 1992 article on Anglo-Saxon paganism conjectures, in reference to this decree, that the Northumbrians and even the more southerly English peoples may have 'picked up the custom of tattooing from the older inhabitants of Britain'.[27] This speculation is reminiscent of earlier scholars' claims that the insular Celts must have picked up the practice from even earlier inhabitants, but Meaney wants to stigmatize the insular Celts with the nasty habit, while Jackson and Zimmer wanted to blame the supposedly non-Celtic, non-Aryan Picts.

It is clear that the combination of the words 'cicatrices' and 'staining' in the letter of the Papal legates refers to a sort of tattooing, though the legates are more interested in the nature of the marks rather than the specific process or designs used. Were the legates then mindful of the use of the word *stigmata* in *Galatians* 6:27 and positive references to body marking elsewhere in the Bible? While it is reasonable to assume that some sorts of tattooing may have been acceptable to the Anglo-Saxon clergy, the evidence is insufficient to allow us to determine the extent either of the practice or of the church's tolerance for it. One well-respected scholar, however, has conjectured that tattooing may have been evidenced at the very highest levels of the Anglo-Saxon Church – even on the person of St Wilfrid, the sometime bishop of York.[28]

William of Malmesbury, writing of the 'savage' pre-Normans in his twelfth-century *Chronicles of the Kings of England*, does not provide for the acceptable sort of tattooing which is mentioned by the Papal Legates; his perspective is much more akin to the blanket condemnation and implicit horror of the classical authors and Isidore. The words he uses to describe the tattoos also suggest a classical source, though William is apparently not, like the classical authors, describing Celts:

> In general, the English at that time wore short garments reaching to the mid-knee; they had their hair cropped; their beards shaved; their arms laden with golden bracelets; their skin marked with punctured designs [*picturatis stigmatibus cutem insigniti*]; they were accustomed to eat excessively, and to drink until they vomited. These habits they imparted to their conquerors, as to the rest they adopted their manners.[29]

In fact, although the Papal Legates and other sources, including William of Malmesbury, appear to be describing Anglo-Saxon communities in their references to tattooing, it is not clear whether they are referring to an Anglo-Saxon custom, to an insular Celtic custom that had been adopted by Anglo-Saxons, or to a practice continued by insular Celtic sub-communities either within or on the margins of one of the Anglo-Saxon kingdoms.[30] But whether they were Anglo-Saxon or Celtic these communities were, apparently, tattooing. Furthermore, the bifurcation between evil pagan tattoos and good Christian ones, which is implicit in the Bible, is clearly articulated in the decree of the Papal Legates in AD 786.

One possible Irish source for 'good' Christian (*stigmata*) tattoos is *The Cambrai Homily* which is found in an eighth-century manuscript.[31] Stokes and Strachan translate: 'are n-airema futhu ocus airde cruche ar Chríst' as 'that he may receive stigmata and signs of the Cross for Christ's sake' and, if they are right, this certainly seems to be a reference to the good sort of stigma. It suggests that devout Christians should receive physical marks which convey Christ's crucifixion. It is not clear, however, what form these marks would take – marks/scars/tattoos on their hands, chest and feet; signs of the cross on their foreheads; a combination of these; or something else altogether. In any case, while it is possible that the process by which one would receive these marks might have involved tattooing, the words that normally convey 'tattoo' in medieval Irish, *rind* and/or *crechad*, are not used. Furthermore, the *Dictionary of the Irish Language* notes that the translation here of *futhu* as 'stigmata' is controversial.[32]

If tattooing were as prevalent as the glosses of the Canterbury School and the decree of the Papal Legates suggest, and if it were as concentrated in the Celtic populations as the classical authors, Isidore, and the Rand glossary imply, then we might expect to find large numbers of tattoo references in medieval Irish literature. But our expectations in this regard are frustrated. The medieval Irish saga tradition is, as far as I can tell, bare of references to tattoos. This silence is curious. Certainly there is ample opportunity for references to tattoos in the sagas, and the love of the fantastic which characterizes much of the saga literature makes us suspect that if the story-tellers knew anything of tattoos they would have used them to their advantage. Collingwood and Myers, in their 1937 study *Roman Britain and the English Settlements*, suggested that tattooing, like the custom of using chariots in warfare and fighting naked in battle, lingered on outside the Roman province but eventually died out. Nevertheless, while the practices of using chariots and rushing naked into battle are amply evidenced in the Irish sagas as well as the classical sources, tattoos appear only in the latter, and not frequently even there. One of the most conspicuous silences in this regard occurs in a section of the *Táin Bó Cualnge*, when Íliach mac Cas rushes to the aid of the wounded Cú Chulainn. Íliach is a Cruithne warrior, stark-naked, riding in a chariot, and bent on severing heads. There is no mention, however, of tattoos. So too in *Tógail Bruidne Dá Derga*, where the descriptions of characters go into unflattering and sometimes even scandalous detail. In this tale, even when words such as *rind, crechad* and *errad* are used in close proximity to each other and in connection with uncivilized practices such as *fáelad* ('were-wolfing') and *díberg* ('plundering'), and with men who are coloured red even to their teeth, they do not seem to refer to the practice of tattooing.

Nevertheless, as Kuno Meyer pointed out over 80 years ago, potential references to tattooing in insular Celtic literature do occur in texts outside the saga tradition such as the late-ninth-century *Cormac's Glossary* and the eighth-century poem *The Caldron of Poesy*.[33]

The word *crechad* in *Cormac's Glossary* seems to suggest the tattooing of criminals and/or the use of tattooing as a punishment, a tradition in the Persian, classical and perhaps also the insular Celtic world.[34] The *Caldron of Poesy* reference, however, is a different story. Liam Breatnach translates the relevant passages as: 'I being white-kneed, blue-shanked, grey-bearded Amairgen' and he translates the gloss to blue-shanked as: 'a tattooed shank, or one who has the blue tattooed shank'.[35] While obviously related to the passage in *Cormac's Glossary*, this reference implies, considering Amairgen's status elsewhere in the tradition as a judge and prophet,[36] that Amairgen has high rather than low status. The use of the tattoo to show high social status is consistent with the interpretations of tattooing among various barbarian peoples found in classical accounts. In her 1995 book *In Search of the Picts*, Elizabeth Sutherland repeats the hypothesis that the symbols on the Pictish standing stones may once have been used by the Picts for tattoos, and she connects these symbols with La Tène and the early Scottish Iron Age.[37] But, as Isabel Henderson pointed out nearly twenty years ago, while this theory is not at all impossible, especially in light of classical references to the Calydonian boar as a facial tattoo, and the elaborate animal shapes on the Scythian warriors, there is, as yet, no solid evidence for such a connection.[38] Amairgen, in any case, although he claims to have taken on many animal shapes himself, does not specify what shapes are 'tattooed' on his leg.[39] P. L. Henry, in his edition of the story, does not use the word tattoo at all; he translates *gairglas* as 'livid shanked' and includes the translation 'cauterized shank' in a note. Henry conceives of Amairgen's text as a conflation of oral and written/religious and lay traditions, and it is conceivable, especially in light of the story of Túan mac Cairill, which I will discuss presently, that this mediation is connected with his blued thigh.[40]

Some of the most interesting references to tattooing in the medieval Irish literary corpus occur in that remarkable collection of mythology, pseudo-history and biblical pastiche known as *Lebor Gabála Érenn*, 'The Book of

Invasions of Ireland'. Two of these *Lebor Gabála Érenn* references were transcribed from continental sources. The one explains the etymology of the place name Poitiers as coming from the founders' custom of tattooing:

> They [the Cruithne] went afterwards over Roman territory to Frankish territory, and founded a city there, called Poitiers; derived from *pictis*, from their [*rintaib*] tatu-marks.[41]

This excerpt contains a clear example of the word *rind* meaning tattoo. There is also a connection established here between the proper name Cruithne and tattoos, but the connection is through the Latin word *picti* (painted) rather than the word *cruth* (shape). This would seem, supposing that one knew of the hypothetical connection, to be the ideal place for the etymologically minded redactor to explain that *cruth* could refer to tattooed forms. Such an omission suggests that no such etymology was current in the medieval period.

The second reference, as Rolf Baumgarten has pointed out, is simply a borrowing and an ingenious elaboration of the reference to tattooing by Isidore of Seville. The final sentence of the following excerpt suggests that the monastic reaction to the contention that their ancestors, and possibly even their contemporaries, tattooed was anxiety.[42]

> The Scots are the same as the Picts, so called from their painted body, as though *scissi* [cut], inasmuch as they are marked with an impression of a variety of devices by means of iron needles and ink. Moreover the country is called Ériu from the heroes. Let anyone who reads this sweat![43]

While the above excerpt, being largely copied from Isidore, does not add substantially to our body of evidence, it does at least indicate that the word *stigmata* was clearly understood to refer to tattooing in Hiberno-Latin literature. The final reference to tattooing in *Lebor Gabála Érenn* is more innovative; it associates inscribing traditional information on the body with literacy, Christianity, and civilization. This reference concerns the transmission of lore from the oral tradition via Túán mac Cairill.

> it was written upon their knees and thighs and palms, so that it is corrected in the hands of sages and righteous men and men of learning and historians, and is upon the altars of saints and righteous men from that day to this; so that the authorities stitched all knowledge down to this.[44]

Although it is difficult to determine the exact meaning of this passage, I read it as a metaphorical reference to tattooing as an act of cultural preservation. It combines the oral explanation of transmission, found in texts such as 'The Settling of the Manor of Tara',[45] with the literary link described in the Fenian tales as when Patrick's assistant Brocán records Caoilte's tales of ancient Ireland in writing. Túán, who has been alive for centuries and, like Ameirgin, has undergone various incarnations (including one life as a deer and one as a salmon), seems to have dictated different parts of his story at different times to the various saints. The account of the saints absorbing and incorporating the oral traditions which are passed down to them is conflated with the literal inscribing of the story on vellum, and the result is an image of the saint as book and the saintly skin as manuscript. According to this reading of the passage, Túán's account was literally transcribed on the bodies of the saints by the scribes. The saints, then, like Túán, become receptacles of that knowledge, but unlike Túán, their knowledge is also recorded in letters and can convey their knowledge even after they die – when their bookish remains are placed on their altars and the altars of other learned men. The sages, learned men, righteous men, and historians are the redactors who study and preserve the saintly volumes. If this reading is correct, then we must imagine Túán having waited some years for his dissertation to be published, for the manuscript could not have been 'stitched together' until each of the saints had died and the skin had been cut out and then bound together. Each saint seems to embody a folio which was bound together in the vellum manuscript, perhaps the multi-layered *Lebor Gabála Érenn* itself – though the fact that it is placed upon altars suggests that the volume being referred to includes the Bible (perhaps with the *Lebor Gabála Érenn* as an appendix).

The saints then, are the vehicles through which the history of Ireland is incorporated into the Biblical tradition and translated into letters (the whole story being imprinted as a text in the minds of and on the bodies of the saints). This notion of the saintly body as text is manifest in the Irish and the continental Christian traditions – in both the Old and New Testaments the word of God is inscribed on the faithful.[46] It is also analogous to the stigmatizing of St Francis of Assisi and Elisabeth of Spalbeck in the thirteenth century, where the body is conceived as a parchment marked with signs which convey a holy text.[47]

There are descriptions of writing upon saintly bodies elsewhere in the hagiographic tradition as well. The metaphor of the body as book upon which words can be written or carved has been traced from classical to modern literature in some detail by Ernst Curtius. One of his examples is St Eulalia from Prudentius, who 'likens the wounds which the torturers inflict on her to purple writing in praise of Christ'.[48]

The recording of Túán's story on the bodies of the saints is an elaborate form of the trope of body as book, which is used elsewhere in the medieval Christian tradition, combined with the notion, found elsewhere in *Lebor Gabála Érenn*, of tattoo as a defining custom in insular culture. Túan's story also incorporates the stigmata, which are conceived of as signs of God's chosen grace and mark the wearer out as divine exemplars of the word.[49] The blue scar that the angel leaves on Saint Columba's side by means of a whip seems to be a sort of imprinting of the 'glass book' upon the Saint's body – a sign both of Columba's wilfulness and of his special servitude to God – and has a similar function.[50] In fact, this figure as it is used in reference to *Lebor Gabála Érenn*, not only helps to explain the origin of the text, it also accounts for the variety of recensions (Patrick's tattooed skin might be thought of as recension one, Columba's as recension two, etc...),[51] and reflects the cultural fusion which Mark Scowcroft explains is the heart of *Lebor Gabála Érenn*.[52] The trope, which involves the marking and eventual skinning of the saints, may also incorporate the punishments of crucifixion and flaying.

This final reference to tattooing is richer and stranger than the other two references in *Lebor Gabála Érenn*, but it is also less straightforward and does not involve the words *rind* or *stigma* as do the earlier references. Nevertheless, the *Lebor Gabála Érenn*, *Cormac's Glossary*, and the *Caldron of Poesy* demonstrate that there are references to tattoos in medieval Irish and Hiberno-Latin literature, and there are two primary associations which characterize these references – the two different characterizations of tattoos which are implicit in the Bible and explicit in the decree of the of Papal Legates in 786. First is the tradition that tattoos are indicative of paganism, illiteracy and criminality. Second is the reading of tattoos implicit in the Túan episode, which connects them with literacy, Christianity and civilized culture.

Another source which contains the material for both of these readings of tattooing is the text with which I began this study, the *Vita S. Brigitae*.[53] In this story, Brigit is met by a renegade king named Conallus and his gang of ruffians, all of whom are marked *stigmatibus malignis* 'by wicked tattoos'. Brigit frees them from their murder oaths and miraculously removes their stigmata by blessing them.[54] She tells them that because of their stigmata, either the 'evil' ones which she removed or because of 'holy' signs that she replaces them with, they will be protected from others, and others from them, by God.[55]

In a doublet of the Conallus episode, which occurs just a few lines later, another group of men having *stigmata diabolica* on their heads approach Brigit and seek her blessing for their plundering. She, on the contrary, asks them to cease and desist. To which they reply that they, not surprisingly, cannot remove their stigmata. But in the end, they too, thanks to the power of God and Saint Brigit, are able to efface their tattoos. While the *signa* signs that are associated with *laicus* or *díberg*, may, as Richard Sharpe has suggested, indicate that the wearer was bound by a murderous vow that he had to fulfil before they were removed, the word *stigmata* (which in all occurrences we have examined so far has meant a permanent mark – a tattoo or a wound) seems to convey that the wearer has been initiated into a way of life. Certainly the brigands' interaction with Brigit is not, as Sharpe argues, simply an odd 'contrivance' – the fact that they ask Brigit for her blessing may indicate that in the world of the narrator, murder outside the tribe is something that they might reasonably expect a religious leader to condone. One of the messages of this passage is that the pagan customs that had heretofore been culturally acceptable were, now that Brigit and Christianity had arrived, unacceptable.

Groups such as these seem to have been made up of junior warriors who functioned outside the respectable communities of Irish society. In his 1986 article 'Juvenile Delinquency in Early Ireland,' Kim McCone compares such groups to the present-day British skinheads, and suggests that the woods and mountains of Ireland served the same function as the football stadiums of today.[56] Among these groups tattooing indicates that one is a part of a particular community, and at the same time distinguishes the wearer from members of the general populace. The extent, type and placement of tattoos among members of these groups may also indicate status and suggest battle prowess. It is clear in the *Vita S. Brigitae* that stigmata are not, on a literary level at least, respectable in Christian Ireland, and it is meant to be a particular tragedy that Conallus, the oldest son of a king, has come to Brigit with his head tattooed. It is possible that the stigmata in *Vita S. Brigitae* signal the difference between the temporary and the permanent state. Is it also possible, as the phrase *stigmata diabolica* suggests, that the tattoos distinguish good *féinnidi*, who only pillage outside of the tribe, from evil *díbergaig* who pillage both at home and away? It is perhaps most probable that the relationship between stigmata, *fénnidi* and *díbergaig* is not quite so clear-cut – except in so far as the latter sometimes wear them but the former do not.[57]

In any case, Brigit removes their evil tattoos by means of a sort of baptism, and thereby alters their allegiance, first freeing them from the conspicuous and presumably indelible marks of their blood-lust and slavery to demons, and then blessing them with the signs (which may or may not be visible) of their servitude to God.[58] There is a link between the new marks which Conallus and his gang wear by the grace of Brigit, in that, in a later passage, his enemies see him and his troop sitting in clerical fashion with a fire in their midst and *libros apertos coram eis*, 'books open before them'. The marks that Brigit gives them seem somehow to enable them to become literate, and they are bookish too in that Brigit makes their brows palimpsests by replacing their rebarbative marks with holy writ. She, in effect, revises them for publication.

The tattoos mentioned here are located on the head, like those mentioned by Claudian in association with his personified Britain, though on the forehead rather than on the cheeks. Other classical sources, however, do mention tattooing of the forehead in association with Britons.[59] Though the 'stigma' used by the gangs mentioned in the Brigit story are not described, a boar or wolf image or some other symbol of military prowess and/or wildness would certainly seem appropriate in context. But, whatever the kind of *stigma* which was marked on the foreheads of the gangs, Brigit is able to efface them, and her feat here is similar to classical accounts of miraculous facial tattoo removals.[60] Brigit's removal of tattoos is also consonant with her repeated healings of permanent injuries by means of holy water, especially skin conditions such as leprosy.[61]

Tattoos, then, are visible on the vellum of Irish and Hiberno-Latin literature, even as, judging from classical and medieval accounts, they must have at one time been visible on the skin of some insular Celts. While, judging by the literary evidence, it is likely that some Celts did tattoo, it is important to note that the classical accounts refer not to Celts in general, but rather to insular Celts, *Scotti*, *Britani* and *Picti*, and probably, even here, intend particular tribes within these groups.

References to tattoos in the classical and the medieval world, as we have seen, associate the practice with both Christianity and with demons, with both civilization and the forces of disorder. The classical references to tattooed Celts convey either their savagery or their nobility; while some medieval references such as the report of the Papal Legates from Britain in 786 distinguish between acceptable Christian tattoos and unacceptable pagan ones. These interpretative dichotomies are evidenced in the Irish and Hiberno-Latin sources as well. In some of these sources they are associated with captivity or punishment, while in others they seem to designate high social status within the tribe. In still other sources tattoos are more strictly definitional – they are what make the insular Celts special, and the *Britani*, *Scotti* and *Picti* are named for them.[62] Tattoos were also used in the literature as creative metaphors, as the image of the human body marked with letters which preserve and convey pagan and/or Christian tradition. The insular Celtic tattoo can be in one context a mark of iniquity and subjection to evil powers, and in another a sign of Christian virtue and subjection to Christ. While we may hope to find further such references to tattoos and tattooing in medieval Celtic literature, especially by paying special attention to the words related to *stigma*, *rind* and *crechad*, it is possible that no clearly legible references will be found in the Irish or Welsh sagas. Those references, if they did exist, seem to have been as radically transformed as the *stigmata* on the foreheads of Conallus and his followers; though perhaps, if we look long and carefully enough, more traces may be visible after all.

4 Wearing the Universe: Symbolic Markings in Early Modern England

JENNIPHER ALLEN ROSECRANS

In the spring of 1609, Simon Forman, a prominent London medical-astrologer, 'made the characters' of Venus, Jupiter and Cancer on his left arm and right breast. The only surviving record of this act is a brief note in the second volume of his 1611 *Volumen Primum*, an alchemical commonplace book, composed of personal diary notes, medical case studies, alchemical notations and astrological treatises, which were possibly written for publication in manuscript or in print. Under the heading of 'Karacters', Forman commentated generally on astrological and celestial symbols, and cited specific empowered astral letters and characters. In the midst of cataloguing the relationship of the planets, the elements and the fixed stars to their correspondent astrological characters, Forman wrote,

> If a man, in a special hour observing the course of heaven, will better his constellation and impress in his body the character of a planet star sign, or angel that it shall there abide and be seen ever after, Let him do it as I shall teach him.[1]

After this corporal revelation, Forman returned to the original course of the work, and quoted several Latin phrases from John Repperus on the influence of consonant astral characters. Before illustrating the celestial characters themselves, however, Forman resumed his discussion of his astral marks:

> Nota: The characters on my left arm I made them 1609 the 24 day of march . . . when 7 degrees of [Cancer] was ass[endant], and they are these [Venus, Jupiter, Cancer]. I made them the quau Regis wherein [Sun] was dissolved of them . . . /The characters . . . on my right breast I made 1609 when 26 of March . . .[2]

According to Forman's calculations, Venus, Jupiter and Cancer were the astrological bodies that governed his horoscope. By impressing the

'Sequuntur figurae literarum divinarum', engraving from Henricius Cornelius Agrippa von Nettesheim, *Three Books of Occult Philosophy* (1535) (London, 1651), showing the divine characters for the planets.

correspondent characters of these three celestial entities upon his arm and his breast, Forman believed he would be able to harness the power of his horoscope, and alter the course of his life. He particularly sought this power because he wished to alter the destiny of his body in this life, and possibly in the afterlife.[3] Which particular sign or symbol for Venus, Jupiter and Cancer Forman employed, and how he wished to control the fate of his body, however, were not recorded in his manuscripts. Whether he inked his arm with the traditional sign for Venus (♀) or with one of the divine characters for Venus, Forman firmly believed that by marking his flesh with the proper astrological symbol at the precise astrological time, he would be able to determine his own fate. Moreover, he believed that it was the permanency of these markings, which would 'abide and be seen ever after' even in death, that invested him with the power to guide his life, both in this world and the next.

The permanency of the astral symbols scribed on Forman's shoulder and chest was achieved with special ink that Forman devised and concocted himself. He spoke to the means and to the kind of this ink and to the permanency of his markings in 'Colloures of the Stone', which also was bound in the second volume of the *Volumen Primum*. Forman wrote of this ink and its celestial efficacy:

> Nota per Forman 1608 Jun 22/ I dissolved gold filed, in the water of sall Armoniak [sodium chloride]; the gold dissolved the water looked very yellow. I put out a little of it in my hand, and it dried a little up on my hand, and I wiped it away, and there was no thing seen, but an hour after I washed my hands and saw nothing. And an hour more after that my hand began to look reddish tawny or purple; and afterward the more I washed the deeper red or purple tawny like russet it was, so that it came to fresh colour & would not away by any washing in four days after. It is the only thing to make characters w[ith] on ones body in an hour of any planet.[4]

We know that with this colour recipe Forman permanently etched three symbols upon his skin, but we do not know the means by which he accomplished these markings. His notebooks did not detail whether he punctured or incised his shoulder and chest with the ink, or if, in fact, he employed any traditional method of tattooing. To test the efficacy of his indelible ink recipe Forman merely put some on his hand, wiped it away and then waited. To mark his flesh he may have merely effected the same method. All that Forman recorded was that he somehow permanently altered both his flesh and his destiny by inking himself.

Corporal alterations like Forman's were not unknown in the early modern period. In fact, writing on the body, both permanently and ephemerally, was fairly common in magical, medical and religious practices. Although tattooing itself was not a widely practised custom in sixteenth- and seventeenth-century England, there was an array of subcultures that authorized certain types of somatic marks and tattoos. Long before overseas customs of tattooing landed in the British Isles, a host of miscellaneous body inscriptions was catalogued in the occult texts, the magical treatises, the medical compendiums, the personal notations and the popular literature of early modern England. The question must be raised, however, about the relationship between marking the flesh and tattooing it. Does this array of magical, medical, religious and popular somatic scholarship record a nascent stage of early modern tattooing, or does this evidence merely attest to the range of early modern symbolic writing customs that preceded the advent of the tattoo in the British Isles? The answer lies in how we understand the tattoo in the early modern period. If it is the penetration of ink under the skin that specifies the tattoo, then this disparate scholarship yields no clear record of tattooing. If, on the other hand, permanence and indelibility also define the tattoo, then certain magical markings can claim this character. Unfortunately, the extant sources that speak to inking and to incising the flesh are too scattered and too mundane to have left a consistent mark on the historical record. Given the paucity of early modern evidence that speaks directly to the placement of ink under the skin, we cannot assume that every indelible or temporary mark recorded in the medical, magical and popular literature of this period can be labelled as a tattoo in the contemporary sense. However, the sources do indicate an array of early modern corporal practices that bear a close affinity with the religious tattoos known to have been acquired by sixteenth- and seventeenth-century English pilgrims, and that may provide a link between indigenous and extrinsic versions of the practice.

Although these eclectic inking traditions are not known to have coalesced in England into a 'tattoo culture' as such until the later eighteenth century, the extant recorded range of indelible and temporary corporal inking practices does demonstrate a strong correspondence between known tattooing practices and similar domestic forms. One example of such an affinity is John Bulwer's 1653 *Anthropometamorphosis*, a text dedicated to describing corporal habits from around the world. Although Bulwer detailed the tattooing practices of 'the Samians', 'the Egyptian Moors', 'the Inhabitants of Mangi, Sierra Leone, the Cape of Lopo Gonsales and the Island of Candou', the peoples of 'Mozambique, Ethiopia, Cape of Bona Speranza, the Kingdom of Bemi, Seal Bay and Siam', and 'the Brazilians and the Floridians', he made no mention of English inking practices. Bulwer's only commentary on the state of English corporeality was by way of attacking the fashions of the English gallant. Referencing the Virginian men who 'pounce and raze their Faces and whole Bodies',[5] Bulwer wrote,

> The slashing, pinking, and cutting of our Doublets, is but the same phansie and affectation with those barbarous Gallants who slash and carbonado their bodies, and who pinke and raze their Satin, Damask, and Duretto skins.[6]

Moreover, believing the fashions of the English gallant that mimicked the corporal practices of the peoples he studied to be born of the same impetuses and ungodly conceits, Bulwer commented,

And I think it were not impossible to prove, that there was never any conceit so extravagant, that ever forced the Rules of Nature; or Fashion so mad, which fell into the imaginations of any of these indicted Nations, that may not meet with some public Fashion of Apparel among us, and seem to be grounded upon the same pretended reason.[7]

Like Bulwer, who wrote of foreign inking practices but only acknowledged English corporal customs in terms of apparel, the anonymous author of *A Wonder of Wonders: or, a Metamorphosis of Fair Faces voluntarily transformed into foul visages* wrote of ancient English inking customs, but not of contemporary ones. The author of this slight treatise briefly spoke to the English history of inking the flesh only so he could compare and slander the women of his age who painted and patched their faces. Although disapproving of the 'heathen' men and women 'who here inhabited' and 'used this Art of Painting and Spotting their outward skins', the unknown author praised the customs of the 'ancient Britains and Picts' who bedecked themselves only in times of war in order 'to afright their enemies', when compared with the base reasons of 'pride' and 'wantonness' that drove the women of his day to so mark their bodies.[8] Although the *Anthropometamorphosis* and *A Wonder of Wonders* illustrated an array of very different worldly somatic trends, neither text spoke of contemporary indigenous English inking practices, save for the cosmetic fashions that *A Wonder of Wonders* critiqued. These texts, however, were but two of a panoply of anthropological and historical texts written in this period that at once spoke to external tattooing acts and at the same time denied England's rich symbolic bodily marking culture.[9] It is difficult to believe that the tattooing customs that authors like Bulwer discussed did not cross the waters that separated England from the rest of Europe and the Americas. But even if they did not, and even if the state of English inking practices consisted merely of stories of foreign lands and of myths of ancient times, the precedents for English modern symbolic tattooing were certainly set within the early modern period, with its affinity for indelibly marking and inking the body with magical, medical and religious signs and symbols.

In the early modern record, the largest subculture that advocated the philosophies and the practices of corporal inscription were the practitioners of the occult arts. For these would-be magi, the inking of the flesh was a very distinct and a very carefully recorded part of magical action. This documentation, which was generally clandestine and limited in its nature, served as the basis for occult practice and meditation in the medieval and early modern periods. Forman's richly detailed manuscripts were no exception. He documented inking his flesh so that his fellow magians could learn from his theurgy: 'Let him do it as I shall teach him.'[10] The rediscovery of Forman's writings invaluably broadens our current understanding of both early modern magic and early modern corporal markings. Such texts record the actual implementation of occult philosophy and of training manuals. Although Forman's manuscript is the only known example of English astral inking by a magus, it animates the most intelligently ambitious and controversial use of symbolic inscriptions – the astral tattoo.[11] Occult corporal markings were steeped in controversy not only because marking the flesh altered the 'Image of God', but because astral markings in particular imparted on their bearer an array of supernatural, if not demonic, powers.

The occult philosophy behind Forman's choice to ink his body permanently was drawn from a very arcane and contentious milieu. Natural magic in the early seventeenth century was perhaps at the peak, or just past the peak of its intellectual and cultural influence. During the Renaissance, scholars like Agrippa, Ficino, Bruno, Pico and Paracelsus stripped magic of its old medieval tradition and demonic unorthodox character, and rebuilt it with a new pious Neoplatonic purpose. This 'new magic', which both reflected an enlivened curiosity about the workings of man, the world and the universe, and placed him as the focus of such operations, became one of the central elements of early modern culture. Widespread belief in the macro-microcosmic Neoplatonic worldview that God created a universe where both the celestial world and the terrestrial world possessed 'all things . . . in all' helped to validate this new magic. This new natural magic, premised on 'the others in the one and the one in the others', in turn reaffirmed man's beliefs that every terrestrial and celestial thing possessed an 'essential virtue distilled by God', that every entity in the natural, the celestial and the intellectual worlds was composed of the same virtues and ideas, and that they all obeyed God (see illus. p. 53). Moreover, this hierarchy of sameness, where superior entities were merely purer and more powerful iterations of the inferior, meant that every entity possessed the power to affect and effect every other.[12] Occult adepts aspired to harness that power. The question that the 'magical renaissance' raised was not whether magic permeated all aspects of the early modern universe, but whether it was moral and lawful for magicians to engage with such forces.

To understand further the 'new magic' and those would-be magi who conjured it, a brief examination of the philosophies of occult magical practice in this period is essential. In 1535, Henricus Cornelius Agrippa von Nettesheim published his *Three Books of Occult Philosophy*. This compendium was the most complete and practical repository of Neoplatonic and ancient magical philosophies ever produced. Drawing upon a vast array of Egyptian,

Greek, Roman, Arabic, Jewish and medieval writings and lore, this trilogy premised three types of magic: terrestrial, celestial and angelic or intellectual. Although Agrippa's *Three Books* did not directly discuss the use of astral inscriptions, it elaborated the corporal foundation of terrestrial, celestial and angelic magical writings upon which they were premised. According to Agrippa, terrestrial magic was the collation and codification of Neoplatonic philosophies and natural applications. Based on the similitude of terrestrial things, *Three Books of Occult Philosophy* offered numerous examples of earthly natural magic: if a person desired to increase their boldness, they employed the heart of the cock, since the boldness of the cock never wavered; to increase watchfulness they were to use the eyes of a night owl. For a person to absorb the inherent virtue of the prescribed entity, it was 'dried, and bound to the arm of him' in the form of an amulet, a ring, a talisman, or a gamahe.[13] To arrest the magical effect, the object would be 'taken off from him'.[14] Similarly, wearing rings infused with a lizard's ability to regenerate its eyes protected against cataracts. Since God created all things in various proportions of the same virtues and elements, terrestrial magic merely aligned a more powerful entity with an impoverished one. In this manner, the distillation of the cock's boldness was the efficacious remedy for timidity.

In the sixteenth and seventeenth centuries, while Catholicism and Protestantism (in all of its various guises) clamoured for control of the Church of England, medieval popular magic quietly evolved into the 'new magic' of the Renaissance. The two religious camps, in addition to denouncing each other as heterodox, condemned this new magic as blasphemous and superstitious. The Catholic Church forbade the magical arts because they placed the power to manipulate the divine in the hands of ordinary men. The Protestant Church assailed magic, with its relics and icons, as a form of popery. The result was a cacophony of condemnations. While Protestantism attacked the Catholic Church for mechanistically mediating the divine on the behalf of man, Catholicism impugned magic for the same practices. As the Catholic Church charged Protestantism with abandoning Church ritual and the holy sacraments, Protestantism censured early modern magic for employing those same rituals and icons. While each religious camp made a great noise about the magical elements within the other, their attacks upon actual magic and its applications in early modern society were generally mild. As people's religious beliefs were questioned and denounced, and as their Church moved from Catholic, to Protestant, to Catholic, to the Church of England, people were often left without access to their own traditional religious means to heal the ailing body, to fortify themselves against spiritual infection, or to find the cause and remedy for misfortune. Magic and

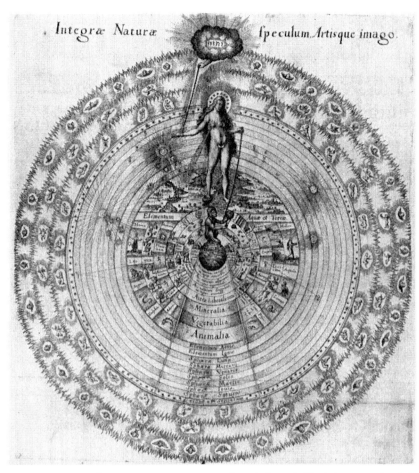

Integræ Naturæ Speculum Artisque imago, engraving from Robert Fludd, *Utriusque cosmi maioris scilicet et minoris metaphysica* (Oppenheim, 1617).

the occult, although censured in the wars of religion, never faltered in their efficacy or in their accessibility. Moreover, the instability of 'official' religion guaranteed that the people would not turn away from magic. The incomplete doctrinal conversions and incoherent evangelical revisions of both Churches, in fact, ensured that the people would turn to magic. Throughout the early modern period, then, charms, talismans and characters remained constant and vital weapons in the people's armoury of spiritual, medical and social defence. As religions clashed, magicians and folk practitioners continued to dispense their terrestrial magic without pause and without much social or cultural criticism, save from the Church.[15]

In dispensing natural magic, however, the practitioner was often faced with a paucity of prescribed terrestrial entities: lion's hearts and the bone of a man never touched by the ague were uncommon in the early modern larder. In such instances, to complete the prognostication or the healing the adept turned to celestial magic. If the heart of a cock was unavailable, than the magi called upon its correspondent superior entity, and invoked the boldness of Aries (Mars). To conjure the intangible celestial entity, practitioners relied upon its symbol or character: the visible mark that represented the invisible power.[16] Celestial magic, like terrestrial natural magic, worked through the flesh; instead of the dried eyes of a night owl, however, a seal or set of characters was applied, and 'from them that virtue, or power' was derived.[17] The power of symbols and characters was similarly called upon when an adept desired a more powerful result, or aspired to communicate with the angels. Intellectual or angel magic differed from its terrestrial and celestial siblings because it conjured divine power not for earthly means, but in order to effect change in both the terrestrial and celestial worlds. Almost everyone – Protestant and Catholic, nobleman and husbandman – perceived this form of magic, which sought to manipulate and control divine power, as extremely subversive. Although Forman was rather vague as to how his three markings affected his body, his desire to control the destiny of his corporal self after death was blasphemous. His aims went far beyond the ordinary religious condemnations of magic; they made the employment of sigils and amulets the very inscriptions of heresy. This was magic at its most blatantly apostatic. This was the magus not as Prospero, but as Faustus – the priest-like magician who tried to usurp the power of God to alter His will in the most crucial arena, the afterlife.

The occult ceremonies of this Faustian magic were detailed in *of Occult Philosophy, or of magical ceremonies: the Fourth Book*.[18] In this book, the basic corporal recipes of Agrippa's terrestrial and natural celestial magic, where correspondent virtues were absorbed through the flesh, were applied to the occult aims of angel magic. It is in this union of somatic magical philosophy and occult practice that Forman's choice to ink his arm and breast can be contextualized. Describing the seventh stage of the first occult ceremony, the author of *of Occult Philosophy* instructed:

> And on the seventh day, which is the Sabbath, let him being washed and fasting, enter the circle and perfume it, and anoint himself with holy anointing oil, by anointing his forehead, and upon both his eyes, and in the palms of his hands, and upon his feet.[19]

Ink and paint were not the only media used to inscribe astrological characters on the flesh, on holy linens, or on parchment. Many ceremonies, like this one, relied on holy oils, blood or perfumes for these purposes. Much like the placement of the cross upon the forehead during Catholic High Mass, 'anointing' in this passage probably referred to the writing of predetermined characters with a blessed salve. Further in the passage, this stage of the ceremony is amended, to instruct the adept that, 'as often as he enters into the circle', he should 'have upon his forehead a golden Lamen, upon which there must be written the name Tetragrammaton'.[20] The Lamen was a piece of metal, wax or paper inscribed and coloured with numerous divine names, seals and characters, determined 'according to the rule of the numbers', and held to the forehead with a 'clean linen'. Pressing the Lamen to the flesh protected the magi from evil spirits, and helped to summon forth good ones to do the magi's bidding. Forman's inscriptions were merely a more permanent iteration of this philosophy.

Central to the conjuring of angels was this ritualized writing of predetermined characters. According to Reginald Scot, a self-made authority on the 'lewde dealing of witches', in order to bind the spirit Bealphares to truthfully answer questions and to reveal the locale of secret treasure the conjurer must 'abstain from lecherousness and drunkenness, and from false swearing, and do all the abstinence that he may do' for three days. On the third day, wrote Scot, the conjurer 'must be cloathed in cleane white cloathes . . . and beare with him inke and pen, wherewith he shall write this holy name of God almightie in his right hand ✠ Agla ✠ & in his left hand this name ✠ ♊ + ▽ ✠ . . .'.[21] In addition to the inkings of the conjurer's hands, the binder was to have particular words and figures drawn upon his clothes. Only with the appropriate preparation of empowered inscription, according to Scot, could the power of the spirit be evoked.[22] Not only did the body, or the things that touched the body, serve as a canvas for these inscriptions, but the locale of the invocation also required similar chirography. As encapsulated in the third scene of Christopher Marlowe's 1604 *Doctor Faustus*, the orchestration of celestial power hinged on the occult circle:

> Within this circle is Jehovah's name
> Forward and backward anagrammatiz'd,
> The breviated names of holy saints,
> Figures of every adjunct to the heavens,
> And characters of signs and erring stars,
> By which the spirits are enforc'd to rise.[23]

According to occult prescription, the circle was prepared much in the same manner as the Lamen – it was composed of, and framed by, divine names, characters and pentacles 'agreeing to the work' of the particular ceremony.[24]

This empowered occult circle did not, however, protect the magus from the influence of spirits (particularly bad ones) while outside its circumference. One magus, in fact, included in his binding spell the explicit instructions that he was not to be harmed in any manner once he left the safety of the circle:

> O N[ominum] noble & loving spirit as thou art a king & hast under the ministers & subjects which do obey thee/ I being the image of God & servant of the same true & everliving God, by the authority of my function calling which thou knowest is honourable. O N[ominum] together with my humanity & baptism, do exorcise & charge thee make haste come & appear unto me, & enter into the circle & bound with I have p[ro]vided for thee in this place & distant from his holy circle wherein I now stand & that thou have no power to hurt me nor my fellows nor any living creature inhabiting under the ☾ globe & upon the face of the earth, with fire, lightening, thunder, nor water, nor by any other means, here to I charge thee by virtue of the blessing wherein my baptism at the font I was blessed in the name of the father & of the son etc, Amen.[25]

Due to the limited and temporary nature of the occult circle, which had to be rewritten for each invocation, and due to the insecure nature of incantations that hinged on the promise of a beguiling and capricious spirit, many magical adepts pursued more indelible sources of power. These magi, who summoned the angels not to locate a lost treasure or to cure a client's palsy but in order to control celestial power, required immutable and immediate access to the invisible. While John Repperus always wore a ring that was inscribed on its inner side with celestial characters to provide this access, Simon Forman inked the appropriate characters on his flesh. These means provided constant protection and uninterrupted manipulation of the supernatural. There was no guarantee, however, that a ring would remain on the body after death, or that it would be reconstituted at the resurrection. Permanent markings, on the other hand, would 'be seen ever after'.

The physicians of the early modern period similarly employed corporal writing. Inscriptive medicine, like natural magic, which imbued one entity with the power of another, relied on terrestrial and celestial sympathies to heal the ill or the injured. A mixture of magic, science and religion, medicine in medieval and early modern England deployed amulets, charms, talismans and gamahes, as often as it did herbal and surgical remedies. Unlike terrestrial and celestial magic that invoked specific virtues from particular entities, much of what the medical wizards scribed on the body or on paper that would touch specific parts of the body possessed only remnant significance.

Unless the physician was also a practising magus, like Forman, Richard Napier, William Lilly, or John Booker (who were among the most famous medical-astrologers of their day), the corporal character remedies generally prescribed by local practitioners bore little resemblance to the original empowered recipes. To cure the ague one physick advised: 'Write these words: "Arataly, Rataly, Ataly, taly, aly, ly," and bind these words about the sick man's arm nine days, and every day say three *Pater Nosters*.'[26] To cure 'all manner of falling evils' another physick recommended taking

> the blood of his little finger that is sick, and write these three verses following, and hang it about his neck, 'Jasper fert Mirrham, Thus Melchoir, Balthazar Aurum, Haec quicum secum portat tria nomina regum, Solvitur à morbo domini pietate caduco.'[27]

Although these incantations contained debased elements of occult magic and remnants of Christian prayer, they possessed little of the original correspondent powers of either.

One of the oldest and most influential sources of such inscriptive medicine in medieval and early modern England was John of Gaddesden's *Rosa Anglica practica medicine a capite ad pedes*. Although written in Latin, this 1314 medical compendium was phenomenally popular. Gaddesden was known for his poetical and appealing writing style, and the *Rosa Anglica* made him quite famous in his day. His medical influence was reflected in Chaucer's *Canterbury Tales*. In *The Prologue*, the tales' physician was noted to be a man of superb skill and vast knowledge:

> With us there was a Doctor of Physick,
> In all this world never was there one his like.
> [...]
> Well knew he the old Aesculapius
> And Dioscorides, and Rufus knew
> Old Hippocrates, Hali and Galen
> Serapion, Rhazes, and Avicenna
> Averroes, John of Damascus, and Constantine of Afer
> Bernard, and John Gaddesden, and Gilbert.[28]

Throughout the medieval and the early modern periods, Gaddesden's text was a core source of practical medical advice.[29] In the case of a toothache or sore jaw, Gaddesden recommended:

> Again, write these words on the jaw of the patient: 'In the name of the Father, the Son and the Holy Ghost, Amen. + Rex + Pax + Nax + in Christo Filio', and the pain will cease at once as I have often seen.

If this failed Gaddesden recommended a second form of symbolic writing: 'Again, draw characters [of the Blessed Trinity] on parchment or panel and let the patient touch the aching tooth with his finger as long as he is drawing, and he is cured.' In addition to these remedies, making the 'sign of the holy Cross' on the aching tooth and on the patient's head during Sunday mass kept 'them from pain in the future' and cured 'that which may be present'.[30]

Medicinal corporal inscriptions were not tattoos – they were not permanent and they did not penetrate the flesh. Nevertheless, the symbolic imagery many practitioners prescribed to heal their patients certainly reified the ascent of, and perhaps gave rise to, the advent of the symbolic tattoo. For the medieval and early modern physician and patient, corporal writing embodied magical and religious belief. Much in the same way that there was a ubiquitous tenet that all things in the universe, both terrestrial and celestial, were composed of the same virtues and properties, people believed that religious and astral symbolism drew their mystical powers from the same well. For Gaddesden and later practitioners, drawing a cross on the forehead of a man maddened with headache effected a result not just because of the divine influence of the cross, but because if done on a day appropriate to the patient's constitution and under the planetary rule of that portion of the body, the potency of the result was assured. Texts and images devoted to this fine balance between medicine, astrology and the map of man's body abounded in the period because according to the macro-microcosmic worldview, 'there is no member in man which hath not correspondence with some star sign, intelligence, divine name, sometimes in God himself the Archetype'.[31] In 1599, *The Key to Unknowne Knowledge* recommended, for instance, following these astrological determinants for the placement of charms, herbals, or for surgery when treating a patient while the moon was in Aries: '♄ the breast, ♃ the belly, ♂ the head, ☉ the reins, ♀ the fat, ♀ the legs, ☽ the knees'.[32] John Woodall, in his 1639 surgical thesis, similarly believed that amputations performed on a day when the moon was waning, the stars were in the proper alignment and a prayer had been said were more likely to be successful.[33]

Like the magico-medical texts, the remnant miscellaneous records of corporal marks in the early modern period are steeped in occult and religious symbolism. A famous French account translated into English in 1711 chronicled the attempts of one 'Monsieur Oufle' to 'render himself belov'd' by the woman he loved. To possess this woman, Monsieur Oufle was known to have tried 'many superstitious practices', not the least of which was 'fastening to his neck certain barbarous words', which were 'incomprehensible to us, and even to those who invented them'. Monsieur Oufle followed these directions:

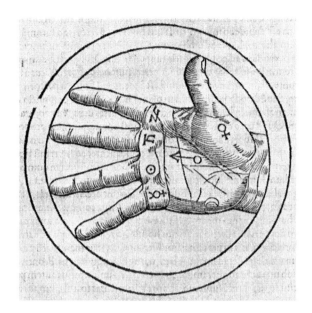

Untitled engraving, from von Nettesheim, 'On the Proportion, Measure and Harmony of Man's Body', *Three Books of Occult Philosophy* (London, 1651).

'Fix about your neck these words, and these crosses † authos † a aortoot noxiotbay † gloy † aperit.' According to the text, Monsieur Oufle was successful in his pursuit, although his eye soon turned elsewhere.[34] Also relying on powers gained from marks upon their flesh were the 'Salutadores'. This group claimed to be able to cure severe distempers and other ailments because of 'a mark' they were born with in the shape of a half wheel upon their chests.[35] Like the Salutadores, the 'Salvatori or Saviours of Italy', who claimed 'themselves related to Saint Paul', impressed on their flesh 'the figure of a serpent'. The Salvatori claimed this mark to be 'natural', although it was 'really artificiall'. The Salvatori boasted that their marks lent them great powers over animals and immunity to venomous serpents and scorpions. We are assured, however, of the falsehood of their claims.[36] The idea of man's power over the animals harks back to Agrippa, who wrote of a character 'imprinted on man', which allowed him to work the 'miracle' of animal dominance.[37] Many in the early modern period also believed that symbolic characters not only engendered power in the bearer, but that certain marks, albeit those inscribed on inanimate bodies, engendered life. Denying that such creation was possible, one anonymous author wrote:

> Tis pretended that Albertus Magnus made a machine which replaced a man entire, having work'd thirty years on it without intermission, to forge it under clues, Aspects and constellations; the eyes, for instance, when the Sun was in the sign of the Zodiac correspondent to those

Parts; which he cast of Metals mixt together, and mark'd with characters of the same signs and planets, and their diverse and necessary
Aspects; and so the Head, the Neck, the Shoulders, the Thighs and the
Legs form'd at several times, and more united and fastened together in
the shape of a man; which were able to reveal to the said Albertus the
solution of all principal difficulties. Henry de Assid and Bartholomy
sibylia, affirm it to have been compos'd of Flesh and Bones, but by Art,
not by Nature.[38]

Agrippa's *Three Books of Occult Philosophy* included a similar though less
detailed account of astral inscriptions generating life.[39]

The diverse symbolic inscriptions catalogued in the early modern occult
texts, the magical treatises and the medical compendiums recount a well-
established history of inking the flesh during this period. These accounts,
however, cannot firmly demonstrate indigenous indelible marks that penetrated the flesh as separate from inking influences that came from overseas;
we may never know for certain the origin of English customs of tattooing.
The only definitive account of early modern symbolic tattooing comes from
the travel journals of the pilgrims who trekked to Jerusalem, marked their
stay with tattoos, and returned to the British Isles.[40] For these world-
travellers, the symbolic tattoo was a celebration and purpose unto itself,
unlike the occult magi, the medico-magians and the physicians for whom
astrological or religious inkings represented astral empowerment, medical
healing, magical effect or life-giving force. We may never know for certain if
traditional tattooing methods crossed the waters that surround the British
Isles. We do know, however, that a host of men, who recorded the Jerusalem
tattoo both on paper and on their own flesh, did cross those waters. The
uncertainty of the processes of Forman's astral tattoos, whether his marks
were achieved by using similar methods of puncturing the skin with 'two
very fine needles, ty'd close together' as was done with the Jerusalem tattoos,
should not eclipse his inkings from the history of tattooing in early modern
England.[41] The history of astral corporal inscriptions, along with the
panoply of other ephemeral and indelible symbolic inkings of the period,
is vital to a full history of the evolution of tattooing in England. Only by
animating these endogenous magical, medical and religious corporal practices can all the precedents for the tattoo, its aetiology and the cultural
contexts of its inscription be fully realized.

5 The Renaissance Tattoo

JULIET FLEMING

[1]

> It is the oddness of a structure that is at issue.
> LACAN

According to Arnold Rubin, tattoo artist and theorist who popularized the term, for the past quarter-century the West has been enjoying a 'tattoo renaissance'; a movement characterized by refinements of conception (such as the influence of Abstract Expressionism, and the introduction of 'photo-realistic' tattoo, black graphic 'tribal' styles, Japanese designs, and imagery adopted from the mass-media); by technical developments such as single needle techniques and an extended palette; and by the refinement of procedure and equipment facilitated by the rise of mail-order suppliers, newsletters and conventions. Unlike earlier or less elite tattooists, artists of the tattoo renaissance may have professional art training and some association with the larger art world. They increasingly specialize in large-scale, custom designs and recognize and value each others' work. 'Being a tattoo artist', they say, 'is different from being a good tattooist.'[1]

But the tattoo renaissance comprises not so much the rebirth or development of technique as the social relocation of a practice; the elevation of tattooing into a socially elaborated art form is coterminous with its gentrification. As a consequence, Western tattooing is now divided against itself in terms of class. On the one hand, it advances serious claims to be considered a 'high' art whose products are governed by canons of taste and knowledge, and shown in galleries and museums. On the other hand, tattooing remains, in theory and in fact, a demotic practice whose products include prison- and home-made tattoos, as well as those done in commercial studios to more or less standard designs. The difference between 'art' tattooing and the 'rough neck, silly aspects' of the commercial trade is one on which tattoo artists such as Rubin insist.[2] But they also acknowledge that this difference is not absolute. For tattoo art not only redeploys the codified motifs of commercial practice (the 'international style'), but the perceived importance of tattoo as an artistic medium derives in part from its articulated deracination vis-à-vis middle-class aesthetic values. Tattoo art understands itself to be, at some level, *outré*: like similar movements before it, its renaissance is predicated on a culture clash of which it is the reified effect.

The re-engrossing of the scandalous affect that the middle-class projects on to its 'outlaws' has been a standard high cultural practice. In the case of tattooing, the results are predictable. To its own practitioners and clients, tattoo art now figures the domain of authenticity – of the properly expressive, and (as the precipitate of 'opposition') of the individual. So Rubin considers the tattoo to be the repository and expression of 'unconventional, individualistic' values;[3] while for Michael Bakaty and others it is 'the only form of human expression we have left that has magic to it. Everything else is academic.'[4] Tattoo artists may even dismiss the work of commercial tattooists on the grounds that it is the derivative product of reproduction and commodification – procedures understood to be inimical to the work of art.[5] Indeed, the desire to class tattooing among the arts drives some of its elite practitioners to read ritual, supernatural, and therapeutic elements into their own work with the same 'striking lack of discretion' that Walter Benjamin attributed to the early theorists of film.[6] Which is only to say that the therapeutic effect that often accompanies the acquisition of a tattoo within our culture is explained by tattoo artists using intellectual protocols that have been borrowed, at least in part, from more established accounts of the ethical and therapeutic functions of art.

Within tattoo's new representational economy, its traditionally marginal social status and its association with ancient or primitive cultures enhance its value as a form of expression whose 'low' or atavistic character allows it to function as a conduit for unconscious or instinctive forces. Here the archaic, pre-individual drives of the Freudian unconscious are re-interpreted, and given new valence as the creative 'drives' of individuals alienated from contemporary 'mass society'. As Governor Jerry Brown testified at the opening of California's Tattoo Expo in 1982:

> Once the power of the tattoo [was] intertwined with those who chose to live beyond the norms of society . . . Today the realm of the outlaw has been redefined: the wild places which excite the most profound thinkers are conceptual.[7]

Under the aegis of the California Expo, tattoo put its 'wildness' (here troping, among other things, the middle-class erotics that attached to Brown) to work in support of the liberal-libertarian coalition represented by the State Governor.

Tattoo's uncanny power to affront (and so arouse) the liberal subject is a power of horror that largely coincides with the special effect identified by Julia Kristeva under the name of 'abjection'.[8] To the person without tattoos, this horror articulates itself in the first instance around the question of permanency. The 'problem' with tattoos, we say (as if we were all being forced to get one, this minute) is that they are indelible – 'You can never get a tattoo off.' The striking persistence of this complaint indicates its support within the social unconscious. The fantasy (since, even before laser technology allowed their removal, it was always possible to write over, and so change, a tattoo) is one that admits in the first instance to the negative possibility that the subject is named on the body. (The debate about tattooing is thus in part a debate about whether 'individuality' can survive certain modes of representation.) The suggestion that identity is constituted, not in the depths, but at the outer surface of the subject, is experienced by the cartesian *cogito* as a type of claustrophobia: *nominor ergo sum*.[9] So the thought of something sticking to the skin is ever a deep affront; even within a comic register it evokes Hercules trapped inside the poisoned shirt of Nessus. A protective covering that displaces and so destroys that which it should protect, the tattoo can be thought of as a poisoned (that is, poisoning) name: like other names, it wounds by threatening to reduce the subject to a function of itself.

Tattoo artists and practitioners, on the contrary, understand their art as being 'anti-repressive'. Tattooing in prison is felt to be an affirmation that (at least) this body is yours; while artists such as Don Ed Hardy differentiate their practice from that of earlier American tattooists by invoking their own departure from the use of 'flash' or pattern sheets. Where once customers chose tattoos from such sheets and so 'had to fit their individual psyche into pre-congealed images that were often very out-of-date', today's tattoo artist functions as 'a kind of therapist: a vehicle to help people channel their unconscious urges to the surface'.[10] British tattooist Chinchilla argues that she can see, as her clients can not, what 'crawls beneath their skin . . . everything I ink on people is already inside them, their history, sleeping creatures or saints, I only open up the skin and let it out, succubus, cherub, bike, snake, Betty Boop with a dildo'.[11] It is at this moment in the tattoo renaissance – when tattooing comes to see itself, in Kristeva's terms, as a form of semiotic writing – that women enter the field as its practitioners and customers. Arguing from an identity position predicated on the assumption that women have privileged access to the semiotic (that mode in which the drives of the pre-Oedipal phase manifest themselves through, but against the grain of, language) female tattoo artist Jamie Summers was able to pull rank on the pro-feminist Hardy in the 1980s by complaining that, in spite of his own claims, his 'mastery of technique and tendency towards intellectualization' produced only 'highly accomplished surface decoration, rather than the revelation of interior states' which had come to be her own sole objective.[12]

This debate between Summers and Hardy demonstrates the extent to which tattoo artists can remain wedded to a classical, idealist aesthetic that is strikingly at odds with the nature of tattoo. To tattoo is precisely to 'decorate' the surface, to produce the skin *as* surface, to suggest that, in the deft form-ulation of Michel Thevoz, 'there is no body but the painted body, and no painting but body painting'.[13] Because Chinchilla accords less privilege to 'inner depth' (and understands what depth there is as inhabited by such historically contingent forms as Betty Boop), she is able to make fuller account of the skin as a writing surface on which ideas are enmeshed in matter. Chinchilla's formulation of the tattoo as an inner demon at once expelled and held at the border of the subject also provides a usefully precise figure for abjection. In Kristeva's work, the abject is a boundary phenomenon. Neither inside nor outside, at once 'an excluded ground' and 'a border that has encroached upon everything', the abject is 'something rejected from which one does not part'.[14] Both conceptually, and in fact, a tattoo is caught in the same impossible situation:

> the defining feature of tattooing is that it is the making of indelible pigmented traces which are inside or underneath the skin . . . behind what seems like a transparent layer . . . The basic schema of tattooing is thus definable as the exteriorization of the interior which is simul-taneously the interiorization of the exterior.[15]

Lodged on the border between inside and outside, the tattoo occupies the no-place of abjection.

Abjection can also be thought of as a boundary effect within the func-tioning of the psychic apparatus itself: as something midway between the procedures of symptom-formation (understood as the somatic expression of something repressed) and sublimation (the deflection, without repression, of a drive). This interim position between symptom production and sublim-ation is one that is attributed to the tattoo when it is understood as a self-inflicted wound – at once a mark that abjects the bearer, and an assertion of control over abjection.[16] One of Chinchilla's customers stressed the therapeutic aspect of such wounding: 'I feel that what one does is ritualistically abrade the skin over the spot where a mark already existed. This, that rose through my muscle and psyche had always been there.'[17] Here tattooing exemplifies

Kristeva's definition of the artistic experience as something 'rooted in the abject which it utters and by the same token purifies'.[18] At the frontier of what is 'assimilable, thinkable', functioning to collapse the boundary between subject and object, tattooing is (to those who have no fear of names) an act of catharsis *par excellence*.

However constructed, tattoo's claim to effectively represent the interior of the psyche is one of the things that permits its elevation into an art form in the West. Another is the irreducible authenticity – the aura – that a tattoo carries as a result of its 'unique existence at the place where it happens to be': the simple fact that because its medium is the living body, a tattoo cannot be reproduced.[19] (Of course, looked at from a different angle, the fact that tattoo takes the living body for its medium, and so proposes that there is nothing about that body or the person in it that is more unique than itself, is precisely what disqualifies it from being considered art.) But the special consequence of tattooing as an art medium – perhaps the radical principle of its function as art – may finally depend on its evocation of the geometrical concern that structures Kristeva's formulation of abjection, and may be said to comprise the simple proposition that is a figure in two dimensions. This figure may be variously thought of as one that is all surface, or one whose inside is also its outside (an instance of 'the intimate exteriority or "extimacy" that is the Thing' in Lacan's important discussion of the wall paintings in the caves of Altamira).[20] As a creature of the surface, a tattoo is an example of the first: as a disturbance to that surface, it is an instance of the second. Even where it is not deliberately recursive – a woman with a tattoo of a woman (with the tattoo of a woman) embracing death – the tattoo is an image of regression without recession, a geometrical paradox that marks the impossible profundity of the surface on which it is inscribed.[21]

In *The Skin Ego* Didier Anzieu tests two dependent hypotheses: 'what if thought were as much an affair of the skin as of the brain? And what if the Ego – now defined as a Skin Ego – had the structure of an envelope?'[22] Anzieu begins his argument (one he sustains through the display of an astonishing and convincing array of cutaneous fantasies) with the observation that the organ of consciousness, the cortex (Latin: 'bark', 'shell' or 'rind') not only sits as 'a sort of cap' on the white matter of the brain, but is embryonically a development of the surface of the early foetus, an introverted and reticulated 'skin'. 'We are faced then, with a paradox: the centre is situated at the periphery'.[23] Anzieu notes this paradox is replicated in Freud's model of the psychic apparatus, according to which the ego 'is not merely a surface entity, but is itself the projection of a surface'.[24] To cite, as Anzieu does, Paul Valéry, 'We burrow down in vain, doctor, we are . . . ectoderm!'[25] Valéry's proposition 'C'est qu'il y a de plus profond dans l'homme, c'est la peau' has important resonance within the work of reconception that constitutes modernism and post-modernism. It is a proposition illustrated by the recurrence of the figures of fold, veil and fan of Derrida's Mallarmé; as well as in Derrida's own important concept of the hymen ('the fold in a lining by which it is, out of itself, in itself, at once its own outside and its own inside; between the outside and the inside, making the outside enter the inside and turning back the *antre* or the other upon its surface'); in the rhizome and fold of Deleuze and Guattari; and in Lyotard's work on discourse and figure.[26] But the uncanniness of the profound surface whose primary figure is the skin is not new in modernism: indeed, one might consider it to be one result of the replacement of the 'flat' plane of medieval representation with the perspectival space of the Renaissance. Within this new, Euclidean space, the skin functions as a Derridean supplement, the material remainder that haunts the objective spatial depth within which the Cartesian subject is driven to locate itself.

So Michelangelo's famous portrait of the artist as a flayed skin on the wall of the Sistine Chapel (1535), and Juan de Valverde's drawing of an anatomized figure carrying his own pelt (1560) seem, today, to be freighted with surplus violence, one that resides in the revelation of two specific facts.[27] The first, revealed by the successive removal of surfaces that comprises the art of anatomy, is that the body is nothing *but* surface. The second is that while death happens in three dimensions, the skin, in two, can survive.[28] The uncanny aspect of the undead skin may be confronted in the comparatively recent story of Alfred Corder, sentenced to be hanged and dissected for his notorious murder of Maria Marten in 1828. After death Corder's body was skinned, tanned and used to bind a presentation copy of the printed account of his life and crime.[29] So treated, the skin becomes the material embodiment of abjection. When, in tattoo, the skin gives its own strange half-life over to a newly 'living' image, it similarly asks and complicates the question of what becomes of our mortal envelope, either at the Resurrection or at the morgue.

But there is another dimension to the intellectual distress for which tattoo stands as a figure. For although we say, with horror, 'a tattoo lasts forever' – as if, within our cultural or psychic economy, permanence were a recognized evil – most tattoos last only as long as the body endures, which is to say not as long as ink on paper. It may be that disapprobation of tattoo's permanence has a political, as well as a psychic, dimension. For where classical economic theory recognizes three types of property; the intellectual, the real or 'immobile'(land) and the moveable (chattels), tattoo announces itself as a fourth type: a property that is at once mobile *and* inalienable. And here inalienability shows itself to be a disconcerting quality in property, as if not only the value but the *propriety* of property depended on its capacity to be exchanged. As is suggested by the popular narrative of the tattooed man who ends up on the wall of an unscrupulous art dealer, a tattoo is a property that, for a variety of ethical and practical reasons, cannot be sold.[30] Tattoo thus readily connotes a blockage in the free circulation of commodities that is understood to constitute economic health in the West: it is partly in this capacity that it has always been used to figure both the improvidence of the class that does not possess, and the culpable economic naivety of native peoples.

[II]

> Pain and history seem tied together.
> *Tattoo International*

According to popular tradition and the OED, the word 'tattoo' made its first English appearance in James Cook's account of his voyages to the Polynesian basin, published in London in 1769. Historians locate the origins of contemporary European tattooing in Cook's return from his South Sea Islands Voyage of 1774 with the tattooed Tahitian known to the British as Omai; the 'noble savage' whose appearance sparked a tattooing vogue among the English aristocracy.[31] It is one of the gaps in the history of Western tattooing that the movement of tattooing from the centre to the margins of British culture has been assumed (as a 'trickle-down' effect), rather than documented. Equally unaccounted for in the history as it stands is the alacrity with which certain groups of Europeans, from ships' crews to the monarchy, apparently adopted the practice in the eighteenth century. For the Europeans had already encountered and documented tattooing in the Americas, Asia and Africa in the sixteenth and seventeenth centuries – in these earlier instances, or so the account runs, without being tempted to try it for themselves.[32]

The most useful recent account of the history of tattooing in Europe is Alfred Gell's brilliant analysis of tattooing as an encounter phenomenon. Gell argues that Western notions about tattooing derive from the overlay of perceptions of tattooing as a 'stigma of the class Other' (the tattooed sailor or criminal) with 'perceptions of the practice as characteristic of the ethnic Other – the tattooed native'. But Gell is concerned with Western tattooing only in so far as its practices and assumptions inform surviving European descriptions of tattooing in Polynesia; and he follows standard accounts of Western tattooing when he begins his own with the assumption that 'tattooing, as it is now practiced in Western countries, originated as a consequence of European expansion into the Pacific'.[33] I propose, instead, that tattooing was occurring in Europe at the same time that European travellers documented its presence in the Americas, Asia, Africa and later in the Pacific. The possibility that Polynesian tattooing reinflected, rather than began, an indigenous practice of European tattooing will not in itself explain the particular social patterns that it has subsequently assumed in the West. But it may enable us to see tattooing more clearly, both as the symptom of a colonial encounter, and as an instance of a cultural practice that is typically under-registered by the societies in which it occurs.

Performance artist Genesis P-Orridge recently outlined a self-consciously 'alternative' history for British tattooing:

> The Romans found the Britons covered in . . . tattoos. The heritage of the pagan Britons was to be heavily tattooed, but of course we're not told of our tribal, integrated, celebratory culture in school. The history has been stolen and turned into a perversion called Christianity.

Like Jamie Summers, P-Orridge understands tattooing as an instance of the elevation of the semiotic into a principle of signification: the tattoo or cut is a 'symbolic key' that 'makes you open to your own unconscious'. P-Orridge goes on to argue that societies that practise tattooing and scarification have been and will be characterized by a benign relational ethics, and to suggest that, before the coming of the Romans, the Britons maintained a balanced relationship with the environment.[34] For Britons both Ancient and New Age, it seems, tattooing evidences man's proper and ethical acknowledgment of the semiotic processes of life and death.

This 'alternative' history of British tattooing is not in serious conflict with the accounts that locate its genesis in the eighteenth-century contact with Polynesia: there is room for both in a history of Britain. But it does bring into view an important set of meanings that structure demotic tattooing in Britain today, where 'Celtic' designs may be used to articulate engagement with, for example, the concerns of Scottish nationalism, or with the particular type of environmentalism associated with Wicca. Besides, as it happens, tattoo's alternative history is largely correct. In the years leading to the accession of James VI of Scotland to the English throne, the antiquary William Camden (newly interested to argue for the tribal unity of the British people) marshalled evidence from classical and other sources to prove that both the Picts and the insular Celts had been 'painted peoples', set apart from later invaders by 'their staining and colouring of their whole bodies' with woad, and 'their *cutting, pinking,* and *pouncing* of their flesh'.[35]

'Listing', 'rasing', 'pricking', 'pinking', and 'pouncing' are the interlinked English terms for tattooing before the middle of the eighteenth century: Samuel Purchas says of the Algonquian Indians that 'the women . . . with an Yron, pounce and raze their bodies, legs, thighes, and armes, in curious knots and portraytures of fowles, fishes, beasts, and rub a painting into the same, which will never out'.[36] The English term 'pounce' was associated with writing as well as with face-painting: pounce is a powder used to dust cheeks, transfer embroidery designs through a perforated pattern or prepare parchment to receive writing. To pounce may be to bruise, puncture, emboss or engrave; to slash or jag the edges of a cloth for ornament; or to polish or erase. A pounce may be an engraving instrument, a tattoo or a 'pink'. Pinking (the cutting out of holes, figures or letters, to display skin, undergarments or linings of a different colour) is a mode of ornament readily associated with excess; its depravity (which consists in the interesting proposition that is a *superfluous taking away*) is regularly adduced in late sixteenth-century attacks on sartorial excess. Finally a 'list' or 'race' is a slit or scratch, a cut that marks. But to rase is also to remove by scraping or rasping, to erase. Remarkable in this early modern constellation of terms for tattoo is the fact that they each propose a logic of the mark whereby one can mark by detraction, detract by addition. In this they register one of the formal paradoxes that structures today's aversion to tattooing.

In his *Historie of Great Britaine* (1611), a book whose frontispiece depicts a tattooed ancient Briton, John Speed echoed Camden's account of ancient British tattooing:

> Solinus likewise speaking of the *Britaines* saith, their Country is peopled by *Barbarians*, who by means of artificial incisions of sundry formes, have from their childhood divers shapes of beasts incorporate upon them; and having their markes deeply imprinted within their bodies, looke how their growth for stature, so doe those pictured characters likewise increase . . . These skarres by Tertullian are tearmed *Britannorum stigmata, The Britaines markes* . . . and of this use of painting both the Britaines had their primitive derivation, and the *Picts* (a branch of British race) a long time after, for that their accustomed manner, were called *Picti* by the *Romanes,* that is, the *painted* people.[37]

Like Solinus and Camden before him, and many after him, Speed is arrested by the paradox of the tattoo as an image fixed on a moving, in this case expanding, surface.[38] Later in his account he reproduces and glosses Claudian's description of Caesar's military triumph over the Picts – '*Perlegit exanimes*

Picto moriente figuras: On dying Picts he reads the breathless shapes, as if the *Beasts* so lively portraited on them, seemed to lie dead together with the murdered bodies of the *Picts*.'[39] Redolent of sympathy for the Picts, Claudian's proposition, underlined by Speed, is that as the tattooed image 'lived' on the skin, so it should 'die' in a gesture of respect for the body that supported it. The empathy of the proposal depends on its acknowledged impossibility; an impossibility borrowed wholesale from the strange object (one that may be equally thought of as a dead image on a live skin, or as a live image on a dead skin) that is a tattoo. The larger question of a tattoo changing as the body changes, expanding or contracting in all its parts without entirely altering their relation to one another, is a formal proposition of some consequence: one dealt with in the field of geometric topology under the rubrics of diffiomorphism and homeomorphism; and one that Lacan uses in his discussion of anamorphosis to illustrate his formulation of the gaze as something excessive to perspectival optics.[40] But in the work of Speed and his contemporaries, the formal proposition of an object that moves and grows, but can never change, takes on a primarily political dimension: one within which the tattoo comes to stand as the sign of the irreducible difference between Europe and its others.

For the antiquaries and their sources, tattooing and body painting among the ancient Britons went hand in hand with the further distinguishing tribal practices of gynarchy and nakedness. The fact that the Picts were, as Tacitus puts it, 'subject to the government of women' was fodder to the antiquarian argument that the Picts were descended from the ancient Britons: 'neither [tribe] ma[king] any distinction of sex for government, or exclud[ing] women from bearing sceptre'.[41] Writing at the end of Elizabeth I's long reign, Camden and Speed may have felt there was nothing especially barbaric in the ancient British tolerance for female rule.[42] But when he addresses himself to the legendary nakedness of the Picts and Britons, Speed follows his sources in concluding that his ancestors went naked through their ignorance of cloth manufacture and other rudimentary arts of civilization, as well as through a desire to display their body markings. In Speed's account, that is, the tattoo is the mark of the Briton as barbarian.

Even now, little is known about Pictish civilization and culture: a few inscriptions aside, written sources are more or less limited to classical accounts of the Picts as primitive barbarians, and (for the period after the conversion) the sparse comments of Adoman and Bede.[43] But these sources are almost unanimous in their claims that both the Picts and other ancient British tribes tattooed; and the recent discovery by archaeologists of Scythian and Pazyrak bodies with extensive tattoo work may indicate that the element of fantasy in classical accounts of British tattooing resides less in the assertion that the barbarians tattooed, than in the implication that the Roman soldiers did not.[44] The accuracy of the record aside, Speed's apparent purpose in invoking ancient British tattooing ('to propose unto the eyes of our now glorious and gorgeous *Britaines*, some generall draughts of our poor and rude progenitors') is to demonstrate the ancient identity of the British 'race': a national group marked and set aside by its use of tattoo and body painting.[45] But the tattoo also marks a different, and conflicting, national concern. Housed in tents, dressed in skins and eating sparely; ignorant of God, agriculture and the value of gold, the Picts of the antiquarian account bear striking resemblance to the New World inhabitants whose existence was fast becoming a focus of British attention at the end of the sixteenth century. Under the pressure of this moment of encounter, the figure of the tattooed Briton finds itself pressed into the service of the newly emergent discourse of comparative ethnography.

The first volume of Theodore de Bry's famous work *America I* (Frankfurt: de Bry, 1590), published simultaneously in Latin, English, French and German, reprints Thomas Hariot's account of the English expedition to Roanoke of 1585, *A briefe and true report of the new found land of Virginia* (London: R. Robinson, 1588), together with thirteen illustrative engravings.[46] Largely based on paintings of the South-eastern Algonquians made by John White, artist recorder to the first Roanoke expedition, the series also includes two engravings based on the work of Jacques Le Moyne de Morgues, artist to the earlier French expeditions to Florida of 1562–5.[47] A fuller set of Le Moyne's images of the Timucua people, with his written commentary on them, and his own account of the attempted French colony, was published by de Bry as *America II* (Frankfurt: de Bry, 1591).[48] White and Le Moyne both recorded the practice of tattooing in their paintings of the native Americans. At least as engraved by de Bry, Le Moyne used tattooing in his paintings to posit an unexpected similarity between the body decoration of the Timucua, and the slashed, pinked, and rased clothing of the French. Le Moyne's account of Laudonniere's attempt to establish a Huguenot foothold in Florida is unusually sensitive to the impact made on Timucua by the arrival of the French. So while he points out to his reader that 'istos Regulos, eorum que uxores, corporis cutem puncturis quibusdam varia picturas imitantibus ornare' ['All these rulers and their wives decorate the skin of their bodies with a kind of tattooing, in imitation of various painted designs'], Le Moyne also records that the Timucua were 'somewhat astonished when they noticed the difference between the smoothness and softness of our bodies and theirs, and the unfamiliar clothing we wore'.[49]

Theodore de Bry (after Jacques Le Moyne de Morgues), Engraving showing the Timucua and the French colonists, from *America II* (Frankfurt, 1591).

De Bry (after Le Moyne de Morgues), Engraving showing the Timucua and the French colonists, from *America II*.

In Le Moyne's work, the difference between the Europeans and the Americans is produced through the proposition of an underlying similarity: European and American figures are often represented in very close juxtaposition, or in poses that reflect each other. The paintings are vulnerable to the charge that they 'idealized' (that is, 'Europeanized') their American subjects: the majority of them were probably reconstructed from memory following Le Moyne's dramatic escape from the colony; and they are not held to be of the same ethnographical value as the work of his contemporary John White.[50] But Le Moyne, whose characteristic style is that of a gentle but sustained mannerism, idealizes European as well as Native American figures; and does so as part of a deliberative enquiry into the question of what it means to be civilized. So he advises readers that Christians have much to learn from the Timucua in terms of temperance, and 'deserve to be handed over to these base uncivilized people and brutish creatures to learn restraint'.[51] The proposition that civilized peoples may learn civility from the uncivilized is a conventional piece of social criticism: it is nevertheless part of a serious attempt to theorize the ethical consequences of a colonial encounter.

John White did not include the arrival of the Europeans in his record of Roanoke: only two surviving paintings show scenes of the colonists, and those are of Puerto Rico.[52] Thomas Harriot, with whom White worked closely to compile a full account of the area of the Roanoke landings, took a markedly functionalist view of Algonquian culture. The first edition of his *Briefe and true report of the newfoundland of Virginia* (1588) was addressed to the English 'Adventurers, Favourers, and Welwillers of the action', and assures them that 'in respect of troubling our inhabiting and planting, [the Algonquians] are not to be feared; but . . . shall have cause both to feare and love us, that shall inhabite with them' (Sig. E1v). Arguably, it was precisely Harriot's and White's refusal to concern themselves with their own relationship to the Algonquians that renders their account of Native American culture more ethnographically accurate than that of Le Moyne.

White's illustrations corroborate Harriot's account of body painting and tattooing among the Carolina Algonquians: according to De Bry's comments on the images, 'the Princes of Virginia . . . ether pownes, or paynt their forehead, cheeks, chynne, bodye, armes, and legges'; while Secotoan women of rank are similarly 'pownced', with the addition of a 'chaine' around their necks, 'either pricked or paynted'.[53] De Bry's apparent uncertainty as to whether the body markings of the various Algonquian tribes were 'pricked' and 'pownced' or 'painted' has led Paul Hulton to argue that 'tattooing was probably confined to the women, while painting was used widely by both sexes'.[54] In fact de Bry's hesitation concerns the distribution rather than the incidence of tattooing among the men and women of the different Algonquian groups; and he argues further that the Algonquian warriors had 'marks rased on their backs' for purposes of identification.

An engraving of these marks, together with a key linking them to the names of different chiefs, is the final image in the series illustrating 'the fashions of the people' in *America I* (Sig. D4v). De Bry then concludes the volume with 'Some Picture of the Pictes which in the olde tyme did habite one part of great Bretainne', in order, as he says, 'to shew that the Inhabitants of great Britain have bin in times past as savage as those of Virginia' (Sig E1). In his introductory remarks to these engravings, which show three heavily tattooed Picts, and two untattooed Ancient Britons 'from neighbouring tribes', de Bry implies the images were copied by John White from 'a oolld English cronicle' (Sig. E1). The engravings are accompanied by a commentary which details the weapons, ornaments, hairstyles and body decorations of the Picts; and explains, in accordance with the engravings, that the Picts 'did paint all their bodye'; the men affecting suns, monsters and snakes (Sig E1v); while the women wore moon and stars, figures of animals and abstract designs (Sig E2v). But the image which was to prove the most memorable to his contemporaries was de Bry's 'Truue picture of a yonge dowgter of the Pictes', an engraving which shows a female nude wearing a sword, holding a spear, and 'painted over all the body . . . of sondrye kinds of flours, and of the fairest that they cowld feynde'.[55] *Pace* de Bry, this image at least is based on the work not of John White, but of Jacques Le Moyne, whose painting 'A Young Daughter of the Picts' is now in the Yale Center for British Art. This painting is anything but a historical record of Pictish life. In fact, executed as it was in the same years in which Camden was working on his account of the tattooed ancient Britons, 'A Young Daughter of the Picts' functions to destabilize the antiquarian record by producing, in most improbable guise, an image of one of its cherished, but tentative ideas. To the extent that this image pretends to be an objective, ethnographic record of ancient British life, it also functions to display the wilfulness of ethnography itself.

Le Moyne's Pict stands to the front of a landscape, in the mid-distance of which can be seen the people and, improbably enough, the buildings of a small but prosperous Pictish town. She stands in a relaxed but artificial pose, her face turned half right, her body half left; her right hand on her

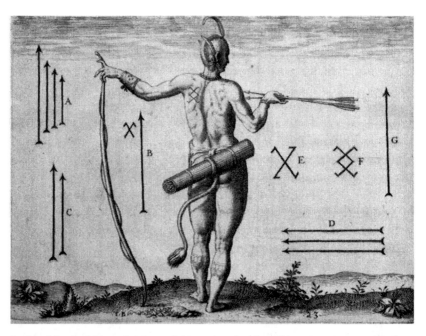

De Bry (after Le Moyne de Morgues), Engraving showing Algonquian tattoo marks, from *America I* (Frankfurt, 1590).

hip, she carries a slim spear in the left. Her carefully tended hair falls in virgin profusion down her back; while except for an elegant iron necklet and girdle, from the last of which a curving sword depends from the impossible support of a golden chain, she is naked. Most striking, of course, is that the young Pict's body is painted or tattooed from neck to ankle with a variety of flowers, among which Paul Hulton has identified the single and double peony, delphinium, hollyhock, heartsease, double columbine, orange lily, tazetta narcissus, cornflower, rose campion, yellow-horned poppy, mourning iris, tulip and marvel of Peru.[56] Hulton points out that, when the painting was made, the last three varieties had only recently been introduced to Western Europe from America and the Balkan peninsula. He concludes 'it was anachronistic indeed of Le Moyne to adorn a Pictish maiden with such newly arrived flowers'.[57] But Le Moyne, author of a volume of woodcuts of beasts, birds and plants intended for decorative patterns, and responsible for a large group of exquisite watercolour drawings of plants (now in the Victoria and Albert Museum), would certainly have known what he was doing in decorating the body of an Ancient Briton with the marvel of Peru. The deliberate anachronism is one in a series of gestures designed to mark the wit of this thoroughly mannerist painting.

In its entirety, Le Moyne's painting constitutes a series of visual and verbal puns, ranging from a joke concerning the impropriety of 'painting' (touching) a nude; to a meditation on the sixteenth-century English word 'pink', which signifies not only a tattoo, beauty or excellence, but also a flower.[58] As a 'pink', the young Pict is herself an instance of the *flors florum*, the 'flower of flowers' which is the conventional floral trope for heavenly and/or earthly love.[59] In its insistent proposition that woman is like a flower – a proposition which involves both a reversal between form and content, and a self-conscious refusal to distinguish between the real and the figural – Le Moyne's painting reveals itself as the painting not of a woman, but of metaphor itself. Its purpose, in brief, is to evoke admiration for the impossible achievements of art.

'A Young Daughter of the Picts' was painted in London, *c.* 1585–8, while Le Moyne was living in Blackfriars as a Huguenot refugee. While the painting may, Paul Hulton suggests, owe something in style to the miniatures of Hilliard and Oliver, in conception there is little like it among contemporary English paintings.[60] Certainly Le Moyne's wit was lost on his peers, or at least hidden from them by de Bry, who bought the painting from Le Moyne's widow, and engraved it as an illustration of the historical appearance and manners of the Picts. De Bry's elliptical comment on the engraving may indicate his own reservations about this use of Le Moyne's image: according to him, the daughters of the Pict were

Jacques Le Moyne de Morgues, 'A Young Daughter of the Picts', c. 1585–8, watercolour and bodycolour touched with gold, on vellum. Yale Center for British Art, New Haven (Paul Mellon Collection).

painted over all the body, so much that noe men could not faynde any different, yf they had not use of another fashion of paintinge, for they did paint themselves of sondrye kinds of flours, and of the fairest that they could fende.

Like Le Moyne, who had suggested that Timucuan tattooing was done 'in imitation of various painted designs', de Bry is uncertain how to distinguish between tattooing and the use of body paint. But the larger problem he is facing here is that, according to his own evidence, girls are tattooed with flowers, women with animals and planets.

The paradox was given sharper formulation by Speed, who in reproducing four of de Bry's engravings, two of the Picts and two of neighbouring British tribes, added tattoo work to the female Ancient Briton. Speed comments:

By these varieties of picturing (if some have not misinformed us out of their alleged ancient *Authors*) those people so distinguished themselves, that their *married women* were knowne by having pictured on their shoulders, *elbowes*, and *knees*, the heads of some four beasts, as Lions, Gryphons, etc. On their belly, the Sunne spreading his beames: on their *Pappes*, Moones and Starres etc. On their *Armes, thighes*, and *legges*, some other fancies of their owne Choice. But for their *Virgines*, their whole body was garnished over with the shapes of all the fairest kinds of flowers and herbes; which (to speak indifferently) could but yield, though a strange, yet no unpleasing aspect . . . yet, this scruple will not easily be removed (if it be true, *that from their childhood their prints increased with their bodies*) how those, who being *Virgins*, had no prints but of hearbes and flowers, becoming *Wives*, were so easily transformed into Beasts or heavenly creatures.[61]

A marginal note identifies the source of possible 'misinformation' as 'the Appendix to Harriot's Virginia'; all the same, Speed is happy enough to reproduce and further disseminate the error, which now takes the form of a conundrum. A tattoo is forever, a virgin is not: a tattooed flower may grow

De Bry (after Le Moyne de Morgues), 'Truue picture of a yonge dowgter of the Pictes', from *America II*.

with the body, but it cannot grow into an animal or star. Standing, in Speed's account, in the place that Derrida calls the hymen ('Neither future nor present, but between the two'), the daughter of the Pict suggests not so much the developmental trajectory of ancient or primitive peoples, but their irrevocably barbarian status. Looking back over Britain's hybrid past, Camden had been moved to take stock of his present moment:

> Since that for so many ages successively ensuing, we are all now by a certain ingraffing or commixtion become one nation, molified and civilised with Religion, and good Arts, let us medi[t]ate and consider, both what they were, and also what we should be.[62]

In his comments on the figure of the young female Pict, Speed introduces a wrinkle into Camden's account of the progress of British civilization, using the isotopic property of the tattoo (which may grow, but cannot change) to illustrate the impossibility of getting from past to present, or from America to Europe, while remaining the same. In so doing he raises the spectre of an incommensurability that is no longer confined, as Le Moyne confined it, to the structure of the signifier, but has become instead a question of cultural codes.

Within the terms of the uneven cultural grammar that is the ground on which the early modern antiquarians began to work out a discourse of British national sentiment, the tattooed ancestor stands for a barbarian past that is at once acknowledged and disavowed. That tattooing, the *Britannorum stigmata* as Camden calls it, is the fetish permitting this avowal-that-is-not-one explains, I think, the curious combination of levity and anxiety with which tattoos are treated in the antiquarian account, as they have been treated ever since. But the fact that the early modern English described tattooing in other times and places as a foreign practice, one whose technologies and functions were unknown within their own culture, should not be taken as evidence that they did not tattoo themselves. For *pace* Camden, and others after him, tattooing survived the coming of the Romans and Christianity to Britain.

Famously, tattooing is prohibited in *Leviticus* 19: 28 ('You shall not make any cuttings in your flesh for the dead, nor print any marks upon you'). But in his letter to the *Galatians* 6: 17, St Paul seems to suggest that tattooing is an acceptable sign of Christian commitment; one that may, indeed, be preferable to circumcision: 'For in Christ Jesus neither circumcision availeth any thing, nor uncircumcision . . . From henceforth let no man trouble me, for I bear in my body the marks of the Lord Jesus.' The practice of branding or tattooing for Jesus was recorded by the fifth-century Greek historian Procopius of Gaza; by the seventeenth-century traveller Fynes Moryson; and by Emile Durkheim and others as a practice still extant within the Eastern

Church in the twentieth century.[63] Reviewing the evidence for tattooing in medieval Irish and Hiberno-Latin literature, Charles MacQuarrie concludes that tattooing in medieval Europe had a bifurcated set of associations. On the one hand it was associated with the wounds of Christ (with what, after St Francis, came to be known as the stigmata) and with the writing that appears on Christ's thigh in *Revelations* 19:16; on the other it was associated with paganism and outlawry.[64] In AD 786 Hadrian's Papal Legates reported tattooing among members of the church in Northumbria; an 'injury of staining' ('tincturae injuriam') they condemned if done for purposes of pagan superstition, but were prepared to allow if undergone for the sake of Christ.[65] William of Malmesbury stressed the second, derogated meaning of tattoo when he described the English at the time of the Norman conquest 'laden with golden bracelets, their skin tattooed with colored designs' (armillis aureis brachia onerati, picturatis stigmatibus cutem insigniti); and went on to suggest that they imparted the barbaric practice to the invaders.[66] But throughout the medieval period it was common practice for pilgrims to have themselves tattooed in Jerusalem, returning home bearing indelible marks as evidence both of their journey and of their commitment to the service of God. The Jerusalem tattoo was a common sight in fifteenth-, sixteenth- and even seventeenth-century Europe. As the English traveller George Sandys recorded in his eye-witness account, 'They use to mark the Arms of Pligrims, with the names of Jesus, Maria, Ierusalem, Bethlehem, the Ierusalem Crosse, and sundry other characters.'[67]

Although the Reformation technically put an end to pilgrimages from Protestant countries, travellers continued to make the difficult journey to Jerusalem from Scotland and England. Protestants though they were, the majority went on to receive tattoos, either at the site of the Holy Sepulchre in Jerusalem, or in Bethlehem, which seems to have been something of a tattoo centre.[68] According to Edward Terry, who was with him when he died in India, Thomas Coryat had had a Jerusalem cross put on his left wrist, and a cross, three nails, and the inscription *Via, Veritas, Vita* on the right while in Jerusalem. Coryat evidently wore his tattoos with pride, understanding them as a type of stigmata, as Terry recounts:

All these impressions were made by sharp *Needles* bound together, that pierced only the skin, and then a black *Powder* put into the places so pierced, which became presently indelible *Characters*, to continue with him so long as his flesh should be covered with *skin*: And they were done upon his Arms so artificially, as if they had been drawn by some accurate *Pencil* upon *Parchment*. This poor man would pride himself very much in beholding of those characters, and seeing them would often speak those words of St Paul, written to the Galatians, Gal 6. 17 (though far besides the Apostles meaning) *I bear in my body the marks of Lord Jesus.*[69]

Fynes Moryson and his brother, who visited Bethlehem in the company of some French pilgrims, took pains to avoid getting tattooed, since it was a procedure they associated with the Roman church:

> And when our *consorts* at Bethlehem printed the signe of the Crosse with inke and a pen-knife upon their armes, so as the print was never to bee taken out, wee would not folow them in this small matter, but excused our selves, that being to passe home through many kingdomes, we durst not beare any such marke upon our bodie, whereby wee might bee knowne.[70]

But another Scotsman, William Lithgow, one of James I's courtiers, had no such qualms, and received extensive tattoo-work in Jerusalem. There he elaborated a standard pattern (a Jerusalem cross) with some devices of his own designed to celebrate the union of the Scottish and English crowns:

Engraving of William Lithgow's tattoos, from his *The Total Discourse, of the Rare Adventures etc.* (London, 1640).

In the last night of my staying at Jerusalem, which was at the holy grave, I remembring that bounden duty, and loving zeale, which I own unto my native Prince; whom I in all humility (next and immediate to Christ Jesus) acknowledge, to be the supreme head, and Governour of the true Christian and Catholicke Church; by the remembrance of this obligation, I say, I caused one *Elias Bethleete*, a Christian inhabitour of *Bethleem*, to ingrave on the flesh of my right arme, *The never-conquered Crowne of Scotland*, and *the nowe inconquerable Crowne of England*, joyned also to it; with this inscription, painefully carved in letters, within the circle of the Crowne, *Vivat Iacobus Rex*.[71]

In the 1640 edition of his text, which he dedicated to Charles I, Lithgow included a woodcut illustration of his tattooed cross and crown, and described a third tattoo which he now claimed to have had added beneath them:

Returning to the fellow two piasters for his reward, I fixed these lines for King James

> Long may he live, and long may God above
> Confirm, reward, increase his Christian love:
> That he (bless'd king of men) may never cease
> To keep this badge, the sacred prince of peace.
> And there's the motto of his maiden crown
> *Haec nobis invicta miserunt*, ne'er won.[72]

Lithgow's tattoo is particularly interesting in that it is partially detached from its religious context as it matches Cross with Crown, and the name of Christ with that of James I ('Prince of Peace').

In the figure of William Lithgow, returning tattooed to the English court, we can no longer refuse to recognize the Renaissance tattoo. Our certainty that the British did not tattoo themselves during the early modern period marks us as the descendants of Camden and Speed, British men and women for whom tattoo is visible as the mark of an ethnic status we have long claimed, as a nation, to have outgrown. If the tattoo now has a generalizable function across different cultures it is precisely to stand as the mark of 'foreignness': Gell notes that at the moment of encounter, the Polynesians thought of tattooing as a foreign practice – as one adopted, for example, from a different island in the archipelago, or from the European sailors who, increasingly tattooed, moved among them.[73] The tattoo may be thought to have achieved its status as the mark of strangeness or barbarity by force of analogy, since it is itself caused by the introduction of a foreign body under the skin. As such, it stands as a ready figure for the border skirmishing that defines conceptual relations between the inside and the outside of social groups, as well as between the inside and the outside of the body. Such formulations, however, depend on an historically specific, Cartesian, conception of the embodied self, and its relation to the signifier; and may be less pertinent to the early modern period.

To those who witness it from the outside (that is, from positions of historical, cultural or social distance), the tattoo appears as a scandalously prosthetic act of naming – one that labels, rather than divines, the essence of a person or thing. So when Harriot argues that the Algonquian warriors wear tattoos 'whereby it may be knowen what Princes subjects they bee', the warriors appear to us to be dispossessed of their capacity for self-determination even as their identity is recognized.[74] Here the tattoo marks the self as foreign because it forces an encounter with the fact that names support (indeed constitute) the identity of the subject. To the extent that the early modern English were more at home with the importance of names than we have since become, they were also more at home with tattooing; more able, that is, to read it as one naming practice among many. Speed, for example, readily imagines the Picts' tattoos as the honorific mark of rank – the 'badges of their Noblenes, thus endamasked'; while Simon Forman, the Elizabethan astrologer, branded himself on the left arm and right breast with the astrological 'characters' that governed his destiny, in order, as he said, to 'better his constellation'.[75] It could be said that in early modern England all men and women were marked, because the operations of the names that possess were still understood. Names cause identity retroactively: within a culture that does not resist this fact they may, after all, divine the truth of what they label. The seventeenth-century identification of tattooing as something foreign or barbaric heralds the replacement of this culture and its naming practices with one that newly reprehends the capacity of language to involve itself with what it describes. Under the aegis of this new order, where the signified is held to exist before signification, a continued belief in the efficacy of names and the value of material signs appears fetishistic. It is consequently projected on to the barbaric other, and ever after read back as that other's sign.

6   Curiously Marked: Tattooing and Gender Difference in Eighteenth-century British Perceptions of the South Pacific

HARRIET GUEST

In 1776, Joshua Reynolds exhibited his full-length portrait of *Omai* at the Royal Academy in London. Omai (or Mai) came from Raiatea, an island not far from Tahiti, and had arrived in England in 1774 on board one of the ships commanded by James Cook on his second circumnavigation of the globe. His appearance fed and encouraged the 'great curiosity' that had been stimulated by accounts of the Pacific islanders after Cook's first voyage to the southern hemisphere; a curiosity that Reynolds's portrait brings into focus.[1] For the painting can be understood both to represent and to smooth over the internal ambivalences that European powers project into colonialist expansion in the South Pacific, and which I want to begin to explore in this essay.

[I]

It is difficult to compare Reynolds's *Omai* to contemporary portraits of European subjects because his exoticism inflects the otherwise perhaps familiar terms of his representation. This is not a private or intimately sociable image, comparable to some of Reynolds's portraits of fashionable women, or men in repose. But nor is it a portrait which indicates any social or public command. Though, as Bernard Smith has pointed out, the islander assumes the pose of the 'self-confident patrician',[2] that pose seems here to indicate the incongruity between domestic conventions of representation and exotic subject, for the figure demonstrates patrician authority only in ambiguous command of the spectator's gaze. His gesture does not seem to invoke the respectful attention of the spectator, but rather to spread out for display some of the tattoos on which so much European curiosity focused. The dignity of the figure seems to be that of an orientalized 'noble savage', cleansed of characteristics that might mark his origin or history, and effaced by being endowed with what a recent biographer considers to be the 'somewhat negroid features' of 'an African princeling'.[3] The generalization of the

Sir Joshua Reynolds, *Omai*, 1775–6, oil on canvas. Castle Howard, Yorkshire.

image seems to make of Omai a blank figure, available to that diversity of inscription that George Forster commented on in European assessments of his character. He wrote that: 'O-Mai has been considered either as remarkably stupid, or very intelligent, according to the different allowances which were made by those who judged of his abilities.'[4] The blankness which made it so difficult to assess or judge Omai may however be exceeded or punctured in Reynolds's representation by the implications of those tattoos. They may mark his figure with the signs of a specifically colonialist curiosity that perceives the islander in terms that resist generalization, and that exoticize his image. Exoticism, I suggest, inscribes its object with an acultural illegibility, isolated from any coherence of origin. Exoticized subjects are characterized as sports, marked as singular tokens lacking any significance beyond that of a fragmentary and unrepresentative (perhaps unrepresentable) insularity. If Reynolds's portrait effaces those features of Omai that might distinguish him as an individual, or as a representative of his people, replacing them with the more generalized image of 'a youthful Oriental sage', then the tattoos seem to mark his specificity, removed from any context that might make it intelligible.[5] They seem to signal an exoticism that may be the key to the peculiar mixture of fascination and indifference that characterizes colonialist representations of the people of the South Pacific.

Joseph Banks had wished to bring an islander back with him as a souvenir of his trip to the South Pacific on Cook's first voyage. He noted in his journal that the government could not be expected to take an interest in this project, but, he added:

> Thank heaven I have a sufficiency and I do not know why I may not keep him as a curiosity, as well as some of my neighbours do lions and tygers at a larger expense than he will probably ever put me to.

His notorious remarks on 'the amusement I shall have'[6] from this scheme indicate the private status of ethnological curiosity, and, in the allusion to private zoos, emphasize the extent to which that curiosity thrives on the isolation of its exotic object, on the colonializing displacement or dislocation of its object from any signs of the personal estate or cultural context that might produce legible or potent significance. Banks's curiosity seems to demand the unmediated access that John Rickman alluded to in his account of Cook's last voyage, where he lamented the inadequacy of 'the feeble pencil of a fribbling artist' to represent the islanders. A more gratifying object of study might have been provided, he suggested, by 'the importation of a native from every climate', to stock an academy with 'living pictures'.[7] The generalization of landscape, clothing and physiognomy that makes an orientalized figure of Omai in Reynolds's portrait may be marked specifically by the colonialist curiosity animating Pacific expansion, which demands that its objects be presented stripped of context, and feeds on the wondrous exoticism which that nakedness enforces.[8]

The project of Pacific exploration is in some senses exceptional, and perhaps unrepresentative in the history of European colonialism, because it was perceived to depend on curiosity. A voyager commented, in an account of the South Pacific published in 1793, that the islanders'

> remote situation from European powers has deprived them of the culture of civilized life, as they neither serve to swell the ambitious

views of conquest, nor the avarice of commerce. Here the sacred finger of Omnipotence has interposed, and rendered our vices the instruments of virtue.[9]

The writer alludes to what he sees as the criminal vices of Fletcher Christian and the *Bounty* mutineers, which he argues might inadvertently work to civilize or enlighten the islanders. He imagines that the mutineers, isolated as a result of their rebellion, might establish proto-European communities in the Pacific. He suggests that European powers more usually fulfil what is understood as their imperial destiny as a result of avarice or ambition, which find as it were their moralized expression through the incidental imposition of 'the culture of civilized life'. In the South Pacific, where the desires that animate conquest or commerce find no gratification, the hand of Providence has to resort to more explicitly vicious means. But what is I think significant, in this reflection on late eighteenth-century European expansion, is the suggestion that the under-determined nature of European interest in the South Pacific makes the moral conflicts and inversions involved in spreading the 'culture of civilized life' much more apparent, much more explicit. The British repeatedly articulated their interest in the South Pacific in terms of the under-determined and ambiguously transactive notion of curiosity – what Boswell identified as 'the enthusiasm of curiosity and adventure', experienced when 'one is carried away with the general grand and indistinct notion of A VOYAGE ROUND THE WORLD'.[10] The sense that this project is somehow set apart from the ambitious views of conquest, trade and settlement by the whimsicality, licentiousness or enlightened and scientific purity of curiosity seems to point to an internal and domestic ambivalence about the demarcation of vice from virtue, and perhaps even of domestic from exotic, that may be projected in Reynolds's image.

Omai was perceived by Cook to be 'dark, ugly' and therefore 'not a proper sample of the inhabitants of these happy isles, not having any advantage of birth, or acquired rank; nor being eminent in shape, figure, or complexion'.[11] Omai was not a proper sample or specimen because he was physically 'ugly', dark and obscure rather than patrician. He was the appropriate object of a feminized 'curiosity, levity and lewdness',[12] rather than of public or political recognition, and that exclusion from representative status may be figured in Reynolds's image in the prominent marking of his tattoos. The tattoos inscribe the generalized figure that Reynolds portrays with an apparently incongruous ethnographic specificity, an authenticating 'air of truth',[13] inviting to the curious investigations of the natural philosopher or collector of exotica. The dignity or 'benign authority' which recent critics have attributed to the figure's stance seems to be marked by those tattoos as the gesture of self-display appropriate to the private zoo or fairground exhibit, the exotic spectacle, rather than to the public position of the patrician. The reinscribed tattoos mark the notion of Omai as 'a simple barbarian' whose transportation to 'a christian and civilized country' would 'debase him into a spectacle and a maccaroni, and ... invigorate the seeds of corrupted nature by a course of improved debauchery'.[14] They stigmatize Omai as the authentic object of a curiosity that finds its gratification in the singularities of nature and culture.

My discussion suggests, then, that the marking of Omai's hands in Reynolds's portrait indicates that the islander's gesture is appropriate to his exotic and unrepresentative status, for his tattoos are incompatible with any patrician authority his posture might seem to imply. It is as though they indelibly blacken and stain the transparent legibility of that classical stance. In this essay I want to explore the exoticism inscribed in tattoos, and in what were seen to be comparable marks of scarification and incision, in late eighteenth-century British perceptions of the islanders of the South Pacific. In writing on the South Pacific in the early nineteenth century, and in the late 1790s, tattoos were frequently represented as analogous to clothing, as a sort of textured surface that is integral to the body, but that also veils and conceals it, and lends it, perhaps, a kind of parodic social propriety. In the earlier accounts from the 1770s and 1780s which I will be considering here tattoos are perceived to have an ambiguously physical texture. One of the most frequently cited accounts of Omai's buttock tattoos, for example, compared them to veneer inlaid in mahogany, as though they were a part of the body's surface, but confirmed its exotic difference.[15] Tattoos in these earlier accounts, I suggest, mark the intersections of discourses of the exotic and domestic, and of gender difference – of discourses which also move ambiguously between physical differences, and differences of culture or of manners. In order to explore these implications of tattooing, I want to look briefly at Joshua Reynolds's use of the subject in one of his influential Discourses on the theory of art.

[II]

In the Discourse which Joshua Reynolds delivered to the Royal Academy in December 1776 he argued, in what was a striking departure from his earlier severity on the subject, that ornament could justifiably be represented in high art because its local interest and appeal 'procures lovers and admirers to the more valuable excellencies of the art'. He claimed that:

Though we by no means ought to rank these [ornaments] with positive and substantial beauties, yet it must be allowed that a knowledge of both is essentially requisite towards forming a complete, whole, and perfect taste . . . in them we find the characteristical mark of a national taste; as by throwing up a feather in the air, we know which way the wind blows, better than by a more heavy matter.

This seventh Discourse employs an extended analogy between the use of ornament in painting and fashions in dress, both of which Reynolds suggests are signs of customary 'national taste'. In relation to both, he seems to advocate a sort of cultural relativism, which means that though the judicious spectator sees ornament or fashion as merely an arbitrary or accidental distraction from universal truth with its 'substantial beauties', he can nevertheless value their charms as an expression of national character. So he argues that in the encounter between a fashionable European and a Cherokee man, 'whoever of these two despises the other for his attention to the fashion of his country, which ever first feels himself provoked to laugh, is the barbarian'. He suggests that each man will reveal the extent of his civility, the degree of his civilization, in the respect he shows for the other's national character.[16]

At this stage of his argument, however, Reynolds introduces some exceptions to this new tolerance for accidental detail. He writes that all

fashions are very innocent . . . The only circumstances against which indignation may reasonably be moved, is where the operation is painful or destructive of health, such as some of the practices at Otaheite, and the strait lacing of the English ladies.[17]

The Tahitian custom which was repeatedly associated with pain and the risk of infection was, of course, tattooing. It seems that this custom, along with the restrictive stays worn by fashionable English ladies, licenses the spectator to depart from his civilized respect for ornament or fashion as the sign of national character, and allows him to give vent to the sort of passionate prejudices which, in the encounter between the fashionable man and the Cherokee, had indicated barbarity. These ornamental customs perhaps bite too deeply into the smooth surface of the body to be tolerated as expressions of customary second nature. Instead Reynolds suggests that they reveal an unhealthy physicality which is more properly the subject of the lectures of 'the professor of Anatomy'.[18] Reynolds's seventh Discourse, then, charts a descent from the substantial beauties of universal truth, to the more meretricious charms of local or national custom, which are contrasted with apparently pathological adornments of tattoos and stays; and that descent also signals changes in the identity of the masculine spectator, who is dignified by the first, seduced by the second, and it would seem physically repulsed or even barbarized by the third.

Although portraiture is not the kind of high art form that Reynolds has in mind in this seventh Discourse, his argument may illuminate the intriguing omission of Omai's tattoos from the conversation piece by William Parry that Banks commissioned at around the same time as Reynolds's portrait of the islander. Here Banks is shown gesturing towards the unmarked – untattooed – hand of Omai, and his gesture seems to emphasize that the figure is here identified, not by the ambiguous ornaments of ethnographic particularity or national character, but through his presentation in the isolated vacancy appropriate to the spectacle of the exotic. The black background, which throws the figure of the Tahitian into relief, contrasts with the richly elaborate colours of the right-hand third of the canvas, where Daniel Solander sits. Solander had travelled with Banks on Cook's first voyage, and catalogued the collections of the British Museum in accordance with the Linnaean system, and it is presumably in his role as a natural philosopher that he is represented here, apparently poised to record and classify the curiosity that his patron Banks discovers to him. The figure of Omai is posed, perhaps again with ambiguously orientalized dignity, or perhaps as though he had been caught in transition, the turn of his body suggesting that his

William Parry, *Omai,*
Joseph Banks and Dr
Solander, 1775–6, oil on
canvas. Private collection.

attention has been diverted from the other men, and redirected downwards, towards the artist and spectator. His face seems open to the spectator's curious gaze, and isolated in contrast to the apparently unselfconscious absorption of Banks and Solander, engaged in the mutually interesting tasks of observation and display. The warmth and detail of what looks like an oriental rug on the table at Solander's elbow, and the depth of the rural scene behind him, may indicate the displacement from the Tahitian, fixed against that flat blackness, of the ornaments that constitute national or ethnic identity. For the physical definition of the draped Tahitian figure seems emphasized by the naked and unmarked surface of the ornamental spectacle he presents.

The nakedness of Omai is perhaps most directly indicated by the contrast between his prominent display and the apparently modest figure of Banks. Banks's proprietorial gesture, and the tidiness and restraint of his dark suit, seem to indicate in him a masculinity that stands aloof from the colourful display of his protégés, and that distinguishes his patrician authority from their peripheral and dependent positions. Reading the painting in the context of Reynolds's seventh Discourse, it may seem as though the more luminous and colourful figures of the two protégés cast the sober-suited Banks in the position of the civilized spectator, invested in a national identity continuous with that of the universal connoisseur. It may seem as though, in particular, the Tahitian were the sign, the ornament, that indicated Banks's worldly tolerance and national difference – the grounding of his comparativist cosmopolitan taste in moral righteousness. Omai is the ornament he tolerates, does not ridicule, but in relation to which he establishes his own superior difference. The clarity of the contrast between patron and islander may to some extent depend on the erasure of Omai's tattoos, for that blankness seems to bring into focus, into relief, the inscription of the whole figure of the Tahitian as exoticized spectacle. He is the feminized object of a philosophical curiosity that does not need to call attention to the marks of exoticization because it so clearly isolates him and indicates his deferential inferiority to the two Europeans.

The contrast between this painting and Reynolds's image, I suggest, focuses primarily on the difference between the terms in which they present the islander as curious spectacle. In Reynolds's portrait, I argued that the tattoos can be understood to indicate the curious and exotic status of the figure, and to deny the apparent authority of his solitary pose. Whereas in Parry's conversation piece, it is the relations between the three men that produce the singular spectacle of the Tahitian's exoticism. I have suggested that these images of Omai can best be understood in terms of the gendered constructions of civilized and national taste in the theory of painting in the mid-1770s. Specifically, I think that they are marked by the instability of gender produced by the valorization of customary national identity. For in Reynolds's seventh Discourse the notion that national character is based in custom appropriates to masculinity what had been defined in his earlier Discourses as a feminizing and sensual taste for ornament. The sensual taste for ornament and spectacle that distinguishes the figure of Omai might in this context seem uneasily close to that of the masculine spectator seduced by national taste. I suggested that in Reynolds's image the apparent oriental dignity of the islander is stigmatized as exotic, and thus excluded from this unsettling proximity, by the reinscription of the tattoos that punctuate the generalized dislocation of the figure. In Parry's painting, Omai is isolated as a naked spectacle of exotic curiosity. In both paintings the presentation of Omai as curious spectacle might be understood to prompt that fascinated distaste that contrasts his physicality with that of the spectator who allows himself to be seduced into adopting national ornament and identity.

In the 'Thoughts on the Manners of Otaheite' which he wrote in 1773, Banks indicated that a blurring of gender definition similar to that produced by the taste for national ornament in Reynolds's seventh Discourse was central to his conception of the difference between civilization and barbarism. 'Us Europeans', he argued, treat 'our women' with an attentive regard which produces in them 'beauty as well as those Elegant qualifications of the mind which blending themselves in our manners make the Commerce between the Sexes so much more deligh[t]ful to us than to the inhabitants of Africa or america'. This thought alludes to the axiom of Enlightenment philosophy which makes the treatment of women the index of civility – an axiom that can imply that masculine civilization varies in its degree of maturity or progress, whereas femininity describes a universal constant. That implication is perhaps more nearly explicit in what Banks goes on to write about tattooing. He writes that both the men and the women of Tahiti 'have a singular custom of inlaying under the skin certain figures in black', and he observes:

> I am inclind to think that as whiteness of skin is esteemed an Essential beauty these marks were originaly intended to make that whiteness appear to greater advantage by the Contrast Evidently in the same manner as the patches used by our European beauties.

The feminizing elision of the comparison between male and female Tahitians and European beauties works to endorse a homogenized and universal notion of feminine vanity untroubled by the cultural specificities of ornament that distinguish masculine fashions in Reynolds's Discourse. Banks's argument, in these thoughts, celebrates the feminized manners of 'Us Europeans' as indications of a high degree of masculine civilization, and it thus clearly distinguishes between the desirable achievement of feminization, and the natural femininity of those who are barbarized, and excluded from civilization, though their commerce may be necessary to its manners. If Banks's accounts of tattooing seem more tolerant than Reynolds's, this may be because he is more comfortable with the notion of an absolute distinction between civilization and barbarity, which allows him to assimilate feminized qualities of mind to the manners of European men, while attributing physical sensuality to exoticized femininity. In Reynolds's Discourse, in contrast, the sensuality of taste for ornament that distinguishes masculine national identity seems much closer to the sort of feminine physicality which he seems only able to repel with moral indignation. These rather different notions of modern masculine identity are, I want now to suggest, important to the way tattooed bodies are perceived in the Pacific by European voyagers, as well as to the images I have discussed.[19]

[III]

I will look at some written accounts and pictorial representations of the South Pacific in the late eighteenth century, and consider them in the context of the constructions of national and civilized masculinity that I have been discussing. But I want to begin by looking at some perceptions of anthropophagy which seem to me to provide a paradigm for the relations between domesticity and exoticism that inform those constructions. In 1773, ten men from the crew of the *Adventure* died at Grass Cove in the South Island of New Zealand. James Burney led the party which discovered their remains, and took these to be 'most horrid & undeniable proofs' that they had been cooked and eaten.[20] Perhaps the most lurid account of this incident was provided in one of the accounts published without the sanction of the Admiralty. Burney's party, according to this journal,

> found several of their people's baskets, and saw one of their dogs eating
> a piece of broiled flesh, which upon examining they suspected to be
> human, and having found in one of the baskets a hand, which they
> knew to be the left hand of Thomas Hill, by the letters T. H. being
> marked on it, they were no longer in suspence about the event.[21]

Burney wrote that what he had seen could 'never be mentioned or thought of, but with horror',[22] and his father observed that after his return to London he 'always spoke of it in a whisper, as if it was treason'.[23]

The moral indignation that marks Burney's response, and that is promoted by the melodramatic fascination of the journalist's account, is perhaps similar to Reynolds's response to tattooing. It is an impassioned but moralized response that forms an important constituent of European national identities, and produces a distinction between islanders and Europeans that is constructed primarily in terms of moral and physical differences. The investment of customary and national significance in the appropriate responses of moral disapproval or horror is indicated in the various narrative elaborations on Burney's findings by voyagers who were not present. Among the recognizable remnants that Burney took back with him to the ship was a head, which because of its 'high forhead' was believed to be that of the captain's servant, 'he being a Negroe'.[24] But later narratives describing the events believed to have taken place at Grass Cove represent this man as having been the last to die, and emphasize that he 'must certainly have felt the most horrid sensations' at what he saw and anticipated, as though this horror confirmed his European, blanched, and sympathetic identity.[25]

The disapprobation that confirmed the common sensibilities of national identity is not, however, present in all of the voyagers' accounts, nor, perhaps, the only response that seems available to Burney. Probably the most influential of the various reflections on the practice of anthropophagy that resulted from this voyage were those given in Cook's published account, which seem to be marked, on the one hand, by the sense of moral and physical distance apparent in Burney's comments, and, on the other, by the implication that the practice is in some respects analogous to treason as an articulation of a markedly political discourse. Cook wrote that the people of the South Island of New Zealand lived 'dispersed in small parties, knowing no head but the chief of the family or tribe, whose authority may be very little'. He claimed that the social isolation and dislocation he perceived resulted in continual personal danger and warfare, and argued that 'were they more united under a settled form of government, they would have fewer enemies, consequently this custom would be less in use, and might in time be . . . forgotten'.[26] The practice is constructed in terms which represent it as a violation of the ideal unity of the social and private body, as though cannibalism replicated social dispersal and dismemberment on the bodies of those killed in battle. It seems to indicate an almost anarchic state of social and private disarticulation and incoherence, which Europeans can speak of only in whispers, as though it were a treasonable secret.

The second set of terms in which Cook articulates his thoughts on anthropophagy is, I have suggested, one which represents the practice as the object

'Representing the landing of part of the *Adventure*'s crew in search of their Companions who were murdered and eaten by the Savages of New Zealand', illustration from John Marra, *Journal of the* Resolution's *Voyage* (London, 1775). National Library of Australia, Canberra (Reese Nankivell Collection).

of that moral disapprobation that is a constituent of the community of national custom in Reynolds's Discourse. It is these terms, I think, which inform Cook's comment that 'At present, they [the New Zealanders] have but little idea of treating others as themselves would wish to be treated, but treat them as they *expect* to be treated.' Cannibalism, he suggests, results from a failure to perceive others as like ourselves, a failure of sympathy, which he believes can best be remedied by 'connexion or commerce with strangers'. He explains that 'An intercourse with foreigners would reform their manners, and polish their savage minds.' The contrast here is between savage isolation and civilized sympathy and sociability; between an asocial and therefore amoral condition which permits 'inhuman and savage' practices and the social and national communities which enforce European moral prejudices.[27] Cook's account suggests that cannibalism might be seen as one of the 'ancient customs' which have been 'handed down . . . from the earliest times',[28] and which, because it is a custom, points to the possibility of a more coherent political organization among the islanders. But it also suggests that cannibalism can be seen as the sign of an inhuman isolation that can only be mitigated or moralized by colonial intervention.

These perceptions of the islanders as either lacking government, or lacking civilized humanity and sympathy, seem to inform perceptions of tattooing, incision or scarification as manifestations of 'ancient customs'. Representations of the islanders' tattoos in the sketchbooks of the artists on Cook's voyages most usually show elaborate designs loosely framed by outlines that suggest isolated parts of the anatomy, disarticulated knees, thighs and buttocks – or the profiles of lightly sketched faces, as in these drawings by Sydney Parkinson and Herman Spöring. These two men were both employed to depict specimens of flora and fauna on the first voyage, and there seems to be little variation from the technique appropriate to botanical and zoological draughtsmanship in these representations of tattoos as curiosities fixed for the perusal of the natural philosopher. Parkinson's more fully worked-up drawings of the New Zealanders are similarly disarticulated. The images that were engraved for the posthumous publication of his Journal, showing the faces of Maori men 'curiously tataowed, or mark'd, according to their manner', are precise maps of elaborate facial incisions which seem dislocated from the features they adorn, or fixed in transient and impassioned expressions that are represented as mask-like.[29]

There is an incoherence in these drawings that may manifest the dislocation and discontinuity Cook attributed to the social formations of the New Zealanders, and that is, I think, apparent in voyagers' written reflections on Maori tattoos. The surgeon on the first voyage, for example, wrote of incisions he found 'extreamly curious' on a man's forehead, looking

> as if a plate for example had been graved with numberless little flourishes confined within two arched lines, and empressed upon the part; and each little curve thus mark'd out, not by a simple line or superficial black mark but really indented in the Skin.[30]

The perception of elaborate facial incisions as analogous to engravings is not unique to this account, and it may have been implicit in Rickman's comments on the islanders as 'living pictures'. It may seem to imply that the islanders are beyond representation in their exotic isolation, that they are, as it were, already the only possible image of themselves, already ethnologically specified to a degree that makes representation and cultural assimilation redundant. That exotic specificity seems opposed to the sense of shared national identity that taste for ornament encourages in Reynolds's seventh Discourse. The precision with which the surgical anatomist or botanical draughtsman marks the islanders' image indicates his technical skill, and

Sydney Parkinson, 'Black stains in the Skin called Tattoo', 1769, pen and ink. British Library, London (Add. MS 23920).

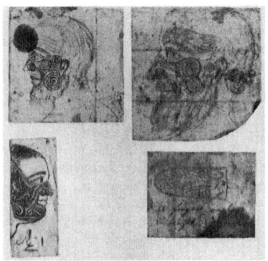

Herman Spöring, 'Black stains on the Skin called Tattoo', 1769, pencil. British Library, London (Add. MS 23920).

Sydney Parkinson,
'Portrait of a New Zeland
Man', 1769, pen and ink
and wash. British Library,
London (Add. MS 23920).

thus marks the knowledgeable and scrupulous accuracy of observation as a characteristic of the innocent and unclouded eye necessary to correct taste.

The representation of tattoos in some degree of isolation from the body they mark, in European texts, seems peculiarly interchangeable with the perception of them as 'really indented in the Skin'. It seems to substitute for the legible cultural significance of the civilized body defined by custom an inscribed and indented skin that is here not quite the object of distaste or disapprobation, but which is perceived to be appropriate to the taxonomies of surgical anatomy or botany. The dislocation and incoherence of these indentations seems to indicate here the excessively masculine or savage absence of convivial civility and sympathy – in contrast to, for example, the initials on the hand of Thomas Hill, which confirm the former coherence of his bodily identity and legible social place. Hill's tattoos seem to indicate a contrasting legibility in part, at least, because they had been inscribed in Tahiti, as accounts of the discovery of the hand emphasize. Their immediate decipherability points to the relative civilization of the Tahitians, and the approximation of their society to European notions of sympathetic sociability.[31] The engraving of the discovery of the European's tattooed hand, published in the unauthorized journal I quoted from earlier, represents the dissevered member as the focus for cohesive relations of what might be described as convivial horror among the European party. For the civility of the Europeans is indicated both by the degree of horror they express, and by the fact that their emotion is shared, that it confirms their common social identity. But the hand, poised as it were between barbarous incoherence and customary legibility, seems also to indicate the disarticulation and meaningless physicality attributed to the New Zealanders absent from the image, and to point up their 'inhuman and savage' guilt, their tasteless greed.

Those drawings which represent incisions as integral to the expression of the face they adorn – for example, William Hodges's image of an 'Old Man of New Zeland' – seem in contrast to indicate a kind of sentimental appropriation which perceives in tattoos the marks of private and individual character. The old man seems to be attributed the kind of dignity in resignation that marks the English rural poor in, for example, Gainsborough's images, and not the spectacular exoticism or ambiguously patrician authority that characterizes Reynolds's more formal and public representation of Omai. In Hodges's drawing, the inscription of the man's brow, in juxtaposition with his earring, may indicate the ornamentation appropriate to ancient customs whose cultural specificities are respected by the civilized spectator, who thus indicates his dispassionate and superior detachment. They mark the New Zealander as the sentimentalized object of a survey which gestures towards an ideally comprehensive universality in its capacity for humanizing and perhaps civilizing assimilation.

These different figures of tattoos as marks of incoherence or of characteristic integrity may all, in a sense, manifest European perceptions of ornament as a sign of feminization. In Banks's 'Thoughts' on the tattoos of the Tahitians, as I have already noted, physical adornment was represented as feminizing in its universality, and European accounts of the tattooing operation in the late eighteenth century feminize those undergoing the process with varying degrees of explicitness. In the large oil paintings produced by the artists who travelled with Cook, it is exclusively feminine bodies that are inscribed with tattoos or scarifications. John Webber's *Portrait of Poedua* and William Hodges's *View taken in the Bay of Otaheite Peha* both clearly gender the representation of bodily ornament. Representations of the New Zealanders, in drawings and in written accounts, are much more ambiguous in their gender than these images of the 'softer' Tahitians, and there are no large oil paintings of tattooed male Maoris from this period. Perhaps their representation in the more private and readily textualized spaces of the

William Hodges, *Old Maori Man with a Grey Beard*, also known as *Old Man of New Zeland*, 1773, chalk. National Library of Australia, Canberra.

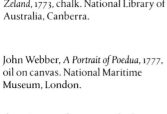

John Webber, *A Portrait of Poedua*, 1777, oil on canvas. National Maritime Museum, London.

drawing and engraved plate works to reinscribe their tattoos in a register of exotic production more immediately accessible to acultural feminization.

Hodges's and Webber's large paintings seem to allude to that construction of the relation between femininity and ornament that is apparent in Reynolds's Discourse, and which informs the observations of John Ledyard, who served as a corporal on Cook's last voyage. He wrote:

> I observe that among all nations the Women ornament themselves more than the men: I observe too that the Woman wherever found is the same kind, civil, obliging, humane, tender being . . . I do not think the Character of Woman so well ascertained in that Society which is highly civilized & polished as in the obscure and plain walks of life . . . Climate & Education makes a greater difference in the Character of Men than Women.[32]

Ledyard's remarks on ornament and gender bring into play the difference between Banks's and Reynolds's notions of modern masculinity, as that might be defined in terms of its national or civilized identity. The notion that women are more suited to the obscure and plain walks of life implies that they are somehow more natural than men, and are corrupted and deformed from that natural simplicity by civilization and polish. It implies that women are more markedly differentiated by their condition than are men, who therefore appear to be more universally accessible to civilization, and more capable of abstracting themselves from their circumstances. It seems that women are too much the impressionable creatures of circumstance, and that they are therefore excluded from that moral community that forms civilized masculine identity. The argument, on the other hand, that education and climate differentiate men, whereas women are everywhere the same, alludes to that construction of national and masculine character which excludes femininity because it is universal, unmarked, and as it were extranational. Women in this context appear to be either beneath or prior to national and customary second nature – somehow too essentially primitive to be fashioned into that cultural form. The appearance of continuity between these different gendered discourses seems to depend on the initial observation that women everywhere 'ornament themselves more than the men' – an observation that is contradicted most directly by accounts of New Zealand and the South Pacific. The remark seems as it were to consign women to the peripheral status of the accidental and contingent. Men may be differentiated by nationality, or by the degree of civilization that is attributed to them, but that difference almost looks like uniformity when it is contrasted with the variously ornamented forms of femininity. Ledyard's remarks adopt a strategy analogous to that of Reynolds's seventh Discourse: men may be universally uniform in their dignified humanity, or distinguished by diverse national identities, but the differences between those civilized and national identities are as nothing compared to the physical variousness and characteristic sameness of women, which conceals their incoherence of definition.

It is this incoherence that is I think manifested in European appropriations of tattooing in the eighteenth century. Joseph Banks, like John Ledyard, Sydney Parkinson, and many of the other voyagers, was tattooed during his stay in Tahiti,[33] marking what has often been described as the inauguration of a nautical tradition – a tradition which might seem to punctuate the chaste detachment of civilized masculine identity, and to emphasize that feminizing attachment to ornament implicit in the definition of masculine national identity. The European voyagers seem to have perceived in the tattooing and scarification of the islanders they encountered the signs of the intersections of ethnicity, gender, age and social station, which they thought were elaborated according to individual fancy. They thought, for example, that there might be a customary or ritual connection between a particular attainment – say, puberty – and the adornment of a particular part of the body. But they usually suggest that the designs that make up the tattoo are arbitrary and whimsical, dependent on what they saw as the vagaries of personal experience and choice. They conceived of tattoos as the markers of an esoteric diversity which could be imitated and appropriated, or assimilated, perhaps, in the context of that relativistic universalism that Hodges's image seems to indicate.

John Elliott, who travelled on the second circumnavigation, recollects in his memoirs of Tahiti that he and his companions particularly admired the warriors of Bora Bora – men whom Cook thought troublesome and anarchic. Elliott writes that these men had

> particular marks tattooed on the Legs etc. We therefore called them the Knights of Bora Bora, and all our mess conceived the idea of having some mark put on ourselves, as connecting us together, as well as to commemorate our having been at Otaheite.

Elliott's messmates had a star tattooed on the left breast, and called themselves the 'Knights of Otaheite'. He notes that they intended to keep their badge secret, but 'we no sooner began to bathe, than it spread halfway through the ship'.[34] The tattoos Elliott describes seem to mark the appropriation of what are conceived of as signs of ethnic or national identity to a secret and exotic position that is excluded from customary or national definition. The notion of a brotherhood of knights seems to allude to that sentimental fondness for Gothic institutions which is important to, for example, Edmund Burke's conception of custom, but here those chivalric orders are identified with the esoteric orders of the men of Bora Bora, and they thus seem to stain the Europeans with a kind of exotic perversion of domestic and national identity. Several of the *Bounty* mutineers were distinguished by the badge Elliott describes, and one of them combined this star with the tattooed mark of 'a Garter around his Left Leg with the Motto Honi Soit Qui Mal Y Pense'.[35] This is the aptly parodic perversion of a custom, endorsed (as Reynolds had argued customs should be) by 'the high and powerful advantages of rank'.[36] Here that custom becomes the insignia of national identity that coincides with the sign of the exoticization of the civilized body.

7 *Godna*: Inscribing Indian Convicts in the Nineteenth Century[1]

CLARE ANDERSON

Tattooing in Asia has a long history. In the fifteenth century, the traveller Nicolo Conti recorded how inhabitants of the Irawadi Valley (Burma) 'puncture their flesh with pins of iron, and rub into these punctures pigments which cannot be obliterated'. A century later, Tavernier wrote that the women of Banjera (East Bengal) tattooed their skin 'in such a manner to appear as though the skin was a flowered fabric'.[2] The origins and meanings of such tattooing, commonly known as *godna* (or *godena*), are both obscure and diverse. Decorative tattooing among the indigenous tribal (*adivasi*) populations of the Indian subcontinent has existed for centuries. Nomadic communities tattooed themselves as a mark of identity, assuring their recognition as they wandered from place to place. Nineteenth-century anthropologists detailed how tribal *gond* women, for example, patterned their legs with a variety of symmetrical tattoos in indigo or gunpowder blue.[3] Designs were said to include animals such as tigers, monkeys and birds, which had totemistic connotations.[4] *Banjara* (traders) and *gadia lohar* (ironsmiths) in Rajasthan wore a particular design on the face.[5] Marking the body was also said to be a sign of ritual status. Among the tribal *abors* of Assam, the presence of a tattoo was necessary to marry.[6] The absence of tattoos on young Burmans' thighs was emasculating.[7] Male *dhangars*, an *adivasi* group from the Central Provinces, branded – rather than tattooed – five marks on the lower arm with a hot iron, as a sign of initiation to manhood.[8] Tattooing and branding were also used as a curative for physical ailments. Some communities branded themselves with burning wood, in the belief that it would make their joints supple.[9]

Tattooing was also fashionable among some caste Hindus. This may have been due to its appearance in the *Ramayana*. Lord Krishna tattooed his four

'Tatoo Designs'. British Library, London (T 49126).

totems – the shell, wheel, gada and lotus flower – on the faces and limbs of his
wives; Vishnu tattooed Lakshmi's hand with drawings of his weapons, the
sun and the moon, promising to protect those who copied the design from
evil.[10] Tattooing may also have been bound up with the consolidation of
gender relations, with tattoo marks seen as effective in curbing female sexual
desire, described as eight times as strong as that of men. It may also have
been a facial disfigurement, introduced at the time of the Mughal (Muslim)
incursions from the late Middle Ages, to prevent attacks on and facilitate the
easy recognition of abducted Hindu women. Indeed, Koranic law reflects the

idea that the marked body cannot be exposed before the sacred. Purely decorative tattooing is therefore taboo amongst Muslims.[11]

As in the case of tribal groups, the meaning of tattoos amongst caste Hindus varied. For Hindus, tattoos, which were believed to survive death, were seen as evidence of earthly suffering which would be accepted in heaven as penance for sins. Particular tattoos would also facilitate the recognition of family members. Marking the body could also have religious connotations. Some Hindu facial tattoos were connected with religious fasting and rites of purification.[12] Brahmin Vishnavites were sometimes branded on the shoulders. Indian Christians were also tattooed. Both Roman Catholics and the Syrian Christian community of Kerala had birds tattooed on the arms and thighs as symbols of the Holy Ghost.[13] Beliefs sometimes also reflected those already established among indigenous populations. Tattooing was, for instance, seen as a means to good health. Thus Hindu women were sometimes tattooed over the spleen and liver to avoid having still-born children. Tattoos were also seen as a cure for rheumatism or injury.

Tattooing was also a means of status differentiation, marking particular rites of passage. Among caste Hindus, it was largely confined to women. Designs varied, but commonly included tattooing on the forehead with sun, moon, star and crescent designs. The forehead had particular significance in the Indian context, with its marking a sign of respectability.[14] The higher the caste, the fewer the designs. The association between tattooing and caste status may have led to the eventual decline of tattooing, as low-caste groups sought to emulate the relative absence of tattoos among higher castes as a means of social mobility, or sanskritization.[15] In a clear illustration of the gendering of the practice, tattoos implied a woman's chastity and fidelity.[16] It was said that in nineteenth-century Bengal a respectable Hindu would not take water from the hand of a girl who did not wear a tattooed *bindi*. The implication was that such women were amoral.[17]

Tattooers themselves varied from region to region. In Rajasthan, they were almost always men; in East Bengal and Bihar, they were predominantly women from the *natura* tribe, known as *godnaiti*.[18] The pricking instrument usually consisted of three or more needles tied together with thread. The pattern was first traced on to the skin with a small pointed stick which had been dipped in the prepared ink. The skin was then washed and a coat of ink rubbed over the surface. Coconut oil was sometimes applied to alleviate the pain and prevent swelling. The fee was either a few *annas* or a gift of rice, plantain or betel nuts, with the amount or quantity dependent on the complexity of the design.[19] Tattooing could be agonizing. One traveller wrote of 'dreadful screeches' when young *gond* women were tattooed.[20] In Burma, opium was sometimes smoked to alleviate the pain.[21]

That sources from the fifteenth to early twentieth centuries reveal so much about the marking of Indian bodies reflects the persistent fascination with the meaning of tattooing and branding. In the late nineteenth and early twentieth century, travellers, anthropologists, district commissioners and colonial officials alike documented and interpreted the significance of what to them was a signifier of India's 'otherness'.[22] In particular, tattooing became a means to identify and distinguish caste, perceived by Europeans as the principle of Indian social organization. Many tattoo designs thus came to be conceived as 'caste marks', with their design and frequency seen to denote precise social status.[23] Tattoos were also used to establish connections between different social groups. As a result of the nature of their tattoos, for instance, the *dômba* caste found in Madras was seen as sharing ancient origins with another caste group, the *dôms* of North India.[24] Neither was the significance of tattoos to European criminologists from the 1870s lost in the Indian context. Just as in Europe tattoos facilitated the recognition of Lombroso's so-called criminal man, so too attempts were made in India to use tattoos to recognize particular 'criminal' castes and tribes.

In 1871, the Criminal Tribes Act consolidated almost 100 years of the development of British perceptions of criminality in India to provide for the registration, surveillance and control of particular social groups. Criminality was viewed as hereditary, with some castes and tribes considered to consist exclusively of *janam chuars* (criminals-by-birth).[25] Following this, the Secretary of State for India, Herbert Risley, undertook a massive ethnographic survey of the Indian districts. Phrenological and other physical bio-data were collected, supporting a pseudo-science which contributed to the development of an anthropometry of the soul.[26] Risley also called for accounts on the nature and frequency of tattooing. Each district commissioner was asked twelve questions concerning its meaning and significance. The gender of those most frequently tattooed was investigated; the favoured part of the body for tattooing recorded; and the designs analysed. Risley's disappointment that tattooing was neither viewed as hereditary, nor connected to ritual worship or 'criminal ceremonies', was palpable.[27]

Tattooing did, however, play a significant role in social reproduction by reproducing social and political types.[28] With decorative tattooing largely confined to tribal *adivasi* groups, many of whom fell under the auspices of the 1871 Act, the connection was made between 'savagery' (which had been associated with tattooing since the first European encounters with the tattooed Polynesian world)[29] and hereditary criminality. One colonial report described the *dôms*, for example, as 'the lowest of the outcasts ... with their presence in any district or part of a district always marked by a decided increase in thefts, robberies and dacoities [gang robberies]'.[30] The recognition of such thieves and dacoits was, of course, facilitated by the fact that they wore particular types of tattoos. Later directives given to the police in the Panjab noted that the *baurias*, a 'notorious wandering tribe', could be recognized by either three brands on the body (if male) or five tattoo marks on the face (female).[31] Yet such groups resisted this stigmatization, enlarging or changing their tattoos in order to counter the marks of identification recorded by the police. The physical description of those under suspicion thus often conflicted with the newly unmarked or differently marked self.[32]

STIGMATIZATION AND IDENTIFICATION: EUROPEAN
PRACTICE AND COLONIAL EXPANSION

Tattoo marks have long been used for the stigmatization of particular social groups. Tattooing was used by the Persians and later the Greeks and Romans for punitive purposes, and delinquent slaves in late antiquity were tattooed, as were criminals, soldiers and prisoners of war.[33] In ancient India branding was also commonly used as a punishment. Brahmins, high-caste Hindus who were expected to maintain a particularly high level of morality but who were exempt from corporal punishment, were marked on the forehead for various offences. For adultery or unlawful intercourse they were branded with a picture of the female genitalia. Excessive drinking was represented with a liquor sign; theft with a dog's foot; and murdering another brahmin with a picture of a headless man.[34] Evidence of punitive tattooing during this period exists elsewhere in Asia. In Burma, for instance, offenders had a circle tattooed on the cheek or a description of their offence inscribed on the chest.[35] As late as the 1890s, one traveller in the remote provinces of Mongolia and Tibet wrote of his meeting with a man tattooed on his left temple with the symbol of the crime for which he was suffering the punishment of exile.[36]

Bodily markings were thus a means to stigmatize and to identify. This was also the case in Europe, where the branding of galley and other public slaves was the norm until the nineteenth century. The 1532 *Carolina* penal code – still in operation in seventeenth- and eighteenth-century Germany – provided for the branding of convicts. This type of marking literally scorched dishonour on to the face.[37] From the mid-sixteenth century, galley slaves in France had the letters 'GAL' branded on their shoulders. In early modern and modern Europe, petty thieves were commonly branded with a 'T'. One convict of 'radically bad and infamous character' at Moreton Bay (Van Diemen's Land), William Saunders, was marked 'thief' on the forehead prior to his transportation.[38] In a crude form of tattooing, *katorshniki* (public slaves) in Siberia had 'KAT' pricked on to their cheeks and forehead and gunpowder rubbed into the wounds; a practice not abolished until 1863.[39] Between 1810 and 1832, when branding was abolished in France, convicts sentenced to forced labour had the letters 'TP' (*travaux perpétuels*) branded on to their bodies.[40] Transported British army deserters had a small 'D' burnt into their left side; as did a number of soldiers court martialled while on service in nineteenth-century Australia.[41]

These practices were extended into the colonies as European empires grew. As in Europe, the use of tattooing and branding was crucial to facilitating control over slave populations. Slaves in the Americas, West Indies and Indian Ocean were routinely branded for insubordinate conduct. Under the Barbados Code of 1688, copied by settlers in the Windward Islands (St Lucia, St Vincent, Tobago and Dominica), slaves could be branded with a hot iron as punishment.[42] The repressive Code Noir (1723) in the French Indian Ocean colony Ile de France (Mauritius) directed that maroon slaves would be branded on the shoulder.[43] In the Danish Virgin Islands a slave ordinance of 1733 decreed that leaders of slave deserters would be 'pinched thrice with a hot iron' before being hanged.[44] Indian slaves were also tattooed by their owners.[45] When two slave boys – Sam and Tom – absconded in Bengal in 1784 , the ensuing 'wanted' poster noted that their right arms were marked just above the elbow – away from normal view, but visible enough for easy identification – with the initials of their master, J. H. Valentin Dubois.[46]

Bodily marking was also integrated into colonial penal codes, such as that introduced in those areas of South Asia under East India Company control. One of the principles of Islamic penal practice in pre-colonial Indian law was *tazir* (*tashir*): discretionary punishment which sometimes involved humiliation by shaving the offender's head, blackening their face or parading them around on an ass. *Tazir* took the rank of the offender and other mitigating factors into consideration during sentencing. This was highly offensive to Western perceptions of uniform punishment. Islamic law was thus replaced by a new 'humanistic' interpretation.[47] The Enlightenment philosophy of the social contract was embraced; punishment could not be discretionary if it were to act as a deterrent. One form of punishment much appreciated by humanists was public works. Prisoners were both economically useful and a highly visible lesson for the general population, 'a focus of profit and signification' as society itself became a theatre of punishment.[48] Life and term convicts were commonly sent out on public works in colonial India, building and repairing roads, bridges, government buildings and even their own lodgings. After 1792, they were also transported overseas to East India Company and colonial territories, including Aden, the Andaman Islands, Arakan, Malacca, Mauritius, Prince of Wales Island and Singapore, where they performed similar tasks. Colonial expansion necessitated a cheap and, preferably, controllable labour supply in order to build the infrastructure required for socio-economic development. Convict labour was both, and thus highly desirable.[49]

Convicts themselves had their identity as a prison labour force literally inscribed on their person. After 1797, life convicts, perjurers and forgers in the Bengal Presidency had their name, crime, date of sentence and court by which convicted – in the vernacular – tattooed on the forehead.[50] Term prisoners were also marked after 1807, a decision revoked in 1817 when it was again decided that lifers alone should suffer the punishment.[51] The 1797 regulations were later extended to South India as the areas around Madras were ceded to the East India Company. After 1803, life convicts there were tattooed on the Bengal model; from 1816, the regulations were extended to term convicts.[52] As in Bengal, the principal aim of the enactments was the reapprehension of escaped convicts.[53] It was also a non-capital punishment viewed as suitable for serious offenders of high caste (especially brahmins) whose execution, it was feared, would lead to social unrest. In one case, a brahmin convicted of murder was banished from Company territory having had the figure of a headless man tattooed on his forehead.[54] The practice itself thus coupled European penal practices with Indian cultural norms in order to facilitate colonial control.

The Hindi verb godna (godena) means to prick, to puncture, to dot, to mark the skin with dots, to tattoo. It is also used to refer to marks of tattooing. A godni is a tattooing instrument; a godnawali a tattooist. Invoking the piercing which godna involves, the word can also mean to wound (or lacerate) a person's feelings.[55] In Bengal, the process is also known as ulki, probably deriving from the Sanskrit word khud, meaning to dig, bore or engrave.[56] In Kerala, tattooing is known as pacha kuthuka (pricking with a green colour).[57] The meaning of godna in colonial penal practice later changed. Early regulations concerning the marking of prisoners with godna specifically referred to indelible blue markings, made from the same blue dye (burnt indigo mixed with soot) employed in tattooing at this time.[58] Godna later came to mean the branding of criminals, with goda the word for a branding iron.[59] Its shifting meaning is, however, by no means unambiguous. The process may have evolved to integrate aspects of both, with convicts being branded and the wound coloured with indigo dye.

The first references to 'branding by *godna*' were made in 1830, when thugs were marked in this way in the Sagar and Narbada Territories of Central India, where William Sleeman's campaigns against thuggee were concentrated.[60] Thugs were believed to be professional, ritual murderer robbers for the goddess Kali and could be arrested simply for being thugs rather than for any specific offence. If marked with the words 'convicted thug', on the forehead or back, after their release from jail old offenders could be recognized should they be arrested for a second time.[61] Those sentenced to transportation for life had the word marked in English letters; those for confinement for terms of years in the vernacular.[62] The use of the English language for lifers was to facilitate their recognition – as thugs – by their British jailers and overseers. To be sure, thugs were often treated differently in the penal settlements, with special rules for their pardon and/or release sometimes applied. Marks in the vernacular for those sentenced to a limited term provided a warning of their 'profession' to potential future victims.

Later commentators, including the Superintendent of Convicts in Singapore, J. F. A. McNair, referred to *godna* as branding with a hot copper iron.[63] By the time Philip Meadows Taylor published his bestseller, *Confessions of a Thug*, in the 1830s, there was no doubt as to his view of the procedure. This

'Tattooed Thugs'. British Library, London (ADD 41300). There is no evidence that thugs – or other prisoners – were tattooed beneath the eyes in the manner that this sketch suggests.

account, which did much to contribute to the orientalist construction of thuggee by feeding into the reader's desire for the exotic 'other', has Meadows Taylor writing in the person of the central character, Ameer Ali, a thug:

> 'Ameer Ali . . . I had trusted thee . . . but thou hast deceived me . . . thou art a Thug and a murderer. Still, because I have a lingering sentiment of kindness towards thee, I do not seek thy death . . . Yet thou canst not be released without a mark on thy brow that men may know and beware of. Throw him down,' cried he to the attendants, and let him be branded!
>
> They threw me down . . . I struggled, yet it was unavailing; they held my arms, and my legs, and head, and a red-hot pice [sic] was pressed upon my forehead; it was held there as it burnt down to the bone, ay my very brain seemed to be scorched and withered by the burning copper. They took it off, and raised me up. Allah! Allah! the agony that I endured – the agony of pain, and, more than that, of shame – to be branded publicly that the world might think me a thief – to have a mark set on my forehead that I must carry to my grave – a mark only set on the vile and on the outcasts from society . . . I bound my turban over my still burning and aching brow, so that man might not see my shame.[64]

The allusion to the marking of Cain would have been obvious to the book's British readership. After Cain kills Abel, he is 'marked' by God before being sent into exile.[65] The humiliation of branding was clear. For high status Muslims, like the fictional Ameer Ali, the punishment was particularly pronounced: permanent marking is explicitly forbidden by the Koran. In addition, whilst the shame inflicted by *godna* affected all, the association of tattooing with low caste almost certainly made the punishment equally offensive to certain Hindus.

Despite the various regulations relating to tattooing/branding, *godna* was never standardized. In Madras, despite repeated directives from the Supreme Court (1815, 1816 and 1823), regulations were not always enforced. Even in regions where *godna* regulations were in place, such as the Bengal Presidency, there were often difficulties in finding appropriate officials to serve as tattooers. Fearful that Indian tattooists would not perform the task effectively (or worse still would fall prey to bribery in some 'Indian conspiracy'), some convicts destined for transportation overseas were marked on arrival in Alipore Jail in Calcutta, rather than at their place of trial, as was the usual practice.[66] This was also the case in Madras, where convicts were frequently tattooed at Chingleput Jail – rather than in the district in which convicted – just a few days before their shipment to the South-east Asian penal settlements.[67]

'Thugs and Budhuk dacoits',
c. 1839–46. British Library,
London (P2572/3). These
pictures, sketched on board
the convict ship *Phlegethon*,
more accurately reflect the
practice of *godna*. Murdan
Khan and Multhoo Byragee
Jogee, both thugs, are the only
tattooed convicts. This is
probably because of either the
nature of their offences or the
fact that they were under
sentence of transportation
for life, rather than for a term
of years.

In other cases, convicts were sometimes tattooed only with part of the description required by the regulations. Descriptions such as *ji banna boddh qaid* (life imprisonment) alone were not uncommon.[68] Neither was the punishment adopted throughout the areas of India under East India Company control. By the time the Bombay Code was formulated in 1827, there was a growing aversion to the practice, for reasons which will become clear. Thus there was never any provision for tattooing or branding offenders in the Bombay Presidency.[69]

It is clear that marking convicts on the forehead was an irrevocable prescription of criminal identity. Indeed, *godna* was primarily perceived a deterrent to convict escape, a particular risk as prisoners were worked outside jail or in the penal settlements. Marked convicts were unable to pass themselves off as free persons and their identity was thus easily verified. This facilitated the recapture of escaped convicts, either by local communities in India or local populations in the penal settlements. These included the Malays of Singapore and slaves, creoles and the Indian community in Mauritius.[70] A mark on the forehead was often the only way in which convicts could be distinguished from free Indians or other settlers.[71]

The failure of the Bombay Government to adopt the tattooing/branding of life convicts was much criticized. In Mauritius, for example, which received convicts from Bombay rather than Bengal after 1830, there was an explosion in convict desertion on the island.[72] The fact that Bombay convicts were not marked with *godna* on the forehead, coupled with the increase in indentured Indian immigrants in the colony, meant that convict escapees (maroons) were able to elude capture by blending in with the free population.[73] Some convicts were even able to pass themselves off as indentured labourers. One maroon convict was found living on a sugar plantation, where he was employed as a servant. The Mauritian Chief of Police lamented: 'planters ought to ascertain who persons really are before they take them into their service'.[74] This was not an isolated case. Another convict was discovered ten years after his escape quite by chance in the Immigration Depot with an immigrant ticket bearing a false name.[75] A third man was employed for nine years after his escape, his master claiming to have been ignorant of the fact that his employee was a convict.[76]

The colonial authorities at the penal settlements along the Straits begged the Bombay Government to reconsider its position. The lack of indelible markings on Bombay convicts made it impossible to distinguish them and this had real implications for the maintenance of penal discipline.[77] The Governor of the Straits Settlements wrote in 1842 that a mark on the forehead – however slight – deterred escapes and facilitated recapture.[78] Given the growing concern with transportation as a 'reforming endeavour', however, the presence of an irremovable symbol of criminal identity was falling from favour. A parallel debate was taking place over the merits of the punishment of flogging, which left marks of the whip (korah) on the offender's back. He thus became a daghi (marked man), which prevented his return to honest labour.[79] Similarly, if tattooed/branded, a 'reformed' (or even released) convict would still be recognized by his godna marking as a common criminal. The Bombay authorities, considering the issue some 40 years after its inception, thus turned down several requests from the Superintendents of Convicts in the penal settlements to introduce godna into their legal code.

ESCAPE AND IDENTITY

On 27 October 1846, a fisherman (koli) from Bombay was tried for the crime of being an escaped convict returned from transportation, Shrawun Sokacha. Convicted of gang robbery with force, Sokacha had been shipped to Aden in 1842, at this time a common destination for Indian convicts, who were put to work on the roads there.[80] In June 1845, he was one of 64 convicts who rose up against their guards and absconded. Although most of the convicts were quickly recaptured, a handful, including Shrawun Sokacha, managed to escape inland and were said to be hiding there. The Sultan guaranteed that he would return Sokacha to Aden, in exchange for a not inconsiderable reward of fifteen German Crowns. Despite his concerted efforts, Sokacha never arrived back in Aden.[81]

In 1846, Ramma bin Balloo Powar, Bombay Police Constable, came across a group of kolis. The men were discussing Shrawun Sokacha's return from transportation. They stated that he was living with his sister near Bombay and had assumed an alias of apparently Arabic origin – Bappoo bin Gunnoo – to hide his true identity. Although the kolis were clearly drunk, they insisted their allegations were not without foundation. Powar went to the place where Sokacha was said to be hiding and arrested a man who claimed to be Bappoo bin Gunnoo. The man was subsequently brought to trial.

The trial hinged around whether Bappoo bin Gunnoo's identity – as claimed by the kolis – could be substantiated, in the face of confused and contradictory evidence. The court proceedings began with the trial judge reading out the indent made when Shrawun Sokacha was originally transported: 'Light complexion and has two scars – one on each arm – and one mark on the right knee; height 5 feet 3 1/2; age 35'.[82] Gunnoo was then paraded before the court and physically examined. The judge remarked that he appeared much younger than he should have been, if the recorded 35 years in 1842 were correct. Equally, apart from a few small marks, his arms and right knee were not scarred. Neither was his complexion particularly light. It was possible – if a little unlikely – that the scars had faded over the previous four years. The original description of Gunnoo's light skin colour was more subjective, although it was remarked that it may have darkened since the indent was made. Indeed, transportation usually followed a prolonged period of debilitating imprisonment, with prisoners commonly spending several months awaiting their trial and the chartering of a convict ship. The most unequivocal evidence was Gunnoo's height, which corresponded closely with Sokacha's original measurement.

The confusion over Gunnoo's physical identity was exacerbated by the conflicting testimonies offered by witnesses called to the stand, some of whom claimed to recognize him, while others were not so sure. This was compounded by the lapse of time since his original conviction. With so much conflicting evidence – and the further possibility that Gunnoo had been targeted for some grudge against him – his identity remained unclear and he was acquitted.

The trial of Bappoo bin Gunnoo coincided with the ongoing debate in Bombay on the merits of marking the forehead to facilitate the recapture of escaped convicts. The trial judge believed that Gunnoo *was* the escaped convict Shrawun Sokacha and was persuaded that convicts sentenced to transportation for life in Bombay should be marked in order that they might be positively identified in the event of their escape, stating that an escaped convict would have 'neither home nor safety'. Significantly, he did not pre-clude marking the less visible shoulder or back for the purpose of identification rather than immediate recognition.

Godna was never adopted in Bombay, however.[83] With the Bombay Government standing firm on the issue, and in the context of shifting attitudes towards penal marking, Bengal and Madras also abolished the practice.[84] In 1849, the marking of convicts was banned throughout those regions controlled by the East India Company. No indelible marks of any kind could be made, or renewed, on any part of the body of any convicted offender.[85] The Act was passed with very little comment.[86] In the absence of tattoo or brand marks, colonial administrators found other means of differentiating convicts in the penal settlements. In the Andaman Islands, where a permanent settlement was set up in the wake of the 1857 Indian uprising, particularly 'dangerous' offenders wore a shirt and *dhoti* marked with red cotton thread. For the first five years of their transportation, all convicts wore a metal ring inscribed with a number around their neck.

Oblong tickets denoted a gang robber (*dacoit*).[87] Thieves wore a small red badge on their chests.[88] Clothes and necklaces were easily removed though. Faced with the same problem of convict desertion as Superintendents in the Straits Settlements, the Andamans' authorities repeatedly called for the reintroduction of *godna* marks, in a less conspicuous place, where they could be identified on closer examination.

A large number of the first batch of convicts sent to the Andamans escaped shortly after their arrival in 1858. Subsequently, the first Super-intendent of the Penal Settlement, James Walker, suggested that each convict's right forearm be branded before their departure for the islands. The letters 'P.B./L' would denote life convicts and 'P.B./T' term convicts, the 'P.B.' denoting Port Blair, the administrative headquarters of the settlement. After their arrival, Walker suggested, the convict's number – the key to tracing their name, caste, crime and sentence through the settlement's records – would be placed beneath the letters, producing a mark such as: 'P.B./L/1085'. The proposals were never adopted.[89] After two cases of convicts escaping the Andamans by sea, the Superintendent again proposed in 1870 that life prisoners be branded. A broad arrow would be burnt on one shoulder or forearm and, as proposed in 1858, 'P.B.' on the other. As a sure means of detection, he hoped that such a measure would deter convicts from escaping. Again, the Government of India refused to sanction what was by then repeatedly described as a 'barbarous practice'.[90]

REDEFINING THE 'CRIMINAL SELF': CONVICT RESPONSES TO GODNA

As a dramatic, highly visible prescription of a criminal identity, it is unsur-prising that convicts made attempts to cover, remove or even rewrite their *godna* markings. There is no evidence that they became a 'badge of honour' as was the case in Brazil, where runaway slaves, branded with an 'F' on the shoulder, proudly displayed proof of their resistance to authority.[91] In the Indian context, turbans were worn low over the forehead to hide *godna* marks.[92] Hair was also grown in such a fashion as to conceal them. Cultural norms relating to dress and physical appearance thus became a means through which convicts were able to mask the identity assigned to them by colonial penal codes.

More dramatically, scarification and attempts to permanently remove rather than conceal tattoos were not unknown. Caustic preparations were certainly familiar – if not widespread – in imperial Roman times.[93] As we have seen, 'criminal' tribes in India enlarged or changed their (voluntary) tattoos in order to conceal the marks of identification recorded by the police. The physical description of those under surveillance thus conflicted with the newly marked or unmarked self.[94] Indian convicts too attempted to remove their *godna* markings. *Godna* was sometimes completely effaced by convicts.[95] In other cases convicts attempted to lighten – and thus minimize – their tattoos. Thus in 1817 it was directed that convicts should only be tattooed early in the morning. It was easier for prison guards to keep watch over newly tattooed convicts during the day, and prevent them from defacing the inscriptions. This was more difficult to prevent at night. The same 1817 order directed that if convicts removed their markings, even partially, they were to be redone immediately.[96]

Alongside attacks on *godna* markings, innumerable transported convicts used aliases in place of the names recorded in the convict indents. While this was equally common among unmarked convicts, the significance of aliases is magnified in the case of tattooed or branded convicts. An assumed alias could contradict a convict's given – and inscribed – name. After the first Andaman settlement was transferred to Prince of Wales' Island in 1805, for example, a number of convicts insisted that their names be re-recorded, claiming that those ascribed to them by the authorities were incorrect. Such correct, or preferred, names in some instances conflicted with those inscribed on the forehead by colonial officialdom.[97] A new name was thus a means to reject the inscriptions of colonial authority.

COLLABORATION AND ADAPTATION IN THE COLONIAL CONTEXT

Tattooing and branding were established cultural practices in pre-colonial India. The use of tattooing as a punishment at that time was bound up with other sanctions of shame and humiliation. Given that bodily marking was also a familiar punishment in Europe, it is unsurprising that the East India Company used it in its own penal codes. This was a punishment consistent with both European metropolitan and Indian practices. However, *godna* extended the marking of the body, common to Europe, to the marking of the forehead, which already held a special significance in South Asia as a penal, cultural, or caste marker. In both Europe and the subcontinent, the effect of *godna* was to stigmatize and facilitate control over certain populations. Additionally, in the later nineteenth-century context, as in Europe, the colonial authorities in India used the presence of voluntary tattoos in their attempts to categorize and survey particular 'criminal' populations.

Yet this is not an unrefined history of colonial oppression, largely because the 'colonial project' was not a uniform one. The imperatives of convict administrators in the penal settlements were often frustrated by those of British officials in the Presidencies themselves. The former sought the effective management of convicts, which they believed to be facilitated by *godna*; the latter, increasingly, to limit it as incompatible with the goal of reforming offenders. More broadly, it is clear that *godna* did not sit easily with British attempts to morally justify their presence on the subcontinent, by abolishing such 'barbaric' practices as *sati* (widow immolation) and female infanticide.[98] As a result of this, and of the practical difficulties inherent in tattooing relatively large numbers of prisoners, there was no consistent policy relating to *godna* across the Company-controlled Indian Presidencies. Moreover, where such policies did exist, they were not uniformly applied.

Perhaps most significant is the revelation that *godna* did not render convicts powerless. Those convicts whose foreheads were marked attempted to resist, redefine or rescript their inscriptions. Continuity in cultural practices – the use of turbans or the growth of hair, neither of which was prohibited in the penal settlements at this time – ensured that *godna* markings could be effectively covered. More dramatically, convicts made attempts to deface or even remove the marks, with some degree of success. Their use of aliases, contradicting official naming and inscribing, were an even more direct rejection of colonial authority. The renaming of the self was symbolic in reaching beyond the constructions of colonial knowledge. Thus, despite *godna* marks, convicts were able, to at least some degree, to redefine their own identity.

8 Skin Deep Devotions: Religious Tattoos and Convict Transportation to Australia

HAMISH MAXWELL-STEWART AND IAN DUFFIELD

All convicts disembarked in Van Diemen's Land between 1817 and 1853 were examined and a description of their physical appearance placed on file. Thus, we know that James Regan was a 28-year-old hairdresser from Leeds with hazel eyes and brown hair and whiskers. We also know that he was tattooed on his right arm with his own initials, 'J R' followed by a heart and the initials of two relatives 'MR' and 'RR'. On the inside of the same arm he also sported three stars, a half moon and a fish. On his left arm he was inscribed above the elbow with a man on a cask of rum. He was also marked on his breast with a star and crucifix.[1]

THE BODY CORPORAL AND THE BODY RELIGIOUS

Through the process of transportation convict bodies were transformed into sites of exploitation. This was achieved through a number of mechanisms. In simple economic terms the convict's body was expropriated by the state, turning each individual from a wage labourer into a production device; to be maintained to be sure but also, like an idle or vicious horse, to be disciplined by the bit, snaffle and whip.[2] Convicts were highly aware of this reshaping process. Back when penal transportation was to the American colonies, convicts' conversion into semi-commodities was apparent, through acts of sale between entrepreneurial contractors who shipped them and planters who purchased their labour services for their sentence terms.[3] An American precursor to the later transportation ballad 'Van Diemen's Land' makes this convict awareness explicit:

> In short time men up to us came,
> Some ask'd our trades and others ask'd our names.
> Some view'd our limbs and others turn'd us round,
> Examining (like horses) if we were sound.[4]

The 'Van Diemen's Land' version further intensifies this equine trope:

> The very first day we landed
> All on that fatal shore
> The planters they came round us
> About three score or more
> So they harnessed us up like horses
> And fit us out of hand
> And they yoked us to the plough my boys
> To plough Van Diemen's Land.[5]

Another version of 'Van Diemen's Land' has the variant, 'And *sold* us out of hand'.[6] Taken literally, this ballad conveys multiple misinformation. In the Australian penal colonies, convicts were not sold but assigned to settlers, and by the state, not private entrepreneurs. Unlike in the Chesapeake, there were no 'planters' in transportation period New South Wales and Van Diemen's Land; in these colonies, the term was not used even of large land-holders. Nor did settlers yoke Australia's convicts to ploughs, which in the earlier decades were drawn by oxen, not horses. The ballad 'Van Diemen's Land', however, vividly conveys convict *understandings* of the social meanings of the bodily transportation experience. In Van Diemen's Land and New South Wales, big free landowners became the officially preferred recipients of assigned convict labour, as also of grants of 'crown' (i.e. Aboriginal) land, thus enjoying one of history's more spectacular free lunches. In early colonial Australian power relations and political economies, they occupied a broadly comparable position to colonial Chesapeake planters. Arguably, Australia's penal colonies were 'a perversion of the planters' frontier . . . [utilizing] disciplined and cheap labour comparable to the negro slave of the planter'.[7] While this remark ignores the important variables of differing unfree labour systems, it perhaps unintentionally reveals why popular understandings sustained the American ballad's horse trope into 'Van Diemen's Land'.

In the later penal transportation 'systems'[8] the state increasingly used bio-data in the shaping process.[9] The need to 'know the subject', or anyway to persuade both 'observer and participant' that the state was all-knowing, had twin imperatives.[10] One was largely mechanical. A recorded description of each convict was essential for surveillance purposes. When Van Diemen's Land prisoners absconded, notices including their hair, complexion and eye colour, height, scars, tattoos and place of birth (which indicated probable accent), were reprinted in the *Government Gazette*, from information in carefully compiled *Description Lists*,[11] as was the case with the bushranger James Regan.

308   THE HOBART TOWN GAZETTE,

Abbott-street, and on the north east by that street to the point of commencement.

George Fox.

A	R	P
1	0	21

Town of Ross.

Bounded on the south by 795 links along an allotment located to Charles Sutton from the Esplanade to Church-street, on the east by 147 links northerly along Church-street, on the north by 745 links along an allotment located to John Iles westerly to the Esplanade, and on the north west by the Esplanade to the point of commencement.

JOSEPH HONE,
Chairman.

NOTICE.

SURVEY OFFICE,
2nd May 1838.

THE new Road through Epping Forest being open for the use of the Public, it is proposed to close the old line of road where it passes through the property of James Crear, Esq.

All persons, therefore, who may have any objections to the measure are requested to communicate them to me in writing, on or before the 4th June next.

G. FRANKLAND,
Surveyor General.

NOTICE.

NOTICE is hereby given, that the next Sittings of the Court of Requests for the District of Campbelton, appointed for Friday the 4th of May, will not take place until Friday the 18th of May.

G. G. EMMETT,
Registrar of the Court.

REWARD!!!

100 SOVEREIGNS
AND
CONDITIONAL PARDON
To any Convict not holding such Pardon,
OR
A FREE PARDON
To any person holding a Conditional Pardon.

Police Office, Hobart,
27th April 1838.

WHEREAS, a most barbarous Murder was perpetrated on the body of Robert Morley, on the 12th day of April last, at the house of Mr. Thornell, in the Police District of Campbell-town. And Whereas, at an Inquest afterwards held on the body of the said Robert Morley, a verdict of Wilful Murder was returned against two persons unknown, and also against George Thomas, or Thompson, as an accessory thereto. THIS IS TO GIVE NOTICE, that I am authorized by His Excellency the Lieutenant Governor, to offer the Reward of 100 SOVEREIGNS and of a recommendation to Her Majesty's mercy for a Conditional Pardon to any Convict not holding such Pardon, and a FREE PARDON and a like sum to any person holding a Conditional Pardon, who shall cause each or either of the said offenders to be lodged in safe custody. The said George Thomas, or Thompson, is believed to have been formerly in the service of Mr. William Kearney, near Richmond, and has been recently employed by Mr. Connell, of

Jacob's Sugar Loaf, (his description is given underneath) and one of the other persons unknown, is strongly suspected to be James Regan, who absconded on his way from Ross to Campbell-town, whilst in custody, on the 10th day of March last, and who was, some short period prior, in the service of Mr George Carr Clarke. The description of the third man is also hereunder given

M. FORSTER,
Chief Police Magistrate.

Description of George Thomas, or Thompson.—Height, 5ft $7\frac{3}{4}$; lost a front upper tooth; in one arm has pricked with ink, or something of the kind, F M J T and 1832 in figures.

Description of James Regan, per Elphinstone 1.—Trade, hair; dresser, height, 5ft $2\frac{1}{2}$, age 28, complexion brown, hair and whiskers brown, head oval, visage oval, forehead high, eyebrows black, eyes hazel, nose and chin medium, native place, Leeds. Remarks— J R M R heart R R half-moon 3 stars fish inside right arm, crucifix star on breast, man cask of rum above elbow, man woman fish.

Description as nearly as may be ascertained of the Third Man.— Height 5ft 8, thin made, well proportioned and active, long face, high cheek bones, rather pale, dark brown hair.

NOTICE

Respecting the Reward of One Hundred Sovereigns and Conditional Pardon or Free Pardon.
Police Office, Hobart,
30th April 1838.

IN reference to the Public Notice from this office under date

Reward notice for James Regan, a convict wanted for murder and illegally at large, from *Hobart Town Gazette*, 4 May 1838.

The state also needed to gather information about convicts' labour skills, to facilitate their allocation to appropriate work locations. The second imperative, however, was psychological. The desire to 'know' the convict was driven by the need to accumulate power over its subject. In order to re-embody the prisoner within a deferential landscape it was necessary to strip away her/his agency. Once paraded, degradingly near-naked, under the omnipotent-seeming official eye, prisoners starkly experienced themselves as humiliated subjects of disciplinary knowledge.[12]

Convict subjection to the official gaze occurred repeatedly between original sentencing and full deployment under the colonial convict management 'system'. From the early 1820s, convicts were physically described before warehousing in the British hulks. This was repeated immediately prior to embarkation for Australia. Before disembarkation at Sydney or Hobart, they were stripped, scrutinized by the so-called 'board of health', and their appearances again filed.[13] Additionally, from 1842, description recording was routinized in the British arrest process.[14] Regular practices of description and humiliation thus punctuated the enforced journey to colonial penal existence. At each gateway, the convict became the subject of official superiors' gaze, an instrument of state power. This process aimed to strip the convict body of agency and load it with chains of moral inferiority, a point reinforced by the categorizing term 'convict', that is, somebody convicted of a crime. Unlike 'prisoner', or 'government servant' (which the transported themselves preferred), 'convict' highlighted immoral sin as well as legal guilt. In intent, the whole 'system' was a moral barometer, where all would enter at one level and thereafter be morally calibrated.[15] Degrees of pain or indulgence subsequently experienced depended upon future conduct. Under the assignment 'system', fully in operation from the early 1820s until the late 1830s, all newly arrived prisoners were either assigned to private employers or retained in skilled government production or services work.

Persistent refusers to doff their caps, keep their traps shut and obey their masters with alacrity, or who worse still committed thefts or repeatedly absconded, were cast into the grinding mechanism of the 'system's' digestive tract.[16] This network of road gangs, chain gangs and hard regime penal stations existed to break the back of the 'wicked' by enforced toil on labour, intensive capital infrastructure works and primary resource extraction.[17] At these ultra-coercive locations, convict gangs were welded into production units under the barking orders of overseers, backed by magistrates' summary powers to impose floggings, irons, solitary confinement in dark cells on bread and water, and sentence extensions of up to three years. As well as reducing convict bodies to the role of collective machine, these gangs occupied a corporeal landscape, associated in the official and dominant class mind, with both pain *and* sin. Only 'wicked' convicts, supposedly, were sent to these places.[18]

Under the probation 'system', introduced into Van Diemen's Land in the early 1840s, newly arrived male convicts performed gang labour for a probationary period. The term varied according to length of sentence for which transported.[19] Diligent, docile men were promoted to paid employment after their probation period. Contrary conduct earned probation extensions and demotions to second and third class gangs. The promotion and demotion criteria operated by probation station superintendents and religious instructors, acting in tandem, were:

> FAVOURABLE CATEGORIES – clever, well informed, cheerful, contented, simple, cleanly, obedient, industrious, faithful.
> UNFAVOURABLE CATEGORIES – ignorant, stupid, revengeful, hardened, sullen, cunning, thievish, restless, dirty, disobedient, idle.[20]

Thus any convict challenging or evading the regime could drop into the 'Unfavourable Categories'. Preaching reinforced the point. Throughout a convict's penal existence, the catechist's proselytizing drone was repeatedly in earshot. At probation stations, the religious instructor was required to perform Divine Service twice on Sundays, before the assembled gang. Every other day, he was to conduct prayers before the gang was mustered in and out of work.[21] At all levels of the 'system' it was common for a religious service to follow muster roll-calls. As in slave societies, catechizing techniques attempted to inculcate humbly deferential duty to superiors. Here are two specimens from Jamaica, used by white Dissenting missionaries:

> Is it right for servants to steal from their masters?
> No, because God has commanded us 'Thou shalt not steal.'
> Even if they are not observed?
> But God sees and will punish them.
> How are thieves punished in this world?
> By being whipped, confined, banished and sometimes hanged.
> But is this all the punishment they are subject to?
> No, if they repent not God will punish them with hellfire for evermore.
>
> Was [Onesimus] a good and dutiful slave?
> No, he was a very bad one, for he was a thief and a runaway.
> And how did the slave behave after his repentance and conversion to Jesus Christ?
> He behaved himself well and was profitable to his master.
> Does religion produce the same effect now on slaves that have it?
> Yes, they neither rob nor run away, but are good servants.[22]

The hectoring, admonitory tone here would have been drearily familiar to transported convicts, especially those in probation gangs and at penal stations. So would the second extract's scriptural reference, chosen to subdue the catechized.[23]

In April 1821 the Anglican parson and magistrate Robert Knopwood preached at a hanging at Clarence Plains. *The Hobart Town Gazette* approved his sermon's text: *Proverbs* 14: 9, 'Fools mock at sin'. Knopwood thus highlighted the consequences of disrespecting religion and made 'a demand for moral and social obedience'. His auditors included convicts attending church under compulsion.[24] Rev. William Schofield, a Wesleyan Missionary Society export from England and official chaplain at Macquarie Harbour, 1828–32, selected texts carefully for use during his distinctly unfruitful mission there.[25] *Proverbs* 12: 1, 'Whoso loveth instruction loveth knowledge: but he that hateth reproof is brutish', informed his preaching one Sunday in 1830. He rubbed the convicts' noses in his gloss on this text:

> After illustrating what is implied in loving instruction and that the Gospel Ministry is imminently adapted thereto, and that the Even^g School for them had been made useful in instructing the ignorant. I called upon the attention of those who had adopted a Brute like conduct, who were unable to read, but nevertheless had not availed themselves of the means afforded, all listened apparently with great attention, and I hope some good was done.[26]

Clergy, as professional moral entrepreneurs, also propagated representations of convict irreligion and moral squalor among the dominant classes. The Benedictine William Ullathorne informed the 1837 Parliamentary Select Committee into Transportation that few prisoners 'had any idea of the doctrine of the Trinity and the first principles of Christianity, though they were called Christians baptized'. If, for him, the average convict knew little of religion, those condemned to penal stations were far worse. At Norfolk Island, he said, it was 'habitual language' for convicts to call a 'bad man' a 'good man' and anyone 'ready to perform his duty . . . a bad man'. He concluded: 'There is quite a vocabulary of terms of that kind, which seem to have been invented to adapt themselves to the complete subversion of the human heart.' The committee sought clarification: 'In short, by convicts, evil was designated good, and good as evil?' Ullathorne responded, 'yes'.[27]

The regimes of penal station chaplains – state employees ranking as civil officers – were highly articulated to subordination and control. At Macquarie Harbour, with the warm approval of Commandant Butler, Schofield imposed rules on convicts in his Wesleyan 'class'.

> 1st rule – This meeting admits only of those who have found peace with God or who have a strong desire to obtain it, which will be evidenced by their doing no harm by avoiding evil of every kind, such as taking the name of God in vain, profaning the day of the Lord, lying,

quarrelling, fighting, rendering evil for evil, doing unto others as we would not wish to be done by in change of circumstances.

2nd – That they shall continue to evidence their desire of salvation by their regular attendance on the means of grace if practicable searching the Scriptures and doing good to all to the utmost of their power by instruction, reproof, exhortation and prayer.

3rd – By rendering obedience to the powers that be Honour to whom Honour Fear to whom Fear.

4th – Not to speak evil of anyone in his absence nor hear anyone do it, without reproaching him, consequently if any member does wrong, by commission of sin, or omission of duty, he shall tell him of his fault alone, if he doth not regard it, he shall then report him to the minister before the accused but if he doth not report it, he shall be no longer a member.[28]

Note that the third of these rules was a doctrine of utter submission to secular authority and the fourth established a duty to monitor and inform on fellow convicts. Such rules help explain paltry convict membership of Schofield's Wesleyan class. Grovelling and informing as membership requirements might diminish *any* mission's appeal, let alone the appeal of a penal station mission.

As well as chastising those fallen from grace, religion also provided a route for 'reformation'. The reformed convict first had to admit to being, in Schofield's words, 'one of the vilest of the vile'. That implied acceptance of the justice of the regime under which the convict suffered. The aim was to impose the values of the system. Thus, the good/penitent thief became the man who bent his back and did his duty. Sermons preached to the condemned on the gallows served the same purpose. Knopwood's sermon admonished those assembled to witness the execution of four bushrangers, John Oliver, Robert Hunter, Joseph Potaskie and John Hill: 'Happy, however, is it for you, that a door of hope, with regard to futurity, still remains open. Salvation is obtainable even for malefactors: and attainable too, in the same way, as for other men.'[29] At the ultimate official body modification device, the gallows, the coercive arm of the state was reinforced by clerical exhortations.

While the administration stressed that the transported's only hope of salvation was gratefully to grasp the guiding paternal hand and submit, convicts stubbornly located hope elsewhere. Love tokens and tattoos richly inform us about this.[30] In both media anchors abound, sometimes followed by the word 'hope'. Anchors symbolizing hope have biblical origins in *Hebrews* 6: 19: 'Which hope we have as an anchor for the soul, both sure and steadfast, and which entereth into that within the veil.'[31] Images of Hope were painted, transfer-printed, indented, moulded and inscribed on to the surfaces of a large range of everyday objects manufactured in the late eighteenth and early nineteenth centuries. Often the virtue Hope (always female) appeared clutching an anchor, as illustrated on the sample of skin from Guys Hospital museum. 'Hope & Anchor' was (and remains) a common English inn name and sign. While to some this beery instance may seem a degeneration or even abuse of true religion, semiotically it bears witness to how profoundly

Piece of tattooed skin showing Hope and anchor. Here the virtue Hope doubles as the woman on the quay waving a merchant navy ensign and clutching a letter. Guys Hospital, London.

biblical language and related iconography suffused the broad base of English popular culture in our period. Likewise, Faith, Hope and Charity commonly figured in Staffordshire Pottery wares.[32] Graphically, hope was frequently contextualized by a fully rigged ship sailing into the distance, a design much utilized on objects manufactured to supply departing sailors with appropriate souvenirs for wives, lovers, relatives and friends. The 'Hope' exchanged was for a safe return, a sentiment explicitly expressed in a range of related objects which bore pictures of a sailor and a woman beneath the words 'A Happy Return'. John Bailey, a lighterman arrested in Middlesex, was one of many convicts who arrived in Australia with a tattooed version of this design. He was inscribed on his right arm with a man and woman followed by the words 'Welcome home Jack'.[33] Hope for a safe return also took an overtly religious form. William Thornton, a ploughman from Beckley in Oxfordshire, was inscribed with the verse, 'Every ill – May God protect a sailor still.' Given his occupation, it is possible that this tattoo had been acquired specifically for the voyage to the Antipodes.[34] While pictures of 'Hope' are quite common on convicts we have only encountered one tattoo which depicts another of the virtues. James Henry, a seaman from Jedburgh in Scotland who had served as mate on an East Indiaman, arrived in Van Diemen's Land tattooed with a picture of 'Faith'.[35] As far as convict bodies go, however, 'Charity' was conspicuously absent.

Convict-made artefacts bore similar designs, further revealing how strongly this iconography, with its rich cultural meanings, was embedded in plebeian beliefs. Thus, a love token fashioned from a George III cart-wheel penny in the hulks in 1843 is inscribed with the following text: 'W/Mollet/Aged * 13/Trans/Ported/7 * Year/1843'; followed on the reverse by the line 'For/Get * Me Not', surrounded by hearts, anchors and diamonds. For this thirteen-year-old about to voyage into the unknown, it was important to leave some remembrance behind. The token signifies far more, however, than affection for an unknown relative or friend. The 'forget me not' and anchors being mutually reinforcing, Mollet's token also held open the hope of reunion.[36]

In similar vein much sense can be made of convict tattoos if the word 'hope' is substituted whenever an anchor is encountered. Thus, James Peatfield's tattoo 'J. P. and an anchor' could be read as 'I have Hope'.[37] Similar tattoos abound on the bodies of convicts, as in just two further examples. Joseph Summerfield arrived on the *Southworth* in 1830, tattooed with 'J. S. and Anchor'; Robert Vetch on the *Chapman* in 1824, inscribed with 'R. Vetch anchor and 2 laurels inside his left arm'.[38] Richard Franklin varied this image with a tattoo of a man carrying an anchor. This can be read literally as 'I carry my hopes with me.'[39] Conversely, James Banican arrived on the same transport as Franklin, tattooed on his left wrist with 'JB anchor upside down', suggesting perhaps hope forlorn.[40] While these tattoos are silent concerning the *nature* of convict hopes, others are more forthcoming. Duncan Smith, sentenced to transportation in Glasgow in 1845 for stealing a purse and money, sported on his breast a woman holding a balance and an anchor. This suggests Smith had some hope in justice, perhaps reinforced by the desires inscribed inside his right arm: 'man and woman, health, love and liberty'.[41] Other tattoos appear to be more consciously religious. Cornelius Hickey was tattooed on the lower part of his left arm with 'crucifix, anchor, H'.[42] Taking the H to stand for Hickey, a plausible reading here is 'I have hope in salvation through Christ's sacrifice on the Cross.' Similar examples include William Silvester, sporting the tattooed string, 'anchor sun & moon stars WS & crucifix'; and William Hoyle, who was inscribed with 'W x H anchor Cross'.[43] Henry Abrahams's tattoo, however, perhaps best describes the importance of anchor tattoos in convict culture: 'without hope man is nothing'.[44]

Recently, Alan Atkinson has queried the utility of convict tattoo records, because of their snapshot quality, frozen by the colonial eye's shutter.[45] This certainly reminds us who controlled the observation process. The Board of Health had its clerks record certain physical traits, ignore others. Occasionally, it is possible to see official decorum intervening in the description process. Robert Dudlow, who arrived at Hobart on the *Phoenix* in 1824, was described as bearing an 'anchor' and the letters 'CUN' on the back of his right hand. The clerk started to record the next letter, changed his mind and inserted instead, 'indecent word'.[46] This may have been done by a convict clerk to assuage superiors and shield himself from rebuke or worse. Was he placing a bob each-way, by correcting the entry whilst leaving Dudlow's obscene jest perfectly transparent? The obscenity's force is intensified by proximity to a device embedded in popular religious culture. It seems Dudlow was not so much ignorant of religion as hostile to moral regulation in its name by agents of the state.

There are indications that much beyond the state's ken could be inked beneath prisoners' skins. Joy Damousi has recently described Mary Smith's tattoos as 'JL heart and star inside her left arm, and John Roach JL heart on the inside of her right arm'.[47] Reference to other tattoos reveals that 'JL heart' is almost certainly a mis-transcription of 'IL heart', short for 'I love to this heart' (also written as I heart L).[48] This (probable) mistake is not of Damousi's making. Her source was the official notice of absconders in the *Hobart Town Gazette*, 6 January 1837.[49] Error could have first occurred during the description recording process; when the Convict Department drafted the absconding notice; or in type-setting at the press. If official processes might garble a common tattoo, then perhaps much else is garbled too. For us, the official gaze, although formidable could not produce anything like totalized power. Yet some would disagree. Evans and Thorpe have recently written:

> it must be remembered, tattoos were equally a vital aid to surveillance, for they provided an almost infallible means of identification in this area before finger-printing and therefore a foil against escape and resistance . . . Thus, dependent upon our reading of their context, we can equally view a tattoo as a means of controlling bodies [or] as a sign of their subversiveness.[50]

Similarly, though a shade less emphatically, James Ross wrote of the convicts, in an essay on prison discipline inserted in his 1833 Hobart almanac:

> strange to say, these people very commonly employ much of their time on the passage out in puncturing with gunpowder, their hands, arms, and breast with various letters and figures, which being indelible, often assist the constables in apprehending them.[51]

SUBVERSIVE TATTOOS, JOKES AND POPULAR RELIGION

Ross's evidence that convict tattooing was common aboard ship en route to Australia is supported by our quantitative data. Of a sample of 939 women arrested in Paisley, Scotland, January 1841 – November 1847, only six were described as tattooed. The rate among Paisley's arrested men in the same period was slightly higher, 78 out of 2,161, still less than 4 per cent.[52] By contrast, of 1226 male convicts sentenced in Scotland and disembarked at Hobart, 1840–53, 26 per cent sported tattoos.[53] Records of over 2,000 female convicts transported from Britain to Van Diemen's Land in the 1840s reveal 25 per cent as tattooed upon arrival. The rate among women transported from Ireland was much lower. Over 800 descriptions of Irish female convicts yielded only four references to tattoos, three on women arrested in Belfast, which had strong cultural ties to the West of Scotland. Significantly, tattooing continued apace once prisoners had been landed on the 'fatal shore'. Our data on a sample of 744 prisoners secondarily convicted in and transported from New South Wales to the penal stations at Port Arthur, Van Diemen's Land and Kingston, Norfolk Island, reveals that 40 per cent were tattooed.[54] There appear, therefore, to have been strong associations between convict transportation and body modification by tattoo.

The colonial state often had the last laugh over the effects of convicts' tattoos, but well short of Evans and Thorpe's almost infallible surveillance technology. Tattoos can be made to disappear. William Baker arrived at Hobart with an older tattoo on his left hand and wrist obliterated by over-pricking with blue marks.[55] Other prisoners, originally transported to New South Wales and later colonially reconvicted and shipped to Van Diemen's Land, arrived in Hobart inscribed with numerous new designs but often strangely lacking tattoos that had been recorded on arrival at Sydney.[56] Over-tattooing allowed endless cat-and-mouse games with state surveillance records. Such ploys did not always revolve around obscuring original designs. Sometimes, older markings were allowed to remain visible, to create 'in your face' effects on the official gaze. The upper left side of Aaron Page's chest is a good example. He had been 'branded' 'D' for 'deserter' and sentenced to transportation for seven years by court martial in Nova Scotia, for absence from his regiment for 24 hours. On arrival at Hobart aboard the *Anson* in 1844, the 'D' had been embellished by a 'Union Jack pricked on it'.[57] Either this was a defiant graphic joke or Page was an undiagnosed half-wit. Evidently some prisoners understood the advantages of their bodies' innate plasticity,[58] for frustrating or defying the state. Thus Angus Mackay, trans-ported on the last convict ship to arrive off Hobart, bore his name followed by a 'broad arrow', the symbol of government property.[59] Both Mackay's and Page's jokes appear to be about ownership. The state asserted rights over the convict's body but the convict could always reassert self and agency through tattoos defying that act of expropriation. When state power was made visible, as by 'branding' the person with a 'D' or marking convict clothing with a broad arrow, this inevitably created further opportunities for a pin-prick artist's gallus wit.

Several scholars have recently discussed the incidence and even some-times power of convict laughter, mimicry, parody, satire and rough wit.[60] The totalizing power of the colonial state, underpinned by clerical and lay religious professionals, to construct hegemony, had to be rejected by convicts if they were to make space for their own agency. James C. Scott gives an excellent theoretical underpinning to this point.[61] For him, however, 'The question of whether a clear act of insubordination has occurred is not a simple matter, for the meaning of any action is not given but socially constructed.'[62] In this respect, clergy were an ideal target for the convict weapon of mockery, as the solemnly humourless manner in which they exer-cised their authority over the transported made them very vulnerable to it. If much of that mockery was behind clerical backs, even that tended to nullify their efforts, which were of real importance to the state. Without such weapons, any attempt by convicts to bargain with the 'system' might merely strengthen 'the invisible ideological shackles which bound the prisoner within a system of naked exploitation'.[63]

The importance of convict tattoos' adjustability is that, while the state attempted to anatomize convict bodies through the processes of description and inscription, many of those bodies were being adapted by enterprising intended subjects of power. In this, religious tattoos played a striking role. Not only were they among the most common on convicts' bodies but where bible texts occur, they are often the very same passages employed by clergy and catechists to dragoon convicts into submission. Thus, William Shemmett arrived on the *William Miles* in 1828, tattooed with several religious scenes (including Christ on the cross together with a centurion and Mary Magdalen), plus a line from *Luke* 18:13, 'God have mercy on me a sinner.'[64] While a casual reading suggests that Shemmett had swallowed the state and clergy's denigrating agenda, the full Biblical text of the parable of the Pharisee and the Publican allows a different meaning to emerge. The Pharisee publicly thanked God on the steps of the temple, loudly proclaiming his gratitude that he was not sinful like Publicans. By contrast, the Publican lowered his head and 'smote upon his breast saying, God be merciful to me a sinner'. The next verse, reads: 'I tell you, this man went down to his house justified rather than the other: for every one that exalteth himself shall be abased; and he that humbleth himself shall be exalted.' The text is highly susceptible to an antinomian reading. It is not hard to decipher whom convicts, typically from the social stratum most affected by antinomian popular religious beliefs, might regard as the latter-day Pharisees of the penal colonies.

Other convict tattoos appear latent with similar messages. George Dakin arrived in Van Diemen's Land in 1827 inscribed with *Proverbs* 14:9, 'Fools make a mock at sin.' The next line of *Proverbs* 14:9 is 'but virtue is found in the righteous'. Like Shemmett's tattoo, Dakin's can be interpreted as turning the establishment view of virtuous righteousness on its head.[65] For any middle-class moral entrepreneur, clerical or lay, who scorned Dakin for being a felon, risked being seen as a fool. This is extremely close to the description of convict culture on Norfolk Island delivered to the Molesworth Committee report by Ullathorne.[66] Of course, Ullathorne's assumptions about good and evil also require reversing in the light of such tattoos as Dakin's. Our reading of his tattooed text is strengthened by the convicts' knowledge that 'fools mock at sin' was employed by the Rev. Knopwood, and doubtless other colonial clergymen, to enforce the social and moral legitimacy of brutally coercive disciplinary practices.[67]

ABSENCES AND VARIABLE PRESENCES IN
CONVICT TATTOOS

A serious gap must be conceded in our method of exploring the meanings of convict religion through tattoos. Religious tattoos are frequently found on transported men but, anchors apart, are very rare on transported women. Indeed, the authors' only current example of a woman tattooed with a crucifix, Prudence Sweenie, was never transported. A 25-year-old tavern keeper, arrested in Paisley in July 1843 for 'breach of the act for the prosecution of smuggling', she was fined and released.[68] Among 513 convict women transported to New South Wales in 1831, David Kent found but four tattooed with crucifixes.[69] Popular religious beliefs and practices surely existed among convict women but cannot be explored through their tattoos, although a potentially useful by-product of this negative finding is the existence of a clearly gendered cultural variable in embodying religion. Kent's four women pale into numerical insignificance against numerous men adorned with crosses and crucifixion scenes. National breakdowns of our sample are informative. While male convicts transported from Ireland were less likely to be tattooed than those from Britain, 38 per cent of the tattooed Irishmen sported a cross or crucifix. This compares to 20 per cent of all tattooed English male convicts and a mere 8 per cent of tattooed Scots. When broken down by religious denomination the figures are even more striking. Only 5 per cent of transported Scottish Protestant men were embellished with crucifixion scenes, compared to 37 per cent of tattooed Catholics sentenced in Scotland. Scottish convicts who gave their religion as 'Protestant' were not necessarily less religious than their Catholic fellow transportees, but appear influenced by Calvinist understandings of the sin of idolatry.

No doubt some of these designs were tattooed long before arrest in Britain or Ireland. Others were explicitly connected to the process of transportation. John Green, tattooed with 'half moon 7 stars aged 22 Crucifix', was also officially recorded as aged 22 on arrival in Van Diemen's Land.[70] This is in every sense a 'transportation tattoo'. Given the nature of the transportation process it seems unlikely, however, that convict experience did not affect the reflexive and social meanings of tattoos, no matter when executed. If this was so for those transported once, then it was doubly so for those colonially convicted a second time and shipped to the confines of a penal station. To pick at random the record of one secondary transportee, William Poole was re-transported to Norfolk Island in 1846 where in the following four years he was punished 51 times. Almost his entire sentence was spent in solitary confinement or labouring in leg irons. In addition he was beaten six times, receiving in all 199 strokes of the lash.[71] Convict descriptions of floggings are more vivid than the laconic entries in the convict department offence registers. William Green, who received 100 lashes in the early 1840s for a failed attempt to abscond from Port Arthur, later related: 'I was flogged until I was dead, I may say, to the world. When I came to my recollection I found myself smothered in my own gore.'[72] Davis recalled a flogging that John Ollery had received at Macquarie Harbour in the early 1820s:

> he pleaded very hard to be forgiven on the score of illness but it was all to no purpose he was tied up and punishment went on amidst the most Heart rendering screams and cries for Mercy but his appeals was made to men that never forgave a Lash.[73]

John Mortlock succinctly summarized the effect of solitary confinement: 'of course the brain is the seat of pain – very dreadful'.[74] Given the levels of pain meted out to re-transported prisoners it is of real importance that 23 per cent of those tattooed were marked with a Cross or Crucifix.

Evans and Thorpe have recently characterized flogging as an emasculating ordeal, through which the figure of authority 'grew concomitantly in power, like a Leviathan', as each violent stroke cut into the back of the prisoner.[75] To ram this home, they quote Robert Hughes:

> Next to homosexual rape, flogging was the most humiliating invasion of the body that could befall a prisoner . . . to be stripped and tied to a triangle, like an owlskin nailed to a barn door; to hear, through the battering pain, the quartermaster-sergeant slowly calling out the strokes; this was to be drowned in powerlessness. It left the prisoner consumed with worthlessness and self-hatred.[76]

This, however, was not the effect a flogging had on Thomas Warwick, the Macquarie Harbour blacksmith. On Sunday, 30 March 1828, Rev. William Schofield preached to the assembled convicts on 'the sufferings of Christ and particularly him being scourged and that he died to save the vilest of the vile'. The very next day Warwick was given 50 strokes for 'having 2 iron wedges in his possession'. He later told Schofield that the association of his own punishment with the torments of Christ had made such an impression upon him that he had determined to join the Wesleyans.[77] As Raboteau has written of slaves, identification with Jesus, the archetypal 'Suffering Servant', could be a powerful weapon. When a flogging is viewed this way, the tables are reversed: the more degradation inflicted on the flayed bodies of the subordinated, the more moral power the targets of abuse can draw from their tormentors.[78] John McCarthy literally illustrated that, during each of his six

Piece of tattooed skin showing Christ crucified. Guys Hospital, London.

floggings at Macquarie Harbour. On every occasion, the assembled convicts would have seen two passions. First, there was McCarthy hanging limp from the triangle, his 'Back like a Bullocks liver and . . . his shoes full of Blood'. Secondly, there was the passion pricked out on his blood splattered chest: 'Crucifix Our Saviour bleeding on it [and] an angel with a cup catching the blood.'[79]

Some convicts appear to have drawn parallels between their own and Christ's sufferings by placing their initials in proximity to representations of the passion. John Flinn bore on his right arm the symbol of the passion, 'a lamb bearing a cross', and on his left arm 'a Crucifx a man and a woman' and his own initials; Stephen Kelly was marked on his left arm with 'IHS Crucifix' and his initials; John O' Niell with 'IHS J.O.N. cross and star'.[80] In a differing but equally poignant reference to Christ's passion, Christopher Inglesby was tattooed on his left arm with several small crucifixes and a slain lamb.[81]

CONVICT APOTHEOSIS?

The convict poet Francis MacNamara also likened prisoners' torments to Christ's. In his 'A Convict's Tour to Hell', the lines 'and many others by floggers mangled/And lastly by Jack Ketch strangled' are used to cue the appearance of Christ who promptly admits Frank the deceased convict bushranger into Heaven. This is only after Frank has been expelled from hell by Satan as patently unfitted for the place, and delayed at the gates of Heaven by farcical bureaucratic demands from St Peter for his 'certificate' (any constable could demand that an ex-convict show his freedom certificate).[82] It should come as no surprise that in this text, the original inventor of gaols, Captain Cook, informers, policemen of all ranks, overseers, convict department officials and colonial governors are consigned to Hell. Some convicts were inscribed with devices that can be interpreted as similar reflections on death and salvation. James Dunn was tattooed with 'IHS death head and cross bones', while John Oldershaw, who was transported twice from England to Van Diemen's Land, arrived on his second voyage with his chest marked with a Crucifixion above the words 'Prepare to meet thy God.'[83]

One way to escape from the more extreme earthly torments that befell some convicts was to follow Christ to Golgotha. Prisoners appear to have abhorred suicide; recorded incidents are rare.[84] There are several recorded cases, however, of penal station death pacts, in which two convicts agreed that one should kill the other. Schofield believed he understood prisoners' preference for this method of release. The survivor would be sent to Hobart (or in New South Wales, Sydney) for trial and execution. Through the assistance of a chaplain in the condemned cell, and the application of many earnest prayers, such a man might 'obtain pardon through the death of Christ'. Execution would swiftly follow trial and the prisoner would have obtained release without consigning his soul to Hell by suicide.[85] Even his consensual 'victim', one supposes, might hope to escape eternal damnation on a technicality. Our analysis of convict religion suggests that such plots may have been a little thicker than Schofield twigged. That Christ was first flogged and then executed by the authorities of his day is suggestive enough, but he was also tried with two thieves. Moreover, the penitent thief was admitted into the Kingdom of Heaven. No wonder Joseph Lamb, another thief, was tattooed with 'Love God for he is good to all.'[86] The ultimate irony is that the state may have played an unwitting role in facilitating some prisoners' desire to play this line of thought through to its logical end. After all, Parson Knopwood's surviving execution sermon approaches its conclusion with the words: 'O Blessed Jesu, who didst not disdain to cast an eye on the penitent thief on the cross, despise not these thy servants, who are now shortly to suffer a like ignominious death.'[87]

No wonder then that when three prisoners were led on to the scaffold at Macquarie Harbour in February 1825, they casually kicked off their shoes into the assembled convict witnesses, whilst calling out farewells that were 'like a party of friends who were going a distant journey on land'.[88]

9 Body Commodification? Class and Tattoos in Victorian Britain

JAMES BRADLEY

THE VALUE OF A TATTOO

In the Victorian world of commodities the Western tattoo was a strange object. Tattooing took place, more often than not, within the framework of a transaction of goods and services that involved the tattooed and the tattooer. The transaction was usually financial, although on convict hulks and in transports and prisons, it often involved the exchange of contraband goods. So far there is no difference between a tattoo and any other commodity – clothing or jewellery, for example. But what after the completion of the transaction? Unless perishable (food or drink bought for consumption), the vast majority of goods had a lasting, if depreciating, exchange value, hence the second-hand market in clothes. Tattoos were neither perishable, nor were they comparable with commodities that retained an exchange value. In nineteenth-century Britain there was no meaningful second-hand market in tattoos. This is not to say that the acquisition of a tattoo did not add value to the body. Where tattoos were used to create extraordinary bodies for display in side- or freak-shows, the process invested the body with a value it previously did not possess.[1] But the instances of tattoos creating wealth for anyone but the tattooer were sufficiently rare that the phenomenon of a commodity with no exchange value beyond the initial transaction demands further exploration.

Victorian tattooing is, in an oblique way, reminiscent of Clifford Geertz's interpretation of Balinese cock-fights as 'deep play'. He revised Bentham's concept of utilitarianism to explain the Balinese predilection for betting more than could 'reasonably' be afforded upon the outcome of such fights. Bentham regarded such behaviour as irrational. The pound that could be won was outweighed by the fortune that could be lost. For the community as a whole, the marginal utility of the combined stake was massively negative, and the outcome was net pain. By the logic of utilitarianism, deep play was immoral and should be outlawed. Geertz, however, gave Bentham's concept a twist. Individuals and collectivities do participate in deep play, and not because of any essential irrationality.[2] At stake in cockfights were matters of status within the family group and the wider community. 'Irrational' gambling upon a contest between two birds had a goal beyond winning money: nothing less, indeed, than the production and reproduction of social order.

Victorian tattooing was like deep play. For the tattooed individual loss of money exceeded value added to the body. It was, from a Benthamite perspective, an irrational act. But the inhabitants of Bentham's world did get tattooed. This meant ignoring the threat of pain, the danger of infection, and the stigma that was occasionally integral to this ambivalently received practice. The tattooed individual acquired a mark that was almost certainly indelible, something that had to be lived with for the remainder of his or her days. Tattooing signified more than a financial transaction in the realm of commodities. For the tattooed individual, it was an act at once intimate, emotive and symbolically significant. It encoded irremediably, at the boundary between the body and the world, nothing less than social relations.

IDENTIFYING THE AFFLICTED: THE REPRESENTATION AND
REALITY OF THE VICTORIAN TATTOO

The anthropologist Alfred Gell attempted to develop an epidemiology of tattooing for Polynesia. It is not overly apparent whether he deploys the term 'epidemiology' figuratively or literally. On the one hand, he suggests his usage is metaphorical. On the other, he states that tattooing 'does indeed have a pattern of occurrence, which resembles the uneven, but at the same time predictable, incidence of an illness'.[3] From the historian's perspective this second, more determinist, position is attractive. Would it, therefore, be possible to develop a predictive epidemiology of tattooing in the Victorian era? The simple answer is that we cannot meet the stringent requirements necessitated by this rigorously statistical methodology. Throughout much of the nineteenth century tattooing as a British custom was barely visible, and where it was – in scanty literary sources, criminal records, and medical literature – an accurate inference of its incidence within the wider population is impossible. If, however, the various representations of tattooing and the tattooed are examined, a coherent picture emerges of the groups most affected: criminals, members of the armed forces and certain segments of the upper classes.

By the end of the nineteenth century tattoos had increasingly become associated with criminals. This outcome was a function of the penal system's machinery. In the first half of the century, detailed physical descriptions were integral to the observation and identification of individuals transported to the penal colonies. Thus on arrival in the Australia, for example, the tattoos of each convict were scrupulously recorded in Conduct Registers. These were then used to identify absconded prisoners.[4] Following the abolition of transportation in the 1850s, British penal and policing systems continued to rely upon similar methods of identification. During the 1860s, when the 'problem' of the habitual criminal was first delineated, tattoo descriptions were an important component of individuating recidivists: the Habitual Criminals Act (1869) established the *Register of Distinctive Marks* which provided detailed listings of the tattoos of previously convicted criminals. As late as the 1890s, many years after the introduction of photography, senior policemen remained firm in the conviction that tattoo descriptions were an invaluable weapon against the repeat offender.[5]

The longstanding presence of tattoo descriptions in criminal records did not create the simple equation 'tattoo equals criminal'. Indeed, until the 1890s, and then only in a piecemeal way, tattoos were neither regarded as membership cards for the company of thieves, nor as symptoms of the criminal body riddled by the hereditary disease of crime. Henry Mayhew, for example, chief architect of the criminal class and besotted with the idea that criminals shared a culture distinct from that of the well-behaved masses, refused to make the connection between criminals and tattoos, despite an open invitation to do so. Following a visit to Millbank Penitentiary, he recounted the words of a warder who noted that 'many of the regular thieves have five dots between their thumb and forefinger, as a sign that they belong to "the forty thieves"', adding that tattoos were more commonly found upon criminals than upon their law-abiding counterparts.[6] Mayhew's curiosity remained blunted and he failed to elaborate the matter. Later observers of the same phenomenon were less circumspect. They too, however, resisted the urge to criminalize the practice, preferring to adopt a comparative approach which sought to identify the environmental conditions shared by the different populations purportedly affected by endemic tattooing – criminals, sailors, soldiers and, at the end of the century, men and women of fashion. It was generally agreed that confinement, boredom and emulation, experienced singularly or jointly, were the necessary pre-conditions for the practice.[7]

Caplan has demonstrated that, whereas on the Continent Lombrosian criminal anthropology led to a partial and uneven pathologization of criminal tattoos, in Britain environmental explanations predominated.[8] This was partly a function of a separate British intellectual dynamic that 'between the 1860s and World War I generated [its] own biologized concepts of the "habitual criminal" and the "moral imbecile"[9] – concepts developed without reference to tattoos. By the 1890s, however, Lombrosian criminology had made limited inroads into British social thought, impacting upon the discourse that informed the interpretation of criminal tattooing.[10] In the late-Victorian context an observer was, therefore, beset by tensions between hereditarian and environmental explanations of the practice, and between British and European criminological traditions.

Havelock Ellis's commentary upon tattooing in his early work *The Criminal* is illustrative of the hybrid, and frankly messy, ideas that flowed from the working-out of these tensions. Although 'sceptical of Lombroso's indiscriminate enthusiasm',[11] he was sufficiently influenced by the Italian to use *L'uomo delinquente* as a template for his own commentary on criminality. At the same time, his approach was marked by an ambivalence towards Lombroso's crude determinism, to the extent that 'his text recapitulated the ambivalences of English criminal science in both embracing and hesitating before the physical indications of criminality'.[12] Ellis knew that British criminals were tattooed, relying in particular on Greaves's research in Derby Prison which had revealed that of 555 persons admitted, 41 (including one woman) were tattooed, an incidence of around 7 per cent. Ellis reported that Greaves had found that those tattooed 'were chiefly soldiers, with a few miners and sailors'.[13] The low rate of tattooing should have been enough to deflect Ellis from either criminalizing or pathologizing tattoos. His concluding remarks derived, however, from the combined wisdom of the adversaries Lombroso and Lacassagne, resulting in an uncomfortable conflation of biological and environmental explanations. He allowed that '[i]dleness often explains it among prisoners, shepherds and sailors'.[14] But he also felt that pathological 'vengeance' produced criminal tattooing. Ellis's account, therefore, separated the 'pathological' tattoos of the hereditary criminal, and the 'normal' environmental tattoos of the rest – a perfect example of the English intellectual tradition of finding the 'middle' or 'third' way.

The low incidence of tattooing in Greaves's 'sample' hardly proved that tattoos were either common among the criminal population or a defining mark of the individual criminal. Rather it reinforced extant weak occupational correlations. Perhaps an analysis of inmates untattooed at admission but tattooed on release would have revealed that the practice was embedded in prison culture. Was it possible, however, that what Greaves was really observing was the extent to which tattooing was endemic within popular culture itself? Might we be able to infer the scope of tattooing among the working classes, urban or agricultural, from its occurrence in the convicted population? The physical descriptions forming a part of the aforementioned Australian Conduct Registers provide some clues. Prior to the late 1840s, these gave a detailed picture of each convict's body – the location of injuries, deformities, physical and mental abnormalities, scars, marks and tattoos. Bradley and Maxwell-Stewart have demonstrated that 308 from 1,179 (26 per cent) Scottish male convicts transported to Van Diemen's Land between 1840 and 1853 were tattooed.[15] These figures do not, however, allow the extrapolation of an overall incidence of tattooing among working-class males in mid-century Scotland. And the same conclusion would hold fast should a similar methodological exercise be carried out upon transportees convicted elsewhere within the British Isles. For while Nicholas *et al.* have argued persuasively that the transportees were not part of a criminal residuum, but were drawn representatively from the British working class,[16] we are probably witness to nothing other than the impact of transportation itself upon the convict body. The operation of the system provided conditions rife for endemic tattooing that disappeared with the introduction of the panopticized penitentiary: long hours unsupervised in shared close confinement; the collective trauma of mass exile; the proximity to seafaring culture; and the necessary admixture of court-martialled soldiers with members of the civilian population.[17]

If tattooing was widely practised among the urban working class, it remained cloaked in invisibility throughout the period. No commentator emerged to document its occurrence. While invisibility does not imply non-existence, the one professional – the medical practitioner – whose gaze fell frequently upon the skin of working-class bodies, dead or alive, did not observe tattoos with a regularity that required utterance: at least, this is so in accounts of tattooing contained in medical jurisprudence textbooks. It was only following the Tichborne trials of the 1870s that tattoos featured in such tomes at all. The byzantine trials sparked by the claimant Orton drew the attention of medical jurists towards tattoos as a means for establishing personal identity. Pre-Tichborne, there had been little point in commenting upon what had no obvious legal use. Even so, post-Tichborne tattoos were of interest only in so far as they provided a possible avenue for establishing the identity of corpses and impostors and there were no attempts to correlate their existence with particular fragments of the general populace.[18]

Over the next twenty years a subtle change occurred. Medical jurists gradually identified tattooing with sailors, soldiers and (occasionally) criminals – but not the wider working class.[19] Glaister, a Glasgow surgeon and forensic medical expert, was specially qualified to comment upon this matter. By 1893 he estimated that as a police surgeon he had examined around 300 corpses,[20] and by the publication of his medical jurisprudence textbook in 1902 he had seen many more. His observations of the quick and the dead led him inductively to the conclusion that tattooing was 'mainly prevalent among soldiers, sailors, and a certain class of civilians associated with both classes'.[21] Either the widely held commonsense knowledge of tattooing's sub-cultural *demi-monde* had somehow transmitted itself to his mind, adulterating his scientific faculties, or he had actually observed this pattern. The former should not be ruled out: scientists and medical practitioners have often shaped their explanations to fit *a priori* assumptions.[22] In the absence of concrete evidence, however, we must award him the benefit of the doubt. But his words need not be the sole testimony. The tattooist George Burchett, reminiscing about the docklands of East End London at the turn of century, described his clientele as consisting of 'sailors, dockers and other rough diamonds'.[23] Another London tattooist, David Purdy, writing towards the end of the nineteenth century, identified a similar pattern: 'I believe it to be a common thing among soldiers and sailors.'[24]

The association of tattooing with sailors is a minor trope of Victorian literature. Sherlock Holmes's powers were proved to Watson's satisfaction when the former identified correctly, and with no prior knowledge, a retired sergeant of Marines. The sceptical Watson was astounded, but Holmes explained '[e]ven across the street I could see a great blue anchor tattooed on the back of the fellow's hand. That smacked of the sea.'[25] Throughout the nineteenth century tattoos were most associated with sailors. In popular literature, where tattoos appeared, they usually signified the seafarer. Rider Haggard's humorous novel *Mr Meeson's Will* has as the dynamo of its plot the tattooing of a will upon the lily-white back of a ship-wrecked maiden. The tattooer was, of course, a rough and drunken sailor.[26] His arms were covered 'with various tattoos: flags, ships, and what not'.[27] Another prime slice of late-Victorian pulp fiction recapitulates the association. Fergus Hume's *Tracked by a Tattoo*, a crude distillation of Wilkie Collins's best novels blended with slight echoes of the Tichborne case, presents the detective Fanks questioning an ex-servant, Mrs Prisom, about her dead master:

'Sir Francis was a Sailor? I suppose when he went to sea and came home a middy, he had anchors, and ships, and true lovers' knots, and such like things tattooed upon his skin.'

'He just had,' replied Mrs Prisom laughing. 'He had quite a fancy for that sort of thing. He told me he learnt how to do it in Japan, and very clever he was at drawing such pictures on the skin.'[28]

If the comments of interested parties were accurate, tattooing was an endemic feature of life on the ocean wave. Thus, the *Lancet* noted in 1851 'the voluntary tattooing of seamen'.[29] The Duke of Cambridge, during a parliamentary commission on military discipline (1868–69), compared the 'branding' (tattooing) of army deserters and bad characters with 'the marking most sailors do to themselves as a matter of amusement'.[30] The matter was also discussed in both houses of parliament. Mr Guest, defending 'branding', reiterated the common defence that '[i]n reality, it implied nothing more than the tattooing to which nearly all sailors voluntarily submitted', a point emphasized by Viscount Bury – '[a]lmost every sailor in Her Majesty's fleet bore similar marks'.[31]

The connection between tattoos and the sea was not chimerical. Many are those who have described the practice's importation from Polynesia following Cook's 1770 voyage to the South Seas.[32] The American historian Ira Dye, however, believes that it must have predated the early 1770s, arguing that by the end of the century tattooing was so prevalent throughout the American merchant and naval fleets that its introduction a mere twenty years earlier was an impossibility.[33] Nevertheless, both versions pinpoint seafaring culture as the cradle of the modern Western tattoo. Burchett's memoirs indicate that a century later shipboard tattooing remained ingrained in the fabric of British naval culture.[34] He noted, however, that by then it had become acceptable for officers, like the fictional Sir Francis, to undergo the operation, quoting a complaint by Commander C.W. Cole that there was, in 1883, 'a prominent and perennial mania of tattooing and almost all young officers of the squadron are bitten by the mania'.[35] The experience of Prince Albert Victor and Prince George of Wales corroborates Cole. During their visit to Japan they observed that many of the local Japanese tattooers came on board their ship the *Bacchante*, 'where they took up their quarters for two or three days, and had their hands full with tattooing different officers and men'.[36] Tattooing had transcended rank, becoming part-and-parcel of the general shipboard experience.

Unlike sailors, nineteenth-century literary sources fail to portray soldiers as tattooed. But other evidence suggests that it was as common among the land forces as it was in the navy. Indeed, the records examined by Bradley and Maxwell-Stewart reveal that the incidence of tattooing was significantly higher for soldiers than non-soldiers (48 per cent compared to 32 per cent). Tattooists like Sutherland Macdonald and Burchett believed that many of their customers were army men and Macdonald himself learnt his craft while serving in the Engineers.[37] As with the navy, tattooing was initially connected with the lower ranks (although Roger Tichborne sported a tattoo while in the 6th Dragoon Guards during the 1850s, this was a relic of his schoolboy days),[38] before spreading to the officer class.

The scope and dimensions of army tattooing are most visible in medical reports. It was first identified as a medical problem after Lister's 'discovery' indicated that sepsis might follow unhygienic practices.[39] In 1862 the French naval surgeon Berchon announced that tattooing, 'generally supposed to be unattended with danger', might cause death. As a consequence the French naval authorities attempted to discourage the practice among its crews.[40] It was not until the 1880s, however, that physicians identified a risk that syphilitic infection might result from contact with an infected tattooist's needles, and it was officers of the Royal Army Medical Corps who reported the majority of incidents. Initially, a single case was recounted, but news of 'mass' infections soon came to light.[41] Most notable was an outbreak in 1888 at the Portsea barracks, Hampshire, involving twelve infected soldiers, all from the ranks of the same regiment. Barker, an Army Surgeon, conjectured that the source was a single tattooer.[42] A few months later, H. R. Whitehead communicated a similar event, showing that Portsea was not an isolated event.[43]

Due to the detail with which Barker described the incident, we are afforded an insight into the economy of tattooing among the lower ranks. Recalling the demi-metaphor of epidemiology, we see the quasi-dermatological illness of the tattoo spreading plague-like through a segment of the regiment, followed swiftly by the real disease of syphilis, which asserted its ascendancy by transposing its own mark upon the crudely etched tattoo patterns. The culprit was assumed to be a discharged soldier, granted the ethical anonymity of the initial 'S'. He was a hawker about the barracks, with a set repertoire of tattoos: 'twenty patterns on paper, mostly female figures, printed in copying ink, each pattern being able to be used about six times'. He applied the tattoo by wetting 'the pattern with saliva before applying it, to obtain an impression'. Barker believed the medium of infection was his saliva, not from the application of the patterns, but rather through his habit of cleaning the needles and mixing the ink with spittle from his syphilitically ulcerated mouth.

In all 23 soldiers were known to have visited 'S'. Nine failed to show symptoms. Of these, Barker believed at least four had previously been infected with syphilis and were therefore 'inoculated' against the disease and 'unlikely' to show the symptoms again. A further two had deserted but had, according to their comrades, developed sores prior to desertion. The dates on which the 23 were tattooed, and the distribution of infected to non-infected, is revealing (Table 1).

TABLE 1 Distribution of infected and non-infected soldiers in the Portsea outbreak (1888)

DATE	INFECTED	NOT INFECTED	TOTAL
18 May	2	0	2
1 June	1	0	1
15 June	2	1*	3
29 June	2	0	2
1 July	1	0	1
23 July	0	1	1
1 August	0	2	2
5 August	3	1*	4
6 August	0	4	4
11 August	1	0	1
23 August	0	2	2
TOTAL	12	11	23

* deserted before examination and counted as cases where syphilis was not contracted, but indications existed that they developed sores post-tattooing. Source: BMJ, 1 (1889).

Only four were tattooed on a day when 'S' failed to operate on another member of the regiment. A large imaginative leap is not required to visualize the men attending 'S' together in mutually supportive groups of two or more. For tattooing in this context was an experience to be shared among barrack-mates. When observers pinpointed emulation as a motive for tattooing they were envisioning the snowball effect apparent at Portsea. Thus it could spread rapidly through a regiment, affecting large numbers in a short time. All members of the ranks were threatened and a prior lack of tattoos made the individual more susceptible: of the infected twelve, only four had been previously tattooed.

Barker commented that over the three-month period '[m]en in the same regiment [were] tattooed, but not by S., [and] did not contract the disease',[44] implying that over this period a figure far in excess of 23 soldiers from the same regiment had been tattooed. On the basis of a full complement of c. 750 troops, and assuming a corps of officers, the incidence of tattooing among the ranks over a relatively short time amounted to a figure in excess of 5 per cent. If we assume, in line with Barker's testimony, that many of the soldiers were previously untattooed, this figure represents an approximation of the quarterly growth rate in tattoos, rather than the overall rate.

Just as medical practitioners were revealing the putative dangers of tattoo-ing, it was diffusing, as if by metastasis, to the officer class. The pattern of

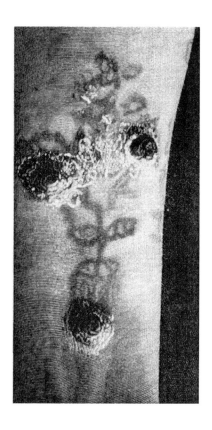

Syphilis erupting on the arm of a soldier over a recently tattooed flower-pot, from *British Medical Journal* 1 (1889).

dispersion recalls that of the navy. The higher ranks had not 'caught' tattoos from crude barrack-room hawkers like 'S'. Rather, the most potent influences were a blend of imperial travel and peer pressure. Bolton insisted that 'many officers and men' stationed in Burma were tattooed by Burmese methods.[45] Lord 'Bobs' Roberts, for example, was said to have developed an enthusiasm for tattooing during service in Burma.[46] From that time, he encouraged the practice among his officers, asserting that the tattooing of regimental crests not only aided the identification of the dead on the battlefield (tragically realized for Roberts when his own son died in the Boer War with a regimental crest meticulously reproduced upon his arm by Macdonald),[47] but also encouraged a suitably martial *esprit de corps*.[48] Bolton, Burchett and Macdonald confirm that Roberts's words were heeded and, catalysed by the Boer War, tattoos became an ever more widespread affectation among officers.

Tattooing did not remain the preserve of soldiers, sailors and criminals. At some time around the late 1880s fashionable society was gripped by a tattoo craze. By 1889 Macdonald's Jermyn Street studio had been inundated by wealthy Londoners. Macdonald himself, when questioned about the social composition of his clientele, replied '[m]ostly officers in the army, but civilians too. I have tattooed many noblemen, and also several ladies'.[49] Burchett identified the origins of the craze with the patronage of Edward, the Prince of Wales.[50] 'Bertie' had first been tattooed in the Holy Land, during his tour of 1862, although knowledge of this event did not emerge until 1881.[51] Apparently, he insisted that his sons be tattooed by *Hori* Chyo on their visit to Japan.[52] Later, returning to Europe via the Holy Land, the future George V wrote to his mother that he and his brother had been tattooed 'by the same old man that tatoed [sic] papa & the same thing too the 5 crosses'.[53] Whether royal patronage really provided the stimulus for fashionable acceptance is debatable.

From the mid-1890s, several journalists cast their eyes upon the phenomenon of the newly tattooed upper classes. One of these, Gambier Bolton, was typical of the new tattooed. The son of the Reverend James Jay Bolton, he was educated at 'private schools' and Cambridge, and married a daughter of Colonel Evelegh, C.B. He styled himself a 'public lecturer and writer on (popular) Natural History'. He travelled widely in Europe, North America and Asia, and accompanied the Duke of Newcastle on his tour round the world (1893–4). According to *Who Was Who* he wrote *A Book of Beasts and Birds* (1903) and *The Animals of the Bible* (1901).[54] His 'Pictures on the Human Skin', written for *Strand* magazine in 1897, revealed that, like army and naval officers, his own marked body was a function, in part, of his travels. Among other tattoos, he possessed a 'Sacred' dragon from Burma and a spider's web inscribed by Chyo. He collected tattooing artefacts and anecdotes from around the globe. But he was also a client of Macdonald, and the final illustrations in the article show the vivid outcome of this encounter. The mass of Bolton's back was covered with a finely detailed falcon, while around his shoulders was coiled an exquisite permanent necklace – a snake in green, red and black.[55]

If Bolton was the epitome of the tattooed gentleman, the public was given no shortage of other high-class role models to follow. Bolton's piece obliquely referred to princes and nobles but did not name names. R. J. Stephen's 'Tattooed Royalty', published a year later in *Harmsworth Magazine*, did. His informant was another London-based society tattooist, Ted Riley, '[than] whom no artist has tattooed more distinguished people', including the Grand Duke Alexis of Russia, Prince and Princess Waldemar of Denmark, Queen Olga of Greece, King Oscar II of Sweden, the Duke of York, Lady Randolph Churchill and the Duke of Newcastle.[56] Riley claimed to Stephen

Gambier Bolton's tattooed back and neck, from *Strand* magazine (1897).

that the list was far far longer. Significantly, Stephen's article was subtitled 'Queer Stories of a Queer Craze'. The iteration of 'queer' cannot escape notice. Stephen, or his editor, expected the magazine's readership to find the subject matter peculiar, in a 'look what the toffs are up to now' way. Indeed, the 'toffs' were presented by him as being almost as alien as exotically tattooed 'savages'.

BODY COMMODIFICATION: TATTOOS, CLASS AND CONTEXT

In the absence of hard evidence, the Otherness integral to Stephen's account signposts tattooing as a phenomenon way beyond the ken of the respectable middle classes. We must, therefore, conclude that it was limited, in the main, to the groups examined above. Consequently, on the most basic level, tattoos acted as a badge of social and cultural differentiation that separated the tattooed from the non-tattooed. On a deeper level, however, social and cultural homogeneity did not unite the tattooed, for the subject matter and aesthetic style of the tattoos created a fault-line that divided the classes. Compare Purdy's description of tattooing with 'The Gentle Art of Tattooing' from the *Tatler* (1903). Purdy's world is a realm of sewing needles and wooden blocks:

> When pricking in, you must always prick the needle in straight. Place the points of your needles over the lines of the figure you have drawn on a person's arm then place your left arm round it, so as you have it in the palm of your left hand, then you can hold tight till further orders. When you have done this you can then commence pricking, but when you find the flesh is limp, you must leave off pricking till you can hold it firmer with your left hand; which you will be able to do after you have given your hand a rest.[57]

This laborious, almost militaristic, description reveals a world of manipulated flesh and drawn blood – one where the tattooer must always ensure that his needles are clean.[58] The arm is manipulated, held and pinched. The needle is pricked into flesh. The tattooed subject risks pain and infection. Purdy thus presented an insight into the informal practice that took place in the schoolyard, barrack-room and between the decks – a self-help manual for hawker's like 'S'.

The *Tatler* related something different. Here tattooing was a 'gentle art', the height of fashionability, and the antithesis of Purdy's rough technique.[59] The sewing needle was replaced by an electric machine (invented by Samuel Reilly in New York in the 1870s) that tickled, not unpleasantly, the skin's surface. Thus described, the technique ignored the penetration of the outer skin that was essential to the operation, and pain was virtually eliminated. Burchett concurred. He used an anaesthetic and insisted that tattooing was 'practically painless, even agreeable'.[60] These factors made it not entirely unsuited for daring 'ladies' – the tattooist Alfred South, quoted in the *Tatler* article, said he had tattooed 900 out of a client-base of 15,000. For the beautiful people, of whatever gender, obtaining a tattoo was tantamount to buying a new frock. And unlike its rude counterpart, the operation took place in the comfortable environs of the 'studio', the place of artists and photographers.

Just as the two worlds affected bodies differently, so they created two separate aesthetic orders. Purdy's style was direct and simple: '[i]t would not be amiss to take the Tower Bridge, or the Imperial Institute. Or one of her Majesty's Battleships, and the Houses of Parliament'.[61] The 'gentle art',

OPPOSITE 'The Gentle Art of Tattooing: The Fashionable Craze of Today', with several examples of the new aesthetic style, from *The Tatler and Bystander* (1903).

THE GENTLE ART OF TATTOOING

The Fashionable Craze of To-day.

AFTER ARCHIBALD THORBURN
A design on a sportsman's wrist

The tattooing craze which first broke out in America has now come to this country, where its chief exponent is Mr. Alfred South of Cockspur Street. During his career Mr. South has operated on upwards of 15,000 persons, including about 900 English women, the designs in a great number of cases being of a most peculiar description. There are some instances where ladies have had the inscriptions on their wedding rings tattooed on their fingers beneath the ring. Ladies who like to keep pace with the times may be adorned with illustrations of motor cars. Another device is that of a figure of Cupid disappearing into the depths of a pewter pot. This picture, which has been tattooed on the skin of one woman only, is entitled "Love gone to pot."

A MESSAGE OF PEACE
On the arm of a peeress

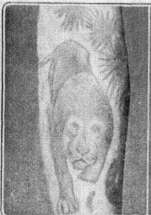

THE BLOOD TRAIL
After Nettleship's famous picture

LION ON THE PROWL
A design on the arm of a cavalry officer

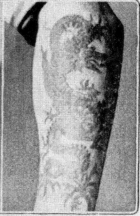

THE CHINESE DRAGON
On the arm of a well-known general

THE DOLPHIN AND THE MAID

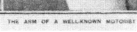

THE ARM OF A WELL-KNOWN MOTORIST

A MAJOR'S SWORD ARM

however, created ornate and elaborate designs: analogues of oriental ornaments, for example, and occasionally, on a grander scale, reproductions
of works of art.[62] We might almost be observing two unrelated practices
producing two radically divergent meanings.

Working-class Jewellery
Purdy's literal designs were part of a long tradition revealed to the historian
in criminal records. The convicts transported to Australia wore their tattoos
either as identity tags or jewellery. Bradley and Maxwell-Stewart have
demonstrated that the most common designs sported by Scottish convicts
were either strings of initials or rings. Thus, over 115 convicts had their own
initials inscribed upon their bodies. The contemporary view of the motive
for this practice was fear of an anonymous death, particularly at sea.[63] Of
these, however, 36 had their initials embedded in longer strings often
punctuated by the heart, symbol of charity and love. Such tattoos contain
deeper meanings than mere dog tags. One example will suffice to illustrate the point. James Milne bore the following inscription upon his arm:
'RMAWBMSM hearts & darts JM'.[64] 'JM' clearly represented Milne himself,
while 'BM' and 'SM' were almost certainly members of his family. 'RMAW' is
probably an acronym, that may plausibly be instantiated for the sentimental
refrain 'Remember Always'.

In cases such as Milne, the tattoos represented a bond between the body
of the individual and the object towards which the individual's emotions
were expressed. This object might, of course, have been a church, nation,
regiment or a ship, but, as with Milne, it most commonly involved other
people. Here tattoos acted symbolically as emotional signifiers implying
a strength of attachment and a token against absence. These signifiers
produced in turn two different effects. In the first instance, the tattoo was a
sometimes public, sometimes covert, display of connection, demonstrating
through a blood sacrifice that a relationship penetrated beneath the skin –
the body's boundary with the wider world. In the second instance, it was as if
the tattooed individual was protecting him- or herself against separation:
should separation occur the tattoo then acted as a vicarious physical
presence for the absent other.

Another class of tattoo, by marking the moment of specific life-events,
served similar functions. Symbols of celebration (pipes and bottles), mourning (figures by tombs), and even dates of trial and transportation were
tattooed on some.[65] As with the other images, these were powerful devices
of remembrance, not unlike the lockets, rings of hair, and household objects
possessed by middle-class Victorians. The key to understanding lies in the

meaning of possessions. Mary Ann Brennan's oft-cited tattoo is relevant here.[66] When she was transported she had the following verse inscribed upon her arm:

> William Jesse
> When this you see remember me,
> And bear me in your mind,
> Let all the world say what they will,
> Speak of me as you find.[67]

The most striking feature of this verse is not its sentimentality, but that it was well known in nineteenth-century Britain. Maxwell-Stewart has located it, or variants of it, on a number of items manufactured through the length and breadth of Britain in the period 1760 to 1860.[68] These objects were intended as keepsakes: puzzle jugs custom-made for weddings and rolling pins intended as gifts from departing sailors to wives and lovers. It further transpires that the verse was inscribed upon convict love tokens, small coins reshaped as keepsakes.[69] Brennan, like many other working-class people, had few possessions. The most precious and most mobile possession was the body itself. Beyond small portable objects, mobility and poverty denied soldiers, sailors and prisoners the possibility of owning physical *memento mori*, 'the jewellery, watches and silverware' which were 'amongst the most mobile of all Victorian things'.[70] Tattoos provided a substitute for jewellery, or other material possessions: a means of articulating emotion to, and forging attachments between the body, the self and others.

Inconspicuous Consumption: The New Aesthetic Order
Some working-class tattoos were, in all probability, purely decorative. The straw-hatted man seated on a barrel drinking, and the tableau of sun, moon and seven stars fall into this category, although they are also open to other exegeses: the sun, moon and seven stars representing the pre-Darwinian cosmos with religious undertones, while in captivity the drinking man served as a reminder of less careworn days. Similarly, while the new aesthetic breed of tattoos appeared more explicitly decorous, they contained deep meanings that related to the client's capacity to consume. During the latter part of the nineteenth century the tattoo had become commodified, a package that could be bought from the set location of the tattooist's studio. The new tattoo was highly detailed, a fine act of draughtsmanship. And because the process of inscription was a time-consuming operation, it was costly (sometimes more than twenty guineas).

It was the entrepreneurial *nous* of the tattooist that made the new aesthetic viable. Macdonald's tactics were exemplary. Apart from his artistic ability, he understood the need to create a suitable environment for his wealthy patrons. The West End location of the 'studio' – in reality the super-intendent's office at the Jermyn Street Hammam – meant that his clients need not remove themselves from their social milieu. Indeed, the Hammam (annual ticket eight guineas, single session four shillings), provided a lush oriental backdrop to the Asian-associated art of aesthetic tattooing – the Turkish baths themselves, complete with a hairdresser, the services of a firm of chiropodists, and a café serving 'Oriental' dishes as well as Occidental refreshments, made it a haven of Eastern titillation.[71] Macdonald's studio provided all the comforts that could be expected from this setting:

> Luxurious cushions, resting here on a divan, the familiar needles with their gaily decorated handles and the little hypodermic syringe, not to mention the ever-ready box of cigarettes and the accompanying cooling drinks.[72]

Burchett could not compete with these ornate surroundings, but knew it would be as well to move his studio closer to the centre of London and the wealthier end of the market.[73]

The right social setting was not, however, enough. The tattooist had to present himself as a respectable man operating in hygienic surroundings. Macdonald's chief ploy was to insist that there were amateur tattooers who scratched patterns badly ('tattooers'), and skilled professionals ('tattooists').[74] Burchett was also acutely aware of the need to present a respectable front. Once he became a full-time tattooist, he portrayed himself as akin to a medical practitioner: adopting a white coat and emphasizing hygienic practices. This was not unpractical. As tattooing became increasingly repre-sented by members of the medical profession as a medical problem, the outward display of hygiene was a necessity. But, medicalization was as symbolic as it was practical. Burchett evidently conceived himself as repro-ducing the style of doctor-patient epitomized in Harley Street practices. This required a certain deference which kept the patient-client in control of the transaction, in what has been termed 'bedside' medicine.[75]

It was not, however, the professional tattooists who created the initial demand for the new tattoo. As we have seen, army and naval officers obtained their tattoos while serving overseas. In this sense, the newly commodified tattoo was the product of colonialism. Their 'ethnic' tattoos were on a par with those acquired as souvenirs by the businessmen and other globetrotters who visited Chyo's studio. As such, the tattoo obtained in the colonial realm was tantamount to the physical appropriation of the subject culture. Likewise, the 'influence' of Japanese tattooing upon Macdonald, Riley and Burchett amounted to the appropriation of an aesthetic.

For many officers, the new tattoo stood for something more than a souvenir or fashion accessory. It was an expression of the martial spirit, where the ability to control physical discomfort acted as a mark of fitness to serve. Neither should we discount Roberts's insistence upon *esprit de corps* as a motive force for regimental tattoos. This is not so far removed from working-class jewellery, with the badge of service connecting the physical body to the metaphorical body of the regiment. An officer's regimental tattoo was, however, differentiated from that of a private by elaborate detail, ornate style and cost. It was a symbol of the ability to consume conspicuously – still an essential skill for the Victorian army officer.

As the tattoo craze in Britain and North America reached its peak in 1899, Veblen published *The Theory of the Leisure Class*, a liberal critique of capitalism which focused upon the reproduction of status through conspicuous and often 'wasteful' consumption. Veblen believed that 'no line of consumption' afforded 'a more apt illustration' of his theory than dress.[76] Both men's and women's fashion signified conspicuous waste (expenditure 'in order to be reputable must be wasteful')[77] and conspicuous leisure (the demonstration that an individual had no need to engage in productive labour). Tattooing played no part in Veblen's analysis, although the craze was integral to the culture upon which he had cast his critical eye. Perhaps tattoos were too inconspicuous: for the most part they were hidden beneath clothing, revealed only at the individual's discretion. But the new tattoo, if inconspicuous, was a leisured and luxurious form of consumption. In 1897, Riley informed Stephen of two special commissions upon which he was working. The first was a reproduction of Landseer's picture 'Dignity and Impudence', which on completion was to measure 12 inches by 9. The other was a copy of Constable's etching 'Mrs Pelham', tattooed upon the chest of 'a Scotch baron'. These copies were achieved in painstaking detail. Riley estimated that the reproduction of a famous picture took up to 80 hours in twelve sittings, at a cost of over 24 guineas.[78] Many of the other designs were oriental in inspiration – dragons being a favourite. These echoed the style of paintings and vases imported from China and Japan, as well as copies made in Britain. It is probable that a detailed tattoo would have cost as much as, if not more than, many of these oriental *objets d'art*.

In Veblen's terms such tattooing was an exercise in 'wasteful' consumption, but its inconspicuousness implied that the impulse for consumption ran deeper than the outward display and emulation of fashionable clothing. There was nothing trivial about this form of tattooing, for it indicated the

A regimental crest by Sutherland Macdonald, from *Strand* magazine (1897).

depth to which economic relations infiltrated the tissues of the body. The commodified and packaged tattoo provided a novel way of reshaping the body within the boundaries of fashion and taste. That many of the designs remained covert, hidden beneath clothing, suggests that the new tattoo also spoke to the tattooed about their ability to consume. This is not to say that the aesthetic designs were devoid of meaning, empty of content beyond the act of consumption. We should avoid the romantic and essentializing impulse to interpret working-class tattoos, by contrast, as somehow more authentic than their bourgeois counterparts. The new tattoos spoke volumes and could serve emotive and meaningful functions. Is it a coincidence, for example, that the naturalist Bolton covered his skin in animals? But, just as the new aesthetic may have articulated similar bonds of attachment to its crude working-class counterparts, it also uttered softly to the financially wealthy self statements like: 'I have travelled'; 'I can spend'; even, 'I have taste'.

BODY COMMODIFICATION?

In several respects the old-style pin-prick tattoo of the working-class sub-cultures, and the finely detailed tasteful decoration of the new aesthetic were shaped by similar emotional concerns. But the similarities should not deflect us from the extent to which tattoos both spoke the language of class, and reproduced class and status upon the surface of the body. As indicated at the outset, in purely economic terms tattoos did not, for the vast majority, add value to the body. But they did have a value as vicarious objects of material culture. For the mobile and/or enclosed populations of soldiers, sailors and prisoners the cost of the tattoo was less than the object it substituted. For the conspicuous consumer, the leisured traveller, the globetrotting businessman or the army officer, it could cost more than the equivalent object in material form. For both, the body was remoulded by the culture and economy through which it moved. Tattoos did not commodify the body, but they did indicate the extent to which commodities, however valueless in utilitarian terms, impacted upon the body, producing and reproducing divisions of class and status.

10 'National Tattooing': Traditions of Tattooing in Nineteenth-century Europe

JANE CAPLAN

[1]

The history of tattooing in nineteenth-century Europe would be significantly less accessible were it not for the interest shown in the subject by contemporary medico-legal experts and criminologists. Their assiduous, at times obsessive researches have bequeathed a rich archive of images as well as a more patchy account of the conditions under which tattoos were acquired and the motives for their acquisition. The most celebrated collectors of this data were the criminologists Cesare Lombroso (1836–1909) and Alexandre Lacassagne (1843–1924), whose investigations of tattooing in Italy and France became public in the 1880s and launched an important international debate between the Italian and French schools of criminology. This debate, as is well known, turned on the physical symptoms of criminality and the degree to which these could be attributed to atavism or degeneration, and the criminal character itself to heredity or environment.[1] Although there were thus significant differences in the two criminologists' analyses and conclusions, both were agreed in linking tattoos closely to criminality, and it is that association that became the most familiar lesson of their research. Up to this point, however, in so far as tattoos had been noticed at all, they were not regarded as reliable signs of criminality. More often than not, tattooing was treated by earlier nineteenth-century observers as a foreign habit imported by sailors who had acquired the technique from Pacific islanders in the eighteenth century and had then passed it on to soldiers and manual labourers within Europe. The apparent exoticism of the practice and its popularity among men of the lower classes ensured that (in continental Europe at any rate) tattooing had generally been dismissed as a foolish and uncivilized form of ornamentation – 'a bizarre decoration' borrowed by sailors from 'savages' and propagated by 'idleness and caprice'.[2] Never mind that this interpretation tended to discount lingering evidence of an older though discontinuous history of tattooing within Europe itself. But it established an alternative path associating tattoos with exoticism, savagery and low life, so that when European tattooing was 'rediscovered' later in the century, there was a powerful impetus to read it as either a survival or an eruption of primitive practices.[3]

Although tattoos on convicts had not gone entirely unnoticed before the 1880s, they were not the central focus of these earlier investigations, which were more likely to be conducted in the barracks or hospital than the prison. True, these milieux were, like the prison, types of confined male community at one remove from the conditions of 'normal' life, a fact which no doubt prepared the ground for the later conversion of tattoos from signs of difference to stigmata of deviance. But pioneering German and French pathologists such as J. L. Casper, A. Tardieu and M. F. Hutin were most interested in studying the tattoo in order to assess its value as a means of individual identification and differentiation, not necessarily in criminal circumstances: they investigated, for example, the tattoo's indelibility and the association of particular designs with workers in specific trades.[4] This focus possibly acted as a form of insulation against the bolder premise that tattoos were evidence of the collectively pathological character of a criminal class. It took the emergence of a new discourse of criminology in the 1880s to accomplish this semiotic move, and to lift research to fresh efforts of collection, compilation and analysis.

The arguments advanced by Lombroso and Lacassagne in this second period of investigation form a necessary backdrop to the primary purpose of this essay, which is is to consider the wealth of evidence assembled as a result of the new criminology, rather than the role this evidence played in the debates themselves.[5] But we owe much of the surviving evidence of tattoos to the functionaries in the growing systems of police and prison administration in Europe: to those police specialists and prison or army doctors who took it upon themselves to assist the criminologists by collating and publishing data about their charges, and who thus secured the survival of reams of information about nineteenth-century tattooing, in marked contrast to the shadowy and fragmentary evidence available for earlier periods. Another common form of record in many countries were the descriptive convict lists and registers, prepared by prison and police authorities, which noted the number and character of tattoos on each individual prisoner or convict as part of the standardized descriptions recorded on arrest, admission to prison and so on. These provide a valuable if laborious means for reconstructing the incidence of tattoos, but as raw data they lack any contextual evidence on the character of the tattooing trade, its practitioners and clients, nor do they include any of the interpretive or analytical glosses provided by the medical collectors.[6] Another source of information on tattooing available by the end of the nineteenth century was the product of journalism and popular culture. This usually fragmentary evidence survives mainly in the form of newspaper and magazine stories about tattooed performers and occasional coverage of the more sensational aspects of the practice – stories about tattooed aristocrats and royal personages, for example. Some original tattoo 'flash' – the patterns on offer from professional tattooists – also survives from before World War I, as does ephemera like trade cards and other advertising material.[7]

The extent of nineteenth-century tattoo culture in most European countries was uncovered only by the efforts of contemporary criminological research, even though the primary aim of this research was not the innocent collection of cultural data. Where this effort appears not to have been made – for example, as far as I know, in the Netherlands or in Norway – the task of reconstruction will be much more arduous. Britain presents an interestingly anomalous case in this context: not only was British criminology relatively dissociated from the continental schools, but tattooing was sufficiently normalized that it attracted virtually no official or scholarly attention comparable to that under discussion here. This might in fact be expressed as a causal relationship: because continental criminology was to this extent irrelevant, the tattoo was never pathologized to the same extent in Britain as it was elsewhere in Europe.[8] But for sheer profusion of evidence, including from the more remote regions of Europe, there is nothing to rival the criminological and police literature as a source for reconstructing the history of the tattooist and his clients. Moreover, the tension between the stigmatizing purposes for which this data was collected and the often innocuous character of the evidence itself lends it a poignancy which is absent from the more calculated record of the popular press. The aim of the research was to contribute to the debate about the pathology of the criminal; but the data itself more often bore witness to fact that tattooing was also a popular habit among the male working class in Europe and could not readily be identified with either 'atavism' or 'degeneracy'.

[II]

This ambiguity is already legible in the work of Lombroso himself, much as he may have tried to repress it. From his research in the Italian army in the 1860s, Lombroso had assembled a characteristically fragmented account of the custom of tattooing among specific Italian communities – principally peasants and rural workers in Lombardy, Piedmont and the Marches, and pilgrims to the shrine of Loreto. Among these groups tattooing was in some sense a traditional practice. Although they formed his category of 'the normal', they were not strictly a control group, since according to Lombroso they embodied the survival of 'primitive' Celtic influences. Collectively he characterized them as

> those classes who, like the ocean floor, maintain the same temperature, repeat the customs, the superstitions and even the songs of primitive peoples, and who share with them the same violent passions, the same dullness of sense, the same childish vanity, the long periods of idleness, and in the case of prostitutes the nakedness that among savages are the principal incentives to this strange usage.

Savages, the lower classes, and criminals shared these and other generic motives for tattooing, but

> the first and most primary cause of the diffusion of this custom among us is in my view atavism, and that species of historical atavism that we call tradition, for tattooing is one of the special characteristics of primitive man and those in a state of savagery.[9]

Building on his own and others' subsequent observations of convicts, including military offenders, and of prostitutes (a similarly segregated group), Lombroso went on to assert that 'tattooing assumes a specific character, a strange tenacity and diffusion among the sad class of criminals . . . locked in combat with society', among whom 'the tattoo can be considered, to use the medico-legal term, as a professional characteristic'.[10] Criminals, tattooed in proportions varying from 6 to 15 per cent of the populations studied, allegedly bore these marks 'seven times more frequently' than soldiers, who themselves were 'incalculably' more likely to be tattooed than were civilians. Their tattoos were also, according to Lombroso, more violent or obscene in character, and more likely to be positioned on or near the genitals, as depicted in the single illustration included in the first edition of *L'uomo delinquente*, of a convict displaying numerous tattoos, including several serpents, an image of crossed daggers surrounded by the motto 'Giuro di vendicarmi [I swear to revenge myself]', and a tattooed penis.[11] Later editions included mounting numbers of such illustrations, which showed elaborate combinations of images and inscriptions scattered across the body from neck to toe.[12] The alleged propensity of criminals to get multiple tattoos and place them on sensitive parts of the body also supported Lombroso's argument that they shared with 'savages' a lesser sensitivity to pain. And despite

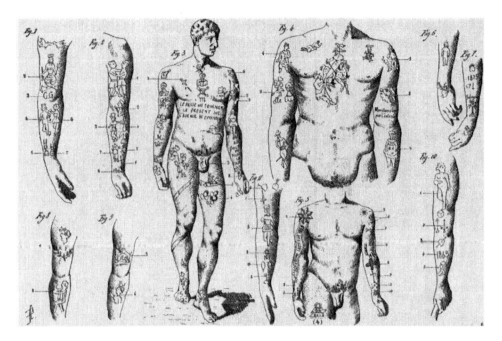

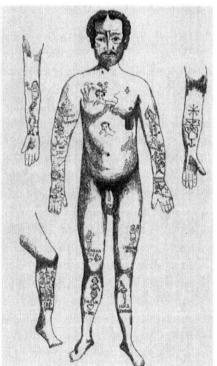

Italian criminal tattoos, from Cesare Lombroso, *L'uomo delinquente* (Turin, 1897).

mounting evidence to the contrary, he continued to argue that it was the worst, most 'savage' criminals who bore the most numerous and indecent images.

If we turn now to Lacassagne, we find initially the more cautious conclusion that '[a] large number of tattoos are the measure of the tattooed man's criminality, or at least the number of his convictions'.[13] 'Men have themselves tattooed as a way of passing the time', he wrote in another early publication, but the number and location of their tattoos 'are a manifestation of that instinctive vanity and need for display that are one of the characteristics of primitive men or criminal natures'.[14] Thereafter Lacassagne's critique of Lombroso became stronger as he expounded his own research at greater length.[15] The intellectual character of this disagreement – between theories of atavism and of degenerescence – need not detain us here, though we should note that the former depended on the idea of an inherited pathology, while the latter was consistent with theories of environmental causation. It is enough to point out that in Lombroso's case, fragmented and disorderly data led him rapidly to firmly tabulated conclusions, while Lacassagne's research suggested a method in which painstakingly assembled and catalogued data were built into a sequential exposition, on the basis of which he eventually advanced a systematic interpretation of the meaning and purpose of tattooing.

Lacassagne argued that the significance of tattoos could not be interpreted with confidence unless a very large number of examples had been collected and analysed. By 1881 he had collected copies of 1,600 tattoo images, traced from life, mounted on specially prepared paper and carefully catalogued according to seven categories of image, ten specifications of location on the body, and so on. He also embedded his interpretation of the evidence in the historical context provided by the earlier French medicolegal research mentioned above. This literature on forensic identification drew Lacassagne's attention to the tattoo as a sign, which his own acute eye enrolled in a long historical series of similarly iconic but morally neutral means of representation and identification: 'hieroglyphs, graffiti, professional emblems found on guild banners and seals, artisans' signatures, and even heraldic imagery'.[16] It was this long sequence of signs that underwrote his proposition that the signs of degeneration represented 'an uninterrupted series' rather than the 'backwards regression' mandated by Lombroso's theory of atavism. As the historical spread of literacy had provided new forms of expression for the educated, the need to exploit 'a materialized expression of metaphor and a language of emblems' had drifted downwards socially, ending up among those 'poorly educated natures' who remained dependent on 'material' means for 'the objective or symbolic representation

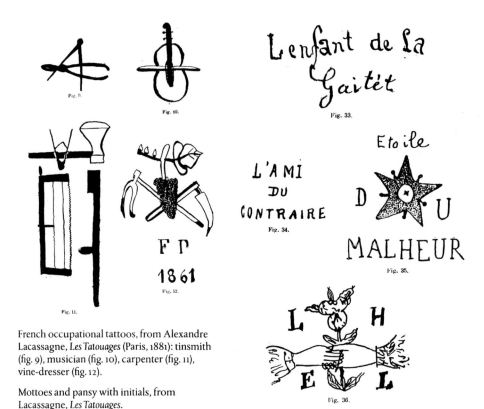

French occupational tattoos, from Alexandre Lacassagne, *Les Tatouages* (Paris, 1881): tinsmith (fig. 9), musician (fig. 10), carpenter (fig. 11), vine-dresser (fig. 12).

Mottoes and pansy with initials, from Lacassagne, *Les Tatouages*.

of an idea'.[17] The traditional symbolism of flowers was invoked here, especially in the figure of the pansy: 'flower of memory and even of hope . . . it is almost the only type of flower on the tattooed'.[18] The tattoo was a way of meeting this need: it expressed simplicity, and no doubt priority on a developmental scale, but not necessarily criminality or disreputability.

[III]

These differences in the sources of interest and the contexts of interpretation persisted as discussion of the significance of tattooing was taken up on a European scale between the 1890s and 1914. The question generated numerous publications in the major European journals of legal medicine and criminology, as well as some substantial monographs – as if to the surprise of the contributors themselves, who sometimes seemed almost to apologize for their curiosity about this peculiar subject. Still, it is not difficult to suggest some reasons for this.

First, there was the sheer visibility of the tattoo. Not only was it intensely provocative – once these images and inscriptions had been noticed, who could resist the temptation to classify and interpret them? – but its investigation did not require any special techniques or equipment, far less a pathologist's slab. Apart from the doctoral dissertations sponsored by Lombroso and Lacassagne at their respective universities of Turin and Lyon, and a few similarly academic studies, much of the original research was the work of ordinary prison or army medical officers who came into daily contact with the tattooed bodies of their charges. For most of them this was probably their sole venture into print: like many nineteenth-century 'experts' they were practitioners not academics, and the goals they set themselves were modest. Anyone could describe a tattoo verbally, and it was not much more difficult to make copies of the images and reproduce them for publication.[19] Once multiple images had been collected, their description and classification required only a reasonably tidy mind and a certain amount of spare time to prepare a piece of written work and submit it to one of the proliferating new journals of criminal anthropology. The tattoo thus offered a readily available means of entering the criminological debates that flourished after 1880. These small-scale researches built into a modest crescendo of publication by the turn of the century, lasting until the debate that sponsored them petered out in the years leading up to 1914.

A typical report would consist of a brief contextualization in the existing literature, a summary of the author's research protocol, and descriptions of the tattoos he had seen, usually catalogued according to Lacassagne's categories or some close variant. Very few authors offered anything strikingly original in the way of interpretation, and some contented themselves with simply listing the tattoos they had found, ostensibly as raw material for others to work on.[20] Feeding this impulse, the editors of the scientific journals themselves were perfectly willing to publish even slight and barely authenticated reports of unusual cases of tattooing, sometimes drawn verbatim from the press: for instance, in the German *Archiv für Kriminalanthropologie* there appeared in 1909 a news item about a worker from Halle with a tattoo of his hero Nietzsche on his lower arm, or in the main Italian criminological periodical a short report on a series of Prussian military images placed obscenely and complementarily on two French brothers ('sodomites and onanists').[21] One can well imagine that, like Lombroso in the 1860s, many prison and army doctors were happy to 'beguile their leisure' by engaging in these modest projects of research. Indeed, like so much else in the police and prison world, their activities formed an ironic parallel universe to that of the prisoners themselves, who had employed their own 'ample leisure' to inscribe the tattoos on their bodies in the first place. The 'idleness' and 'boredom' of men confined for long periods without adequate occupation were persistently identified as the principal motivations for getting tattooed, such that the tattoo became a virtual emblem of unfilled, vitiated time. Understandably, the professional men who occupied their own spare time studying them did not dwell on this parallel, any more than that suggested by the tattooed man's susceptibility to 'imitation' as a motive for his behaviour. But one author pointed out an ironic consequence of the attention he had been devoting to tattooed convicts:

> My interest was one more reason for them to cultivate tattooing, even though I was always at pains to stigmatize this stupid habit [Unsitte]. The fact that I spent time talking to the tattooed prisoners and stuck some of them in front of photographic apparatus seems to have been enough reason for some to get themselves tattooed.[22]

A second point is that even the most dedicated criminal anthropologist was bound to recognize that tattoos had a cultural as well as anatomical character. Unlike purely anatomical features the tattoo, athough a physical image, was not an involuntary or hereditary mark, but was a cultural product acquired in determinate social situations. In some tension with original motives for the research, the tattoo therefore positively incited national studies that could compare the history, the social diffusion and the popularity of the practice in different countries, and the extent to which images were shared across national and linguistic boundaries or were locally specific. France and Italy generated the most numerous studies, and Germany (with Austria) was not far behind, but there were also scattered and sometimes individually voluminous contributions from observers in countries as varied as Belgium, Denmark, Rumania and Spain. Most of the authors were familiar with at least some of the foreign literature, either directly or by report, and many aimed to compare their local findings with those of their foreign colleagues. Thus an internationally cross-referenced discussion emerged in the pages of their professional journals, spurring subscribers to further efforts of investigation.

Finally, the argument about the character of contemporary tattooing was not in itself so complicated or contentious that contributors ran any great intellectual risk by entering it. As already suggested, it was perfectly possible to avoid any deep engagement with the issues. If most writers did line up against Lombroso's theories, this was partly because degeneration was a more plastic concept than atavism, with a greater metaphorical reach and a more capacious plausibility. The original terms of the argument were in any case readily reformulated as the difference between internal (constitutional) and external (environmental) motivations for prison tattooing, which also furthered the distinction that was drawn between the motivation to get tattooed on the one hand, and the specific choice of image on the other. The prison was, so to speak, a site of exchange or overlap between internal and external explanations, offering scope for the discussion of both. And as the Belgian criminologist Louis Vervaeck was to argue in 1906, the concepts of atavism and degeneration were in any case 'very close to identical': the distinction was less important than the fact that 'the two theories make the tattooed individual into an abnormal being, whether this is because he has remained or has become a savage'.[23]

A survey of the national literatures shows that virtually all the Italian research worked with the Lombrosian categories and was confined to the milieux of prison, military jail or licensed brothel. By contrast, in France, Germany and Austria (the countries where most of the other nineteenth-century research was carried out), these conveniently confined and available populations were also the principal object of study, but interest did not always stop short at the prison gate. Although researchers were usually defeated by the challenge of carrying out reliable comparative research in the non-criminal population, they often tried to incorporate evidence of tattooing among non-offenders and reached a somewhat better under-standing of the scope of the practice in the working-class community at large. This led German authors especially to adopt a generally sceptical attitude to Lombroso's more extreme arguments, and a number of their perceptive analyses, notably those by the Berlin prison physicians Baer and Leppmann, entered the canonical literature.[24] It was also typical of both the French and German accounts (unlike the more focused Italian research) to include careful descriptions of the techniques and practitioners of tattooing: these conveyed a strong and informed impression of tattooing as a normal practice in popular culture, fostered by fairground and circus entertainers, popular reportage, and in some countries the tattooing craze that developed around the turn of the century. In Germany, moreover, with its tradition of folklore studies (*Volkskunde*), a more serious interest emerged in mapping the popular history of the custom in Europe, which eventually led to some academic studies of a quality unrivalled elsewhere.[25]

The Italian literature seems to have been less generous in the scope of its vision, except for the attention paid to pilgrim tattooing in Loreto.[26] It is of course possible that this narrower field of observation in fact mirrored real differences between northern and southern Europe, or between Italy and the more established colonial and maritime nations.[27] Nineteenth-century Italy

German tattoos worn by convicts in Plötzensee prison, Berlin, from A. Baer, *Der Verbrecher in anthropologischer Beziehung* (Leipzig, 1893).

was still a country of local cultures and languages, profoundly uneven in its cultural development and resistant to the patterns of diffusion that seem to have carried tattooing across the territories of its northern neighbours. It was precisely the anxiety about this cultural imbalance between 'civilization' and 'savagery' *within* the newly unified country that generated Lombroso's project and hypotheses.[28] At a more prosaic level, it seems at least plausible that a custom that flourished in one locality or region might not necessarily spread beyond it. Italian tattooing may well have remained more tied to existing local traditions – the pilgrim images in Loreto, or the repertoire of mainly Christian images observed on Neapolitan boatmen in 1785 by the English traveller Hester Piozzi, whose description of them as 'Mahometan', 'half-Indian' and pagan discounts the character of the imagery but would have been music to Lombroso's ears.[29]

It is a tribute to the international resonance of the criminology debate that we find contributions to it emanating from so many European countries (not to mention the Americas too). Leaving aside the better-known evidence from Italy, France and Germany, I would like to address here the less familiar literature on Rumania, Spain and Belgium. These more marginal studies allow us to trace the relationship between the indigenous and imported traditions, both of the practice and of its interpretation.

[IV]

We should not be surprised to find that Rumania, with its close cultural associations with France, brought forth research in 1899 that was comparable in scope to Lacassagne's, yet barely ventured beyond his paradigm. The author, Nicolas Minovici, was head of the Rumanian anthropometric service and thus in a position to monitor thousands of individuals who went through this system, as well as hundreds more convicts, prostitutes and asylum inmates – a total of 15,000 people.[30] But so uncommon was tattooing in Rumania – no more than 116 (less than 1 per cent) of Minovici's subjects were tattooed, and the vast majority of convicts were not tattooed – that Minovici could conclude only that in his country tattooing had few indigenous roots and 'no connection whatsoever with atavism and even less with criminals'.[31] He reported indigenous tattooing only among Rumanians in Macedonia who tattooed their children with a cross and their name, allegedly so that they could be identified if killed by Turks. He concluded that tattooing in Rumania was a Greek import, but he was otherwise uninterested in pursuing the anthropological or cultural associations – despite the fact that several of the images he reproduced under the category of 'romantic or erotic emblems' suggested intriguing affinities with folk art.

In fact Minovici was less interested in the criminological than the forensic value of the tattoo, which, following the conclusions of earlier research in Rumania in the 1860s, he saw as an 'unrivalled' sign of identity. A number of the 250 images reproduced in his study showed the same kind of occupational emblems that had interested the French researchers. To Minovici, Lacassagne's principal achievement was that he had restored the tattoo to forensic prominence after the adoption of anthropometric techniques of identification had reduced it to a kind of second-class status. By this time the tattoo had in fact secured itself a place among the repertoire of identificatory techniques or *signalement* ('descriptive particulars' – there is no single equivalent word in English) pioneered by the French police in the 1880s. French police science discounted the significance attached to tattoos by criminal anthropology, and concentrated on their value as a mark of identification on criminals or on unidentified corpses. In the later words of Edmond Locard, the pre-eminent French expert in police science after Bertillon, the tattoo was 'so to speak privileged by virtue of its identificatory power ... [it was] the model and archetype of the distinguishing mark'.[32] Yet, as Locard was to concede, after some 200 pages of discussion, the practical value of tattoos was limited to that of any other 'distinguishing mark'. They might be indelible, but they could still be altered or their number augmented; they were usually concealed and hence did not visibly identify a suspect or quarry. Minovici's claim about the forensic significance of the tattoo was thus in a sense helpless, a gesture towards a potential that the tattoo seemed to embody yet not to realize fully.

Where Minovici picked up the French tradition of identificatory practices, the motif of writing and the lineage of symbolisms advanced by Lacassagne were prominent in Rafael Salillas's 1908 account of tattooing in Spain.[33] Drawing on the hypothesis that tattooing originated from scars received in battle, Salillas traced a double track of 'personalization' that led from this: the heraldic mark which externalized individual personality and was a mark of distinction and honour, but which was simultaneously applied to one's property. His fragmentary evidence suggested the existence of honourable tattooing in the indelible marking of noblemen prescribed by the Code of Castile – an example, like guild tattoos, of tattooing as a primitive form of 'civil register'.[34] But as new and more flexible practices to denote personal distinction replaced decorative and emblematic tattooing, it was the property-marking function that survived, to overwhelm the connotation of externalized self-possession with one of expropriation and servitude.

Salillas's study switched between a partially conjectural account of the generic history and meaning of 'honourable' tattooing on the one hand, and on the other a more focused discussion and interpretation of the contemporary Spanish evidence, read through a double discussion of the convict studies by Lombroso and Lacassagne. The Spanish data, collected from prison and police records, led him to conclude that there was no indigenous tradition of popular or 'normal' tattooing in Spain, since the fragmentary early evidence indicated that if it existed at all it was socially exclusive. He attributed this lack to the absence of Celtic influences in Spain (by contrast with France and northern Italy – he was much taken by Lombroso's arguments on this score), as well as to the Spanish predilection for brilliant clothing and ostentatious adornment, a cultural preference which ruled out the more isolated signals represented by tattoos, medals and honorifics. Salillas also made much play of a sixteenth-century description of the tattooed hearts borne, among other signs of distinction, by the elite of prisoners incarcerated in the Seville prison.[35] Tattooing in contemporary Spain

'Romantic and erotic emblems', from Nicolas S. Minovici, 'Les Tatouages en Roumanie', *Archives des sciences médicales* IV (1899).

Occupational tattoos, from Minovici, 'Les Tatouages en Roumanie': boot-maker (fig. 94), locksmith (figs 95, 97), farrier (figs 96, 98), flower-seller (fig. 99), cabinet-maker (fig. 100) and sailor (figs 101, 102).

was confined almost exclusively to sailors and prisoners – sailors because they were exposed to foreign influences, prisoners because confinement and idleness propagated the practice (the tattooed cadavers sent for dissection were known colloquially in the pathology labs as *presidarios*, or convicts). Even in these groups tattooing was less common than in France or Italy, and it was hardly practised at all among soldiers; the tattooists were more likely than not to be foreigners, and tattooed inscriptions were often in French or obvious translations. Only in the more cosmopolitan port of Barcelona was professional tattooing established, and the city's unusual openness to foreign influence was paralleled by another unusual feature: its inhabitants' preference for political over religious and patriotic symbols.[36]

The influence of foreign tattooing also hovered over an extensive account of tattooing in Belgium by Louis Vervaeck, the chief physician at the Brussels Minîmes jail.[37] Vervaeck's 1906 study of over 14,000 subjects included numerous petty offenders and vagrants who could not be described as professional or recidivist criminals. He also made unusual efforts to extend his researches beyond the prison population itself, and he built up a fascinating picture of a popular custom that had no obvious connections with the prison or criminal underworld.

> Numerous Brussels workers are . . . tattooed, many of them while they were apprentices, while they were idling on a Monday or a holiday; they get tattooed in the bar on a Saturday night, in the street or the countryside, in periods when there is little work, but above all when the military lottery is drawn – then veritable tattooing sessions take place.[38]

The popularity of lottery tattoos – Vervaeck described them as 'le triomphe des chiffres' – was peculiar to Belgium, especially Brussels, where the annual conscription lottery was a ceremonial occasion accompanied by boisterous festivities in the working-class quarters. The inscription of a youth's lottery number on his skin, often embellished with palms, decorated frames, shields, garlands or initials, echoed its installation 'in a gilded frame in a place of honour in the paternal home'. Some even had their number tattooed in several places, while others tattooed the numbers of their close friends or relatives, creating a souvenir of 'these days of their life'.[39]

This honourable form of tattooing – an unusual variant of the barracks tattooing found in most European armies – was perhaps the most deeply integrated into Belgian working-class life, but (and again this was true throughout northern Europe) tattoos were also far from uncommon among manual workers, especially in those heavy trades where men worked with bare arms and torsos – mining, glass-blowing, hauling, building – or among transport workers such as sailors, boatmen and carters. But Vervaeck reported that tattooing was thought to be a relatively recent import into Belgium, probably coming from France (it was commoner among Walloons than Flemings), and it had not yet been professionalized, by contrast with France, Britain and to a lesser extent Germany. The tattooists were workmates or fellow-soldiers, and they were most often rewarded for their work with a few drinks rather than a cash payment. Despite his claim that tattooing was a French import, Vervaeck was also at pains to show how the Belgian tattoo differed in character from those of other countries; it is worth quoting him at length here:

> Our national tattooing is essentially different from that of Germany and France. The latter is exuberant, varied, alive, crude, by turns amusing, sarcastic, vengeful or depraved, its appearance and design characterized

by fantasy and extravagance; while German tattooing is correct, cold, stiff, perfectly executed, mechanical, I would say, to the point that one can see at a glance if a prisoner hails from the other side of the Rhine. Their allegories and their emblems are all alike, stamped from the same die . . . decent both in appearance and meaning. In spite of everything, they emanate only an air of skill and harmony, like a sculpture from which life and spirit are absent. Are these not the typical characteristics of the psychology of the nations who surround us? Belgian tattooing is more modest, more ugly one must admit, less spiritual, but more naive and sincere. When we find on some depraved vagabond a Christ or a Virgin in veneration, or a scene of the Passion, how can we not think of the profound religious sentiments that are rooted in our rural populations? When we see on a daily basis tattoos of military emblems and inscriptions, how can we not recall the national virtues of this little country – attachment to the family hearth and to the motherland, sincere affections, a simple life?[40]

This sentimentalized evidence of popular tattooing led Vervaeck to criticize Lombroso and Lacassagne alike. He judged their theories of degeneration to be essentially indistinguishable, and denied that 'the tattooed man is an abnormal being who is developmentally arrested or degenerate'.[41] But Vervaeck went on to draw a sharp distinction between tattooing as such, 'which has no constant relation whatsoever with degeneration or criminality', and 'the special tattooing which characterizes criminals and the depraved, a kind which bears the obvious imprint of vice and crime'. With this he re-insinuated the degenerationist model by the back door:

Once this distinction is made, we would be entirely in agreement with the Italian and French criminologists in saying that among this minority of the delinquent and the depraved tattooing presents *special* characteristics which suffice to classify the inmate who bears them. Tattooing is extremely common among the truly criminal and develops among them with great facility as a consequence of the degenerative taints, the sexual inversions and the subversive tendencies that are the lot of this sad class of prisoners.

Thus Vervaeck's taxonomy of tattooing embraced three categories: it was to be found among the worst criminals, 'individuals whose state of degenerescence is unquestionable'; among minor offenders, who were only 'weak-minded' and subject to the influence of others; and finally among ordinary working-class Belgians. The latter were 'honest men of healthy stock and unimpeachable constitution', but among them too weak-minded-ness and suggestibility played their part, for even 'honest men' usually got tattooed in circumstances where group pressures were strong and individual will-power enfeebled by alcohol and the desire to please. And whatever the differential distribution and significance of tattooing, the tug of depravity was too hard for even the Belgian evidence to resist. While Vervaeck conceded that it would be impracticable to ban tattooing outright, he argued that it should be generally discouraged, prohibited for young people, and proscribed in the army by severe penalties including 'cauterization by fire' – an extraordinarily harsh suggestion which also contained disturbing implications of branding.

Vervaeck's paradoxical conclusions can be understood as a proposal that the incorrigible offender should stigmatize himself by inscribing a permanent physical mark that announced his criminal identity on his body's surface. With this he only articulated with unusual clarity a view which suffused the tattooing debate more nebulously, and which can be seen as a return of the repressed practice of penal branding and mutilation. Now that the state had abandoned the official marking the body, in the name of progress, humanity and reform, the criminal was being asked to literally brand himself.[42] Yet this was perhaps only consistent with the stated aim of these strategies: to re-make tattooing as that which Lombroso claimed it already was, an irrevocable yet self-imposed stigma of criminality. As Vervaeck expressed his hopes for the future of the tattoo, 'Confining itself to those milieux which in essence tend to glorify it, it will become the true characteristic of the criminal, the depraved, and the degenerate.'[43]

[v]

These investigations of tattooing in Rumania, Spain and Belgium illustrate the extended international reach of the criminological debates of the later nineteenth century, as well as their unintended consequences. Without the stimulus of this debate, it is unlikely that such a wealth of information on the demotic practice of tattooing would have been collected from so many European countries, its images and descriptions thus enabled to outlive the bodies of the subjects of this assiduous research. The internationalization of the investigative project carried another lesson, however. This was the tendency of each author to deny any indigenous sources of the practice and to ascribe it instead to foreign influences – even while simultaneously re-claiming it for a 'national' culture. Thus Minovici held Greeks responsible for tattooing in Rumania, just as Vervaeck credited the French for introducing the practice into Belgium, while Salillas in his turn ascribed the prevalence of tattooing in Spain's coastal regions to imported influences from Italy and France. By the time they were writing these authors may well have been correct in believing that indigenous traditions of tattooing, if they had ever existed, had faded in their countries. Yet it is impossible to miss the fact that their claims only replicated on the national level the argument that had been made for the continent as a whole since the eighteenth century: that the origin of modern European tattooing was not the survival of local traditions but importation from distant and savage cultures. And more than this, for 'imitation' – the quintessential primitive substitute for creativity – marked both the original moment of cultural exchange and the repeated acts of individual inscription.

11 Branding the Other/Tattooing the Self: Bodily Inscription among Convicts in Russia and the Soviet Union

ABBY M. SCHRADER

Bodily inscription was an essential component of the Muscovite and Imperial Russian penal systems. Until the era of Catherine the Great, members of all social estates and people of both genders were subject to various forms of corporal punishment and mutilation – including knouting, branding, and the rending of nostrils – that indelibly scarred the criminal body. Beginning in the late eighteenth century, officials gradually amelio-rated corporal punishment, abolishing some chastisements outright, circum-scribing other practices to members of lower status groupings and exiles, and deeming that certain gendered, aged, and physically deficient bodies could not be subject to floggings.[1] Nonetheless, while corporal punishment was rendered problematic in late eighteenth- and early nineteenth-century Russia and while state servitors began to question its efficacy on diverse grounds, bodily inscription continued to play a central role in Imperial, and later Soviet, criminal spheres. In large part this is because branding not only constituted a central component of the Russian penal complex but was also an important administrative measure whereby officials ascribed status to individuals by literally marking their membership in various social group-ings. In so doing, they sought to exert control over the subjects whom they governed.[2]

In this essay, I trace how officials, rather than conceiving of branding only as a penal measure, came to consider it a tactic for preventing fugitives and vagrants from contesting the rigorous status system that was central to the functioning of the Russian state. Although this approach failed to achieve its stated goals, bodily inscription nevertheless constituted an important marker around which vagrants and fugitive exiles constructed their own subjectivity as members of a corporate group. Analysing the tattooing culture that developed among vagrants and criminals in Russia and the Soviet Union, I argue that the symbolic significance of these forms of bodily inscription can only be comprehended when they are placed in the context

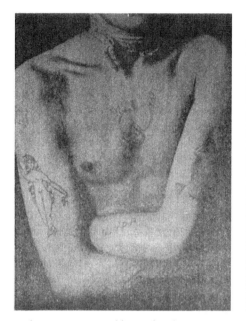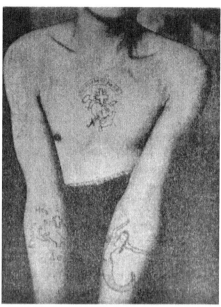

Under-age convicts emblazoned with tattoos, Moscow, early 1920s, from M. N. Gernet, ed., *Prestunnyi mir Moskvy. Sbornik statei* (Moscow, 1924). Note the acronymic tattoos that mark both convicts' lower arms.

of official practices of status-ascription and marking. Russian and Soviet convicts operated within a discursive structure that privileged social status groupings, and therefore appropriated tactics of bodily inscription deployed by Russian officials in an effort to forge their own particular identities and assert ownership over their own bodies. I conclude by suggesting that, because resistance functioned as part of a multivalent complex of power relations, convicts' reliance on tattoos as a means of constructing themselves in opposition to officialdom was necessarily fraught with tension. Studying official cultures of bodily inscription and convict countercultures of tattooing as related and interdependent phenomena enhances our understanding of both processes at the same time that it illuminates the extent to which the body itself constitutes a central text of cultural history.

ASCRIBING STATUS IN IMPERIAL RUSSIA

From the period when state building got underway in the late seventeenth century, Russian autocrats and policymakers began to elaborate a complex system of 'ascriptive legal-administrative categories,' or status groupings (*sostoianiia*), according to which they regulated their society.[3] This process, which began in earnest during the reign of Peter the Great, was essential to his project of constructing a well-ordered police state: formal privileges and honour became wholly dependent upon each status group's service to the state and the autocrat.[4] As Wirtschafter notes, this arrangement, which facilitated Peter's institution of the poll tax, military recruitment and a Table of Ranks into which all nobles were enrolled, 'deeply affected and even transformed social structures and customary relations' in Russia. However imperfectly this system functioned, however much practice deviated from theoretical formulation, and however flexible and accommodating status groupings proved to be, it is nonetheless significant that officials considered it necessary to ascribe to every individual and community a particular legal status in order to administer and ensure the security of the realm. Where individuals and communities did not fit comfortably within pre-existing social categories, policymakers developed new *sostoianiia* to address these deficiencies. Equally significant is that bureaucrats sought to preclude their subjects' resistance to enrolment within these status groupings because they correctly perceived this as a rejection of Russian authorities' power to categorize and govern the lives of those residing within the empire.[5]

In a context in which officials attempted to impose social control by registering individuals and communities in *sostoianiia* and in which such registration entailed the imposition of duties and liabilities such as enserfment, the draft, religious standardization, and the payment of the capitation, vagrancy became a significant form of social protest. As Iadrintsev, a renowned Siberian ethnographer, notes in his 1872 work on criminality and the exile system, 'the Russian masses have long manifested a proclivity towards vagrancy that is rooted in the special circumstances of their historical life'. He explains that 'flight constituted the sole means of evading dire straits and the difficulties presented by life in society . . . [and] . . . the only form of individual protest' available to those seeking to avoid the encroachment of centralizing state power. As such, vagrancy and flight have a long history in the Russian tradition. But the significance of vagrancy was even greater in Siberia than the Russian centre: Siberia 'presented itself, in terms of its physical status and due to its low population density, as perfect ground for vagrancy' and, consequently, waves of Russians, the so-called 'wandering people,' relocated to this borderland in their quest for 'a free life devoid of power and control'. In so doing, they established the first real Russian presence in the region.[6]

Simultaneously, Russian authorities conceived of the Siberian borderland as a dumping ground for convicts and misfits. Exile was established as a central feature of the Russian penal system during the sixteenth century; the goal was to alienate convicted criminals and outsiders from the rest of society. Authorities used exiled convicts as negative 'others' against whom they constructed a definition of what it meant to be a Russian subject.[7] Two types of exile existed in contemporary Russia. Those subjected to the first form of exile – hard labour – had committed serious crimes, such as murder, arson, robbery or brigandage, or were repeat offenders. The state stripped these criminals of their property, proclaimed them civilly dead and banished them to Siberia. Until the late eighteenth century, hard labour supplemented knouting and facial disfigurement for members of all social groupings. The second type of exile, which consisted of resettlement in Siberia, constituted punishment for less serious crimes. It also functioned as a means by which landlords or communities alienated those individuals whom they considered troublemakers by administrative, rather than judicial, order.[8]

The exile system burgeoned with the expansion of the Muscovite State and, later, the Russian Empire, beyond the Urals during the seventeenth and eighteenth centuries. The conquest of the vast, sparsely populated Siberian terrain coupled with the need for manpower to mine its resources made exile an attractive alternative to the death penalty. The concept of using exiles as a source of labour was formally articulated by Peter the Great; upon Elizabeth's abolition of capital punishment in 1754, exile swelled, reaching massive proportions with the 1822 introduction of new regulations governing this system; in the 46 years following this reform, officials transported approximately 350,000 vagrants and convicts to Siberia.[9]

At the same time, in an era when the geographical boundaries of the Russian state were growing less distinct, Siberia's nature as a wild and criminal borderland troubled Russian administrators; officials began to question the status of Siberia, as well as that of the exiles banished to this realm. From the mid-eighteenth century, as autocracy developed in the centre, the exploration of Siberia advanced and officials introduced policies and bureaucratic agencies to improve its administration.[10] Simultaneously, Siberia underwent a demographic explosion: the number of Russians in Siberia nearly doubled between 1770 and 1820 and grew by another 40 per cent between 1820 and 1852.[11]

That officials increasingly deemed Siberia part of Russia and, specifically, a region that promised fiscal and political advantages for the entire state further complicated matters. On the one hand, Siberia was barren, outlaw, and Russia's symbolic 'other'. Yet, simultaneously, officials were beginning to conceive of Siberia as an absolutely essential part of the 'unified Russian state'.[12] As Infantry General Annenkov asserted in 1852, 'Siberia is, for us, not only a place that is other (*chuzhoi*) . . . Siberia is part of Russia, and as such, is one of her most important parts. Completely adjacent to eastern Russia, Siberia is both geographically and politically part of the east, and is its most significant part . . .'[13]

Administrators articulated new regulations to govern exiles in the process of fielding their conflict about Siberia's identity. Understanding that the prosperity and security of Siberia would benefit the entire empire, authorities recognized that the realization of this goal depended in part upon the reintegration of exiles into social structures: not only did officials homestead those sentenced to resettlement or who had completed their labour terms, but they also sought to enrol them into modified versions of the Russian status system that had long existed in the centre.[14] In light of this, they grew increasingly vexed by the problems posed by exiles who took flight from incarceration and, more generally, by vagrancy. That between a fifth and a quarter of all Russians in Siberia were individuals who stood outside the law in one way or another troubled administrators. These officials understood that 'exile, by its very nature, was not particularly well suited to settling [Siberia]' and that it 'necessarily augmented vagrancy to astonishing proportions'.[15]

The severe regimentation imposed on hard labourers, harsh climate and infertile soil, and virtual absence of anchoring structures such as the family engendered chronic vagrancy in nineteenth-century Siberia. While it is impossible to ascertain the magnitude of this problem with any degree of precision, a conservative estimate suggests that one third of all exiles fled at some point. Investigators concur that exiles escaped from every prison, mine, factory and settlement in Siberia and that, over the century, they absconded in the tens of thousands.[16] Authorities never apprehended half of those who ran off; most fugitives who returned to exile camps and prisons were so-called 'seasonal' exiles who never intended to flee permanently; rather, these were individuals who turned themselves in to authorities at the first sign of frost.[17]

During the first half of the nineteenth century, local and central authorities were preoccupied with the material and psychological ramifications presented by exile flight and vagrancy. They were concerned that the measures they imposed, which included flogging both those who escaped and the individuals who harbored vagrants, failed to impede flight.[18] Even more important, authorities considered escape attempts transgressive of the boundaries ostensibly erected by the exile system. They believed that, by evading physical confinement, exiles denied not only the authorities' capacity to punish but also to categorize them.

Fugitive exiles and vagrants engaged in a complex series of pretences. Their primary goal consisted of concealing their real identities and status in order to avoid detection and receive lighter sentences upon surrender. To this end, fleeing convicts commissioned proficiently-stamped false identification papers; bribed officials to look the other way; concealed their brands and scars from anyone who might denounce them; adopted pseudonyms or the names of deceased convicts who were sentenced to less onerous labour terms; and 'exchanged' identities with gullible newcomers.[19] These fugitives

> were individuals who ... lived under various names and who were variously exiles at hard labour, exiles at resettlement, soldiers or peasants, and who then once more became exiles at hard labour, soldiers, and peasants, etcetera.[20]

In a system predicated on the notion that every individual occupied a distinct legal identity, fugitives and vagrants who moved between different categories at will, and who thus defied the ability of Russian officialdom to impute a clear status to them, especially affronted authorities.

This problem was compounded by the fact that fugitives continued to mock the state's power to order its subjects' identities even after they were caught or surrendered to the police. Police registered entire lists of vagrants whom they apprehended under pseudonyms such as 'Ivan Nepomniashchii' (John I-Don't-Remember) and 'Nikolai Bezprozvanii' (Nicholas Without-a-Name). These individuals pretended not to know their origins and parentage (*ne pomniashchie rodstva*), their status, or why they had been exiled.[21] Central and local officials repeatedly complained about these nameless vagrants. By the late 1820s, simultaneous with efforts to improve Siberia's administration and link the region more closely with the centre, officials began to develop various techniques to impede flight and to preclude exiles from concealing their identities.[22]

BRANDING THE 'OTHER'

Since the early eighteenth century, Russian authorities perceived branding as a means of regulating the status of those who sought to subvert official attempts to construct their identities. Ethnographers who have examined Russian customary law note that peasants of practically all regions of the empire had long stamped their animate and inanimate property with initials and other seals, such as crosses, for identificatory purposes that served as a 'mark of collective and personal ownership'.[23] These practices 'evolved into state and official brands' with the centralization of government in Russia;

princes and rulers arguably coopted this popular practice in efforts to assert their ownership over their subjects and the goods that they produced. This process culminated in the 1818 standardization of all official seals, brands and imprints in autocratic Russia.[24] While it is impossible to draw a direct connection between marks of ownership and eighteenth-century penal branding, a provocative correspondence exists between these two types of juridical marks. Indicative of this connection is that the Russian autocracy applied the same terminology to the branding of convicts and the imprinting of official documents and coins, referring to both technologies as *kleimenie* (branding) and the plates used in each case as *shtempeli* (stamps). In each case, the state sought to brand its property in order to exert ownership, and hence control, over it. In so doing, it implicitly attempted to fix the status of this property,

This goal served as the primary impetus behind Peter the Great's 1712 promulgation of an ukase in which he ordered provincial authorities to use a needle to prick a cross on the left hand of military recruits who took flight from his new standing army. Clearly concerned with the ramifications of desertion, Peter decreed that this mark be rubbed with gunpowder to ensure that the cross proved visible and indelible. He enjoined governors to 'proclaim distinctly ... that wherever they see a man who has on his left hand the aforementioned cross, they should capture him'.[25] Authorities enforced this edict, which was made public in 1715, for several years.[26] In 1718, one army captain testified that, under his supervision, one hundred deserters had been beaten and 'stamped on their left hands with the recruits' brand'.[27] However, the ukase provoked considerable controversy and subsequently fell out of use because it entailed tattooing recruits who had not committed a serious offence.[28]

Nonetheless, the significance of this measure resides in the fact that the autocrat considered bodily inscription one means of ascribing resistant Russian subjects with fixed status. This goal also motivated Peter the Great's innovation of the practice of branding convicts with the imperial symbol of the eagle; executioners rubbed gunpowder in the scars left by the red-hot iron stamp studded with needles 'so that they could by no means be erased and so that [the convicts] would be known by this mark until their deaths'.[29] The autocracy standardized penal branding throughout Imperial Russia in 1753, replacing other marks and representations with acronyms. Convicts previously sentenced to death were instead publicly put to the knout and had their nostrils rent and their forehead and cheeks branded with the letters 'V,' 'O,' and 'R' to signify their status as serious criminals (in Russian, a *vor* is literally a thief). The autocracy considered these convicts politically dead and consigned them to exile from honourable society; their scarred faces rendered the outsider status of these convicts visible to all.[30] Branding remained in force with little modification through the reign of Alexander I (1801–25).

Thus, by the early nineteenth century, the practice of branding convicts was well-established in the Russian penal lexicon. Even though branding was a penalty reserved for the harshest criminals in Imperial Russia, it is not surprising that nineteenth-century authorities sought to appropriate this practice when confronted by vagrants and fugitives who attempted to circumvent the categorization essential to the Russian status system. The chief rationale behind branding was that it fixed the status of the marked individual and made it visible to those responsible for policing unmanageable subjects. These were precisely the goals of those who sought to preclude vagrancy.

In 1828, Russian Chief of Staff General Adjutant Prianishnikov suggested that brands be placed on the arms of fugitive exiles whom police apprehended, in order to facilitate identification in the likely event of their subsequent escape. This branding would be extra-judicial; that is, it would supplement floggings and be carried out by a physician's assistant rather than an executioner. This proposal garnered considerable support from Siberian administrators. Nonetheless, the Minister of Justice, the State Council – Russia's highest legislative consultative institution – and Tsar Nicholas I refused to authorize it on the grounds that all branding constituted punishment and, as such, required judicial sanction.[31]

However, while this proposal remained contentious, Nicholas I did ultimately endorse the policy of branding fugitives in 1845.[32] Responding to the outcry of frustrated Siberian officials who found the mounting fugitive problem increasingly unbearable,[33] the State Council ruled that,

> [T]he proclivity towards vagrancy and vice, laziness and parasitism and the desire to evade supervision incessantly lure exiles from their place of settlement or work, and that the only means of putting an end to this dangerous form of disorder consists of branding exiles at hard labour every time they attempt flight.[34]

The State Council left it up to the Ministry of Internal Affairs and Siberia's chief administrators, the governors general, to determine the precise details of this form of branding.

The nature of the recommendations ratified by Nicholas I in 1845 reveal the extent to which authorities were preoccupied with status. While the governors general proposed elaborate codes whereby police could 'accurately determine the name [of the exile] and the place whence he escaped',

Minister of Internal Affairs Perovskii rejected these schemes. Instead, he proposed that the state standardize and mechanize branding practices, marking the shoulders of fugitives with acronyms that denoted their status: exiles at resettlement were branded with the letters 'SB' (*ssylno-brodiag*, i.e. vagrant exile) and hard labourers, with 'SK' (*ssylno-katorzhnik*, i.e. exile at hard labour). This system would fix and render visible the status of every fugitive whom the authorities apprehended.[35]

Equally significant is that Nicholas I approved Perovskii's extension of these branding practices to vagrants apprehended within European Russia.[36] Perovskii rationalized this by citing the problems posed by the fact that over a third of those who took flight from jails, convict labour gangs, the army or serfdom concealed their identities and status.[37] The practice of branding fugitive exiles and vagrants reveals officials' concern that there were people in Siberia and Russia who refused to allow authorities to determine their status. Even when officials stripped criminals of their status as peasants, merchants or nobles they reassigned them to the status of exiles; quite tellingly, Russian law used the same term – *sostoianie* – to refer to all of these identity categories. The status of exile, of course, was a dubious honour, but its position was still fixed and clear under Russian law. Flight, however, represented a rejection of status altogether. This repudiation threatened state order precisely because this order was predicated on the fact that every individual occupied an established social position. Fugitives came and went as they pleased and, in so doing, manifested their refusal to allow officials to determine their identities. Branding anonymous vagrants within Russia and escaped Siberian convicts constituted authorities' efforts to mark status on the bodies of those who otherwise disavowed juridical ascription.

In 1846, immediately after these laws took effect, police branded nearly a thousand fugitive exiles and vagrants; in 1847, this number more than tripled.[38] Yet this measure failed to stem flight and dissuade runaways from feigning amnesia and concealing their true identities.[39] Nevertheless, branding retained considerable significance for how convicts conceived of themselves and ordered their own lives: the policy of bodily inscription imposed by authorities appears to have played a role in shaping how vagrants demarcated their own status and group identity in both Imperial and Soviet Russia. It provided vagrants with one way to mark their own group status in a means that was visible and clearly comprehensible to other denizens of the criminal world. In the process of appropriating the tactic of marking their bodies and constructing a corporate identity for themselves, vagrants and convicts attempted to subvert the power relations inherent in autocratic policies and transform these into a strategy of resistance. Yet this resistance ultimately remained as incomplete as the strategies of power and domination deployed by authorities.

INVERSION AND REINSCRIPTION: VAGRANT CULTURE IN
LATE IMPERIAL RUSSIA

During the late nineteenth and early twentieth centuries, Russian criminologists, ethnographers, and other social scientists became intrigued with the cultural conditions of prison and exile life and attempted to study these on their own terms. Investigators observe that vagrants – *brodiagi* – occupied the most privileged status position within the extremely hierarchical world of the prison. Iadrintsev recognizes that fugitives self-consciously proclaimed themselves 'field nobles' (*polevye dvoriane*), and 'were, as they say, aristocrats among the exiles'. One criminologist, Shreiterfel'd, notes that vagrants 'considered themselves "honoured citizens of the jail," its legitimate offspring and its masters'. Another, Svirskii, remarks that 'the thieving brotherhood, acknowledging their alienation from the world outside the prison, from so-called honest society, attempt[ed] to create for themselves within the prison a niche as a privileged, aristocratic caste'. And Mel'shin, himself sentenced to hard labour, observes that '"vagrant" is the highest title a prisoner [may possess]'.[40] Indeed, these surveys indicate that prison inmates quite explicitly classified themselves, and that, in so doing, they drew on the corporate language of the Russian social order, identifying themselves by the discourse of ascriptive legal status pioneered by Russian officialdom. They employed the very same concept of ranking (*chinstvo*) employed by Peter the Great, considering that 'each rank (*chin*) belong[ed] to a distinct order' and that they, the *brodiagi*, occupied the uppermost station.[41]

A vast array of social practices allowed vagrants to constitute their corporate identity. They paid great attention to upholding their ideals and standards, including 'fearlessness in the face of danger, bravery in times of adventure [and] cleverness sufficient to waylay pursuers'.[42] To accomplish these goals, vagrants fashioned particular cultural forms, including 'their own literature, songs, language, and customs' through which they expressed ideas such as sorrow, heroism, love, friendship, and insult.[43] These modes of communicating with one another took shape over a long period and were passed down from vagrant to vagrant; speaking the language of vagrancy and observing its customs enabled neophytes to establish themselves as community members.[44] Vagrants thus sought to defend and mutually support members of their corporation. To this end, vagrants organized themselves into more or less democratic groupings (*skhodki*) that governed

decision-making, including the appointment of spokesmen, the organization of escape attempts, negotiations with authorities, and daily life in
prison barracks.[45]

The development of the cultural forms that comprised vagrant corporate
identity necessarily took place in a specific socio-political context: vagrants
reacted to authorities' attempts to construct and mark them as 'other'. As
Iadrintsev observed, exile and incarceration functioned as rites of passage
for the vagrant:

> it was here that the vagrant was completely naturalized, that is . . .
> proclaimed worthy of being assimilated as a member of the corpora-
> tion; here he was anointed with all the secrets of the corporation, was
> born into it.[46]

In the process of initiation into the prison milieu, vagrants drew on the same
mechanisms used by official Russian culture, coopting these strategies in
order to resist the autocratic power complex and assert mastery over prison
subcultures. In so doing, they sent a clear message to both authorities and
other, less experienced inmates that they had the power to set the tone of
prison and exile life.

Several examples illustrate this point. First, while vagrants and exiles
more generally sought to evade the state's power to punish, they nonetheless
utilized the very language of punishment fashioned by officialdom when
enforcing discipline in their own ranks. Vagrants developed highly elaborate
judicial codes and established unofficial courts in which they tried those who
transgressed their norms. Mimicking official forms of justice, they upheld
their rule through the use of violence: they appointed their own judges and
executioners and staged spectacular floggings that replicated the structure
and content of trials and executions carried out under state auspices. The
vagrant *skhod* regularly flogged or executed vagrants who spied; denounced
their brethren; compromised with authorities; ran off with or raped their
comrades' lovers; or committed other crimes that flouted the vagrant code of
discipline.[47]

Secondly, just as the social status of Russian elites such as the nobility was
predicated on a series of exemptions from various obligations imposed on
other social groups, vagrants understood that their own elite corporate
identity and status only made sense when contrasted with the lack of privileges possessed by other inhabitants of the prison world. Vagrants refused to
'mix with the other inmates living in their midst', instead attempting to live in
a 'separate society'.[48] Vagrants achieved mastery over the jail by demanding
the most favorable bunks, largest rations, and lightest work details.[49] It was

this process of contrast that enabled them to 'consider themselves higher and more experienced than the rest of the petty masses of the prison world'.[50]

Finally, vagrants utilized a series of markers to render themselves visible to other members of their company. A vagrant who entered a prison for the first time had to be able to convince comrades that he belonged to the aristocracy. He did so in part by upholding the secret rituals of vagrant life. Even more significant, vagrants acquired power from their brands. While vagrants attempted to hide their brands from the police, they openly celebrated these markings before each other, employing these to confirm their pedigree. Consequently, the scarred and branded hard labourer enjoyed great prestige among his peers because his markings established him as an individual possessed of vast experience.[51]

But vagrants took this process one step further by using their own technologies of bodily inscription to underscore their ascendancy in the criminal world – they inscribed tattoos on their own bodies that functioned as 'calling cards' that permitted them to recognize one another.[52] In the process, they sought to transform a practice that marked their social alienation into a source of pride and corporate membership. While authorities believed that the brand underscored official authority because it allowed them to identify fugitives, vagrants reversed the dynamics of this relationship by demonstrating that criminals derived their own counter-cultural power from the brand or tattoo. Even though convicts clearly understood that 'augmenting the number of tattoos on their bodies' by acquiring additional 'marks of distinction' facilitated their capture, they nonetheless considered the tattoo empowering. In their slang, criminals referred to their tattoos as 'regalia' (*regalki*) and used them to signify their 'rank' (*chin*) in the prison world. In the late Imperial Russian criminal sphere, the *skhodka* carefully regulated the tattoo, deeming that only the most seasoned and experienced convict who had distinguished himself 'by virtue of his crimes and bloody deeds' had earned the right to 'show his regalia on his breast' and that only the most fearless vagrants possessed the right to 'reward themselves with ranks (*chiny*)'.[53]

A 'consecration' ceremony that Svirskii witnessed amply illustrates this point. Authorities had captured and sentenced to hard labour one vagrant by the name of Kosoi. Upon his arrival in the camp, the local vagrant corporation greeted Kosoi as a brother and was eager to hear tales about his wanderings while at large in the Siberian taiga. Because Kosoi demonstrated fearlessness in the face of authorities, the vagrant company decided to reward him by inscribing his body. The vagrants' elder, the *starosta*, exclaimed:

Mitka Kosoi, you have escaped from Siberia for the third time, you have passed through many transit camps in your life, and not once have you received the 'macaroni' (the lash), and always, like an honourable thief, you've defended your comrades; therefore, we would like to reward you with 'regalia' so that *everyone will know exactly who you are.*[54]

This act of scarification was highly ritualized and, in many ways, its structure resembled the spectacle of branding: the criminal designated to perform the scarification brandished the blade of his knife before the gathered vagrant public. The vagrants who 'fixed [their] eyes on Kosoi . . . tried to imagine for themselves [Kosoi's] physical suffering' just as convicts who beheld the spectacle of branding empathized with the punished rather than with the authorities carrying out the sentence. Yet, like many criminals forced to submit to floggings at the hands of the police and executioners, Kosoi remained a picture of composure and stoicism, presenting 'the impression that this [scarification] was not at all painful to him' even though 'vermilion blood began to flow down his chest' and the wound was liberally rubbed with salt.[55] The vagrants who partook in this spectacle clearly took pride in Kosoi's bravery in the face of pain, congratulating him in much the same way that the gathered public at the scaffold praised convicts who refused to acknowledge the pain associated with flogging.[56]

The content of the scar with which the vagrant brotherhood marked Kosoi's body also constituted an inversion. The *skhodka* opted to emblazon his body with a pine tree that 'served as a symbolic mark of his vagrancy and convict daring'.[57] In choosing this particular image, Kosoi's compatriots contested the official meaning of Siberian exile, turning it into a place that imbued its vagrant residents with honour rather than shame. Thus, in both form and content, the scarification rite observed by Svirskii accomplished an act of recuperation and reversal: by wresting control of practices associated with official power and reenacting its spectacle, convicts reinforced the idea that they could carve out their opposition to officialdom by assimilating its technologies.

TATTOOING THE SELF

The culture of bodily inscription developed and perpetuated by fugitive exiles in Siberia informed the tattooing practices of twentieth-century convicts. Nineteenth-century vagrants functioned as convenient and appropriate role models for successive generations of outlaws. Observers have noted that the norms expressed by the latter 'did not arise in a vacuum, but were founded on the traditions, customs, and "laws" of the criminal underworld of tsarist Russia' and particularly on the 'centuries old traditions' of vagrants.[58] In large part this was because vagrants had long sought to turn themselves into 'perfect thieve[s]' (*otlichnye vory*), conceiving of theft as a 'profession,' hallmark of elite status in the criminal underworld, and 'essential for membership in the vagrant' corporation.[59] Moreover, the '*Ivany*', professional criminals who were the leading voices in Soviet jails, wished to enjoy the 'limitless respect' of other inmates that had been the hallmark of vagrant status in the pre-revolutionary era. Although the numbers of 'true vagrants' had dwindled during the final years of the Imperial era, their legends and traditions persisted. The '*Ivany*' self-consciously coopted these in setting themselves up as the legitimate heirs of vagrants and fugitive hard labourers.[60]

Twentieth-century denizens of Russian and Soviet criminal underworlds thus sought to insert themselves and their own experiences into a well-developed vagrant folklore and history and to emulate vagrants' ideals and laws. They insisted on absolute solidarity in their ranks; shunned the grey prison masses; only dealt with members of their own groupings; and controlled the prison environment, establishing *skhody* and law courts that enforced their rule in a violent manner. Moreover, like Siberian vagrants, they used prison jargon and an idiomatic song culture that they called 'rogues' music' (*blatnaia muzika*) to communicate with one another and construct their group identity. These cultural practices became essential components of a 'moral credo', which they dubbed 'thieves' laws' (*blatnye zakony*) that regulated convicts' 'relationship to their work, to the prison administration, to other inmates, and to themselves'.[61]

Thus, it is unsurprising that the tattoo retained its significance in this context. Like nineteenth-century vagrants, twentieth-century Russian and Soviet convicts used, and continue to use, tattoos as one means of upholding long-standing traditions, signifying group solidarity, and conversing in a language which they attempt to keep secret from authorities. In a series of interviews conducted in the Dopr prison in Ukraine and in Moscow correctional facilities in the mid-1920s, investigators determined that between 60 and 70 per cent of all inmates who sported tattoos acquired them in jail; generally speaking, they opted to tattoo themselves immediately after sentencing or when they were first incarcerated.[62] Those who studied tattooing practices among convicts from the 1940s through the 1980s reached similar conclusions.[63]

Tattooed convicts conceived of bodily inscription as a rite of passage: they asserted that more seasoned inmates had convinced them that the tattoo

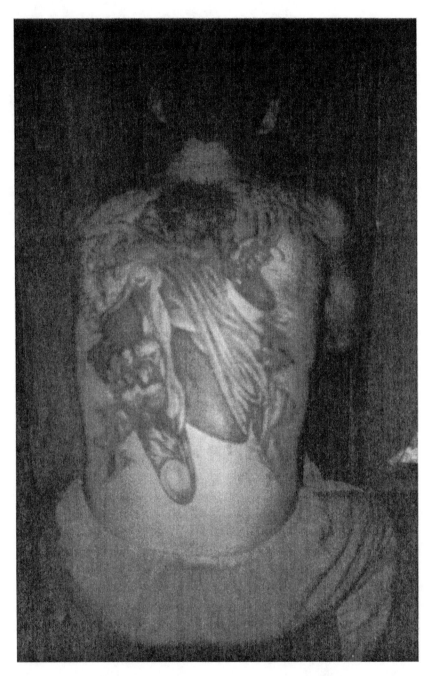

Forensic examination of a tattooed convict at the High Security Psychiatric Hospital, St Petersburg, 1994. Psikhiatricheskaia boln'nitsa so strogim nabliudeniem, g. Sankt Peterburg.

'would inculcate in them a sense of "collegiality"' and enable them to demonstrate that they belonged to criminal groupings by allowing them to 'uphold tradition'. Considerable peer pressure motivated some convicts to mark their own bodies; these individuals deemed that visible tattoos 'testified to their membership in the criminal world'.[64] Convicts placed a premium on tattooing their 'fingers so that [they] would be visible to everyone'.[65] As one inmate asserted, his tattoo enabled him to feel as if he was 'forever anointed' in the criminal underworld of Ingushiia's drug addicts.[66] Another exclaimed that his tattoo, which bore the inscription 'I will not forget my native mother' (Ne zabudu mat' rodinu) brought to mind that he had joined the 'thieves' family, which had become a mother' to him.[67] Thus, as one investigator emphasizes, 'the tattoo functions as a means of self-representation in a distinct clan.'[68]

Like the vagrant brand, tattoos also served as a criminal's 'calling card.'[69] Through the content of their tattoos, Soviet-era convicts conveyed specific socio-demographic information about themselves to other criminals. This included data about their crimes; the groupings to which they belonged and their status within these orders; their penchant for drug use and other habits that authorities deemed deviant; and the brave acts that they had committed in order to uphold their traditions. Convicts considered that the tattoo functioned as regalia that marked their 'ranking' (chinstvo) and attested to the fact that they actively upheld 'thieves' laws'. One convict called his tattoo his 'head dress'.[70] Another affirmed that

> tattooing is for us like evening wear embellished with [official] ribbons; the more we are tattooed, the greater importance we enjoy among our comrades. Conversely, the one who is not tattooed does not enjoy any influence; he is not considered a proper rogue and the gang doesn't respect him.[71]

Like their vagrant predecessors, twentieth-century Russian and Soviet convicts used bodily inscription to wrest control of authorities' power in two important ways. First, rather than allow officials to categorize them as deviant, convicts literally took power into their own hands to convert a mark of shame and deviance into that which endowed them with sovereignty. Thus, while convicts clearly associated the tattoo with the autocratic brand, they inverted official values, deriving considerable power from the idea that this inscription served as a means of marking and constructing their own identities and of ensuring that they remained distinct from honourable society.[72] By marking their own bodies, they perpetuated older Russian traditions that associated the 'juridical mark' and the brand with ownership, implicitly insisting that they owned their own bodies and consequently that the police were unable to regulate their lives and practices. They thus used the tattoo to endow convict particularism with a positive rather than negative valence.

Secondly, convicts actively mocked authorities' efforts to decode their tattoos. While police, representatives of the Ministry of Internal Affairs, medical personnel and criminologists have catalogued tattoos in order to detect and rout out criminality, they concede that this enterprise is largely futile. First, they note that tattoos are poor forensic tools because a convict may choose to mark and remark his body with additional identification-altering designs.[73] Moreover, these forensic efforts are also frustrated by the purposeful multivalence of convicts' tattoos. While, on the one hand, specialists suggest that tattoos provide authorities with a window on criminals' affiliations, they nonetheless recognize that the 'real' meaning of tattoos 'is comprehended only among criminals and drug addicts'. Alferov strives to decipher the tattoos that he encountered among Ingushiia's junkies in the late 1980s, yet ends up conveying the impression that the true significance of any tattoo is ultimately opaque and inaccessible to those outside the criminal's own sphere. He observes that words and images that possess a seemingly clear meaning in Russian express entirely different messages to criminals. For instance, tattoos of churches bearing numerous cupolas signify the number of times an individual was incarcerated rather than Orthodox belief.[74]

Convicts are also fond of using acronyms that subvert the seemingly univalent meanings of the words that they spell. The letters 'TON' do not connote 'tone' for junkies; rather these initials indicate membership in the 'secret society of drug addicts' (tainoe obshchestvo narkomanov); similarly, 'ZLO' does not translate into 'evil' but stands for 'I will avenge all that is legal' (za vse legal'nym otomshu). One specialist in contemporary tattooing practices recounts that an Armenian juvenile delinquent who sported the tattoo 'BOG' – conventionally translated as 'god' – did so not out of religiosity but because it meant 'I've been sentenced by the state' (byl osuzhden gosudarstvom). Moreover, even once observers recognize that these letters constitute acronyms rather than words, this does not mean that they can easily decipher their significance. For example, the tattoo 'SLON' does not mean 'elephant' in the criminal world, but can be translated variously as 'Death to the dogs – they will not be saved,' (smert' liagavym – oni ne spasutsia), 'Rogues love only the state' (Suki liubiat odno nachal'stvo), or 'the heart loves one forever' (serdtse liubit odnu naveki).[75] That tattoos are subject to multiple interpretations contributes to convicts' ability to keep the outside world at bay and thereby allows them to preserve their exclusivity.

Convicts' penchant for employing letters in their tattoos is of great significance. Even illiterate convicts derived meaning from these tattoos, the content of which echoes the acronymic brands employed by autocratic officials in the pre-revolutionary era.[76] The use of letters and acronyms allows criminals to perpetuate vagrants' tradition of actively nullifying the power that the state attempted to exert against outlaws, thereby turning the very technologies of oppression into ones of resistance. On the surface, tattoos such as the aforementioned 'BOG' or 'TUZ' – 'the prison is already familiar' (*tiur'ma uzhe znakoma*)[77] – suggest acceptance of authorities' power to try and convict those who commit offences and in so doing apparently reinforce state power. However, when convicts mark themselves in this manner, they attempt to resist this force by implying that they have control over the process of inscription. Convicts' fondness for tattooing their bodies with eagles, a brand employed by Peter the Great in the eighteenth century, seemingly functions in a similar manner.[78]

Tattooing appears to be a technology whereby Russian and Soviet convicts have asserted power and control over their own corporate identities and traditions. Yet, the point remains that this strategy of resistance reinscribes power relations even as it contests the hegemony of authorities. Russian officials' own ambivalence about the status of Siberia and the alienation of its exile population indubitably opened up space for vagrants to contest the status which authorities imputed to them. The status categories constructed by officials needed to accommodate a certain degree of flexibility, the boundaries of the Russian Empire and Siberia were subject to negotiation, and the project of administering these domains made it necessary for officials to rely on exiles and outsiders to settle Siberia. These ambiguities allowed convicts to draw on official methods of ascribing status in their efforts to constitute their own exclusive corporate identity.

Coopting official discourses concerning status, vagrants reinterpreted these in an effort to forge their own outlaw language of categorization and ranking. They assimilated many of the same technologies used by Imperial officials: they articulated explicit hierarchies, reenacted judicial and penal rituals, and inscribed the bodies of the fiercest convicts. In so doing, they sought to transform the negative valuation with which officials endowed the tattooed outlaw into a source of power and pride. Yet, convicts' unofficial language of categorization and status could never be entirely divorced from the official. Thus, just as administrators were unable to circumscribe vagrancy through branding and thereby monopolize authority over their subjects by assigning them to status categories, so too have convicts been unable to utilize corporeal markings to challenge fully the forces that strove to categorize and alienate them.

Convicts proved incapable of stripping from these technologies the negative connotations assigned to them by Russian authorities. While convict tattoos embody multivalence and thus defy easy interpretation by those unconnected with criminal spheres, they do remain potent markers of the outsider status of those who sport them. Moreover, by assimilating technologies of bodily inscription, convicts also implicitly accept the validity of official strategies of categorization, reinforcing these because they choose to classify and affiliate themselves in their own unofficial corporations even as they refuse to be pigeonholed by authorities. Thus, even as convicts assert ownership over their bodies by inscribing themselves with tattoos in their effort to contest officials' attempts to exert control over their subjects, convicts end up mimicking the very processes of subjection that they seek to undermine. Consequently, Russian and Soviet officials' power and vagrants' and convicts' resistance remain intertwined in a constant dynamic of interdependence; neither strategy can be fully comprehended without an analysis that accounts for the internal structure of the other.

12 On Display: Tattooed Entertainers in America and Germany

STEPHAN OETTERMANN

> He is a lowly guest in the meanest vaudevilles,
> Among the stamping she-devils, with their entwined tattoos.
> Their sharp-pronged forks lure him down the sweet shaft to hell,
> Bedazzled and befooled, but always mesmerized.
>
> HUGO BALL, 1915[1]

> The conference of delegates regrets the display in certain variety
> theatres of female bodies that are to all intents and appearances nude;
> they are celebrated as 'the gospel of beauty' but in fact are nothing
> more than intoxicating displays calculated to poison our youth.
>
> XITH CONGRESS OF THE GERMAN MORALITY LEAGUE, 1902[2]

The true home of the European tattoo – that mark whose very existence has been called into question – is, or rather was, the fairground and the market. It was here that bodies were put on display, and the glory and poverty of European tattooing can be best be measured on the decorated skin of Tsavella, La Belle Irène and the Great Omi.

'SAVAGE CANNIBALS'

Long before the (re)discovery of tattooing in the South Seas and the subsequent renaissance of Western tattooing in the nineteenth century, a common sight in the fairgrounds of Europe was the 'savage' who had been captured at the edges of the world, his body decorated with strange and indelible blue images. The theories that were proposed in those times to explain the meaning and purpose of these images have survived almost to the present day. In 1560, for example, French seamen captured a family of 'Eskimos' on the Greenland coast. The man put up a vigorous resistance and was killed; his wife and child were hauled back to Europe where they were put on exhibition in France and Germany. According to an illustrated handbill describing the 'Eskimo' woman to an astonished sixteenth-century public,

> the figures [on her face] are blue, blue like the heavens; the men put them on their womenfolk so that they may recognize them, for otherwise they traffic with one another like cattle; and these marks are not to be removed again by any means . . . Let us thank Almighty God for his beneficence, that he has declared himself to us by his Word, so that we are not like these savages and man-eaters.[3]

We do not know what became of these 'Eskimos', but the fate of another such 'savage', Prince Jeoly, is well known. Jeoly, or Giolo, was taken from the Philippine island of Meangis by the pirate and explorer William Dampier in 1691, and brought back to England. There he eventually succumbed to the cold, damp climate, and expired in Oxford from chickenpox. But before this he was widely put on show, first as a sensation for the London elite, including King William and Queen Mary, and later, leased to an impresario, to satisfy the curiosity of the gaping crowd at the Blew Boar's Head in Fleet Street. A contemporary copper engraving shows Jeoly surrounded by numerous snakes and other poisonous creatures, and a handbill distributed to the public claimed that

> The paint . . . is prepared from the Juice of a certain Herb, or Plant, peculiar to that Country, which they esteem infallible to preserve humane bodies from the deadly poison or hurt of any venomous Creatures whatsoever.[4]

Twenty-five years after this, two tattooed 'American Princes', allegedly captured 'on the coasts of Brazil' or else 'in Mexico', were offered for sale in London. A German sea-captain, Pecht, bought them and put them on display in France, Italy and Germany.

> Let it be known to all *Gentlemen, Ladies* and Connoisseurs of the *curious*: the two famous wild Indian Princes, *Sauase Oke Charinga* and *Tuskee Stanagee*, are come here to Breslau from the New World of *America*, and are to be greatly marvelled at on account of the many decorations to be found on their bodies. For their bodies are strewn all over with *Hieroglyphic* figures and Indian characters, these being so well drawn that there can be nothing to compare with them.

As always, there were sceptics who did not believe their own eyes: thus a contemporary report commented:

We are bound to point out that it is not entirely proven that these people are true Americans, but may be other personages in metamorphosis, for it is known that there are presently several examples of 'Americans' through whom an advantageous deception has been practised under this supposed name.

In spite of these doubts, the ruler of Saxony, Augustus the Strong, purchased the two Indians for 1000 taler in 1722 and brought them to his court. They were inducted into the protestant faith, and on 6 October 1725 were baptized in the Kreuzkirche in Dresden under the names Friedrich Christian and August Christian.[5] Thus liberated from their 'spiritual and physical slavery', civilized and reformed, the two princes were sent on as a gift to the Tsar of Russia in Petersburg.[6]

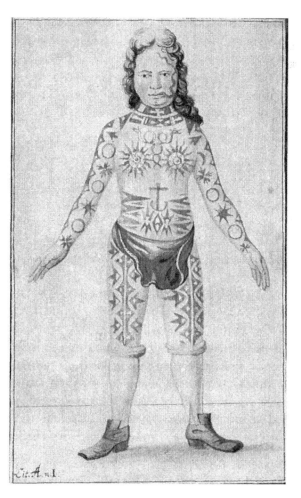

The 'American Prince'
Tuskee Stannagee, c. 1722,
watercolour.

Also 'princes' were the two South Sea islanders who were brought to England later in the eighteenth century, almost as if to illustrate the adoption into European languages of the borrowed word 'tatow'. Omai, the Tahitian prince brought back by Captain Cook in 1774, came to be a national treasure: newspapers printed his life story, the most celebrated artists painted his portrait, the popular theatre made him into a hero and a box-office hit, and learned men counted it an honour to shake his hand (which was not in fact heavily tattooed). Omai returned home with Cook's third expedition to his island, bearing rich gifts that included a barrel organ, an electric generator, a coat of mail and a suit of armour.[7] Some thirty years later, Timotiti, grandson of the famous chief Honu of the Marquesan island of Vaitahu, arrived in London in May 1799. The sixteen-year-old youth was tattooed across his face with a stripe that was supposed to be an admonition to revenge his father, who had been killed and eaten by his enemies. But the intended act of vengeance never took place: Timotiti fell into the hands of a group of ultra-zealous missionaries, who dragged him from one missionary event to another as an example of a particularly spectacular conversion. He died on 2 December 1802 in London, and was buried as John Butterworth, having been baptized with the name of the ship that had borne him away from his homeland.[8]

BORDER-CROSSINGS

The first white person in the long list of tattooed entertainers who imitated the 'savages' and exhibit themselves at fairgrounds was Jean Baptiste Cabris. Born in Bordeaux in 1780, Cabris had joined an English whaling ship in his childhood. When the ship sank off Nuku Hiva (in the Marquesas), he was rescued and taken in by the local inhabitants. Cabris adopted their language and customs; he underwent a crucial step in acculturation when he allowed himself to be tattooed, and he married the daughter of a lesser chief. He had virtually forgotten his mother tongue by the time the Russian admiral Krusenstern's expedition landed on Nuku Hiva in 1804, and had 'gone native to such a degree that his customs and his manner of living and thinking were almost indistinguishable from those of the indigenous people'.[9] Cabris returned to civilization with this expedition. Leaving Krusenstern to sail on to Japan, Cabris left the ship at the Russian settlement of Petropavlovsk, on the Kamchatka peninsula, and together with three other members of the crew took the long land route through Siberia back to Europe.

The strange fate of this man and the novelty of his tattooed body soon attracted wide interest. He performed savage dances in theatres in

Joseph Kabris, native of Bordeaux, 'Vice-King and Grand Judge of the Isle of Mendoça', c. 1818–19, watercolour, from Karl von den Steinen, Die Marquesaner und ihre Kunst (Berlin, 1925).

Moscow and St. Petersburg, and was greeted as a prodigy by all the notables of the empire . . . His facility in swimming, in which he excels almost as much as the natives of Nuku Hiva, has procured him a place as a swimming instructor with the naval cadet corps. Meanwhile he has almost forgotten the language of Nuku Hiva and has made unbelievably fast progress with French. The story of his erstwhile marriage to a royal princess and his heroic deeds on the island have now been embroidered with so many new elements designed for the ears of his European audience that he begins to sound like a second Münchhausen when he starts to tell his tales. At the present time [1811/12] he lives in Kronstadt.[10]

In 1817 Cabris made his way back to France, via appearances in the fairs and markets of central Europe. Under the title of 'Vice-King and Grand Judge of the Isles of Mendocaa' he waited upon Louis XVIII and Frederick William III, and subsequently he became the star of the 'Cabinet des Illusions' in Paris. An article in the *Petite chronique de Paris* reported in 1818 that,

> A farcical scene has just played itself out in a small theatre in the market of Orleans. The director had announced a play in which Munito, the intelligent dog, and the famous tattooed man Joseph Kabris [sic] were to perform together. Enraged that he was supposed to appear with a poodle, Kabris turned the theatre into a battlefield. Whereupon the Grand Judge of Nuku Hiva was hauled off to jail for a night, and then turned over to the municipal police.[11]

Cabris died in Valenciennes in 1821, and was buried there: he had taken great pains to ensure that his body was not handed over to the museum of Douai, which had wanted to prepare it as a scientific specimen.[12]

FANTASTIC BIOGRAPHIES

While Cabris was a genuine crossover between the savage and civilized worlds whose adventure-filled career was (more or less) exactly as he described it to his astonished public, the same could not be said of his immediate avatar. John Rutherford, a Bristolian who moved from fair to fair with a 'travelling caravan of wonders' in the 1820s and 1830s, deliberately constructed his vitae to fit what had by now become the public's declared expectations. He claimed that he had been taken captive by Maoris in New Zealand in 1816 and forcibly tattooed – a procedure that normally lasted over a period of years but which in his case was executed so speedily that he almost died. Following this involuntary initiation he was adopted by the tribe of his tormentors, married the chief's daughter, and became a chief himself. After six years of this captivity, however, he contrived to escape onto a British ship that had anchored off the island, and was able to return home. This nerve-wracking tale, retailed by numerous English newspapers in 1828, helped Rutherford to amass a fair income as he took himself and his story from fairground to fairground. His biography appeared as a book in 1830, under the title *The Great White Chief John Rutherford* (it was reprinted in 1847 and translated into German), and was the source of some confusion in the historiography of New Zealand.[13] For Rutherford's story may have been 'true' by poetic standards, and it had a certain status and logic in the world of fair and circus, but it was unable to withstand the investigations of sceptics and others who were immune to the romantic fantasies of the day. In fact, Rutherford had left his ship voluntarily, had never been taken captive or forcibly tattooed, but was one of the many beachcombers and tramps who were roaming the Pacific islands at the time. The illustration on his handbill shows that his face was tattooed in Maori 'moko' fashion, but the rest of his body was decorated in the Tahitian style, while the designs on his chest had probably been applied on Rotuma (in the Fiji islands).

The first tattooed man to exhibit himself in America was the Irishman James F. O'Connell, whose story was as sensational and murky as those of his fellow showmen in Europe. O'Connell had been living for several years on the small Micronesian island of Ponape when an American ship picked him up and brought him to New York. Immediately after arriving there in 1835, he took an engagement with the circus impresario Dan Rice, and for the next twenty years toured in travelling shows in the eastern and southern states. He probably owed his considerable success to the contemporary best-seller *A Narrative of Shipwreck Captivity and Suffering of Horace Holden and Benjamin Nute*, which went through several editions between 1836 and 1841.[14] In this book Holden, who was not himself a showman, described how a band of savages had captured and forcibly tattooed him and his comrades; the others did not survive the ordeal. They had been tattooed from head to toe, and only Holden's desperate pleas spared his face from the same fate. By contrast, O'Connell did have his face tattooed, perhaps to outdo his literary counterpart, though this was very unusual among the inhabitants of Ponape in whose traditional style he was otherwise decorated. It was said that women and children who encountered him on the road died of shock, thinking they had seen the devil incarnate.[15]

SHOW BUSINESS

To make big business out of a simple piece of skin required the nerve and the commercial genius of a P. T. Barnum, the greatest showman in the world. Barnum had already converted other freaks and sports of Nature and art into the stuff of dreams (and of nightmares), and it was this master of artifice who brought the tattooed out of the disorganized world of the fairground and into the place they henceforth occupied: the sideshow. They took their place as 'characters' among the rest of the circus performers – the midgets, bearded ladies and giants, the 'waistless' women and the fat ladies – and the tattooed man or tattooed lady became a profession. W. L. Alden, an early expert on freaks, described Barnum as the man

> that invented the tattooed business, and for a while it was the best line of business in the profession. Every museum was bound to have a Tattooed Girl, with a yarn about her having been captured by the Indians and tattooed when she was a little girl.[16]

The first tattooed man to be made famous by Barnum, the Greek Alexandrino, remained the most celebrated exponent of the genre in the entire nineteenth century. Alexandrino, who also went by the Turkish name 'Captain Georgi' and the Suliote 'Tsavella', claimed to belong to a race of wild and bold mountain men from the Balkans; with his beautiful and mysterious tattoos, he was the model for all subsequent showmen who exhibited their skin to the public. In Germany he was usually known as 'The Tattooed Man of Burma', while in America he appeared in 1870, 1876 and 1880 as Captain Constantenus, Prince Constentenus, 'The Turk', or 'The Living Picture Gallery' in Barnum's 'Great Traveling World's Fair'. He was paid a thousand dollars a week, and employed his own 'lecturer' who usually began his patter with the words 'And this tattooed man is always much admired by the ladies . . .' Alexandrino was fully aware that his public was intrigued not only by the 388 images of fantastic animals tattooed, in Burmese style, from the soles of his feet to his hairline, but also by his amazing stories: that he was an arms trader and treasure-seeker who had been taken prisoner in the land of the Mougongs and forced to undergo the 'Chinese tattoo torture'. 'Both the images and the man', wrote a German illustrated magazine, 'are an unsolved mystery, a puzzle picture from the Far East, in the truest sense of the word.'[17]

Alexandrino was taken up by scientific and medical societies in Europe, and was inscribed in the medical literature as 'Homo notis compunctis'. As a result, even though he disappears from view after 1892, his image survives in a splendid coloured engraving in Hebra's *Atlas der Hautkrankheiten* (dermatological atlas).[18] His successor was John Hayes, who appeared in 'Barnum and Bailey's, the Greatest Sideshow on Earth'. Hayes, born in Ausonia (Connecticut) in 1864, took the biographies of his tattooed predecessors which had till then been sited in the South Seas or the Far East, and transposed them to the 'Wild West'. His story was that he had joined the army at the age of fourteen as a drummer-boy, and had been taken prisoner during the Indian wars. He lived among his captors for a time, and got married, before finally managing to escape. As proof Hayes displayed his 780 tattoos, which he claimed had been forced on him during a 154-day period of

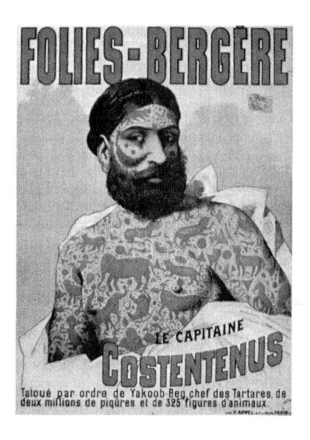

Lithographic poster for
Le Capitaine Costentenus,
Paris, *c.* 1890.

'torture'. In reality, these tattoos were the work of Samuel O'Reilly, the famous American tattooist and later inventor of the electric tattoo machine.[19]

The model for Hayes's tale was presumably the fate of Olive Oatman, whose family had been attacked by a band of Yavapi on the westward trail in 1851. Most of the migrants were killed, but the thirteen-year-old Olive and her younger sister were abducted by the Yavapi and sold to a group of Mohave Indians. In 1856 Olive was identified as a white by a government official near Fort Yuma, and seized back from the Indians (her sister had died in the meantime). Her story became the stuff of Hollywood legend, but, unlike all the tales invented by her successors, Olive Oatman's was true. A contemporary photograph shows her in a black dress, her hair tied back in a tight bun. On her chin – pretty, but incongruous next to her European clothing – are the typical tattoos of a Mohave woman: five vertical lines with two or three triangular designs on the two outer lines. In order to make these rather modest tattoos more marketable, Miss Oatman's promoter published a sensationally written account of her capture, her life among the Indians and her eventual liberation. The book was sold in the course of an extended public 'lecture trip' she made across America; it went through a number of editions, and served as the prototype for the stylized life-stories of her numerous imitators.[20]

Not the first of these imitators, but the first to make an appearance in Europe, was La Belle Irène (Irene Woodward, 1863–1916). She was first seen in Castan's Panoptikum in Berlin, where the German-Polish impresario Rusinski gave out the following version of her life history. La Belle Irène was said to have been born in 1870 in Dallas (Texas), where she lived a perilous life in the 'jungle'. In order to protect her from abduction by Sioux Indians, her father hit on the idea of having his child tattooed in blue and red over her whole body. According to a contemporary observer, these skin decorations betrayed 'a certain artistic taste':[21] they included butterflies, flowers, Indians, suns, eyes, insects, rattlesnakes and eagles, as well as entire scenes drawn from life, such as 'The Sailor's Farewell'. 'A charmingly tattooed necklace' was hung with a medal on which the name Irene was likewise tattooed. There were also proverbs like 'Nothing without labour', 'Never despair', and 'I live and die for those I love', while on her back were emblems for faith, love and hope. The number of individual images totalled four hundred – even her toes were adorned with little stars and crosses – and the whole oeuvre was said to have taken eight years to complete. Professor Dr. Johannes Ranke, who presented La Belle Irène to the Munich Anthropological Society in 1891, found the 'images done in red and blue colour . . . most artistically executed . . . This pretty young woman's skin glows and has the feel of velvet; her nakedness seems beside the point.'[22] The Berlin Anthropological Society too, where she had been presented a few months earlier, judged her to be 'really most artistically tattooed on all visible parts of her body', and only recorded some regret at her modesty: 'She exposed only her naked arms, her neck, shoulders, and her legs to just above the knee, however, since she was wearing a kind of dancer's costume for the presentation.'[23]

La Belle Irène was the last professional tattooed entertainer to secure this kind of scientific audience (apart from anything else, a good publicity stunt). There was already some scepticism at her appearance in Berlin: one of the more well-travelled participants observed that

> in every city in the United states, from New York to San Francisco, in any of the innumerable little dime museums, one can see men and women tattooed from head to toe, along with living and waxwork eskimos, idiots, calves with five legs, leopard-spotted negroes, giants, dwarves, invisible men and albinos. Some horror story is always touted

about their abduction by Indians . . . The tattoos range from the worst kind of amateur work to images of exceptional beauty. The speaker remembers having seen on the back of a blonde girl Murillo's well-known Madonna executed with the greatest artistic skill. Irène's tattoos are far inferior to those of many of her colleagues.[24]

In fact, tattooed entertainers were no longer a rarity in America, though they continued to enjoy public popularity. The most celebrated of these included Miss Stella, Lady Pictura, Mr and Mrs Williams, Calavan (who was also ready to tattoo inspired spectators), Mellivan and Maud Arizona. Around 1900 Frank Howard (d. c. 1920) was appearing with Barnum and Bailey, with a story virtually identical to the one told by his predecessor John Hayes. His sister Annie Howard, who appeared with him, had herself been tattooed by the famous savages of the South Seas – allegedly. In point of fact, she had no more been shipwrecked in the Pacific Ocean than her brother had been a drummer-boy in New England. Her tattoos were the work of the New York tattooist O'Reilly and of her brother; and he himself had been decorated by Steve Lee and the German-American tattooist Martin Hildebrandt.[25]

At first there was a good living to be made in the tattoo entertainment business, with earnings usually in the range of $100 to $200 weekly. Soon, however, it was not enough just to be tattooed. Barnum, with his usual keen nose for business, was already presenting tattooed dwarfs, fat ladies, wrestlers and sword-swallowers in the mid 1880s. From 1890 it was increasingly common to find tattooed Indians who also had to perform as conjurers, mind-readers, jugglers and so on, because the spectacle of their skin alone was no longer enough to attract an audience. In 1900, for instance, 'Austin and Stone's Museum' presented a white juggler whose Indian 'squaw' assistant was 'tattooed with many genuine designs . . . the best North American Indian work ever achieved', as the posters proclaimed. Already in 1880 entire tattooed families were apparently performing, father, mother, children – and pets: one of these families was accompanied by a Great Dane as a special attraction. A certain Captain Burt Thomson tried to imitate this by having a lap-dog tattooed for his sideshow on Coney Island, but it was stolen after the first performance. The public made up for this disappointment by flocking to see a tattooed cow being displayed in another booth.[26]

These excesses were unknown in Germany, which was about ten or fifteen years behind the American tattoo boom. But here, too, countless women followed in the pioneering footsteps of La Belle Irène: Ruth-Sylvia, Surita, the Englishwoman Annie Frank, 'the pearl of the Rhine' Marie Theissen, Alwanda, Wallona Aritta, La Bella Wilhelma, Creola, Jenny, Angelika,

Mia Vera, Bella Angora and so on. The women always gave themselves the most exotic-sounding names, to go with their astounding life-stories and the incredible advertising copy blazoned on their billboards – on Dyita Salome's, for example, one could read

> Salome/known as the Blue Woman/the only living being tattooed in 14 colours/*Oriental Beauty*/Salome's body represents a value of/*30,000 marks*/won awards in Berlin, Vienna, Paris, London, New York, Petersburg etc./Salome will pay/*10,000 marks reward*/to anyone who has ever seen a comparable array of colours on one body.[27]

Among the more famous tattooed performers were the American couple Frank and Emma de Burgh, who appeared in Castan's Panoptikum in Berlin following La Belle Irène in 1890/1. They also performed in France, but were normlly engaged by Barnum and Bailey. On Frank's 'massive and bulging torso' Emma de Burgh could be seen, striking a relaxed pose, above her the words 'Forget Me Not', and wreathed by fruits, flowers and animals; on his left arm Frank had a sailor's head, on his right the bust of a woman wearing a hat, and from his hips to his feet a variety of arabesques 'in the Indian style'. Emma de Burgh, who claimed she had let herself be tattooed for love of her husband, bore a total of 250 designs, with the name of her husband resplendent just above her bosom. Like many American performers, the couple had been tattooed by O'Reilly, though the designs on their backs were allegedly the work of the Japanese *Hori* Chyo of Tokyo, the 'emperor' among the various 'kings' of tattooing. Frank's showed a tapestry-like portrayal of a crucifixion scene, 'Mount Calvary', in subdued colours; Emma's, the 'Last Supper' after Leonardo da Vinci.[28]

Tattooed couples seemed to exert a unique fascination on the public. The de Burghs had many imitators – in Germany, for example, Carlo (originally from Erfurt) and his wife Anita. Rivalli, whose spouse appeared as a conjurer, and who hit the peak of her fame around 1900, reemerged in 1926 as a hideous monster under the title of 'La Bête Inconnue'. The American Mildred Hull, who had allegedly tattooed herself, committed suicide in order to avoid the same fate.[29] There were also of course tattooed men who displayed themselves for a living, but they were less common than the women because they could not count on the public's goodwill and curiosity. A surprising number of tattooed men on the German scene were Czechs, whose main trade was to perform as fakirs, fire-eaters or acrobats. Among them were Roustan, Ramses and Don Manuelo, 'the best and truly most artistically tattooed of men, resplendent in many colours – such beauty, artistry and grace'.[30]

Salome, the only living beauty tattooed in seven colours, c. 1905, German postcard.

EROTIC ATTRACTIONS

In an article on 'Erotic Tattoos' published in the journal *Anthropophyteia* in 1907, Hugo Ernst Luedecke writes about

> the sideshowmen's world . . . a world of the degenerate, of boosters and patter-men, of the tattooed and fakirs (people 'who don't bleed', i.e. when stuck with a knife they are able to remove it so fast that no blood flows) . . . Onetime pimps can be found here often enough – fellows 'on the *qui-vive*', tough, muscular men, lusty and potent, smart and unshockable. Many with a predilection for being tattooed have found that they can now make their living from this alone.[31]

Luedecke was evidently very struck by characters such as William, the fakir Hugo Schmidt, the sailor Mr Line and Frank Marwood:

It is the misery of modern culture that it atrophies the instincts, which
are after all the root of all life. Our poets twitter their love songs, i.e.
they practice intellectual masturbation, instead of pursuing the powerful life of the body; our young ladies expose their breasts in public at
balls and the like, without having the courage to surrender themselves
freely and self-confidently. At least the circles where tattooing reigns
have escaped this kind of half-heartedness. Strong in their instincts,
they acknowledge no law of the reasonable; power and toughness are
their 'love', its enjoyment consecrated by alcohol. And their girls? They
jeer at everything 'refined' or 'intellectual', they suck those who have
these qualities dry to the last drop and leave them with VD as a
memento; they are the 'gilded flies that invade the palaces of the
wealthy' (Zola), but they can love! They love with their instincts: whatever is brutal, mean, strong, instinct merging with instinct.[32]

The world of tattooing so extravagantly praised by Luedecke reached its apogee in Germany in the years before World War I, as is evidenced by the wealth of advertisements in the trade magazine *Der Impresario* as well as numerous souvenir postcards.[33] 'It is the fashion', wrote L. Stieda in 1911,

for many people to tattoo themselves as a means to earn their living. We can see tattooed females in every fairground and exhibition, not excepting the Munich Oktoberfest. They have submitted to the painful torture of tattooing in order to exhibit their body for payment. Usually only the arms and legs are exposed, at most the neck as well – I have no doubt that such women have tattoos on their back and abdomen too, but one is never allowed to see these covered areas of the body, since the police forbid it! The tattoo designs are extremely varied. Sometimes the entire body, or what one can see of it, is covered with portraits: emperors, kings, composers, coats of arms of all kinds, flowers. Most are very pretty and in bright colours. Here tattooing has a genuine material value: it makes money.[34]

In spite of these descriptions, it is hard to locate sources which could tell us exactly how the tattooed artist conducted his or her performance, and how it was received by the audience. What did they actually do? How did they entertain their public? Did they just display themselves, or did they strike poses? Did they dance or sing? Did they narrate their tragic life-history, always the same story over and over again? Or did they sometimes offer a novel variation of some kind? Certainly there were some of these. Celly d'Astra had her tale of forcible tattooing by a Svengali-like master; Hugo Schmidt represented himself as a fakir; Anetta Nerona, who was tattooed with celebrities such as Goethe, Schiller, Bismarck, Kaiser Wilhelm II and Richard Wagner, also performed as a magician, athlete, snake-charmer and musical virtuoso. Similarly, Sabella Anita was also a wrestler and athlete, and touted herself as the 'Blue Woman, today's youngest and most travelled tattooed woman'. Meanwhile, the less professional tattooed entertainers, like the bearded ladies or the less well-endowed fat ladies, probably worked intermittently as bar-girls or barkers in second-rate sideshows and dives, passing by imperceptible stages into prostitution.

Because the women had to undress to some extent in order to show off their body art, their appearances must have had something in common with an erotic show, like an early form of strip-tease. 'Sylvia' seems to have offered her audience a kind of dance of the seven veils, which caused some raised eyebrows. The posters, handbills, trade cards and postcards advertising these performers were deliberately inoffensive, in order to avoid giving the police an excuse to intervene and confiscate them. Working conditions were hard enough in the years before World War I, when local morality leagues were assiduous in their unofficial inspections of fairs and sideshows; they suspected traffic in women and prostitution wherever they looked. Thus 'Suleika, the fantastic tattooed woman', a painting by Otto Dix from 1920, captures better than any printed photograph the mood of the Orient and the harem that was surely intentionally invoked by the exhibition of tattooed women. The Dadaist Hugo Ball paid a visit in Zürich in 1915 to the exhibition of 'Nandl, the Beauty of Tirol', whose trade card depicted her chastely and with downcast eyes, despite her raised dress. In his diary he noted that:

> The name of the tattooed woman is Frau Koritzky, though she calls herself Nandl. She has a closet in a beer-hall, from which she urges

Otto Dix, *Suleika the Fantastic Tattooed Woman*, 1920, watercolour.

guests to come over to her. The fee is 30 centimes, or free for artists. She bares her bosom, arms and upper thighs (decency is not the issue, art tips the scales), and is covered all over with portraits, waterlilies, twining flowers and wreathed foliage. Her husband accompanies her on his zither. On her posterior are two butterfly wings – a delicate and aesthetic touch. Somewhere I once read of a tattooed Indian who had the names of her lovers pricked into her skin. That's not the case here. On the contrary, Nandl's portraits offer a course in the history of German literature and music; they evoke education, not the erotic ... The blue velvet figures in her flesh are not unattractive and offer a kind of primitive satisfaction.[35]

'They evoke education, not the erotic': the dilemma of European tattooing could hardly be described more precisely. Sublimation was the inevitable result of the cultural defamation that overwhelmed tattooing as its alleged association with degeneration and criminality became pervasive. But only in some places did defamation tip over into a more explicit policy of official repression.

A NEW MORALITY

To establish some kind of official control over the curious fascination emanating from the tattoo world – a fascination which viewers found hard to justify even to themselves – authorities resorted to ordinances and bans, in Germany at any rate. In 1911, for example, according to the *Leipziger Rundschau*, the police intervened to ban the appearance of a fully tattooed woman, and official measures against the tattooed were to become even more severe in Germany in the interwar years, as we shall see.[36] Elsewhere tattooed entertainers were left unmolested, though the profession was in any case entering its period of decline. France still had its 'living tapestry', Ricardo; the USA its Betty Broadbent and others – in fact there was still scarcely an American circus which, in true Barnum and Bailey tradition, did not have its 'tattooed lady'. But even there the decline was setting in, announced by the 'World Congress of Tattooed Men' arranged by a New York Dime Museum, which exhausted a satiated public interest. Nevertheless, in 1930 Albert Parry could still count almost 300 tattooed showmen in America.[37]

The finest and most celebrated tattooed showman of these twentieth-century twilight years was undoubtedly the 'Zebra Man', who also called himself the Great Omi, after the Pacific islander whom Cook had brought to England some two hundred years earlier. Before he fulfilled the dream of the

Zebra Man, he was said to have been a major in the English army, who exchanged his uniform for the flea-circus after the war. George Burchett, the 'King of Tattooists', tattooed the Great Omi and tells his story in his memoirs. The process took, with interruptions, more than seven years to complete between 1927 and 1934: three sittings a week, in which no more than three inches a day could be tattooed. Burchett estimates the number of pricks that Omi had to endure in his face and head alone as some fifteen million, plus 500 million pricks over the rest of his body.[38] The finished Zebra Man appeared between the wars in England and America, where he was one of the most highly paid attractions in the entire world of sideshows. His engagements included Ripley's 'Believe It or Not' show, and, in 1954, a last appearance at the 'World Congress of Human Oddities' in London.

The situation had developed very differently in Germany, where a model of clean-cut integrity and discipline squeezed the cultural space available for bodily exhibition. The fashion for tattooed ladies dissipated after World War I, to be replaced by the marble-white bodies of revue girls: instead of a display of ornamented bodies, the display was the chorus-line of drilled, synchronized physiques itself. In 1932 the authoritarian Prussian government headed by Bracht issued a decree that effectively forced public displays out of existence. As the *Berliner Tageblatt* reported in September 1932, under the headline 'Tattooed Girls – Bracht-Decree Nixes Show':

> Fräulein N. had made her way with a variety troupe to Egypt, where she was able to entertain the inhabitants of Cairo and Alexandria with the uninterrupted sight of her fully tattooed body. The troupe's leader also had something unusual to offer: partly from preference, partly as a business proposition, he lived in women's clothes, which made a delightful contrast to his otherwise masculine appearance. Hassan, an enterprising African restaurant-owner, had expected these two attractions to make him a handsome profit. But [when] the whole theatre set burned down (cause unknown) . . . the ambisexual entrepreneur and Fräulein N. had to take ship back to Europe prematurely. They trusted that their homeland would show the same enthusiasm for the special attractions of a tattooed girl as it had in the past. But they had not allowed for the new morality that had meanwhile broken out in Germany, and which now threatens their business.[39]

Fräulein N.'s living was ruined: the finest examples of her skin decoration were located on parts of the body which Bracht's decree had now strictly banned from public display.

One year later, in 1933, a Frøken Ingeborg from Denmark – evidently unaware of the sea-change that Germany had undergone in the meantime – inserted an advertisement in the *Leipziger Zeitung* seeking an engagement for 'the Star of the North ... [the] award-winning best-tattooed woman with her lovely daughter'.[40] It is unlikely that she found employment; and the Nazi purge only became more radical and drastic. Thus in 1938 one could read in a Berlin newspaper:

> The police have received instructions to take the severest measures against this kind of excess in the sideshow trade. These measures are to be heartily applauded. In future, shows that offend against the people's values or contradict the objectives of the National Socialist state will be banned ... The decree empowering the police lists point by point what will be regarded as impermissible from now on. This includes displays of human abnormalities or hereditary disabilities calculated to arouse disgust, for example so-called fish-people, crab-people, bird-people, paralyzed people, animal people ('hay-eaters') and so on. Any performer whose physical or mental health requires it is to be admitted to a hospital or asylum, according to the regulations in force.[41]

This regulation covered tattooed performers as well. Those who could fled abroad, where their talents were still welcomed. How many of those who stayed behind ultimately fell victim to the Nazis' euthanasia program, which killed over 100,000 elderly, incurable or mentally and physically disabled hospital and asylum patients between 1939 and 1941, we will probably never know. But in Germany itself, the climate of disreputability that had surrounded tattooed showmen since virtually their first appearance reached a uniquely murderous conclusion. It wiped this harmless entertainment from the face of the country and, until recently, from public memory and esteem as well.

13 The Changing Image of Tattooing in American Culture, 1846–1966

ALAN GOVENAR

The representation of tattooing in popular culture in the USA has been a barometer of public opinion and its relationship to the growth of the tattoo profession. From the mid-nineteenth century, when tattooing first gained popularity among American sailors and merchant seamen, to the end of World War II, popular studies focused on the origins of tattooing in non-Western cultures, its appeal among the different branches of the military, especially the army and navy, its correlations to social status, and its ramifications in behavioural patterns. During this period tattooing was perpetuated ostensibly as a folk art form with an imagery that was traditional and that reflected different elements of popular culture. This essay considers this ongoing commentary in the popular press in the context of official regulations in the armed forces, the evolving repertory of tattoo designs, and the oral accounts of tattoo artists and heavily tattooed performers in the circus and carnival. It chronicles the demise of tattooing after World War II, and concludes by examining the factors that contributed to the revival of tattooing in the 1960s.

TATTOOING IN THE POPULAR PRESS

The increased popularity of tattooing in Western Europe and the United States in the nineteenth century generated studies of it by anthropologists, physicians and popular writers. Anthropologists, such as A. W. Franks, A. Lacassagne, W. Joest, R. Fletcher and G. R. Stetson, were chiefly concerned with the practice in 'savage' non-Western cultures.[1] By contrast, physicians, such as F. F. Maury and C. W. Dulles, examined the role that tattooing needles might have in communicating syphilis and other diseases.[2] British popular writers, such as Tighe Hopkins, R. J. Stephen, Gambier Bolton and Oliphant Smeaton, tended to have a more historical perspective, discussing the 'savage origins' of tattooing and exploring the 'mysterious' and 'queer' manifestations of the practice among royalty as well as the rank and file.[3]

In America some of the first articles on tattooing appeared in *Scientific American*. The earliest of these articles, by T. W. Dodd of Walsington, England (May 1891), concerned the removal of three 'very indelible tattoo marks by applying nitric acid with the stopper of the bottle . . . just sufficient to cover the stain so as to avoid making a larger scar than needful'.[4] In contrast to Dodd's method, later *Scientific American* articles discuss the methods developed by French physicians, Variot (September 1891), Baillot (January 1896) and Brunet (May 1899).[5] Essentially, the methods proposed by these physicians are similar in that they all involve the use of acids to remove the tattooed skin. It is apparent from these articles that an undetermined number of persons were, as *Scientific American* (May 1899) points out, 'with advancing years anxious to be relieved of the too persistent records which they then no longer look upon as ornamental'.[6]

Between 1891 and 1903 seven further articles on tattooing were published in *Scientific American*. Of these, four dealt with tattoo removal and three with the different cultures in which tattooing was practised, including Australia, New Zealand, Marquesas Islands, New Guinea, Colombia, Canary Islands, Japan, Laos and Burma.[7] Overall these articles are inconclusive and devote little more than a paragraph to each culture, examining the methods of tattooing (by 'burns, incision, and fine punctures') and the formal characteristics of tattoo designs (line, symmetry and pattern). With regard to practices in the West, there are few substantive remarks. Tattooing among Christian pilgrims in Loreto, Italy, high society in Europe, England and North America, soldiers, sailors, thieves and 'lower class' Westerners are mentioned in passing, but never adequately explained. The general tone of disapproval is conveyed in the following comment from a 1903 article:

> Among us, the art of tattooing is left to the lower class; so it is a degraded art. The representations are coarse, and as a general thing, poorly executed. Sometimes the artist is capable of drawing very fine artistic figures that are the admiration of physicians who have an opportunity of seeing them. But such cases are becoming rarer and tattooing has become gross and vile, like every despised art.[8]

The relationship between the popular press and the actual demographics of tattooing in America is unclear. The few available studies took the armed forces as their subject, and this almost certainly skews the findings. In 1908, the anthropologist A. T. Sinclair wrote that tattooing in America was increasing; he estimated that 95 per cent of the 26th US Infantry and 90 per cent of the sailors serving on American men-of-war were tattooed.[9] In 1909, the US Navy issued a circular stating that 'indecent or obscene tattooing is cause for rejection, but the applicant should be given an opportunity to alter the design, in which event he may, if otherwise qualified, be accepted'.[10] Five years later, a naval surgeon, A. Farenholt, made public the results of his twelve-year study of tattooing practices of men in the navy. Farenholt estimated that about 60 per cent of those he observed were tattooed, and reported that patriotic and sea-emblems had become less popular: 'all sorts of lettering, including lucky numbers, important dates, happy mottoes, and wordy tributes to lost comrades or past glories, held first place in the navyman's favor'.[11]

Tattooing had been an acceptable means of expressing devotion and loyalty to country during the Civil War, but by the beginning of World War I, military authorities were attempting to discourage the practice. In 1918, Major General O'Ryan banned tattooing for soldiers in the National Guard Empire Division; according to the New York Times, O'Ryan wanted to upgrade the image of his men.[12] Tattooing was increasingly considered 'barbarous', and unsuitable for 'civilized' armed forces. Moreover, tattoo designs of this period were becoming more erotic. For example, women in tattoos were often nude and posed in a sexually suggestive manner, while in the nineteenth century women in tattoos were usually clothed, although they were sometimes depicted in tight corsets with plunging necklines that accentuated their breasts. In addition to the view that tattoos were immoral, there was also some official concern about hygienic conditions in tattoo shops. Yet Farenholt, in twelve years of study, had not found any evidence of infection, transmission of disease, or blood poisoning due to tattooing.[13]

THE GROWTH OF THE TATTOO PROFESSION

While the popular press was ambivalent about the public acceptance of tattooing, the tattoo profession was beginning to establish itself in cities around America. The earliest recorded professional tattoo artist in America was Martin Hildebrandt, who claimed to have opened his first shop in 1846 and reportedly 'marked thousands of sailors and soldiers' during the Civil War. In the 1870s, Hildebrandt operated an atelier on Oak Street in New York (between Oliver and James Streets). However, little is known about the nature of his tattoos or the designs he used.[14]

In 1875, Samuel F. O'Reilly opened a tattoo shop in Chatham Square in the Bowery section of New York. O'Reilly's career is better documented than Hildebrandt's, though principally through the oral accounts of the tattoo artists he trained, including Ed Smith and Charlie Wagner.[15] His principal contribution to the profession was the invention of the electric tattoo machine around 1890. The electric tattoo machine (patterned after the rotary mechanism of a sewing machine) not only quickened the process and decreased the pain involved, but facilitated greater detail and subtlety in colouration and shading. With the increased technical proficiency in tattooing itself, the quality of the drawings and paintings on which they were based also improved. Tattoo artists during this period were generally trained through an informal apprenticeship system. Aspiring tattooists often solicited the help of established practitioners.

One of the most remarkable tattoo artists working in the early 1900s in America was Gus Wagner (no relation to Charlie Wagner), born in Marietta, Ohio in 1872. Wagner left Marietta in 1896 and spent the next six years travelling around the world as a merchant seaman. He learned to tattoo from the natives of Borneo and Java, and according to an article in the *Marietta Daily Journal* (27 June 1902), he returned to Ohio with his body covered with '264 designs of tattooing upon his skin'. In an article in the *Newark* (Ohio) *Tribune*, Wagner was acclaimed as 'one of the greatest globetrotters in the country':

> Mr. Gus Wagner, globetrotter and tattoo artist brother of Nick Wagner of Pine Street is in the city and will remain here for a short time. For the present, he will locate at 15 South Side of the Square, where all who desire to see his work and to take advantage of this skill can find him. He's an artist in his line and a visit to him will satisfy one that he can do what he claims. Tattooing is quite a fad and many ladies as well as gentlemen have adopted it and their persons bear everlasting symbols of the art. Mr. Wagner came here from Marietta where he tattooed 460 persons, giving satisfaction in each case.[16]

Over the course of his life, Wagner amassed extensive documentation of his travels and exploits in newspaper clippings, letters, business cards, stamps and ephemera that attracted his interest. Later in his life, he assembled these into a leather-bound book, inscribed with the title 'Souvenirs of the Travels and Experiences of the Original Gus Wagner: Professional Globetrotter, World's Champion Hand Tattoo Artist and Tattooed Man'. Wagner never used electric tattoo machines, but instead relied on the hand-carved tools bound with needles that he made as a merchant seaman. These were patterned after the methods used by the indigenous cultures in which he first observed tattooing. His repertory of designs, however, derived more from images of American popular culture of the nineteenth century than

Papa (Gus Wagner) and Mr Neff, Christmas 1940.

from the traditional motifs found in Java, Borneo and in the islands of the South Seas.

Overall, Wagner's tattoo designs are very similar to those made by C. H. Fellowes, who apparently was his contemporary. However, all that is known about Fellowes is contained in his sketchbook and hand tattooing kit, which were found in 1966 by a Providence, Rhode Island, antique dealer and later sold to a private collector. In 1971 a selection of Fellowes' designs were published in a book compiled by anthropologist William Sturtevant. Sturtevant divides Fellowes' repertory into a series of categories: 'America First', 'Sweethearts and Wicked Women', 'For Those In Peril On the Sea', 'Heroes and Other Strangers', 'Over the Bounding Main', and 'Friendship and the Familiar'. Together, these categories elucidate the thematic content of Fellowes' work, but do little to explain the context in which he practised tattooing.[17]

Presumably, Fellowes was itinerant like Gus Wagner, who derived most of his livelihood by making relatively small, isolated tattoos on different people. In Kansas City, Wagner recalled that he tattooed 'lodge emblems' on the arms of hundreds, and that 'about three hundred women have been numbered' among his customers.

A popular idea among women [he said] was to have a beauty spot tattooed on the cheek or chin. If seen, women paste a small square bit of black cork plaster on their cheek or chin to mark a beauty spot. My method of putting it on with black ink is much more substantial. In fact, it lasts a lifetime and can not be removed without leaving a scar.

In an article in the *Kansas City Times* in 1905, Wagner remarked that in addition to small tattoos, he had also

tattooed several persons' entire bodies and charged them about three hundred dollars a piece for it. A job of that kind takes about three weeks if the patient is a good subject. To accomplish the work in that time I work nine hours a day.[18]

In 1906 Wagner began tattooing his wife, Maude Stevens Wagner, in Los Angeles, and by the following year he had completely covered her with tattoos. Together, the Wagners travelled around the country, exhibiting themselves as tattooed attractions in circuses and carnivals, and tattooing others whenever possible. They either rented space in empty storefronts, or set up in other places of business: in one scrapbook photograph, they posed in front of an ice cream shop with banners advertising their skills. Generally, Gus Wagner displayed his repertory of tattoo designs on sheets of canvas and illustration board that he either hung on the wall of his temporary tattoo shops and/or had bound into small books. These designs are generally called 'flash' in the argot of the circus and carnival because of the immediacy of their appeal. Wagner advertised that he used 'the latest colors and antiseptic needles' and provided 'thousands of original designs to select from, including oriental, biblical, lodge emblems, landscape pictures, photographs, etc.'.[19]

Although Wagner was a hand-tattooist, it is likely that most of his contemporaries, like 'Lew the Jew' Alberts in New York and Charlie Western in Seattle, who utilized electric machines, employed comparable designs. Reportedly, Alberts and Western were two of the first tattoo artists to reproduce and sell copies of their designs. Few sheets of flash from the turn of the century have been found, but it is clear from the extent of the Gus Wagner collection that the basic repertory of tattoo designs remained relatively stable through the mid-1960s and, to varying degrees, is still used today.

Essentially, these tattoo designs constitute a folk art form that is traditional and has been transmitted through the generations by word of mouth and imitation. As a folk art, the tattoo is unique in that it not only exists as a design drawn and painted on paper or canvas, but can also be a permanent addition to the skin. The traditional tattoo is drawn in a formulaic way, developing variants over time. As folklorist John Vlach has pointed out,

Tattoo flashes by Gus Wagner,
c. 1900–1930.

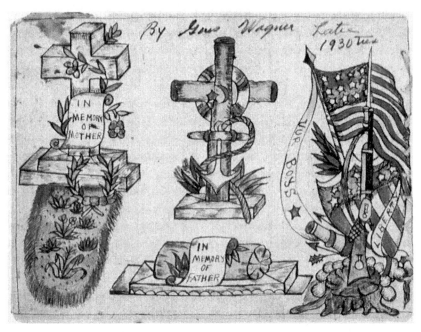

folk artists by definition submit to or are at least very aware of the demands and needs of their audience, and this social coercion promotes not only conformity, but the continuity of tradition and the stability of artistic performance.[20]

The repertory of American folk tattoo designs during the early 1900s included the following: hearts, flowers, daggers, scrolls, women, animals, serpents, birds, ships, occupational emblems, military insignia, and Christian icons and scenes. But over the years, this repertory expanded to include other elements of folk and popular culture. Tattoo artists have introduced new designs, some of which have become familiar enough to be labelled traditional in their turn.[21] For example, one of the most common tattoos during World War I was called the 'Rose of No-Man's Land,' a theme made famous by popular song as well as tattoo. Tattoo artist Leonard St Clair (1912–1980) maintained that this design, featuring the face of a Red Cross nurse, was originally created by New York tattooer, Charlie Wagner, and that the design quickly became traditional, 'copied and re-done by tattooers all over the United States'.[22]

In addition, during the first half of this century, cartoon characters became part of the repertory of American tattoo designs, and in the years since then, tattoos have featured a multitude of cartoon heroes: Mutt and Jeff, Andy Gump, Maggie and Jiggs, Happy Hooligan, the Katzenjammer Kids, Betty Boop, Felix the Cat, Snuffy Smith, Pogo, Mickey Mouse, Donald Duck, Bugs Bunny, Mighty Mouse, Roadrunner, Pink Panther, and an array of other popular images, deriving from both print and broadcast media.

The rapid expansion of this repertory of designs continued to prompt official disapproval of tattooing in the military. In a 1928 interview, Harry Lawson, a veteran tattooer with 35 years of experience (in Honolulu, Norfolk, and various California ports) said that tattooing had declined among sailors because 'them cake-eaters crowded the real men out of the navy'.[23] In 1932, 'Texas Bob' Wicks confirmed the decline in an interview with journalist Albert Parry:

> Yes, the sailors don't care a thing for their country no more. Why, I tattoo flags and Miss Columbia on six soldiers for every one sailor. In the old days, a sailor was every bit as patriotic as a soldier, sometimes having flags and emblems on the back as well as the chest.[24]

According to popular articles of the 1920s and 1930s, military authorities were becoming more conservative with regard to tattooing. Yet it seems likely that a good deal of the confusion surrounding the decline of patriotic tattoos was created by the popular media. For example, an anonymous writer proclaimed in the *New York Sunday Mirror* on 20 March 1932, 'Sailors are *sissies*. They used powder and cold cream', and then quoted the Bowery tattooer Charlie Wagner as saying, 'The fight's all out of 'em.'[25] According to Parry, Wagner denied with bitterness that he ever said anything of the sort. In another interview, Wagner explained that the decline, if there was one, was due primarily to the fact that during the Depression sailors couldn't afford tattoos.

Charlie Wagner at work, The Bowery, New York City, 1920s.

Charlie Wagner was indubitably the most famous of the Bowery tattooers. According to his contemporary, Leonard St Clair, who worked in Wagner's shop in the 1930s, Wagner was initially a talented artist, but the 'environment got to him'.[26] Wagner operated a combination barber-tattoo shop at 11 Chatham Square on the fringes of Chinatown, a neighbourhood characterized by squalid street-life, graphically depicted by Reginald Marsh in his 1932 painting and etching, 'Tattoo-Shave-Haircut'. In a 1922 interview, St Clair recalled:

It was just like the picture. When I was working in his shop, he used to tattoo sailors under the stairway. Now, there were four barbers in there too, you know, leased under Charlie. It was a barber shop, selling hair-cuts for a dime, nickel for a shave. You had to run an oil mop over the floor. You couldn't sweep it. There were splinters all over the place.

In time, St Clair remembers, Wagner 'got to drinking, taking everything in his last days, tattooing anyone who walked in the door, teaching the trade to people he shouldn't have'. Wagner was a 'character', eager to talk to popular writers, but as his practices grew less prudent, the publicity he received became more damaging to his profession.[27]

From the few references in the *New York Times* in the 1930s, it is clear tattooing was also becoming popular among teenagers, a fact which angered middle-class parents and prompted the New York Assembly to pass a law in 1933 making it a misdemeanor to tattoo a 'child' under the age of sixteen.[28] Despite attempts to restrict tattoos, heavily tattooed people were still popular in the circus and carnival. In 1932, the *Literary Digest* reported that there were 300 completely tattooed men and women who exhibited themselves in travelling circuses and carnivals, as well as in urban 'dime museums'.[29] Thus,

Leonard 'Stoney' St Clair at work, Columbus, Ohio, *c.* 1977.

tattooing was brought to areas where people had previously only heard or read about it.

Generally, the circus and carnival employed itinerant tattoo artists who traversed the country during the spring, summer and fall, and usually wintered in the South. During the off-season, they sometimes worked in rented spaces in arcades, pool-rooms, bars and hotels near military bases, bus depots, train stations and other locations where there was a large transient population. Although there were sometimes rivalries between tattooers and heavily tattooed performers, there was also a rather well-developed private communication network, which provided information concerning equipment distributors and good and bad places to work.

TATTOOING IN THE CIRCUS AND CARNIVAL

The most extensive documentation of tattooed people and circus performers during this period is contained in the corpus of photographs collected and sold by Bernard Kobel in Clearwater, Florida. Between 1930 and 1976, Kobel published a catalogue of 'Highly Tattooed Men and Women,' in which were advertised (with descriptive texts) 1,325 photographs (which sold for fifteen cents each). Of these, 93 were photographs of persons who worked as professional tattooed 'attractions'. However, in only some instances were the names of tattoo artists and tattooed people, and the date of the photographs identified. Of the tattooed attractions in Kobel's catalogue, two of the most frequently photographed were Betty Broadbent and Artoria Gibbons.[30] Broadbent was from Philadelphia, and her interest in tattooing began in 1923 when she was fourteen and working as a baby-sitter in Atlantic City. In an interview in November 1982, Broadbent recalled her initiation:

> When I went to the Boardwalk on my days off, I saw a tattooed man, Jack Redcloud. He was the man who had Christ's head and crown of thorns tattooed on his bald head. That's when I decided to get tattooed. I wanted to be independent and to take care of myself. I sure didn't want to go back to school.[31]

Broadbent got to know Redcloud, and he introduced her to his tattoo artist, Charlie Wagner. Wagner was a friend of a circus man, Clyde Ingalls, and when Ingalls learned of the project to tattoo Broadbent, he signed her to a contract before her work was completed. In 1927 Broadbent began exhibiting herself as part of the Ringling Brothers and Barnum and Bailey Circus, where she was billed as the 'youngest tattooed woman in the world'.[32]

In the summer, [Broadbent remembers] I wore a floor-length satin robe and in the winter, a velvet one. The platform lecturer would announce, 'And now, ladies and gentlemen, the lady who's different.' Up till then, nobody had the slightest idea what was different about me. I'd unzip my robe and I'd be wearing a costume underneath, sort of a long bathing suit that came four inches above my knees.[33]

As *Tattoo Historian* writer Judy Aurre has pointed out, Broadbent had a 'respectable act, not like those carnival floozies with one or two tattoos who would bump and grind'.[34] In the early 1930s, Broadbent appeared as a steer rider with Tom Mix. Later she rode jump horses and bucking mules in circuses. At various times, Broadbent took up tattooing herself in shops located in New York, Montreal and San Francisco. Then, in 1937, she left the country to spend two years working independent circuses in Australia and New Zealand. Broadbent continued to work in the sideshow until 1967, when she decided to retire.

Body paint was in vogue then. The youngsters would come in wearing paint and they'd be rude. They'd say my tattoos were just paint. And of course, by then you had to wear little or nothing to attract any attention. I was too old; it wasn't for me. I decided it was time for me to sit back and let the young folks have it.[35]

Like Betty Broadbent, her contemporary Artoria Gibbons had a respectable career as a tattooed attraction in the circus sideshow. However, unlike Broadbent, Gibbons was from a rural Wisconsin area. In an interview in the late 1960s, Artoria recounted the history of her early life and her decision to join the circus:

I was born on a farm in upper Wisconsin, and my parents were very poor. I only went as far as the ninth grade, and when I was fourteen, I decided I wanted to leave home and see the world. I had never been no place in my life, only to the village a couple miles away from our farm and they didn't even have a motion picture show in it. Well, one day a carnival came to the village, and after I done my chores, me and my sister went to see it. We stood outside the freak show and a nice looking guy started to talk to us. I asked could we come in for free. We didn't have any money and he said okay. Well, him and me got to talking. He told me the show didn't have a tattooed lady, and then asked me if I would like to be one. Said that he was the tattoo artist, and if I let him tattoo me, I could join the show and see the world. And that's what I did. His name was Charles Gibbons and he was a couple of years older

Artoria Gibbons, 1930s.

than me. What he wanted more than anything else in the world was to have somebody who could inspire him, and that was me. After I said okay, he started to tattoo me right away and before the next week came around, he had done his first one. It was a little angel on my left wrist.[36]

Soon after her first tattoo, Artoria married Charles 'Red' Gibbons, and they had a 'good life together'. Artoria retired from the Ringling Brothers and Barnum and Bailey Circus in the 1940s, after the death of her husband. However, after twenty years, she was 'bored and lonely, and had the itch to get back to show biz'. She saw an ad in the *Billboard* (now the *Amusement Business*) and joined the Dell and Travis carnival. According to Dean Potter, operator of the Dell and Travis sideshow, working for the carnival was 'quite a come down for Mrs. Gibbons after so many years in the Big Top', although he did add that 'she's happy here and so are we to have her'.[37] He also commented that Gibbons was a religious woman, a Baptist, who went to church regularly; and indeed, Mrs Gibbons expressed her Christian faith in her tattoos, which included numerous reproductions of religious paintings: Leonardo Da Vinci's *Last Supper* across her upper back, Botticelli's *Annunciation* on her arm, and Raphael's angels on her left shoulder.

Circus historian Chappie Fox has remarked that Artoria Gibbons, like Betty Broadbent, made 'an honest living in outdoor show business'.[38] The integrity of this generation of heavily tattooed attractions is readily apparent in many of the photographs in the Kobel collection. The heavily tattooed women of Artoria Gibbons's generation dressed themselves in modest circus gowns. They were often shown standing or sitting in a demure pose. Their tattoos were highly detailed and modelled, and often featured portraits of George Washington and other presidents, as well as details from paintings by European masters, such as Leonardo, Botticelli and Raphael. However, not all tattooed people were as successful as Artoria Gibbons and Betty Broadbent. According to Bobby Librarry, a lesser known contemporary of Gibbons and Broadbent, it became more difficult in the 1930s and '40s for a tattooed person to make a living.

There was too much competition. We were forced to embellish our already heavily decorated bodies with exotic stories in order to compete with each other. Many performers used the popular theme of having been abducted as children and forcibly marked. Circus performer, Miss Mara, ruralized the tale, billing herself as the *Abducted Farmer's Daughter*.[39]

Moreover, as Betty Broadbent pointed out, in the 1940s a woman had to show more of her body. In a 1982 interview, Broadbent recalled that she had to have a St Louis tattooer, Bert Grimm, tattoo her upper legs that had previously been covered by her long bathing suit.[40] By this time, in any case, heavily tattooed people were beginning to lose their audience in the circus and carnival; tattooing had become too common.

ATTEMPTS TO REGULATE TATTOOING

By the 1940s, tattoo equipment and supplies were advertised in popular magazines, such as *Popular Science* and *The Police Gazette*. However, this growth in tattooing precipitated problems, or at least the perception of problems, as attention began to be paid to the hygiene of tattooing, and the question of regulation was raised. The earliest efforts to regulate the hygienic conditions of tattooing were made by tattoo artists themselves. A 1942 *Collier's* magazine article reported that when tattooer Harry Lawson tried to get the city councils of a dozen communities to pass regulatory laws governing tattooing practices, 'no one seemed interested'.[41] World War II was raging, and the efforts to regulate tattooing attracted little attention or support. In fact, the tattooing business was enjoying a wartime boom. In a 1943 article in the *New York Sunday Times*, Charlie Wagner commented that the nature of his clientele had changed:

> Funny thing about war, fighting men want to be marked in some way or another. High class fellas too – men from West Point and Annapolis. Sailors used to be my biggest customers, but now it's soldiers. And fliers. Had a fine chap from the Air Force who wanted to be tattooed for good luck before he took off for India, so I put five 'Happy Landings' on his chest. And he got to India and back safely. Better than a rabbit's foot.[42]

Motivations other than superstition, however, seem to have encouraged servicemen to get tattooed. Tattoos were a means of establishing group solidarity among the members of platoons, divisions, and particular branches of the military. In some instances, tattoos were used to commemorate accomplishments or missions. Some tattoos were a way of expressing devotion to wives, children, family, and country, and easing the separation from home. Others fortified the masculine egos of the wearers or vented the frustrations and anxieties of war. According to tattoo artist St Clair, the most common time for a military man to get a tattoo was after the completion of either basic training or a more specialized kind of advanced training. For example, at Fort Campbell, Kentucky, there was a tradition of 'Jump School' tattooing in the 1940s.

Chutes and boots were popular tattoos around those paratroopers, a lot of patriotic designs. I'll tell you a guy had a hard-time if he had those chutes and boots put on before he took his first jump. That's right. The

Tattoo flashes by Stoney
St Clair, 1940s.

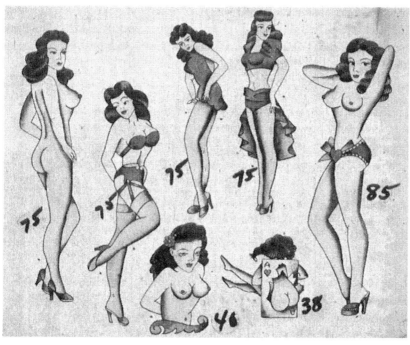

rest of them guys worked him over if he got that tattoo too soon. The tattoo was a mark of accomplishment, and if you hadn't accomplished anything, you didn't deserve the tattoo.[43]

In Little Rock, Arkansas, St Clair recalled working in the 1940s near a 'tank destroying outfit' where the men got 'the head of a black panther with a half-track in its mouth' tattooed on their arms after they finished their training, 'before they were shipped out'.[44] Aside from military and patriotic tattoos, St Clair claimed that during World War II, flowers and scrolls with names were popular as well as were more 'gruesome' designs – grotesque images of skulls, snakes, fire-breathing dragons and grim reapers. Although St Clair was reluctant to generalize about the motivations of his clientele, he did feel that he was 'helping them if it [having a tattoo] was something they craved, something that was on their mind'.[45]

During World War II the interest in tattooing was not limited to the military. In the United States the medical profession became interested in the potential uses of tattooing in plastic surgery. According to an article in the *Saturday Evening Post*, the technique of 'pigment injection,' which involved the process of tattooing, was developed in St Louis by medical artist Gertrude Hance, after eight years of experimentation.[46] Hance discovered that the tattoo machine was especially useful in restoring the colour to the transplanted skin of wounded militarymen. After World War II, some physicians even recommended the tattooing of invisible marks containing information about blood type and allergies. In a 1952 *Science Digest* article, Dr. William Kaufman maintained that if 'atomic warfare' should come,

[an] informational tattoo on your skin might actually be the means of saving your life. Why? In the event of simultaneous atomic attacks on several large population centres in this country, there will be millions of people in immediate need of medical attention – hundreds of thousands of these will need one or more transfusions of whole blood to survive. The medical and surgical care of such casualties would be greatly facilitated if each person could have neatly tattooed onto his skin, certain important medical information – especially his correct blood type.[47]

Although tattooing was gaining some acceptability as a medical aide, there were governmental attempts after World War II to limit the 'unchecked' practices in the population at large. Before the war, several states had passed minimum age laws for tattooing. However, during the war tattooing became so popular and widespread that it became very difficult to enforce any of those regulations. After the war, health authorities, in a combined effort with the police and the courts, began to inspect tattooing practices more closely. One of the first legal actions taken against tattooers occurred in New York City in 1944, when Charlie Wagner was fined for failure to sterilize his needles.[48] In some instances, the social pressure against tattooers was so great that they were forced to close their shops and move to other cities or states more hospitable to their practices.

During their resocialization into civilian life, many military men found that their tattoos, which had been important status symbols while they were in the military, had negative social value at home. St Clair recalled that after World War II, he was confronted by numerous individuals who wanted him to remove the tattoos that they had got when they were supposedly drunk and unaware of the consequences. But St Clair maintained that there were 'considerably more men who returned from the war, proud of their tattoos'.[49] For these men, St Clair believed, the tattoo was 'a form of medal (or maybe, wound), a sign that they had served their country in its time of need'.[50] Despite this, tattoos were losing their significance as status symbols in the military. As early as 1946, a poll conducted at the United Servicemen's Lounge in New York City showed that most of the new recruits were not interested in tattooing.[51] There was a brief respite during the Korean War (1950–53), when patronage of tattooing apparently swelled again. There are no accurate statistics, but the popular articles of the period suggest that the practice of tattooing increased, although it was not as widespread among servicemen as it had been during World War II.

Military regulations seem to have reflected the growing disapproval of tattoos. Once a person is in the Armed Forces, the commanding officer assumes the responsibility for evaluating the 'physical standards' of his men (or women). If the commanding officer determines that tattoos 'limit the effectiveness' of a particular recruit (e.g. by causing him to miss work days as a result of infection), he can recommend that the recruit be prosecuted and punished accordingly. And according to recruiting officers at Army, Air Force, and Navy Examining and Entrance Stations, a person may not enlist in the Armed Forces with an obscene tattoo.[52] Although there are no written standards for what constitutes an obscene tattoo, the Armed Forces Examining and Entrance Station states that the decision usually rests with the commanding officer. Clearly, if the commanding officer is tattooed, the policy towards tattooing is likely to be more tolerant. In the case of clearly anti-social tattoos on the hands or face (e.g. the phrase 'fuck you'), the judgments of commanding officers have been consistent. However, in the case of private tattoos (on the chest, back or legs) and semi-private tattoos (on the arms) the judgments of commanding officers have varied. If the examining officer is in doubt, the person is referred to the Armed Forces Examining and Entrance Station, where a final decision is reached.

THE DEMISE OF TATTOOING AND ITS REVIVAL

By the early 1950s, the popularity of tattooing was clearly in decline. Writing in the magazine *Holiday* in 1953, journalist Rex Bonesteel lamented that

> The venerable art dedicated to skin deep beauty is, unlike its indelible triumphs, fading away. Nothing more fittingly marks the current and sad state of tattooing than the passing of a once famous New York artist, 78-year-old Charlie 'Dad' Wagner, whose death last New Year's Day was almost unnoticed.[53]

Charlie Wagner had been the most widely publicized tattooer in America for more than twenty years, but by 1953 his public image had disintegrated. Wagner's death seemed to mark the passing of an era. The circus, the carnival and tattooing were all struggling for survival in the increasingly suburbanized, family-centred era of the 1950s. American society was changing. Postwar Americans rushed to marry and have families, settling in new suburban areas far away from the city neighbourhoods in which tattoo shops were located. Postwar society emphasized middle-class conformity and material comfort. All of this went against the impulses to tattooing. In this context, tattoos became identified primarily with rebelliousness among adolescents and young adults. Tattoos were considered 'lower class' and deviant, associated with blue-collar workers, drunks, hot rods, motorcycle clubs and street gangs.[54]

Yet in spite of this decline, by the 1950s a popular image of the tattoo was well-established, particularly in cartoons by 'Popeye, the sailor man' and by 'Cookie' in 'Beetle Bailey'. In 1956, the Philip Morris Company decided to create a variant of the tattooed man in advertising Marlboro cigarettes, which had previously been promoted as 'America's luxury cigarette' for women. Sales were down, and the ad agency Leo Burnett Inc. was employed to engineer an image change that would increase the appeal of Marlboros. In a 1959 interview, an executive at the agency commented: 'We wished to show a man who, during some moment – some loose moment – got himself tattooed.'[55] The first tattooed man in Marlboro advertising was a cowboy, a character not usually associated with tattooing. But depicting the true cultural context of tattooing was not a concern of the advertisers. According to sociologist Bruce Lohof, 'the advertising executives asked themselves what was the most generally accepted symbol of masculinity in America, and this led quite naturally to the cowboy'.[56] The cowboy was succeeded by 'he-men explorers, sailors, athletes, and an occasional tattooed, but no less rugged individual in a tuxedo'. In any event, the advertising campaign was highly successful. Hundreds of letters were received by the Philip Morris Company from tattooed people who wanted to pose with a Marlboro. Lenny Bruce even satirized the Marlboro ad in a 1959 performance on the Steve Allen show. During his act, Bruce pointed to the top of his hand (the location of the Marlboro tattoos) and said, 'I'm so bad, my tattoo even moved up my arm.' He then rolled up his sleeve and showed the tattooed heart on his forearm.

In a 1959 *New York Times Sunday Magazine* article, Gay Talese speculated (based on an interview with a Bowery tattooer, Stanley Moskowitz) that there were seventeen million men and three million women each wearing at least one tattoo in the United States – a clientele that supported some 250 tattoo artists. With regard to the motivations of this clientele, Talese could only say that 'it is at least debatable whether today's tattooed types can be herded into generalized classes'.[57] However, he then discussed the 1958 study conducted by a team of psychiatrists at the Oklahoma School of Medicine which concluded (after comparing 65 tattooed subjects at the Oklahoma City Veterans Administration Hospital with non-tattooed men) that the tattooed man is 'more likely to have been divorced, is more of a rebel, has more trouble with society and authority, and is more likely to have been in jail'.[58] In addition, Talese drew attention to a 1959 report issued by the National Education Association in which it was stated that 'potential juvenile delinquents might be spotted as those with male kin who are tattooed'. What Talese did not point out is that these studies were ultimately inconclusive, in that they were based solely on data generated in institutional settings and for a single year, 1958. Still, Talese did accurately characterize the image of tattooing among the widening middle class in the United States, for whom tattoos were associated with deviance and the deviant elements of society: hot-rodders, motorcyclists, prostitutes, juvenile delinquents and irresponsible military men.

In 1959, a study was conducted on a group of 648 submariners at the Naval Research Laboratory at New London, Connecticut, 'to confirm or disprove the theory that tattooed men really were potentially poor material for a branch of the service in which there was little room for maladjustment'.[59] The results of the study showed that 30 per cent of the men were tattooed, and among these, 'psychological tests suggested that while those with one tattoo differed insignificantly from those who were untattooed, men with two or more designs had unresolved sexual and aggressive conflicts'. More-over, 'subjects desiring future tattoos obtain scores higher in the direction of personal maladjustment and conflict than subjects who disclaim the desire to obtain tattoos'.[60] Although this 1959 study did not conclusively show the way in which tattoos correlate with work effectiveness, studies such as this confirmed the popular view that tattoos were indicators of social and psycho-logical problems. Civic groups, in a combined effort with the police, health departments and the courts, moved to make the practice of tattooing illegal, proceeding from the general assumption that tattooing was a deviant activity.

One of the first states to take extensive legal action against tattooing was New York. In 1961, the practice was banned in Nassau and Suffolk counties because of its alleged link to the 1959 viral hepatitis death of a 'boy who had been recently tattooed'.[61] Under the new law in New York, the use of tattoo-ing equipment was restricted to medical doctors. In 1963, the New York Supreme Court ruled that the 1961 ban was unconstitutional and stated that 'qualified artists' could work under sterile conditions. But no regulations existed to establish the qualifications of tattoo artists or the standards for the sterility of their shops, and in the following year, the New York State Appellate Division overturned the 1963 ruling, calling tattooing a 'barbaric survival'.[62] In 1965, a Suffolk County police spokesman stated that a signifi-cantly high proportion of persons who commit primitive crimes (murder and rape) have tattoos, and urged city authorities to gather more data on the nature of tattooed people. In early 1966, the American Civil Liberties Union (ACLU) filed a brief in the New York City Appeals Court, seeking to remove the 1961 ban. The ACLU argued that city health officials had failed to demon-strate the connection between tattooing and the hepatitis outbreak of 1961, and that tattooing was a 'recognized art form' that should be protected by the law. These efforts were unsuccessful, and the Appeals Court upheld the ban in June 1966.[63]

The legal action taken in New York reflected the prevailing antipathy against tattooing. Generally the public conception of tattooing was negative and based on surviving stereotypes from the postwar era, of dirty, crowded shops patronized by drunks. But it is difficult to evaluate the extent to which this stereotype was valid. Some tattooers of that generation, such as Leonard St Clair, say that the stereotype was exaggerated and untrue.[64] Nevertheless, it had enough power that tattooing was eventually made illegal in cities in Oklahoma, Indiana, Connecticut, Massachusetts, Wisconsin, Arkansas, Tennessee, Ohio, Michigan and Virginia.[65] As a result of such repression, tattooers became increasingly circumspect. Many refused to talk to people from the media, especially those from local newspapers and television stations, fearing that they would receive unfair treatment. Some young tattooers thought that by publicly disassociating themselves from older tattooers, they could improve the image of their profession.[66]

When the Vietnam crisis began, there was a resurgence of patriotic tattooing in the armed forces, repeating the earlier pattern established in World War II and the Korean War. In 1962, the *New York Times* reported that American recruits for South Vietnam's new junk fleet were having the phrase 'Sat Cong' (Kill the Communists) tattooed on their chests.[67] St Clair maintained that a number of his customers during the 1960s were military men who still sought traditional, patriotic tattoos such as flags, eagles, marine bulldogs, 'chutes and boots', and other emblems and insignia. But, in a curious reversal of the military associations of tattooing, as public opinion and growing counterculture sentiment increasingly opposed the war in Vietnam, so tattoo designs reflected the change. Peace signs, marijuana leaves, mushrooms, swastikas, motorcycle emblems and other counter-cultural symbols gained fairly widespread popularity. Often older tattooers refused to tattoo these new designs, but some eventually changed their policy because they realized that they would lose business if they did not.

Despite these signs of change, the public image of tattooing in American culture did not shift significantly in the 1960s. Older tattoo artists, such as Leonard St Clair, distrusted the younger generation, who, in turn, rejected the values of their elders. In this context, many tattoo artists guarded their 'trade secrets' and often isolated themselves from their colleagues. Nonetheless, tattooing in the 1960s was beginning to attract the interest of contemporary artists, such as Bruce Nauman, Dennis Oppenheim and Chris Burden, who created 'body pieces' to explore the ways in which the artist could become both the subject and object of the work art.[68] Some younger tattoo artists, like Ed Hardy (who was then a student at the San Francisco Art Institute), started to recognize the need for tattooers to organize as a professional group and to establish uniform ethical and hygienic standards that would finally help to overturn the laws that had been passed to restrict tattooing. These efforts, combined with changing attitudes toward the adornment of the human body in the population at large, did create a context in the 1970s and 1980s for tattooing to ultimately establish itself as a legitimate art form.

14 Inscriptions of the Self: Reflections on Tattooing and Piercing in Contemporary Euro-America

SUSAN BENSON

> In English the notion of 'adornment' suggests the superficial, the
> non-essential, even the frivolous. We often think of adornment as
> an artificially added layer, concealing what 'really' lies beneath. The
> Wahgi concept is rather different. For them, the decorated appearance
> is more often thought to reveal rather than conceal.[1]

It is an anthropological commonplace that every culture's ideas about the
body both reflect and sustain ideas about the broader social and cultural
universe in which those bodies are located. In this passage, the anthropologist Michael O'Hanlon chooses to contrast Wahgi bodily practices with
what may be taken to be the very different ideas about surface and depth,
body and self, to be found in contemporary Euro-America. For us, what is
'outside' or on the surface of the person stands in problematic and possibly
deceptive relation to what is 'inside': it is in the depths of the embodied self
that authenticity lies. By contrast, for the Wahgi, as for many other peoples in
Melanesia, the surface of the body, the 'social skin' as Terence Turner has
called it in another context,[2] is the site of cultural attention and symbolic
elaboration precisely because it is on the skin that personhood is located.
And anthropologists working in Melanesia have made the argument that
these contrasting attitudes to bodily surfaces reflect a central difference
between Melanesian ways of figuring the person and those of the West: the
difference between cultures where persons are explicitly seen as outcomes of
the actions of others and whose own potential for action is to be understood
in terms of relations to others; and cultures where the meaning of personhood and the capacity for action is located in ideas of personal autonomy
and separation.[3]

To accept this argument is not, of course, to assume some kind of simple
dichotomy between the body politics of the West and the rest of the world
(or, as it is framed in some kinds of sociological accounts, between 'modern'
and 'traditional' societies). Any serious consideration of the rich cross-

cultural material on these issues indicates the enormous diversity of ways in which cultures conceive of the body and the relationship between corporeality and the self. Nor does it follow that Western traditions place no emphasis upon the cultivation and symbolic elaboration of the surfaces of the body. This is far from the case, as a wealth of historical material as well as contemporary cultural studies indicates. But it is to suggest that the meaning of such practices must always be understood in a specific cultural context: in the European or American case, one in which ideas about self-realization and self-mastery have come to be increasingly central to conceptions of personhood, one where personhood is conceived in terms of what lies 'inside' but is not 'of' the body (notions of soul, mind or spirit) and where, historically, the relationship between surface and depth has been figured as the relationship between appearance and essence. In such cultures, it might be argued, the skin, the border zone between the bounded self and the social world thought to encompass that self, a membrane that protects but may also conceal, must be a zone of fascination and danger of a particularly charged kind.

Such a conception of the location and character of the self rests, of course, upon a profound paradox. For despite the etherealization of the self and the denigration of mere corporeality that has historically characterized Western conceptions of personhood, it can only be through the body and embodied action that we make visible, to ourselves and others, what we are. As Nicole Loraux acutely remarks in her discussion of Plato's *Phaido* – that text so central to the development of European ways of thinking about body and soul – when Plato wishes to illustrate the beauty of Socrates' immortal soul, and thus the truth of his argument for its existence as something distinct from the body, he must speak of Socrates' body, of his capacity to suffer with grace and die with corporeal fortitude.[4] To scrutinize the body, then, for the signs of what may lie within it or beyond it has been a powerful preoccupation within the Western tradition, one running through any number of important philosophical, medical, or criminological debates, each with their own particular discursive parameters and specific historical preoccupations, each linked in specific material ways to particular structures of power and domination. For, as Michel Foucault memorably insisted, the body is always 'directly involved in a political field',[5] its training and its intelligibility always of concern; the politics of the body is always a practical politics, a question of power as well as epistemology.

In this essay, I want to explore contemporary Western – and particularly English and American – attitudes towards some specific forms of body modification – primarily tattooing, but also piercing, branding and cutting –

as practices that engage directly and explicitly with ideas about skin and self, essence and appearance, and which insistently direct attention to questions of power and control: as practices, in short, which both reflect and seek to negotiate aspects of the body politics of contemporary society. Once powerfully associated with the primitive, the disreputable and the pathological, these practices currently hover on the boundaries of acceptability. It has been argued that over the past 40 years the technical, professional and aesthetic developments of the 'Tattoo Renaissance', as Arnold Rubin termed it,[6] have radically shifted tattooing from a marginal, predominantly masculine practice to a fashionable and decorative art form, while, more recently, body piercing has moved out of the American West Coast sexual underground and the oppositional culture of Punk into the mainstream. While – as we shall see – serious claims are made by some tattoo and piercing enthusiasts for the therapeutic and emancipatory consequences of such practices, it could be argued that for many others – 'the young crowd, the fashion people', as Californian piercer C. M. Hurt terms them[7] – acquiring an elegant celtic armband or a decorative navel piercing reflects little more than a shift in the aesthetics of body decoration, another moment in the restless movements of style which characterize Euro-America in the late twentieth century. Yet it is clear that part of the appeal of the tattoo or of 'advanced' or 'extreme' piercing – and part of the revulsion that many experience when they look at those so tattooed or pierced – turns on the ways in which such practices speak to an inchoate yet powerful set of contemporary concerns around flesh and self.

In this respect it is useful to consider tattooing and piercing in the context of a broader range of practices which signal a contemporary preoccupation with what could be termed 'body-work', with the discipline, transformation and reconfiguration of the flesh. Running, working out, dieting and bodybuilding; the astonishing rise of plastic surgery as an acceptable way to maintain a 'youthful appearance' and acquire a better body; gender reassignment and third-sexing; anorexia and bulimia: whether normalizing, transgressive or pathological, resting upon the deployment of sophisticated technologies or upon physical effort and willpower, what all seem to share is a kind of corporeal absolutism: that it is through the body and in the body that personal identity is to be forged and selfhood sustained.

In some respects, this emphasis upon self-fashioning (in the most hyperliteral sense) appears to confirm much of what is currently written by cultural critics about the plasticity, contingency and motility of identities in the world of 'late capitalism'. If, as many would argue, fluidity, mutability and the capacity for constant reconfiguration now characterize not only the economies of the Western world but also our notions of personhood and identity, we might indeed expect such ideas to be registered in the kind of bodywork under consideration here. Yet in the intense focus upon the body as the manifestation of the will of the subject ('as living canvas to decorate and living clay to sculpt', as a current advertisement for *Bodyplay and Modern Primitive Quarterly* puts it) it is possible to detect a quite different set of preoccupations: with possession, fixity and the stabilization of the self through and in corporeality. Such preoccupations seem to take all too literally the paradox Loraux defines: that it can only be through the body that the individual can understand her or himself to be a self. Identities may be fluid but the too, too solid flesh of the 1990s is definitely *not* melting: indeed much work has gone into ensuring that it should not.

The symbolic elaboration of the surfaces of the body that tattooing and piercing achieve must be understood, then, in terms of the imperatives of this specific cultural context. In thinking about these issues, however, it is important to see these practices not only as a system of signification, as 'scars that speak' in Lacassagne's terms;[8] but also in terms of the processes of bodily inscription that these practices entail. Significant here is what Alfred Gell, in his magisterial account of Polynesian tattooing, has called the 'technical schema' of tattooing: the puncturing, cutting and piercing of the skin; the flow of blood and the infliction of pain; the healing and closure of the wound; and the indelible trace of the process, a visible and permanent mark on yet underneath the skin: 'an inside which comes from the outside . . . the exteriorization of the interior which is simultaneously the interiorization of the exterior'.[9]

Piercing can, I think, be understood in similar terms, although in some respects the end result – an open 'wound', healed yet not sealed, a passage through the skin marked by the presence of metal, material alien to the body itself – demands specific consideration. The ambiguous power of these practices rests – as Gell so cogently pointed out – upon their capacity to open up and seal the boundaries of the body – and thus, by extension, the boundaries of the self. It remains to ask just how and why these practices have come to occupy the place they now have and what they offer for those committed to them. Before considering contemporary practices in detail, however, I want to look briefly at their historical development: for it is clear that this development itself reflects ways of thinking about the skin and its elaboration that are of continuing significance in the present.

The histories of tattooing and branding to be found in publications by enthusiasts or posted on the Internet tend to recapitulate the same fixed points: tattooed Picts and Britons, Coptic religious brands, claims for the widespread tendency for mankind to tattoo, the construction of a universalizing and thus normalizing history of tegumentary intervention. Yet the precise history of such practices in Europe and America is a complex one that has scarcely begun to be written, not least because the evidence we have tends to come from those opposed to the practice, one apparently prohibited within early Judaeo-Christian traditions and – in the case of branding at least – directly associated with punishment and subjection.[10] It seems reasonably clear, however, that it is only in the late eighteenth century that 'the tattoo' (a term directly derived from its Polynesian equivalent, *tatau*) is installed as a significant element in the European cultural repertoire. Originally seen as a practice characteristic of the savage others encountered by Europeans on their voyages of discovery in the Americas and elsewhere, it enters Europe as a residuum of the very particular relations of contact, exchange and appropriation then developing in the South Seas. Received by eighteenth-century mariners in the context of their dealings with Polynesians, the tattoo is quickly reconfigured as the basis of what will become a specifically Euro-American tradition, strongly associated with sailors, with soldiers and with other marginal populations.

In considering this history, a number of issues seem clear. First, that a practice originally developed in a context of exchange – of sexual favours, of goods, of cultural knowledge[11] – quickly became associated with something very different – a defensive and bounded masculinity. Secondly, that the spaces within which European tattooing flourished were precisely those spaces in which the expanding capacities of the nation-state's will to order and regulate male bodies held most powerful sway: the armed forces, the labouring population, the prison: spaces where issues of personal bodily integrity and security were most problematic. In Britain, for example, it was in the institutions of army, navy and prison that beating as punishment survived longer than in other sections of society. Evidence of a culture of tattooing among women prostitutes, a population both subject to the regulatory attention of the state and engaged in a form of work closely associated with corporeal vulnerability, is entirely compatible with this pattern.[12] Thirdly, as Maertens has suggested, these are also populations characteristically stripped of the 'social envelope' in which less marginal others might enfold themselves: families, rooted local ties, the persistence of social relations through time. Tattooing, in short, seemed to offer in its augmentation and elaboration of the symbolic qualities of the skin an additional protective carapace to those most buffeted by the operations of power and by marginalization; and the particularities of inscription seem to speak of the need for belonging, commemoration and defence, as well as of a defiant acceptance of misery and ill fortune.[13]

Yet in this process of cultural flow and transformation the association with the savage is not entirely negated. While the stylistics of tattooing quickly become suffused with a very European set of preoccupations – most significantly, perhaps, with 'the word made flesh', whether political slogan, religious motto or more personal memoranda to the self – extreme and elaborate forms of tattoo are in the nineteenth century consistently associated with the idea of forcible acquisition and with the savage other. Thus in the United States, it seems to have been commonplace for the tattooed women who exhibited their bodies in the circuses and freak shows of the late nineteenth century to claim that their tattoos were the result of capture by Indians – who, very surprisingly, then tattooed religious mottos and roses on their white flesh.[14] Similarly, Horace Ridler, who, between the 1930s and the 1950s, chose to work under the name of 'The Great Omi' (an explicit reference to the Polynesian islander Omai, brought to London by Captain Cook in 1774), received his dramatic 'tribal'-style face and body tattoos from the London tattooist George Burchett, but preferred to say they were the result of capture by New Guinea natives or, at another point in his career, of his membership in a secret Indian cult.[15] Such claims seem on one level – like the argument frequently made that most tattoos were acquired 'on impulse' or while drunk – designed to erase the question of intentionality: after all, no proper European could *want* a tattoo. But they also serve to maintain the symbolic link between the tattoo and its external and exotic past.

Whatever the extent of 'real' tattooing in the past – and evidence suggests that this might be a more complicated issue than one might suppose[16] – the practice is thus clearly associated with the disreputable and the marginal on the one hand and with the primitive and the exotic on the other. These associations, forged into an account of atavistic pathology in the late nineteenth century, bring together two significant tropes in late nineteenth-century Western thought: the idea of the distribution of cultures in space and time in terms of advanced and backward, primitive and civilized; and the idea of the layering of the human psyche, in which the primal, the impulsive and the instinctual is to be found 'beneath' the controlled and the rational exterior of the self. Such associations are carried over into modern tattooing. What is interesting about modern practices is, however, their linking of these qualities not, as in the past, to what should be avoided or despised but rather to what should be celebrated and cultivated.

This shift in sensibility is, however, quite recent. For much of the early part of the twentieth century, tattoo remained a marginal albeit increasingly commercialized practice with a relatively restricted clientele.[17] Electrical tattoo machines, developed in the 1890s, permitted faster and easier work and tattooists were for the most part unconcerned with aesthetic experimentation, working mainly from 'flash', a fixed repertoire of designs displayed on their walls. The result was a highly stereotyped range of images. Such 'old-style tattoos', as they were recalled by Stanley Moskowitz who worked in New York in the 1940s, operated within a well-understood range of representational conventions: 'The patriotic stuff. That was their purpose . . . Or love of their wives, girlfriends. Remembrances . . . Parents . . . They saw their stuff. Something hit them on the wall.'[18]

From the 1960s onwards, however, the organization of the practice, the character of the clientele and the kind of work produced all underwent a marked transformation. While many, perhaps most, tattoo shops remain the province of 'scratchers' – the British term for tattooists of limited skill and little inclination for innovation – and while there continues to be a steady demand for 'old-style' tattoos, increasing international communication, technical innovation and the work of a number of key individuals, many from art school backgrounds, radically transformed the possibilities of the medium.[19] At the same time, the 'tattoo community' became more visible and more organized, with the development of large scale and well-publicized conventions, an expanding number of magazines, books and now websites devoted to tattoo, and – a sure sign of coming of age – publications and museums devoted to the documenting of its own past.[20] Upmarket establishments – and over the past 30 years the number of tattoo establishments has grown rapidly in absolute terms, both in Europe and in America – now offer a great diversity of styles to an increasingly diverse clientele: Japanese, tribal, celtic, photo-realism, fantasy gothic, black and grey work, as well as retro-Americana.

The growth in piercing and related forms of body modification is even more remarkable and its history even more obscure. A widely accepted account would locate its development in the dynamics of cultural transformation in 1970s California, when these practices, rooted in the West Coast sexual underground, began to attract a broader clientele. Encouraged by the Californian Muzak millionaire and piercing enthusiast Doug Malloy (Richard Symington), a network of individuals – including the man who chooses to call himself 'Fakir Musafar' and Jim Ward, as well as Mr Sebastian

Tattoos by Don Juan (Olde City Tattoo,
Philadelphia), 1999.

(Alan Oversby) in Britain – began to expand and professionalize their activities, marketing special jewellery for piercings, developing new techniques
and disseminating information through Ward's magazine *Piercing Fans
International Quarterly*. Like tattooing, then – and the tattooing and piercing
'worlds' are not coterminous but certainly overlap – piercing in the contemporary context has developed its own forms of discourse, communication
and visibility. Initial demand was largely from the complex sexual subcultures flourishing in the aftermath of the liberal climate of the 1960s – in
Jim Ward's terms, 'hardcore leather people, SM practitioners', circles where
piercing continues to be explicitly tied into social and sexual rituals of erotic
pleasure, submissiveness and domination – although 'punk type kids' and
the broader gay population were also attracted to it.[21] By the late 1990s,
however, what many would now see as purely 'decorative' piercings –
earlobe, tragus, nostril, navel and to a lesser extent tongue and eyebrow – are
relatively commonplace, while those conventionally seen as 'erotic' as well as
decorative – nipple or genital piercings, for example – are quite widespread

in many social milieux in Britain and in the United States. 'Advanced' or 'extreme' piercings, however – together with a constantly expanding repertoire of body modifications such as stretching, tongue-splitting, genital modification or metal implants – remain a good deal less widespread, as do practices such as branding, cutting or 'slash and burn' where the processes of acquisition seem as important as the physical trace left upon the body.

RETHINKING THE EXOTIC AND THE DISREPUTABLE

Despite their growing acceptability, both tattooing and piercing continue to be defined by many of those involved as oppositional practices. It is asserted (with some truth) that, given the attitudes of many towards the tattooed or extensively pierced, to engage in such practices is to place oneself 'outside society'; more importantly, however, that these practices *in themselves* transgress or negate something central about the kind of person demanded by 'society' in late capitalism. For many it is precisely the link with the primitive and the atavistic that achieves this transformation. The identification with the primitive and the exotic is thus no longer abjected, but is reconfigured as identification with the authentic, the uncommodified, the pure, in opposition to the corruptions of mainstream society; or, in the case of Japanese tattoo, with the refined aesthetic of an 'ancient civilization'. And for many, to inscribe upon the skin the marks of the primitive other is 'anti-repressive', a way of releasing the savage within or of returning to a corporeal authenticity occluded by the disciplines of contemporary conformity. Coffee-table picture books, movie travelogues, scholarly accounts of the European past or of other cultures, the *National Geographic Magazine*, anthropological pot-boilers, Compton's Picture Encyclopedia: testimony from enthusiasts indicate that all have served as sources for those wishing to re-imagine the relationship between themselves and the non-Western world of tattoo, initiation rituals, constricting belts, penis bolts and so on. But personal travel and the cultivation of international contacts have also been important, particularly around the Pacific Rim and between Europe and South and South-east Asia, increasingly possible in the era of mass tourism and global connections. As in earlier epochs, then, these practices and Euro-American understandings of them must be seen in the context of historically particular patterns of cultural flow, arising from particular configurations of economic power and difference. The history of both tattooing and piercing in the twentieth century is thus thoroughly entangled in the processes of commodification, cultural appropriation and global deracination that many of its more articulate and influential practitioners would oppose.

For the Dutch artist Hanky Panky this wholesale and gloriously indiscriminate appropriation of the world is a sign of the modern: 'there are no limits now because we are *not primitives* – we can mix whatever we want!' Similarly for Ed Hardy, one of the most influential presences in contemporary tattoo, 'real American tattooing' is precisely about 'having all these cultures floating next to each other':[22]

> I think tattooing is the great art of piracy ... it's a totally bastardized art. Tattoo artists have always taken images from anything available that customers might want to have tattooed on them.[23]

In similar spirit, it was Hardy who in the early 1980s incorporated the black and grey single-needle work associated with West Coast Chicano street culture into his 'more custom creations', transforming a style associated with the prison and with low life into another option for an increasingly discriminating clientele. British and American customers can now demand

Tattoos by Don Juan (Olde City Tattoo, Philadelphia), 1999.

(and get) Kandinsky backpieces, Japanese style carp, Micronesian black work or Cholo tears – whatever they wish, raided from 'High Art', 'tribal culture', 1940s cartoons or the barrio. And Hardy, at least, is prepared to accord the same freedom of choice to Japanese kids who in the 1980s preferred 'totally retro 40's and 50's Americana imagery' to what in the US at the time were considered infinitely superior Japanese designs.[24]

In some respects, then, the commodification of these practices and their claims to be 'art' require us to treat them as no different from any other form of personal consumption in the West. In the words of one clear-sighted enthusiast, 'The guy with a $10,000 tattoo and a few thousand dollars worth of body jewellery is no different than the guy in the Italian designer suit wearing a Rolex.'[25]

Yet to limit interpretation of these practices to a simple story of Western consumerism (as if consumerism *were* ever simple) would be to miss precisely that which gives these practices their power: their indissoluble link to corporeality and to corporeal absolutism. For many enthusiasts, tattooing and piercing are distinctive precisely because of the meaning they would attribute to the body in contemporary culture, as 'the only truly precious possession we can ever have and know and which is ours to do with as we will'.[26] The precise relationship between these practices and ideas of possession and ownership remains, however, to be explored in more detail. In the material that follows I have drawn for the most part upon secondary sources and upon the enormous range of personal testimony, commercial advertising and well-established enzines on the Internet, as well as on a small amount of primary research; and the limitations of such material must be clearly acknowledged. In particular, I would emphasize that this is tattoo-talk and piercing-talk, between interlocutors, practitioners and enthusiasts; it cannot address the inchoate and complex ways in which such practices might operate in the life-world. That must be the subject for detailed ethnographic investigation.

SPEAKING THE SELF, RECLAIMING THE BODY

The first and most obvious point to be made is the way in which tattooing and piercing are read explicitly as statements of the self. No longer is tattooing accounted for as drunken impulse or forcible subjection: tattoos, like piercings, are to be 'chosen' after much deliberation. And this is reflected in the designs, which should form a coherent and aesthetic whole on terms decided by the subject. Undoubtedly this reflects a changing relationship between the tattoo and the body: in the words of artist Greg Kulz, the tattoo as 'enhancement, rather than . . . some random overlay'. In particular, designs which incorporate untattooed areas of skin rather than going for 'that blanket coverage look'[27] draw explicit visual attention to the qualities of the possessor's body, to the curve of the hip or the shape of the calf, a shift from an emphasis upon incorporation and wrapping to one of enhancement and display. In doing so, they draw attention not only to the flesh but also to the issue of 'design', the relationship between the intentions of the self and the marked body, the relationship between what lies within the body and the tattoo.

For Ed Hardy, traditional tattoo – 'big sections of tattoo shop flash randomly applied' – is condemned precisely for its failure to meet the complexities of self-realization: in the past, 'people had to fit their individual psyche into pre-congealed images that were often very out-of-date'.[28] Yet it is clear that the issue of the relationship between self and tattoo is not absent in earlier work, as Hardy himself has acknowledged elsewhere, but merely differently configured. The haphazard and incoherent nature of early twentieth-century tattoo reflects lives that were themselves often incoherent and fragmented, 'one thing after another': we should not be surprised by the absence of a master narrative of the self expressed upon the skin. Nor has the meaning of tattoo been altogether transformed. Tattoos continue to act as 'rites of passage' (a term much in use in tattoo-talk), as well as straightforward badges of identity for bikers, sailors, prisoners or gang members. But what certainly is central to a lot of contemporary tattoo and piercing talk is the idea of *individuation*; of the tattoo, as one contributor to the Bodyart Enzine put it, as 'a declaration of me-ness'.[29]

At its crudest, this is expressed in the language of consumer choice, with the body as a thing to be customized by the subject. In the words of an advertisement for a Las Vegas Tattoo business: 'You can change your decor – turn your junk into art. Design a wall, your car, the appearance of your house, or your flesh. You're only limited by your imagination!' For others, however, the relationship between body and self, skin and essence, is a more complex one, and one haunted by the idea of 'limit' which such simple sloganizing refuses.

At this point it is necessary to remind the reader of the technical schema of tattooing and of related practices of body modification outlined earlier in this essay: the piercing of the skin; the flow of blood and the infliction of pain; the healing of the wound; and the visible trace of this process of penetration and closure. In their capacity to enact the interiorizing of exteriority and the exteriorizing of interiority – and to *fix* this mediation in the form of corporeal transformation – these are symbolic practices of great power, permitting a rich and complex meditation on issues of agency, autonomy and control. The 'metaphoric possibilities', as Gell terms them, of such practices are manifold; and the multiplicity of uses to which they are put in the Western context, the diversity in ways of writing and speaking of them, repays closer attention.

On the one hand, contemporary tattooing continues to address issues of augmentation through appropriation, in which images of power are trapped and held, on yet inside the skin. There are the conventional symbols of the Western tattoo tradition (big cats, birds of prey, dragons, dangerous snakes), now supplemented by more fashionable Japanese or tribal iconography (or the iconography of destruction – a grenade, for example, tattooed on the chest 'like armour, protecting me from those who'll break my heart').[30] Others draw on images which reflect an engagement with what Goths and Satanists like to call 'the dark side': skulls, spiders, poison ivy, deadly night-shade, scenes of violence or bondage: the welcoming into the flesh of images of danger and subjection.

Such processes of inscription draw into the self potentialities – fearful or powerful – that are imagined as coming from elsewhere; and thus fix and possess them. This sense of taking what is external and making it internal is also found among those who seek tattoos as a form of memorialization of those loved and lost, 'to remember my friend', as one person put it, 'in a way that is now part of me'. Such incorporation may be taken very literally – mixing a dead brother's ashes with the ink used for the tattoo; or it may reflect a more general identification, as in the case of one Body Modification Enzine contributor who, wanting 'some kind of historical marker', chose to 'brand myself as a Jew'.

Yet tattoos or piercings can also, in the most obvious way, act as a registration of external events upon the self, a 'private diary' as the British performance artist Genesis P-Orridge puts it, or, in Lyle Tuttle's terms, 'a montage of my life'.[31] So Ed Hardy is reported to have said that he would never get his 'crappy old tattoos' covered up because they were connected to events in his past; another artist, Keith Alexander, sees his discarded piercing jewellery in a similar light, as 'a reminder of the long journey I have taken piercing and stretching'.[32] Again, what is external is transformed into something internal to the subject; and memory, a critical property of contemporary self-identity, is externalized and fixed upon the skin. Thus Seattle tattoo artist Vyvyn Lazonga claims that 'Getting pierced and tattooed tends to develop a person's awareness of *memory*: the piercings or tattoos become points of reference that reinforce the self and its history.' And such practices may do more than merely 'remind' or 'reinforce'; they may, as Lazonga puts it, also elicit 'who the person is or is becoming'.[33] In this sense they evoke not the registration of external events but internal depth:

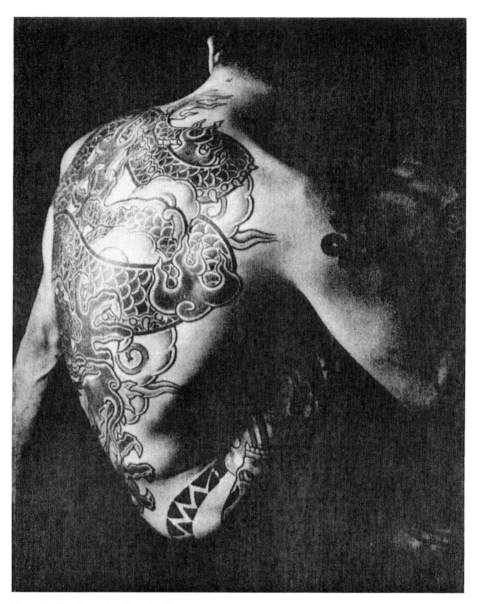

Tattoo by Alex Binnie, Into You, London, 1997.

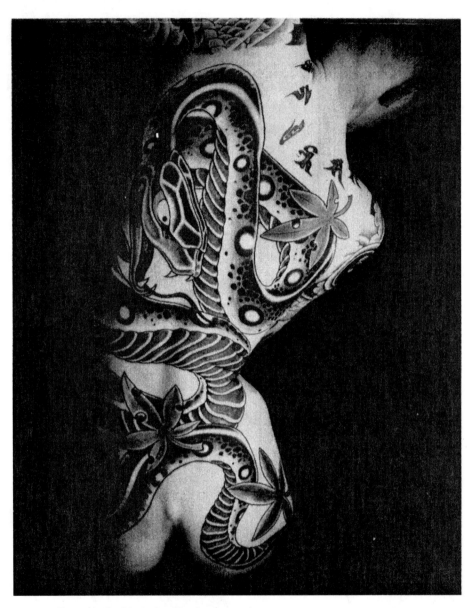

Tattoo by Alex Binnie, Into You, London, 1998.

Chinchilla, the woman tattooing my shoulder, tells me that everything she inks on people is already inside them . . . she only opens the skin and lets it out.[34]

I think modern primitives are *born*, not made. Early childhood experiences only open up the door to what is already inside.[35]

I try not to think of it as *enhancement* so much as an extension of self . . . some piercings reflect the personality . . . Other piercings are supposed to be there.[36]

Letting it in, letting it out: the ambiguities of the process are well evoked by the British artist Alex Binnie:

I think that when you tattoo somebody, something can happen . . . You are physically opening up the body and sometimes it would appear that the mind is opened up simultaneously . . . If you're opening someone up, you are letting something in. You can put information in.[37]

Yet tattooing, piercing or branding can also act as a kind of closure, 'to end something', a way of 'reclaiming' the body for the self. Here the emphasis is upon the marked skin as a defence or seal against its own past, while the violence and pain entailed in the process of cutting or piercing both mimics and expunges a previous violation. What is critical here is, of course, the will of the subject and that the person is 'in control' of the process. In an instructive discussion posted in the summer of 1998 on the RABbit Hole (a site dedicated to body modification matters) on the relationship between self-mutilation and body modification – both, it was recognized, practices common among those who have suffered personal abuse – this was precisely what counted. Self-mutilation is 'addictive', beyond the control of the self, something done in secret which merely repeats the original harm without transforming it; body modification, by contrast is 'done with complete consciousness', 'usually considered for some length of time' and is often publicly witnessed: inscribed on the skin will be the marks of self-possession, not defeat.[38]

CONTROL AND PERMANENCE

In this material it is possible to detect suggestive differences between tattooing and piercing which cannot be fully explored in this paper. The issue of 'control', for example, merely an elusive presence in the ways in which most people write and talk about their tattoos, is much more explicit in the ways in which people write and talk about piercing, cutting and branding, where it is often coupled with a sense of the body as a thing to be bent to the will of the self: 'Making', as another contributor to the RABbit hole debate put it, 'my body fit the mental and spiritual vision I had of it'.

That this vision often draws upon on an aesthetic of penetration and subjection – bolts, chains and spikes, 'shiny metal embedded in defenseless genitalia', as a RABbit participant put it – reinforces this sense of a body to be mastered. So too does the piercing and sealing with studs, rings, spikes or bolts of precisely those parts of the body most associated with the pleasures and dangers of connection to others: lips, tongue, nose, ears, navel or genitalia; and the focus for many of those involved in 'advanced' piercing upon processes where pain and penetration are central.

By contrast, in tattoo-talk the focus is rather on the body as an 'expression' of the self, a site for self-realization. And in this, of course, the idea of the permanence of the tattoo is critical. If in some other contemporary bodily practices – body-building, for example – it is the *work* that the self puts into the body that allows the self to know itself to be a self (and this work must,

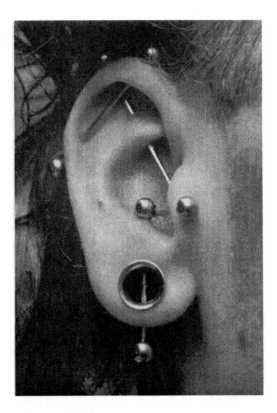

Piercing by Luis Garcia,
Infinite Body Piercing,
Philadelphia, 1999.

of course, be done over and over again) the permanence of the tattoo establishes a different regime, an instantiation of the will in defiance of process and time: 'you can never get it off'. In a fluctuating world, as a Maori man told James Cowan in the first decades of the century, 'You may be robbed of all your most-prized possessions but of your *moko* (facial tattoo) you cannot be deprived.'[39]

The tattoo can thus be linked both to the over-valuation of certain aspects of contemporary Western ideas of the self – the idea of autonomy and self-fashioning – and to their transgression. The inscription of the self on the skin may memorialize the self's past, but in another sense it exists in defiance of time: nothing about the self thus inscribed can ever be discarded or denied.[40] This, in a culture so committed to constant change and innovation, is surely what lies at the heart of the fear of the tattoo, for it is precisely the permanence of the tattoo, its evocation of the private depths of the self upon the surfaces of the body and its non-negotiable relationship to that body, that reminds us of the fixed end-point of all this mutability and self-fashioning, our own death: 'That's what I think really kicks people in the head about tattooing: they see it and they remember they're going to die . . . The permanence hits them, and that is linked to mortality.'[41]

What is distinctive in contemporary tattoo practices is the linking of such assertions of permanence to ideas of the body as property and possession – 'a statement of ownership over the flesh', as one individual put it – indeed as the *only* possession of the self in a world characterized by accelerating commodification and unpredictability, 'the one thing you get in a culture where you are what you do'.[42] The body thus acts not only as a site of personal creativity, but also as a touchstone of authenticity and truth, 'the last artistic territory resisting co-optation and commodification'.[43] And it is within this framework of authenticity and possession that interest in the *pain* expressed by some of those who participate in these procedures must also be understood. Pain, like the tattoo itself, is something that cannot be appropriated; it is yours alone; it stands outside the system of signification and exchange that threatens the autonomy of the self. And, of course, like the flesh itself, pain is conceived of as really 'real'; it speaks its own truth: 'If there had been no pain, then the tattoo on my shoulder might as well have been house paint.'[44]

In the tattoo, then – as in the rather different practices of piercing, branding and cutting described above – we can see attempts to construct what could be termed sealed selves: persons who are, in Shakespeare's memorable phrase, 'lords and owners of their faces', dependent upon no external power.[45] It is in this light that we should interpret the statements found over and over again in the testimony of the tattooed that acquiring the tattoo was 'for me', something to be possessed, not something to be looked at. Indeed in the past (and often still in the present) the pleasures of secrecy and disclosure play a part in the power of the tattoo for its possessor: 'at home I can walk down the street and still be a nobody, and that's where my tattoos kick in. I separate myself from people.'[46]

Now, none of this looks much like the flexible, mutable personhood celebrated in so many post-modern texts: on the contrary what seems to be central is fear of fragmentation, anxiety about boundaries and about the relationship between will and self; the body is the battleground in which such anxieties are played out. Tattoos may be 'scars that speak' but they do not demand a reply: they are an assertion of what is, frozen in the flesh, not an invitation to communicate. Like the Wahgi with whom I began this essay, those who tattoo certainly regard the decorated skin as something which reveals rather than conceals, but this is not a revelation designed to lead into sociality, connection or exchange: it is one established in defiance of these processes. Yet in that very defiance of the connection between self and world, in its acknowledgement of the need to defend the embodied self against external impositions, the tattoo inevitably accords to the world the power to subject:

> The world being as it is, there are few enough things I have control over and this is one of them. It sets me apart from the mainstream a bit, my way of saying there is more to me than the cubicle I work in, the corporate mantras I am poured into daily and expected to conform to.[47]

The tattoo, then, is a consequence of engagement, imagined as detachment: in Euro-America, as in Polynesia, 'The apparently self-willed tattoo always turns out to have been elicited by others.'[48]

Nowhere is this clearer, and nowhere are the profoundly disturbing implications of this position more evident, than in those forms of tattoo still associated with the marginal or the disempowered; those whose scope for action in the world is precisely confined to the capacities of their bodies and whose bodies are most completely subjected to the watchful and regulatory gaze of others. If the fashion among the new middle-class tattoo enthusiasts is for a relatively discreet statementing of the self – decorative yet personally significant – these others make subjection their own, inscribe and redescribe it in words and images upon their flesh, and reflect it back to those around them. As the rapper Tupac Shakur put it, 'Back in Elementary, I thrived on misery . . ./

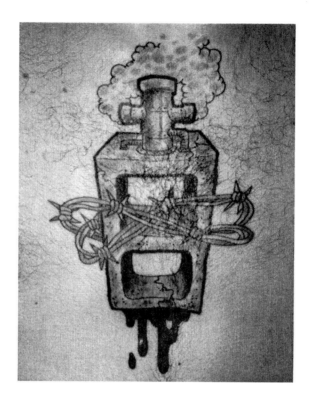

Inside my mind couldn't find a place to rest/Until I got that "Thug Life" planted on my chest.'⁴⁹

As well as 'Thug Life', Shakur's tattoos included images of power and violence, religious iconography, and, amongst others, the phrases 'Only God can judge me'; 'Trust nobody'; 'Notorious Outlaw'; 'Heartless'; 'Fuck the World'; an image of Queen Nefertiti, with the slogan '2 die for'; a machine gun, with the words '50 Niggaz'; and, above his heart, his own name.

Shakur's death, in a drive-by shooting in 1996, can only draw attention to one of the most curious assertions in all of this: that the body is something that we 'really own' – the only thing to be depended upon, the only thing that might defend us against the webs of power that entangle us. For in truth we do not own our bodies, they own us, and the only thing that is certain about our bodies is that they will let us down, that in the end they cannot be mastered or bent to our will. In this sense what these practices bring into sharp focus is the *impossibility* of Western ideas about body and self, and of these fantasies of permanence, control and autonomy that they seek to negotiate. To flee from the dull compulsions of work-discipline and consumerism or to refuse the unpersoning that marginality and oppression entails is something altogether to be admired. Yet to flee into corporeal absolutism is to flee into practices that can, in the end, offer no escape from the wider systems of signification and organization that they seek to reject. The anxiety and the ravenous ferocity that attends our attempts to achieve these unrealizable fantasies of autonomy, to fix the meaning of identity in a manner that cannot be altered upon the skin, has resonances not just for the marked but for all our strategies of corporeality and identity in this world we like to call 'modern'.

References

INTRODUCTION

1 Tattooing is the puncturing of the skin and the insertion of an indelible pigment into the dermis to a depth of between 0.25 and 0.5 cm, by means of a needle or other sharp instrument. The pigment is inserted either by dipping the instrument into it beforehand, or by rubbing it into the punctures. Instruments may be made of many substances, including bone, shell, wood or metal, and needles can be used singly or bound into bundles. This basic technique is found throughout the world, with local variations; modern innovations include more stable pigments, a greater variety of colours, and the electrical tattooing machine (for this invention, see Govenar, Chapter 13, this volume).

2 For further information and extensive references see Arnold Rubin, ed., *Marks of Civilization. Artistic Transformations of the Human Body* (Los Angeles, 1988); Jean-Thierry Maertens, *Le dessein sur la peau. Essai d'anthropologie des inscriptions tégumentaires* (Paris, 1978); W. R. van Gulik, *Irezumi: The Pattern of Dermatography in Japan* (Leiden, 1982); Donald Richie and Ian Buruma, *The Japanese Tattoo* (New York and Tokyo, 1980); Clinton R. Sanders, *Customizing the Body: The Art and Culture of Tattooing* (Philadelphia, 1989); Alfred Gell, *Wrapping in Images: Tattooing in Polynesia* (Oxford, 1993). Older but important works include Wilhelm Joest, *Tätowiren, Narbenzeichen und Körperbemalen. Ein Beitrag zur vergleichenden Ethnologie* (Berlin, 1887); W. D. Hambly, *The History of Tattooing and Its Significance* (London, 1925). Additional references are given in the chapters in this volume, and in the Select Bibliography.

3 It is important here to acknowledge the work of tattoo practitioners and enthusiasts, without whom it would be much harder to reconstruct the history of tattooing. From George Burchett, who learned tattooing at the end of the nineteenth century and practised it in London for half a century, to contemporary tattooists like Lyle Tuttle, Ed Hardy and Michael McCabe in the United States, Alex Binnie in London and Henk Schiffmacher in Amsterdam, tattooists have been crucial in rescuing knowledge and artefacts of tattooing history that would otherwise have been lost. See for example George Burchett, *Memoirs of a Tattooist* (London, 1958); Donald Edward Hardy, ed., *Sailor Jerry Collins: American Tattoo Master* (Honolulu, 1994), and the *Tattootime* series edited by Hardy; Michael McCabe, *New York City Tattoo. The Oral History of an Urban Art* (San Francisco, 1997); Leonard St Clair and Alan B. Govenar, *Stoney Knows How: Life as a Tattoo Artist* (Lexington, KY, 1981). Authors with naval backgrounds have been equally important: see Ronald Scutt and Christopher Gotch, *Art, Sex and Symbol: The Mystery of Tattooing* (London, 1986), and Ira Dye, 'The Tattoos of Early American Seafarers, 1796–1818', *Proceedings of the American Philosophical Society*, CXXXIII (1989), pp. 520–54. The outstanding history of tattooing in Europe and the USA is Stephan Oettermann, *Zeichen auf der Haut. Die Geschichte der Tätowierung in Europa* (Frankfurt, 1979; reprinted Hamburg, 1994); the study by Scutt and Gotch is the best synthetic history in English; and see

also the historical account in Jean Graven, *L'argot et le tatouage des criminels* (Neuchâtel, 1962).

4 Among this growing literature, which has expanded vastly in the 1990s, see e.g. Stefan Richter, *Tattoo* (London, 1988); V. Vale and A. Juno (eds), *Re/Search #12: Modern Primitives: Tattoo, Piercing, Scarification: An Investigation of Contemporary Adornment and Ritual* (San Francisco, 1989); Jeff Jaguer, *The Tattoo: A Pictorial History* (Horndean, 1990); Chris Wroblewski, *Skin Shows*, 4 vols (London 1989–95); Michelle Delio, *Tattoo. The Exotic Art of Skin Decoration* (London, 1994); Amy Krakow, *The Total Tattoo Book* (New York, 1994); Henk Schiffmacher and Burkant Riemschneider, *1000 Tattoos* (Cologne, 1996); Margot Mifflin, *Bodies of Subversion: A Secret History of Women and Tattoo* (New York, 1997); Ted Polhemus, *The Customized Body* (Baltimore, 1997).

5 Gell, *Wrapping in Images*, pp. 1, 3.

6 *Ibid.*, p. 18.

7 See Caplan, Chapter 10, this volume. Thanks to Alex Binnie for first drawing my attention to the concept of nomadism.

8 See Caplan, Chapter 10, this volume and '"Educating the Eye": The Tattooed Prostitute', in *Sexology in Culture. Labelling Bodies and Desires*, ed. Lucy Bland and Laura Doan (Oxford, 1998), pp. 100–15.

9 See also Susanna Elm, '"Pierced by Bronze Needles": Anti-Montanist Charges of Ritual Stigmatization in their Fourth-Century Context', *Journal of Early Christian Studies*, IV/4 (1996), pp. 409–39.

10 The fragments of evidence from medieval and early modern Europe are assessed by Oettermann, *Zeichen auf der Haut*, pp. 14–20.

11 See John Carswell, *Coptic Tattoo Designs* (Beirut, 1958); Henry Field, *Body-Marking in South-Western Asia* (Cambridge, MA, 1958); Edith Durham, *Some Tribal Origins, Laws and Customs of the Balkans* (London, 1928), part III.

12 Catherine Pigorini-Beri, 'Le tatouage religieux et amoureux au pèlerinage de N.D. de Lorette', *Archives de l'anthropologie criminelle et des sciences pénales*, XVI (1891), pp. 5–16, and Italo Tanoni, 'Il tatuaggio sacro a Loreto', *Ricerche di storia sociale e religiose*, XII (1977), pp. 105–19.

13 Thus Pigorini-Beri, *op. cit.*, p. 15, links Holy Land tattooing and the tattoos of Pisan sailors in the late nineteenth century. However, Marcus Rediker's assertion, in *Between the Devil and the Deep Blue Sea. Merchant Seamen, Pirates, and the Anglo-American Maritime World 1700–1750* (New York, 1987), p. 12, that early eighteenth-century sailors marked themselves with 'The Jerusalem Cross' appears to rest on errors in citations from texts by William Dampier and Edward Ward, both of whom refer not to sailors' but to pilgrims' tattoos: see John Masefield, ed., *Dampier's Voyages* (1697) (London, 1906), pp. 494–5, 497, 539–40, and Edward Ward, *The Wooden World Dissected in the Character of a Ship of War* (London, 2nd edn, 1708), p. 101: Ward makes no reference to sailors' tattoos, but rather compares their pride in the 'wales' raised on their flogged backs to the 'Holy-Land pilgrim['s] . . . Jerusalem print'. Lapses of this kind are understandable, but have the unfortunate effect of putting erroneous information into circulation in a field in which there is not much opportunity for corroboration: cf. W. Jeffrey Bolster's citation in *Black Jacks: African American Seamen in the Age of Sail* (Cambridge, MA, 1997), p. 92.

14 Bernal Díaz del Castillo, *Historia Verdadera de la Conquista de la Nueva España* (Mexico, 1939), I, pp. 117, 123. I am grateful to James Krippner Martinez for this reference. The Spanish word here is *labrada*, i.e. worked, carved or embroidered, and I use the latter term in preference to the modern translation 'tatooed' (sic) in the English

translation for the Hakluyt Society by A. P. Maudslay, *The True History of the Conquest of New Spain* by Bernal Díaz del Castillo (London, 1908).

15 Lionel Wafer, *A New Voyage and Description of the Isthmus of America*, ed. L. E. Elliott Joyce (Oxford, 1934), p. 83. Wafer was a surgeon on pirate expeditions to this region in the 1680s. I am grateful to Ignacio Gallup-Diaz for this reference.

16 Dye, 'The Tattoos of Early American Seafarers'; Simon P. Newman, 'Reading the Bodies of Early American Seafarers', *William and Mary Quarterly*, 3rd ser. LV (1998), pp. 59–82.

17 For early imagery, see Oettermann, *Zeichen auf der Haut*, pp. 50–5. The popular illustrated survey by Margaret Lambert and Enid Marx, *English Popular Traditional Art* (London, 1946) is unusual in reserving a place for tattooing as an example of folk art.

18 For tattoos on Prussian and French soldiers, see Johann Ludwig Casper, 'Über Tätowirungen. Eine neue gerichtlich-medicinische Frage', *Vierteljahrsschrift für gerichtliche und öffentliche Medizin*, I (1852), pp. 274–92; and M. F. Hutin, *Recherches sur les tatouages* (Paris, 1853); for tattooing on Indian convicts, Anderson, Chapter 7, this volume.

19 Hester Lynch Piozzi, *Observations and Reflections Made in the Course of a Journey through France, Germany, and Italy*, ed. Herbert Barrows (Ann Arbor, MI, 1967), pp. 229–31.

20 See Jones, Chapter 1 and Fleming, Chapter 5, this volume; Joest, *Tätowiren*, p. 6; R. P. Lesson, 'Du tatouage chez les différens peuples de la terre', *Annales maritimes et coloniales*, 1820, II, p. 290; Otto Lauffer, 'Über die Geschichte und den heutigen volkstümlichen Gebrauch der Tätowierung in Deutschland', *Wörter und Sachen*, VI (1914/15), p. 7; Cesare Lombroso, *L'uomo delinquente* (Milan, 1876), p. 43. A. T. Sinclair, 'Tattooing – Oriental and Gypsy', *American Anthropologist*, N. S. X (1908), pp. 361–86.

21 See the successive parliamentary debates on 'branding' in the British army in Hansard, *Parliamentary Debates*, 3rd ser., CLXV (1862), col. 1988; CLXXIII (1864), cols 1806–14; and CLXXVIII (1865), col. 368, and R. L. Blanco, 'Attempts to Abolish Flogging and Branding in the Army of Victorian England before 1881', *Journal of the Society for Army Historical Research*, XLVI (1968), pp. 137–45; also the discussions of tattooing in nineteenth-century Britain in this volume (Maxwell-Stuart and Duffield, Chapter 8; Bradley, Chapter 9).

22 Carmen Bambach Cappel, 'Pouncing', in *The Dictionary of Art*, ed. Jane Turner (London, 1996), XXV, pp. 378–80. Pieter Jan Tichelaar, 'The Production of Tiles', in Ella Schaap, *Dutch Tiles in the Philadelphia Museum* (Philadelphia, 1984); I am grateful to Ella Schaap for this reference.

23 Scrimshaw has long been prized and exchanged by museums and collectors, but tattoo 'flash books' and paraphernalia have become commodified only in recent years; see the exhibition catalogue *Pierced Hearts and True Love: A Century of Drawings for Tattoos* (New York/Honolulu, 1994).

24 E. Norman Flayderman, *Scrimshaw and Scrimshanders: Whales and Whalemen* (New Milford, CT, 1972), p. 51. See also Nina Hellman, *A Mariner's Fancy: The Whaleman's Art of Scrimshaw* (New York, 1992), pp. 25–6.

25 Flayderman, *Scrimshaw and Scrimshanders*, pp. 62–3.

1 C. P. JONES: STIGMA AND TATTOO

1 This essay represents an updated and less technical version of my article, 'Stigma: Tattooing and Branding in Graeco-Roman Antiquity', *Journal of Roman Studies*, LXXII (1987), pp. 139–55.

2 William J. L. Wharton, ed., *Captain Cook's Journal during his First Voyage round the World made in H. M. Bark 'Endeavour', 1768–71: A Literal Transcription of the Original Mss. with Notes and Introduction* (London, 1893), p. 93.

3 *The New Catholic Encylopaedia*, XIII (New York, 1967), p. 711, article 'Stigmatization'.

4 Konrad Spindler, *The Man in the Ice* (Toronto, 1994), pp. 167–73; on the date, pp. 79–80.

5 Richard S. Bianchi, art. 'Tätowierung', in *Lexikon der Ägyptologie*, ed. W. Helck and E. Otto, VI (Wiesbaden, 1986), pp. 145–6.

6 Leviticus 19, 28, Isaiah 44, 5 (*New English Bible* translation). In general, see 'Tattoo', *Encyclopaedia Judaica*, XV (Jerusalem, 1971), pp. 831–2.

7 References in Jones, '*Stigma*', p. 145.

8 Herodotus, *Histories* 5, 6, 2.

9 Anon. *Contrasting Arguments (Dissoi Logoi)*, 2, 13 (Thomas M. Robinson, ed., *Contrasting Arguments* (New York, NY, 1979), pp. 108–9).

10 Aetius Amidenus, *Tetrabiblon* 8, 12 = Alessandro Olivieri, *Corpus Medicorum Graecorum* VIII/2 (Berlin, 1950), pp. 417–18.

11 Xenophon, *Anabasis* 5, 4, 32.

12 Herodian, *Histories* 3, 14, 7.

13 Herodotus, *Histories* 2, 113, 2.

14 Evidence in Jones '*Stigma*', p. 144.

15 Lucian, *On the Syrian Goddess*, ch. 59.

16 Herodotus, *Histories* 7, 35.

17 Asius cited by Athenaeus, *Doctors at Dinner (Deipnosophistae)*, 3, 125 D (Martin L. West, ed., *Iambi et Elegi Graeci*, 2nd edn, II (Oxford, 1992), p. 46).

18 Plutarch, *Life of Pericles*, 26, 3.

19 Plutarch, *Life of Nicias*, 29, 1.

20 Herodas, *Mimes*, no. 5.

21 Scholiast to Aeschines, 2, 79 (Mervin R. Dilts, *Scholia in Aeschinem* (Stuttgart, Leipzig, 1992), p. 75, no. 170a); Bion of Borysthenes in Diogenes Laertius, *Lives of Eminent Philosophers* 4, 46.

22 Wilhelm Dittenberger, ed., *Sylloge Inscriptionum Graecarum*, 3rd edn, III (Leipzig, 1920), no. 1168, lines 48–68.

23 Aristophanes, *Wasps*, line 1296.

24 Aelius Aristides, *Oration* no. 3, *In defence of the Four*, section 651.

25 'Stigmatization', *Encyclopaedia Britannica*, 11th edn, XXV (Cambridge, 1910–11), p. 917.

26 *Revelation*, 17, 5.

27 John Zonaras, *Epitomated History*, ed. Ludwig Dindorf (Leipzig, 1868–74), III, p. 409; Alexander P. Kazhdan and Nancy P. Sevcenko, 'Theodore Graptos', *Oxford Dictionary of Byzantium* (New York, NY, and Oxford, 1991), III, p. 2042.

28 Peter Burroughs, 'Crime and Punishment in the British Army, 1815–1870', *English Historical Review*, C (1985), p. 570.

29 Petronius, *Satyrica* 103–6.

30 Vegetius, *On Military Matters* 2, 5, 2; *Code of Theodosius* 10, 22, 4.

31 *Code of Theodosius* 9, 40, 2 = *Code of Justinian* 9, 47, 17.

32 David L. Thurmond, 'Some Roman slave collars in CIL', *Athenaeum*, LXXXII (1994), pp. 459–93.

33 Mark T. Gustafson, '*Inscripta in fronte*: Penal Tattooing in Late Antiquity', *Classical Antiquity*, XVI (1997), pp. 79–105; and see Gustafson, Chapter 2, this volume.

34 For de Thévenot's account of his own tattooing in Jerusalem, see Jones, '*Stigma*', pp. 141–2; and Fleming, Chapter 5, this volume.

35 Arne E. Eggebrecht, 'Brandstempel', in *Lexikon der Ägyptologie*, ed. W. Helck and E. Otto, I (Wiesbaden, 1975), pp. 850–2.
36 Dio Chrysostom, *Oration* 14, 18–24.
37 Hippocrates, *Airs, Waters, Places* 20, 1.
38 Evidence in Jones, 'Stigma', p. 152.
39 Lucian, *On the death of Peregrinus*, 28.
40 Martial, *Epigrams* 6, 64, lines 24–6.
41 Diodorus of Sicily, *Historical Library* 34/35, 2, chap. 1, sections 27, 32, 36.
42 Pieter Burman (Petrus Burmannus), *Titi Petronii Arbitri Satyricon quae supersunt* (Amsterdam, 1743), II, p. 197, col. 1. I have not seen Burman's first edition (Utrecht, 1709).
43 Gina Lombroso Ferrero, *Criminal Man, According to the Classification of Cesare Lombroso* (New York, NY, 1911); see also Caplan, Chapter 10, this volume.

2 MARK GUSTAFSON: THE TATTOO IN THE LATER ROMAN EMPIRE AND BEYOND

This is a revised and slightly shortened version of my article '*Inscripta in fronte*: Penal Tattooing in Late Antiquity', *Classical Antiquity*, XVI/1 (1997), pp. 79–105. I am grateful to the University of California Press for permission to reprint.

1 C. P. Jones, '*Stigma*: Tattooing and Branding in Graeco-Roman Antiquity', *Journal of Roman Studies*, LXXVII (1987), pp. 139–55.
2 Pontius, *Life of Cyprian*, 7.1488.
3 For marks – figurative and otherwise – on the forehead in early Christianity, see F. J. Dölger, *Sphragis: Eine altchristliche Taufbezeichnung in ihren Beziehungen zur profanen und religiösen Kultur des Altertums* (Studien zur Geschichte und Kultur des Altertums 5.3–4) (Paderborn, 1911), pp. 70–193; G. W. H. Lampe, *The Seal of the Spirit: A Study in the Doctrine of Baptism and Confirmation in the New Testament and the Fathers* (London, 1951), pp. 1–18, 274–80.
4 Hilary, *Against Constantius*, 11.4–7.
5 Namely, A. Rocher, ed. and trans., *Hilaire de Poitiers: Contre Constance* (Sources Chrétiennes 334) (Paris, 1987), pp. 237–8.
6 Claudian, *Against Eutropius*, 2.342–5.
7 Theodoret, *Ecclesiastical History*, 4.22.
8 Boethius, *The Consolation of Philosophy*, 1.4.18.
9 Theophanes, *Chronography*, a.m. 6285.
10 *The Life of Michael the Synkellos*, 23 (M. B. Cunningham, ed. and trans., Belfast Byzantine Texts and Translations 1 (Belfast, 1991), p. 94). The list of sources is on p. 157, n. 145.
11 Cited in P. Perdrizet, 'La miraculeuse histoire de Pandare et d'Echédore, suivie de recherches sur la marque dans l'Antiquité', *Archiv für Religionswissenschaft*, XIV (1911), p. 83, n. 1.
12 *Theodosian Code*, 9.40.2.
13 David L. Thurmond, 'Some Roman Slave Collars in CIL', *Athenaeum*, LXXXII (1994), pp. 459–93.
14 Gaius, *Institutes*, 1.13.
15 See, for example, Peter Garnsey, *Social Status and Legal Privilege in the Roman Empire* (Oxford, 1970).
16 Tacitus, *Annals*, 15.44.

17 Most texts are gathered in H. Musurillo, ed. and trans., *The Acts of the Christian Martyrs* (Oxford, 1972).

18 Cyprian, *Epistles*, 76.

19 *Collatio legum Mosaicarum et Romanarum*, 15.3.7.

20 Aetius, 8.12; and see pp. 4–5 above.

21 C. Lévi-Strauss, *Structural Anthropology*, trans. C. Jacobson and B. Grundfest Schoepf (New York, 1963), vol. I, p. 257.

22 M. Foucault, *Discipline and Punish*, trans. A. Sheridan (New York, 1979), pp. 25, 26.

23 See Page duBois, *Torture and Truth* (New York, 1991), pp. 69–74.

24 A. Gell, *Wrapping in Images: Tattooing in Polynesia* (Oxford, 1993), p. 30.

25 W. R. Van Gulik, *Irezumi: The Pattern of Dermatography in Japan* (Leiden, 1982), pp. 6–16 and pl. 2, indicates that, in ancient Japan, at roughly the same time, penal tattoos were also placed both on the face and the arms.

26 See the heartbreaking memoir of Lucy Grealy, *Autobiography of a Face* (New York, 1994).

27 See, for example, Maud Gleason, *Making Men: Sophists and Self-Presentation in Ancient Rome* (Princeton, 1995), p. 55.

28 Plato, *Laws*, 9.845d; Plautus, *The Pot of Gold*, 325–6; *Casina*, 397, 401; Cicero, *In Defence of Sextus Roscius of Amerina*, 57; *Against Catiline*, 1.2; Petronius, *Satyricon*, 103.2, 105.11; Scholiast to Aeschines, 2.83.

29 See especially W. Andrews, *Bygone Punishments* (London, 1899), pp. 138–42, and A. M. Earle, *Curious Punishments of Bygone Days* (Detroit, 1968 (1896)), pp. 138–49.

30 E. Kogon, *The Theory and Practice of Hell: The German Concentration Camps and the System Behind Them*, trans. H. Norden (New York, 1979 (1950)), pp. 44–5, and illustrations on p. 297.

31 'Branded women rail at "settling old scores"', *Minneapolis Star Tribune*, 2 January 1994, p. 26.

32 William F. Buckley, Jr., cited in Clinton R. Sanders, *Customizing the Body: The Art and Culture of Tattooing* (Philadelphia, 1989), p. 183, n. 10.

33 Daniel M. Kahan, 'What Do Alternative Sanctions Mean?', *University of Chicago Law Review*, LXIII (1996), esp. pp. 630–53.

34 Again, these are discussed by Jones, 'Stigma'. Herodotus, *Histories*, 7.233.2; Suetonius, *Life of Gaius*, 27.3.

35 Ambrose, *On the Death of Valentinian*, 58.5–7; *Theodosian Code*, 10.22.4 (398).

36 Foucault, *Discipline and Punish*, p. 43.

37 *Ibid.*, pp. 47, 49.

38 Perdrizet, 'La miraculeuse histoire', p. 80, n. 4.

39 J. T. Sellin, *Slavery and the Penal System* (New York, 1976), p. 121; and see Schrader, Chapter 11, this volume.

40 Hans Ebensten, *Pierced Hearts and True Love* (London, 1953), p. 20.

41 *The Digest of Justinian*, 48.19.10.1 (Macer).

42 Henry Chadwick, 'Theta on Philosophy's Dress in Boethius', *Medium Aevum*, XLIX (1980), pp. 175–9.

43 *Revelation*, 19.11–16; quote from 19.16.

44 Victor of Vita, 2.2.

45 Procopius of Gaza, *Commentary on Isaiah*, 44.5.

46 Theophylact Simocatta, *Histories*, 5.10.13–15.

47 Cited in W. Reidel, ed. and trans., *Die Kirchenrechtsquellen des Patriarchats Alexandrien* (Leipzig, 1900), p. 245. Tattooing was also condemned at the Council of Chelsea in 787. See A. W. Hadden and W. Stubbs (eds), *Councils and Ecclesiastical Documents*

Relating to Great Britain and Ireland (Oxford, 1871), vol. III, p. 458; and see MacQuarrie, Chapter 3, this volume.

48 See, for example, Ruth Melinkoff, *The Mark of Cain* (Berkeley, 1981), who treats the manifold interpretations of Cain's mark in Jewish and Christian exegesis.

49 My essay on Paul's *stigmata* and the tattoo in early Christianity is forthcoming.

50 Judith Perkins, *The Suffering Self: Pain and Narrative Representation in the Early Christian Era* (London, 1995), p. 115.

51 *The Life of Michael the Synkellos*, 20.243–4, 247 (trans. Cunningham).

52 Van Gulik, *Irezumi*, pp. 13, 15.

53 M. Thévoz, *The Painted Body* (New York, 1984), p. 80.

54 Nathaniel Hawthorne, *The Scarlet Letter*, 2nd edn (New York, 1990 (1850)), pp. 230, 140, 143.

3 CHARLES W. MacQUARRIE: INSULAR CELTIC TATTOOING: HISTORY, MYTH AND METAPHOR

A longer version of this paper appears in of *Études Celtiques*, XXXIII (1999), pp. 159–89. I owe special thanks to Joseph Nagy, Robin Stacey, Thomas Clancy and William Gillies for advice on matters of translation and argumentation.

1 Richard Sharpe, *Medieval Irish Saints' Lives* (Oxford, 1991), pp. 180–3. See also Sean Connolly, 'Vita Prima Sanctae Brigitae: Background and Historical Value,' *Journal of the Royal Society of Antiquaries of Ireland*, CIXX (1989), pp. 1–40 (31).

2 See Connolly, 'Vita Prima', p. 10.

3 See Richard Sharpe, 'Hiberno-Latin Laicus and Irish Láech', *Ériu*, XXX (1979), p. 81.

4 See C. P. Jones, '*Stigma*: Tattooing and Branding in Graeco-Roman Antiquity', *The Journal of Roman Studies*, LXXVII (1987), pp. 139–55, and his essay in this volume, Chapter 1.

5 For some possible visual evidence of Celtic tattoos see D. F. Allen, *The Coins of the Ancient Celts* (Edinburgh, 1980), p. 147, and Charles Thomas, 'The Interpretation of the Pictish Symbols', *The Archaeological Journal*, CXX (1963), pp. 31–97 (esp. pp. 88–93). It is also possible that tattoos are represented on the naked male figure who appears in the top right corner of *The Book of Kells* page 'Initium Evangelii' (Mark 1:1) (Luzern, 1990), folio 130r. Anna Ritchie, *Perceptions of the Picts: from Eumenius to John Buchan*, Groam House Museum Trust (Rosemarkie, 1994) (Groam House Lecture), has suggested this figure may represent a Pict – the Book of Kells was presumably a product of Iona. Thanks to Katherine Forsyth for this last reference.

6 See Jones, Chapter 1, this volume. A scan of *CETEDOC* for words containing the root *stigma** turns up 126 references, nearly half of which are to St Francis of Assisi. St Francis's stigmata effectively redefined the word for the later Middle Ages. *CETEDOC Library of Christian Latin Texts*, 2nd edn (*CLCLT-2*), ed. Paul Tombeur *et al.*, for the Centre de traitement électronique des documents (*CETEDOC*) and the Université catholique de Louvain (Turnhout, 1994).

7 *Rind*, for example, is the word applied to tattooing in *Lebor Gabála Érenn* (see below) and in 'The Gaelic abridgement of the book of Sir Marco Polo', *Zeitschrift für Celtische Philologie*, I (1897), pp. 392–3. The *Dictionary of the Irish Language* (Dublin, 1913–76, compact edn 1981), R col. 74, ll. 31–6, records that *rindainech* 'is a recognized class of fool or buffoon and conjectures that it may be a compound of the word *rind* "scratch" and the word *ainech* "face"'.

8 *Dictionary of the Irish Language*, C, col. 514, lines 36–61.

9 For example, see Henri Hubert, *The Rise of the Celts* (London, 1934), p. 203; Kenneth H. Jackson 'The Pictish Language', in *The Problem of the Picts*, ed. F. T. Wainwright (Westport, CT, 1956), pp. 129–60; Isabel Henderson, *The Picts* (New York, 1967), p. 33; A. L. F. Rivet and C. Smith, *The Place-Names of Roman Britain*. (London, 1979), p. 281; Thomas, 'Pictish Symbols', pp. 31–97; and F. C. Diack, *The Inscriptions of Pictland* (Aberdeen, 1944). For the association between *cruth* and tattoo see quotation from the seventeenth-century writer Duald MacFirbis in Lloyd and Jenny Laing, *The Picts and Scots* (Phoenix Mill, 1995), p. 122.

10 Heinrich Zimmer, 'Matriarchy Among the Picts', *Leabhar Nan Gleann: The Book of the Glens*, ed. George Henderson (Edinburgh, 1898), pp. 1–42.

11 Nora K. Chadwick, 'The Name Pict', *Scottish Gaelic Studies*, IIX/2 (1958), pp. 146–76 (163).

12 For example Chadwick (*ibid.*) suggests that the accounts of Celtic tattooing were distortions and/or elaborations of Caesar's references to dyeing, that the accounts are connected to the camouflaged (*pictae*) Celtic (and or Germanic) marines (pp. 154, 165), and that, in the unlikely event that they did exist, the markings may have been the result of rubbing into wounds a disinfectant (*vitrum*) which was also a dye and produced an incidental tattoo (p. 176).

13 W. D. Hambly *The History of Tattooing and its Significance* (New York, 1927), pp. 284–6. Kris Sperry, 'Tattoos and Tattooing: Part I: History and Methodology', *The American Journal of Forensic Medicine and Pathology*, XII/4 (1991), p. 313.

14 K. H. Jackson, 'The Pictish Language', in Wainwright (ed.), *The Problem of the Picts*, pp. 129–60.

15 Don Brothwell, *The Bogman and the Archaeology of People* (London, 1986), p. 102 and plate IV. Tamara Talbot Rice, *The Scythians* (London, 1957). Renate Rolle, *The World of the Scythians* (Los Angeles, 1989; first published in German, 1980), pp. 83–6.

16 See H. J. Edwards, ed., *The Gallic War* (New York, 1987), Book V: 14.

17 F. B. Pyatt et al., 'Non Isatis Sed Vitrum Or The Colour of Lindow Man', *Oxford Journal of Archaeology*, X/1 (1991), pp. 61–73. Lindow man II had in an earlier inspection been found to be dye-free. See I. M. Stead, J. B. Bourke and Don Brothwell, *Lindow Man: The Body in the Bog* (London, 1986), p. 41.

18 Edward Echols, trans., *Herodian of Antioch's History of the Roman Empire* (Berkeley, CA, 1961), p. 105; Henie Petrie, ed., *Monumenta Historica Britannica* Part I (London, 1848), pp. lxiii–lxiv; Th. Mommsen, ed., *C. Iulii Solini Collectanea Rerum Memorabilium* (London, 1895), pp. 102–3. Chadwick, 'The Name Pict', p. 160; Johann Matthias Genser, ed., *Cl. Claudiani quae exstant* (Leipzig, 1759; reprint: Hildesheim, 1969), pp. 354–5. O. A. W. Dilke, trans., *Claudian: Poet of Declining Empire and Morals* (Leeds, 1969), pp. 14, 17, 428.

19 W. M. Lindsay, ed., *Isidori Hispalensis Episcopi Etymologiarum Sive Originum. Scriptorum Classicorum Bibliotheca Oxoniensis*, XX (Oxford 1911), sect. XIX, pp. 23, 7 and sect. IX, pp. 2, 103.

20 F. P. Dutripon, ed., *Vulgatae Editionis Bibliorum Sacrorum Concordantiae ad recognitionem Jussu Sixti V. Pontif. Max.* (Paris, 1860), p. 1308. Louis-Claude Fillion, ed., *Biblia sacra juxta vulgatae exemplaria et correctoria Romana*, 7th edn (Paris, 1911).

21 References to stigmatizing soldiers (and armourers) are also made in N. P. Milner, trans., *Vegetius: Epitome of Military Science* (Liverpool, 1996), p. 9. Tattooing is also mentioned in the Theodosian Code 10.24.3. See Clyde Pharr, *The Theodosian Code* (Princeton, 1952). It is possible that the *Romana stigmata* that Gildas refers to in *De Excidio Britonum* are actually 'Roman tattoos'. Michael Winterbottom, ed. and

trans., *Gildas: The Ruin of Britain and other Works* (London, 1978) p. 92, l. 34 and p. 94, l. 29.

22 *Epistolae Beati Pauli Glosate Glosa Interlineali* (Halle, 1910), 20^{v}.

23 *Die Althochdeutschen Glossen*, v, ed. Elias Steinmeyer and Eduard Sievers (Berlin, 1922), p. 119.

24 '383 Theodoret of Cyrrhus, commenting on this biblical passage, notes that certain people tattoo their skin using needles and ink, in reverence of demons': Bernhard Bischoff and Michael Lapidge (eds and trans.), *Biblical Commentaries from the Canterbury School of Theodore and Hadrian* (Cambridge, 1994), p. 487. See also Bernhard Bischoff, *Mittelalterliche Studien: Ausgewählte Aufsätze zur Schriftkunde und Literaturgeschichte* (Stuttgart, 1967), pp. 19–25.

25 See Bischoff and Lapidge, eds, *Biblical Commentaries*, pp. 368–9.

26 David Wilkins, *Concilia Magnae Britanniae et Hiberniae*, I (1737), p. 150. See also Arthur Haddan and William Stubbs, *Councils and Ecclesiastical Documents relating to Great Britain and Ireland*, III (Oxford, 1871), p. 458; and Audrey L. Meaney, 'Anglo-Saxon Idolators and Ecclesiasts from Theodore to Alcuin; A Source Study', *Anglo-Saxon Studies in Archaeology and History*, V (1992), pp. 103–25.

27 Meaney, 'Anglo-Saxon Idolators', p. 115.

28 See Douglas C. C. Young, 'Author's Variants and Interpretations in Frithegod', in *Bulletin Du Cang: Archivvm Latinatatis Medii Aevi*, XXV (1955), pp. 91–2. There is also some speculation that Hereward the Wake may have been tattooed; see Victor Head, *Hereward* (Stroud, Glos., 1995), p. 37.

29 William Stubbs, ed., *Willelmi Malmesbiriensis monachi De gestis regum Anglorum* (London, 1887–9), Book III, part 245, p. 305.

30 See David Pelteret, *Slavery in Early Mediaeval England* (London, 1995), for indications that Celts made up a large part of the slave population of Anglo-Saxon England.

31 Whitley Stokes and John Strachan (eds), *Thesaurus Palaeohibernicus: A Collection of Old-Irish Glosses Scholia Prose and Verse*, II (Cambridge, 1903), pp. 244–5.

32 *Dictionary of the Irish Language*, F, col. 492, ll. 45–51.

33 Kuno Meyer, 'Tätowierung bei den Iren', *Zeitschrift für Celtische Philologie*, X (1915), pp. 400–1. O. J. Bergin *et al.*, *Anecdota from Irish Manuscripts*, IV (Dublin, 1912), p. 49. Liam Breatnach, 'The Caldron of Poesy', *Eriu*, XXXII (1981), p. 62. See Meyer, 'Tätowierung', for 'garrglas' as a word associated with tattooing. The *Dictionary of the Irish Language*, G, col. 95, ll. 57–8, also gives a citation for the word *glass* ('grey-blue') in association with tattoo from Laws 5 108.30: 'crechad glass ar na roscaib' ('blue tattooing on the eyelids').

34 See Jones, 'Stigma', pp. 147–50.

35 *Ibid.* See also P. L. Henry, 'The Caldron of Poesy', *Studia Celtica*, XIV/XV (1979–80), pp. 123–4.

36 R. A. S. Macalister, *Lebor Gabála Érenn: The Book of the Taking of Ireland*, parts 1–5, Irish Texts Society (Dublin, 1938–41, 1956), part 5, pp. 30–47, 106–7, 110–21, 156–9.

37 Elizabeth Sutherland, *In Search of the Picts* (London, 1995), pp. 83, 175. For a fuller and more persuasive account, see Charles Thomas, 'Pictish Symbols', pp. 88–93.

38 See Henderson, *The Picts*, p. 158, for an analysis of this supposed connection.

39 Dáithí Ó hÓgain, *Myth, Legend and Romance* (New York, 1991), pp. 23–4.

40 Henry, 'The Caldron of Poesy', p. 119.

41 Macalister, *Lebor Gabála*, part 5, pp. 178–9.

42 Rolf Baumgarten, 'A Hiberno-Isidorean Etymology', *Peritia*, II (1983), pp. 225–8.

43 Macalister, *Lebor Gabála*, part 1, pp. 164–5.

44 Macalister, *Lebor Gabála*, part 5, p. 225. For another version of this passage see the

last 8 stanzas of a poem of 78 stanzas in Macalister, *Lebor Gabála*, part 4, pp. 280–3.

45 R. I. Best, ed. and trans., *Eriú*, IV (1919), pp. 121–72.
46 For example, *Deut.* 6:6–9 and *Rev.* 3:11–13.
47 Although the texts are usually anything but holy, the potential for tattooing as analogous to writing was also clearly realized in the classical world. C. P. Jones mentions a disputed reference in the lost *Babylonians* to the Samian people as 'lettered' (*polugrammatos*). Jones, 'Stigma', pp. 148, 153.
48 Ernst Robert Curtius, *European Literature and the Latin Middle Ages* (London, 1953), p. 312. Curtius also mentions the story of Cassian (4th century), also found in Prudentius, in which the schoolmaster is literally written on by his angry students with metal styluses.
49 Walter Simons, 'Reading a Saint's Body: Rapture and Bodily Movement in the Vitae of Thirteenth-century Beguines', in *Framing Medieval Bodies*, ed. Sarah Kay and Miri Rubin (Manchester, 1994) pp. 10–23 (11–12).
50 Alan Orr Anderson and Marjorie Anderson (eds and trans.), *Adomnán's Life of Columba* (Oxford, 1991), pp. 188–91. See also Joseph Falaky Nagy, *Conversing with Angels and Ancients* (Ithaca, NY, 1997), p. 138. Túán himself uses the word *crechta* to describe the marks that have been left in his skin during his various adventures in the shape of a fish; see John Carey 'Scél Túáin meic Chairill', *Ériu*, XXXV (1984), p. 102.
51 For what seems to be a depiction of a book as a manifestation of a saintly body, notice the head, feet and hands on the frame of the 'Portrait of Saint John', *The Book of Kells* (Luzern, 1990) folio 291v.
52 Mark Scowcroft, 'Leabhar Gabhála – Part I: The Growth of the Tradition', *Ériu*, XXXIX (1988), pp. 1–66 (p. 12).
53 Sharpe, *Medieval Irish*, pp. 180–3. Book II, paras 37, 38, 40.
54 See Connolly, 'Vita Prima', for a translation of the corresponding passages in *Vita Prima*, esp. sections § 65 and § 68 (pp. 32–4).
55 Peter Cramer, *Baptism and Change in the Early Middle Ages, c. 200 – c. 1150* (Cambridge, 1993), p. 41. See also J. G. Davies, *The Early Christian Church* (New York, 1965), pp. 104.
56 Kim R. McCone, 'Werewolves, Cyclopes, Díberga, and Fíanna: Juvenile Delinquency in Early Ireland', *Cambridge Medieval Celtic Studies*, XII (1986), pp. 1–22.
57 Sharpe, 'Hiberno-Latin', p. 86.
58 Joseph Bingham, *Origines Ecclesiasticae: The Antiquities of the Christian Church* (London, 1845), book 11, chap. 9., sec. 5; cited in A. H. Lewis, *Paganism Surviving in Christianity* (New York, 1892), p. 250.
59 Jones, 'Stigma', p. 150.
60 *Ibid.*, pp. 143–4.
61 I find seven separate examples of such healing; see Connolly, 'Vita Prima', pp. 19, 22, 29, 35, 37, 38.
62 See Jackson, 'The Pictish Language', p. 158, for etymology of Britain from *Priteni: 'the name is presumably Celtic and may mean "the people of the designs," i.e. tattoos'.

4 JENNIPHER ALLEN ROSECRANS: WEARING THE UNIVERSE

1 Simon Forman, 'Of Apoticarie Drugs', c. 1607, f. 586v, in *Volumen Primum*, vol. II, 1609, Ashmole 1494/1, Bodleian Library, Oxford. I am indebted to Dr Lauren Kassell for this reference and the bibliographic details of Forman. For further details on Forman see Lauren Kassell, *Simon Forman's Philosophy of Medicine: medicine, astrology and alchemy in London, circa 1580–1611* (Oxford, 1997).

2 Forman, 'Of Apoticaric Drugs'.

3 This revelation for marking the flesh and controlling his fate is located in Forman's earlier discussion of Repperus and the similar markings Repperus wore on a ring for the same purpose, 'to alter destiny of body'; *ibid.* Aside from Forman's few notations, no other biographical information on Repperus is given.

4 *Ibid.*, f. 402. Forman's recipe for this special ink is similar to other sixteenth-century recipes for gold ink:

> To Make Aurum Musicum
>
> Take one ounce of Salarmoniack [ammonium chloride], one ounce of quick silver [mercury], one ounce of Conterfein [zinc], half an ounce of brimstone [sulfer], bruise the brimstone, set it on fire, but let it not be over hot least it burneth, or become black, then take the Salarmoniack, and the quick silver, being in powder, mix them well together, then mingle them with the brimstone, stir them well and quickly with a stick, till the brimstone becommeth hard, then let it cool, grind it on a stone, and put it in a glass with a long neck well stopped with luttum [lute, typically of clay, to form a seal], and set it in a pan with ashes, make a fire under it, and let it stand half a day, in such a manner, not over hot, till a yellow smoke riseth upon it, and when the yellow smoke is gone, then it is prepared.
>
> Otherwise.
>
> Take an ounce of tin, melt it in a pot, put into it half an ounce of tartarum, and one ounce of quick silver, stir them together, till it be hard, and congealed into a cake, then grind it well upon a stone, put to it one ounce of beaten Salarmoniack, mix them well together, then melt one ounce of brimstone, but make it not too hot, pour the ground powder into it, stir it well until it be hard, let it cool, and do as before is said.
>
> You must temper it thus.
>
> Grind it well, wash it well in clean water out of one mussel shell into another, till it be very clean, then put it into a pewter pot, put some gum water therein, stir it about, and white therewith, let it dry, and polish it.

Jack C. Thompson, *Manuscript Inks: Being a personal exploration of the materials and modes of production* (Portland, OR, 1996), pp. 29–30. For a discussion of classical and medieval ammonium chloride-based inks, see Cyril Stanley Smith and John G. Hawthorne, 'Mappae Clavicula: a little key to the world of medieval techniques', *Transactions of the American Philosophical Society, New Series*, LXIV/4 (1974); for a discussion of ammonium chloride inks and their use in secret and alchemical writings, see Martin Levey, 'Mediaeval Arabic Bookmaking and its relation to early chemistry and pharmacology', *Transactions of the American Philosophical Society, New Series*, LII/4 (1962). I am grateful to Julie Biggs at The Folger Shakespeare Library and Jack C. Thompson at the Thompson Conservation Laboratory for their bibliographical help and information about inks in the early modern period.

5 John Bulwer, *Anthropometamorphosis* (London, W. Hunt, 1653), p. 252.

6 *Ibid.*, p. 537.

7 *Ibid.*, p. 530.

8 Anonymous, *A Wonder of Wonders: or, a Metamorphosis of Fair Faces voluntarily transformed into foul visages: or, an Invective against Black-spotted Faces: By a Well-willer to modest Matrons and Virgins, MISO-SPILUS, i. Qui maculas odit* (London, J.G. for Richard Royston, 1662), pp. 4–5.

9   This idea is explored further by Juliet Fleming, 'The Renaissance Tattoo', *Res*, XXXI 31 (1997), pp. 34–52; and see Fleming, Chapter 5, this volume.
10 Forman, 'Of Apoticarie Drugs', f. 586v.
11 Although there is no direct evidence that Forman's occult marks penetrated his flesh, his three corporal inscriptions were permanent, and I have chosen, therefore, to define his markings as astral tattoos.
12 Robert Fludd, *Mosaical Philosophy: grounded on the essentiall truth or eternal sapience* (London: Humphrey Moseley, 1659), Bk. II, Sect. 2, chap. 4, *passim*.
13 A sibling of the talisman or the amulet, the gamahe was a magically empowered piece of paper or a piece of cloth that was fastened to the body. Particular spells or astrological signs were written on the paper or the cloth that were to be tied to the correspondent part of the body; the anchoring of the spell to the sympathetic body part allowed the magical writing to be in contact with the appropriate conduit of the flesh. Like the amulet or the talisman, it was the contact with the body that enabled the gamahe to have its effect.
14 Henricus Cornelius Agrippa von Nettesheim, *Three Books of Occult Philosophy*, trans. James Freake, ed. Donald Tyson (St Paul, MN, 1997), p. 47.
15 For a further discussion of magic in the early modern period see Stuart Clark, *Thinking with Demons: The Idea of Witchcraft in Early Modern Europe* (Oxford, 1997) and D. P. Walker, *Spiritual and Demonic Magic: from Ficino to Campanella* (London, 1958).
16 Agrippa, *Three Books*, Tyson edn, p. 558.
17 *Ibid.*, p. 562.
18 This book was originally attributed to Agrippa, but the authenticity of that claim is as questioned today as it was in the sixteenth century. Regardless of who penned the work, the text was written concurrently with Agrippa's other writings, and came to be regarded by many as part of the canon of occult texts. The difficulties concerning the authorship of the work are threefold: it was published after Agrippa's death; it is largely a reprint or recontextualization of *Three Books*; and Agrippa's own student, Johannes Wierus, rejected *of Occult Philosophy* as a forgery.
19 Henricus Cornelius Agrippa von Nettesheim, *of Occult Philosophy, or of magical ceremonies: the Fourth Book*, trans. Robert Turner (London: John Harrison, 1655), pp. 62–3.
20 *Ibid.*
21 Reginald Scot, *The Discoverie of Witchcraft . . . written and published in Anno 1584 by Reginald Scot, Esquire. London, Printed by Richard Cotes. 1651* (Suffolk, 1930), p. 241.
22 *Ibid.* Elias Ashmole (although the true author is believed to be Richard Napier) recounted an invocation that similarly mentioned the need to inscribe magical objects as well as the flesh. In his 'Rules and Observations to be used herein' Ashmole/Napier enumerated ten rules, which helped to prepare the magian for the invocation of the spirit Oberon. The ninth rule bade the magi to 'Anoint your eyes with the aforesaid thing [rosewater] before you begin', and the tenth, 'Make a candle of Alleluia virgin wax and write on the candle OBERYON.' Elias Ashmole, *The Invocation of Raphael Oberion Concerning Physick*, attributed to Richard Napier, Sloane 3846, fol. 107, The British Library, London.
23 Christopher Marlowe, *Doctor Faustus*, scene iii, lines 8–13.
24 Arthur Edward Waite, *The Book of Ceremonial Magic* (Secaucus, NJ, 1997), p. 80.
25 Anonymous untitled book of magic, with instructions for invoking spirits, etc., *c.* 1580, p. 190, manuscript collection, V.b. 26, The Folger Shakespeare Library, Washington, DC.
26 Sloane 3846, Sloane Mss, f. 14, The British Library, London, cited in Keith Thomas, *Religion and the Decline of Magic* (New York, 1971), pp. 180–1.

27 'Jasper brought Myrrh, Melcoir Frankincense, Balthazar Gold, whoever carries these three things of the Kings will be saved, if they have faith in the Lord, from the disease of falling' (author's translation). Peter Levens, *The Pathway to Health* (London: John Beale, 1654), p. 215. In 1584 Reginald Scot made a free translation of this age-old charm against the falling evil. In his *The Discoverie of Witchcraft* he wrote, 'Gaspar with his myrh beganne / these presents to unfold, / Then Melchior brought in frankincense, / and Balthasar brought in gold. / Now he that of these holie kings / the names about shall beare, / The falling yll by grace of Christ / shall never need to fear' (Scot, p. 132).

28 Geoffrey Chaucer, *The Canterbury Tales, The General Prologue*, lines 413–14 and 431–6.

29 The text went through four editions, the latest of which was in 1595. There are also fourteen extant manuscript versions, all fourteenth- to fifteenth-century. Although textual popularity does not equal good medicine, the influence of the text cannot be ignored. John of Gaddesden, *Rosa Anglica practica medicine a capite ad pedes*, cited in Logan Clendening, ed., *Source Book of Medical History* (Mineola, NY, 1960), p. 14.

30 *Ibid.*, pp. 84–5.

31 Agrippa, *Three Books*, Tyson edition, p. 345. These astrological assumptions were the base construct for physiognomy in the period.

32 F. Kett, *The Key to Unknowne Knowledge* (London, Edward White, 1599), p. Aiii.

33 John Woodall, *The Surgeon's Mate, or military and domestique surgery* (London, Nicholas Bourne, 1639), p. 401.

34 Laurent Bordelon, *A History of the Ridiculous Extravagancies of Monsieur Oufle; occasioned by his reading books treating of magic, the black art, daemonicks, conjurers . . . written originally in French, by the Abbot B—— and now translated into English* (London, J. Morphew, 1711), fol. 53. This *History of the Ridiculous Extravagancies*, as outlined in its preface, was written in the genre of *Don Quixote* and *The Extravagent Shepard*, which were entertaining fictions published to expose 'those deprav'd by reading Poets, Romances, Books of Chivalry, and other such Trifles, widely distant from Truth, and all Probability'. According to Bordelon, *A History of the Ridiculous Extravagancies* was an extraordinary text because it was a work of non-fiction; Monsieur Oufle, said Bordelon, was a real man who 'believed nothing so firmly, as what appear'd incredible to others' (fol. A2). Although an author of both historical and fictional texts, Bordelon's main interest was encyclopaedic histories of social thought and of social aberrations, or what he called 'curieuses'. *Les Imaginations extravagantes de M. Oufle*, which was first published in 1710, was one of Bordelon's many texts (like his 1692 *Les Diversités curieuses* and his 1699 *Histoire critique des personnes les plus remarquables de tous les siècles*), that made sweeping generalizations and claims, but offered no real evidence or support. Given that Bordelon's field of interest was the social and personal curiosities of interesting men, and that he also wrote great fictions for the stage, it is difficult to know whether *A History of the Ridiculous Extravagances* was a work of non-fiction, fiction, or possibly (and most likely) both.

35 *Ibid.*, fol.148.

36 *Ibid.*

37 Agrippa, *Three Books*, Tyson edition, pp. 591–2.

38 Bordelon, fols 155–6.

39 Agrippa, *Three Books*, Tyson edition, pp. 108–9.

40 For a discussion of pilgrimage tattoos, see Fleming, Chapter 5, this volume.

41 Henry Maundrell, *A Journey from Aleppo to Jerusalem at easter ad 1697* (London, John Bowyer, 1703), p. 73.

5 JULIET FLEMING: THE RENAISSANCE TATTOO

With thanks to Joseph Koerner for suggesting I write on abjection; Phillipa Berry, Joseph Boone, Dympna Callaghan, Stefan Collini, Katherine Craik, Ezra Getzler, Martin Hyland, Rayna Kalas, Charles MacQuarrie, Steven Melville, Francesco Pellizzi, David Rollo and Einar Steingrimsson for information and comments.

1 Marcia Tucker, 'Tattoo: the State of the Art', *Artforum*, May 1981, p. 44. For further details of the tattoo renaissance see Arnold Rubin, 'The Tattoo Renaissance', in A. Rubin, ed., *Marks of Civilization: Artistic Transformations of the Human Body* (Los Angeles, 1988), pp. 233–62; and Clinton Sanders, 'Organizational constraints on tattoo images: a sociological analysis of artistic style', in I. Hodder, ed., *The Meanings of Things: Material Culture and Symbolic Expression* (New York, 1989), pp. 232–41.
2 Rubin, *Marks of Civilization*, p. 258.
3 *Ibid.*, p. 260.
4 Tucker, 'Tattoo: the State of the Art', p. 43.
5 See Don E. Hardy, *Forever Yes: Art of the New Tattoo* (Honolulu, 1992), p. 15: 'Nonexclusionary and defiantly beyond the commodification inherent in all other mediums, tattooing is a universal body language bridging cultural differences with direct expression.'
6 Walter Benjamin, *Illuminations*, ed. Hannah Arendt, trans. Harry Zohn (New York, 1985), p. 227.
7 Quoted in Rubin, 'The Tattoo Renaissance', p. 255.
8 Julia Kristeva, *Powers of Horror: An Essay on Abjection*, trans. Leon S. Roudiez (New York, 1982).
9 Describing the Cartesian *cogito* as 'the presence, inside man, of the celebrated little fellow who governs him, who is the driver', a notion 'already denounced by pre-Socratic thought', Lacan offers instead his own formulation of the subject, a subject properly symbolized by the barred S [$] 'in so far as it is constituted as secondary in relation to the signifier'. The bar may be thought of as the stroke or notch of the signifier that, marking the subject off, situates him as such. The difference between Lacanian and Cartesian models of the self, the one 'marked' and the other not, may be grasped by considering that the Lacanian subject is instantiated *as a tattoo*: 'The subject himself is marked off by a single stroke, and first he marks himself as a tattoo, the first of the signifiers.' Jacques Lacan, *Four Fundamental Concepts of Psycho-Analysis* (1973) trans. Alan Sheridan (New York, 1982), p.141.
10 Hardy, *Forever Yes*, p. 52.
11 *Tattoo International*, CLV (November 1994), p. 11.
12 Rubin, 'The Tattoo Renaissance', pp. 257–8.
13 Michel Thévoz, *The Painted Body* (New York, 1983), p. 70.
14 Kristeva, *Powers of Horror*, pp. 3–4.
15 Alfred Gell, *Wrapping in Images: Tattooing in Polynesia* (Oxford, 1993), pp. 38–9.
16 Gell suggests a socio-historical explanation for the radical bifurcation in the meaning of tattoos: 'whereas in non-hierarchical societies body-markings reveal an immanent self which is inside the body, and can be made to appear on the skin, in hierarchical societies body markings are brands imposed from without, and signify the suppression of the devalued body', *Wrapping in Images*, p. 26. In today's Western societies, where a significant proportion of the population is tattooed, the case is less clear-cut, and the tattoo is understood as being *simultaneously* a

symptom and the effect of sublimation. Italian criminologist Cesare Lombroso touched on the strange double nature of the tattoo in his analysis of the signs of criminality. Arguing that a disposition to criminality was inborn, the result of an ontogenetic deficit, Lombroso included among the signs of criminal tendencies large jaws, high cheek bones, handle-shaped ears, 'insensibility to pain, extremely acute sight, tattooing, excessive idleness, love of orgies, and the irresistible craving for evil for its own sake' (Cesare Lombroso, *Criminal Man*, comp. G. Lombroso-Ferrero [New York, 1911], p. xv). In Lombroso's list, tattooing occupies the place of a hinge between physical symptoms and social characteristics: actively chosen by those who bear them, the tattoo is the product of an irresistible, biological disposition to become tattooed. Lombroso's conclusion, and the deductive method that produced and reproduced it, were taken to their logical conclusion by his contemporary Adolf Loos: 'If someone who is tattooed dies in freedom, then he does so a few years before he would have committed murder' (Alfred Loos, 'Ornament and Crime' (1908), in L. Münz, and G. Künstler, *Adolf Loos: Pioneer of Modern Architecture*, trans. Harold Meek (London, 1966), pp. 226–31).

17 *Tattoo International*, CLIII (June 1994), pp. 10–11.
18 Kristeva, *Powers of Horror*, p. 17.
19 Benjamin, *Illuminations*, p. 220.
20 Jacques Lacan, *The Ethics of Psychoanalysis 1959–60* (1986) (London, 1992), p. 139.
21 Describing the 'propensity for interpreters to regard tattooing as a kind of writing, legible if one just knew how to read it', Nicholas Thomas notes that apprehension of the curvilinear forms characteristic of Maori *moko* as 'scrolls' constitutes 'an effort to read the visual for what it [is] not ... Interpretative desire is defeated from the start if designs take the form of an archaic bearer of writing, a scroll which appears as such only in profile, its text surely there but unnecessarily seen. If only it could be looked at from a different angle, pleads the reader' (Nicholas Thomas, 'Kiss the Baby Goodbye: *Kowhaiwhai* and Aesthetics in Aotearoa New Zealand', *Critical Inquiry*, XXII/1, pp. 93–4. The skin is a two-dimensional surface that at once provokes and defeats a desire for depth.
22 Didier Anzieu, *The Skin Ego*, trans. Chris Turner (New Haven, 1989), p. 9.
23 *Ibid.*
24 Sigmund Freud, *The Standard Edition of the Complete Psychological Works of Sigmund Freud*, trans. James Strachey (London, 1953–74), vol. XIX, p. 26.
25 Anzieu, *The Skin Ego*, p. 60. The figure whose depth is a feature of its surface, or the figure whose surface is, like that of a manifold, without edge, is a recurrent motif in contemporary French theory. It is encountered in the Möbius strip that Lacan chose as an emblem for the journal *Scilicet*; in his figure of the mitre (a self-intersecting surface projected into three-dimensional space) in the seminar on *Identification*; and in the other 'fundamental' topological objects (such as the Klein bottle and the Borromean rings) that organize his late work. Lacan cautions that, in everything concerning topology, 'one must always be very careful to avoid attributing it with any kind of Gestalt function'. But he goes on to demonstrate the pleasure to be gained from imagining biological life's 'touching strivings after topological configurations' (especially when that life form is the erect, uncircumcised penis); and finally insists that only topological considerations can provide us with appropriate images to organize our thought 'when it is a question of something inside that is also outside' (Lacan, *Four Fundamental Concepts*, p. 147). Pressed on his use of topological figures, 'Is topology for you a method of discovery or of exposition?', Lacan replied with enigmatic caution. 'It is the

mapping of the topology proper to our experience as analysts, which may be taken in a metaphysical perspective' (p. 90). In Lacan's writing, the fact that the Ego 'has' (or maybe is thought to have) the structure of the Möbius strip goes some way towards accounting for its perversion and alienation. Anzieu's more complaisant conception of the Ego leads him to consider the Möbius strip configuration as being specific only to borderline states (Anzieu, *The Skin Ego*, p. 124). But both theorists link psychic disturbance, pathological or not, to what they understand as geometrical disturbance; as does Kristeva when she describes *jouissance* as 'a "structure" that is skewed, a topology of catastrophe' (Kristeva, *Powers of Horror*, p. 9). It is here that the question of the appropriateness of using topological figures to represent psychic phenomena may be raised – a question that, for the mathematician, marks a border dispute between the hard science of mathematics and a humanistic discourse that takes mathematical truths either for metaphors, or as models for psychic entities and effects. At issue is the fact that in mathematics topological figures carry no affect: the Jordan curve theorem, for example, demonstrates the difficulty, but not the trauma, of proving that there are such concepts as inside and outside. Viewed from the perspective of mathematics, the purchase that topological paradoxes have on the humanities, their capacity to provoke and model intellectual anxieties, would dissolve as soon as those figures were properly, that is mathematically, understood. But such a view is motivated by suspicion of the productive conflation in Freudian and Lacanian psychoanalysis between bodily organ and image; between causal explanation and hermeneutics. It is consequently a suspicion that disables from the start any attempt to understand Lacan's account of the Cause at work in the midst of the field of hermeneutics. For further discussion see Slavoj Zizek, *The Mestastases of Enjoyment: Six Essays on Woman and Causality* (London, 1994), pp. 29–54.

26 Jacques Derrida, *Dissemination*, trans. Barbara Johnson (Chicago, 1981), p. 229; Gilles Deleuze, *The Fold: Leibnitz and the Baroque*, trans. Tom Conley (London, 1993); Gilles Deleuze and Félix Guattari, *A Thousand Plateaus: Capitalism and Schizophrenia*, trans. Brian Massumi (Minneapolis, 1987); Jean-François Lyotard, *Discours, figure* (Paris, 1971). For Derrida, Mallarmé's fold marks the place at which conventional literary criticism fails, and the work of deconstruction begins: 'Now, if we can begin to see that the "blank" and the "fold" cannot in fact be mastered as themes or as meanings [in Mallarmé], if it is within the folds and blankness of a certain hymen that the very textuality of the text is re-marked, then we will precisely have determined the limits of thematic criticism itself' (pp. 245–6). Lacan's use of topological figures to describe the problematic relation of inside and outside is illuminated by Derrida's discussion of that relation as 'the matrix of all possible opposition', and of writing as the term or practice that 'opens up' the 'very possibility' of these oppositions 'without letting itself be comprehended by them' (pp. 103–4).

27 For a discussion of the difficult conditions under which Michelangelo worked on *The Last Judgment* and the real and fantasized cutaneous discomfort such conditions provoked see R. Leibert, *Michaelangelo: A Psychoanalytic Study of his Life and Images* (New Haven, 1983), pp. 331–60.

28 For a discussion of anatomy as a method for revealing order which causes decay see Devon Hodges, *Renaissance Fictions of Anatomy* (Amherst, 1985).

29 J. Curtis, *An Authentic and Faithful History of the Mysterious Murder of Maria Marten* (London: Thomas Kelly, 1828). The volume is now in Moyses Hall Museum, Bury St Edmunds, England.

30　In the course of his discussion of primitive accumulation, Marx offers a parodic, 'nursery tale' account of the genesis of capitalism, one predicated on a division between the 'frugal élite' and the 'lazy rascals': 'Thus it came to pass, that the former sort accumulated wealth, and the latter finally had nothing to sell except their own skins' (Karl Marx, *Capital*, vol. 1 [1867], trans. Ben Fowkes [New York, 1977], p. 872). The bottom line that presents itself to Marx and, he imagines, to even the most irresponsible theorists of capitalism is the human skin – the commodity in which no one, even the person who owns it, has the right to trade. In actuality the tattooed skin can be bought and sold – but not without raising profound questions concerning human and property rights.

31　For description of the reception of Omai in Britain see Harriet Guest, 'Curiously Marked: Tattooing, Masculinity and Nationality in Eighteenth-Century British Perceptions of the South Pacific', in John Barrell, ed., *Painting and the Politics of Culture: New Essays on British Art, 1700–1850* (Oxford, 1992), pp. 101–34 and Guest, Chapter 6, this volume. For an extended discussion of the impact of European exploration on Polynesian tattooing see Gell, *Wrapping in Images*.

32　Samuel Purchas, *Purchas His Pilgrimage* (London: W. Stansby, 1617) contains many descriptions of tattooing reproduced from the accounts of European travellers (see for example pp. 487, 571, 743, 813, 853, 876, 955, 958).

33　Gell, *Wrapping in Images*, p. 10.

34　A. Juno, and V. Vale, Interview with G and P. P-Orridge, *Research* 12 (1991), pp. 164–81, p. 180.

35　William Camden, *Britannia* (1586) trans. P. Holland (London: G. Bishop, 1610), p. 115. In discussing the history of the Scots, Camden underlines his purpose in arguing for the racial unity of the ancient peoples of Britain; and incidentally demonstrates the difficulty of producing a tactful account of Britain's barbarian past: 'So far am I from working any discredit unto them, that I have rather respectively loved them alwaies, as of the same bloud and stoke, yes, and honoured them too, even when the kingdomes were divided: but now much more, since it hath pleased our almightie, and most mercifull God, that wee growe united in one Bodie, under one most Sacred head of the Empire, to the joy, happinesse, welfare, and safetie, of both Nations' (p. 119).

36　Purchas, *Purchas his Pilgrimage*, p. 955.

37　John Speed, *The Historie of Great Britaine* (1611) (London: G. Humble, 1627), p. 167; see Camden, *Britannia*, p. 31.

38　In Joyce's *Ulysses* D. B. Murphy bears three tattoos, one 'a young man's side face looking frowningly rather ... See here, he said, showing Antonio. There he is cursing the mate. And there he is now, he added, the same fellow, pulling the skin with his fingers, some special knack evidently, and he laughing at a yarn' (James Joyce, *Ulysses* (1922) (London, 1986), p. 156). For a discussion of Murphy's tattoos see J. Levine, 'James Joyce, Tattoo Artist: Tracing the Outlines of Homosocial Desire', *James Joyce Quarterly*, XXXI/3 (1994), pp. 277–300.

39　Speed, p. 182; see also Camden, p. 115.

40　Lacan introduces a tattoo to illustrate 'a dimension in the field of the gaze that has nothing to do with the vision as such', a dimension that may be apprehended operating within 'all the paranoic ambiguities' to which distortion may lend itself. 'How is it', he continues, 'that nobody has ever thought of connecting this with ... the effect of an erection? Imagine a tattoo traced on the sexual organ *ad hoc* in the state of repose and assuming its, if I may say so, developed form in another state.' Lacan, *Four Fundamental Concepts*, p. 88. Lacan's imaginary organ is, in his own argument, something of a chimera: one that is briefly standing in for the 'gaze as such', that is, for the desire that articulates itself through optical distortion. But it is worth remaining with the tattooed penis long enough to note that in the stretching of the tattoo image we confront the propositions that semblance is subject to physical laws, and that the image has an internal structure having nothing to do with appearance.

41 Camden, *Britannia*, p. 30. In *The Historie of Great Britaine*, Speed goes so far as to compare Queen Elizabeth to Bodicea, 'another Great Lady of British race . . . whose juste, wise, and resolute kinde of Government hath justified that Custome of our old *Britaines* and *Picts* . . . that they made no difference for the Soveraigne command, yea, and used to warre under the conduct of women' (p. 183).

42 The association of tattooing with the rule of women reaches beyond its historical justification; where it emerges in the discourse of modern anthropology it is often used to mark the double abjection of native cultures. So Joseph Dowd suggested tattooing was a practice 'which probably originated at a time when the matriarchate was universal and before children came to have individual names. Instead of giving a special name to each member of the family or tribe, all of the same blood on the mother's side were designated by a common tattoo mark' (J. Dowd, *The Negro Races: A Sociological Study* (London, 1907), p. 42). In his 1898 essay 'Matriarchy among the Picts' Heinrich Zimmer also linked the two practices when he insisted that tattooing, like matrilinear descent, was a savage custom not properly associated with the Aryan community: see Charles MacQuarrie, 'Insular Celtic Tattooing: History, Myth, and Metaphor', *Etudes Celtiques*, XXIII (1999), pp. 159–89, and MacQuarrie, Chapter 3, this volume.

43 The question of whether or not the Picts tattooed themselves has not been fully addressed. Part of the evidence for ancient British tattooing, as Claudian, Solinus, Camden, Speed and others point out, is comprised by the Roman name Picti (the painted men) and the ancient British name *Priteni* (people of the designs). See MacQuarrie, 'Insular Celtic Tattooing', pp. 2–10.

44 For an excellent account of tattooing in Greek and Roman Antiquity see C. P. Jones, '*Stigma*: Tattooing and Branding in Graeco-Roman Antiquity', *The Journal of Roman Studies*, LXXVII (1987), pp. 139–55. Distinguishing the practice from branding, Jones argues that the incidence of tattooing for decorative, religious and punitive purposes was sufficiently widespread that 'the word stigma and its cognates could be used in Ptolemaic Alexandria and Neronian Rome to refer to tattooing without any fear of misinterpretation' (p. 140). I am resisting Jones's conclusions that tattooing was confined to the bodies of slaves, criminals and barbarians; and that from the Middle Ages to modern times it was known as a living tradition 'only to travellers to the orient, or, from the late eighteenth century on, in the South Pacific' (p. 155). See also Jones, Chapter 1, this volume.

45 Speed, *The Historie of Great Britaine*, p. 179.

46 The first Roanoke expedition, for which John White acted as official recorder, was led by Sir Richard Greville under the patronage of Raleigh from June 1585 to June 1586. In July 1587 White returned to Roanoke as governor of 'the city of Raleigh in Virginia'. Shortly after his arrival there he went back to England in search of further provisions and assistance; on returning to Roanoke in August 1590, he found the settlement deserted. See Paul Hulton, *America 1585: The Complete Drawings of John White* (Chapel Hill, 1984).

47 Jacques Le Moyne de Morgues accompanied the French commander Réné de Laudonniere on his expedition to Floria in 1563 and 1565. Laudonniere's expedition

journal was published by Hakluyt in France in 1586, and in London in English in 1587 and 1589. Le Moyne left France as a Huguenot refugee some time after 1573, settled in Blackfriars as a painter and engraver under the patronage of Mary Sidney and Walter Raleigh and died in 1588. See Paul Hulton, ed., *The Work of Jacques Le Moyne de Morgues, a Huguenot artist in France, Florida, and England*, 2 vols (London, 1977).

48 Theodor de Bry was a Flemish goldsmith, engraver, and publisher with Protestant sympathies. In 1587 he was commissioned to engrave Thomas Lant's drawings of Philip Sidney's funeral procession; on a return visit to London the following year he purchased le Moyne's paintings from his widow. Two of Le Moyne's Florida paintings are used to illustrate *America I* (1590), which is dedicated to Walter Raleigh; the rest appeared in *America II* (1591): see Hulton, *The Complete Drawings of John White*.

49 De Bry *America I*, Plate 39; translation by Hulton, *The Work of Jacques Le Moyne de Morgues*, p. 151.

50 See Hulton, *The Work of Jacques Le Moyne de Morgues*, p. 70.

51 *Ibid.*, p. 148.

52 Hulton, *The Complete Drawings of John White*, p. 9.

53 De Bry, *America I*, Sig A1v and A2.

54 Hulton, *The Complete Drawings of John White*, p. 28.

55 White is known to have made direct copies of Le Moyne's work, and it is possible that de Bry was working from such a copy when he engraved 'The Truue picture of a yonge dowgter of the Pictes'. For an account of the complicated relationship between the work of Le Moyne, White and de Bry see Hulton, *The Complete Drawings of John White*, pp. 17–18.

56 Hulton, *The Work of Jacques Le Moyne de Morgues*, p. 164.

57 *Ibid.*, p. 57.

58 The sixteenth-century French word *fleurdelise* carries some of the same determinants: Randall Cotgrave's *Dictionarie of the French and English Tongues* (1611) defines the verb *fleurdeliser* as meaning 'to set a flowerdeluce between the shoulders with a hot yron (the mark of a rogue;) also, to flourish, beautify, sticke, set thicke, with Flowerdeluces'.

59 J. Peterson, 'Writing Flowers: Figuration and the Feminine in Carmina Burana 177', *Exemplaria*, VI/1 (1994), pp. 1–34 (24).

60 Hulton, *The Work of Jacques Le Moyne de Morgues*, I, p. 78. Although he seems, like de Bry, to have enjoyed the patronage of Raleigh and the Sidney Family, Le Moyne was still in possession of the painting at his death, which he had also, on an earlier occasion, refused to sell to de Bry. While Hulton concludes that *A Young Daughter* was painted for no occasion other than the exercise of Le Moyne's own virtuosity, it is possible that the painting consituted something of an in-joke aimed at Camden.

61 Speed, *The Historie of Great Britaine*, pp. 180–2.

62 Camden, *Britannia*, p. 110.

63 Fynes Moryson, *An Intinerary* (London: John Beale, 1617), vol. I, pp. 233–4; Emile Durkheim, *Elementary Forms of Religious Life* (1912), trans. J. W. Swain (London, 1976), p. 232. See also J. Carswell, *Coptic Tattoo Designs* (Jerusalem, 1956), and L. Keimer, *Remarques sur le Tatouage dans l'Eqypte Ancienne* (Cairo, 1948).

64 MacQuarrie, 'Insular Celtic Tattooing', pp. 28–9, and Chapter 3, this volume.

65 See A. Sinclair, 'Tattooing – Oriental and Gypsy', *American Anthropologist* N.S. X/3 (1908), pp. 361–88 (369); MacQuarrie, 'Insular Celtic Tattooing', pp. 12–13, and Chapter 3, this volume.

66 W. Stubbs *De gestis regum Anglorum* (Her Majesty's Stationery Office, 1887), vol. II, p. 305.

67 George Sandys, G. (1615), *A Relation of a Journey begun An.Dom. 1610* (London: W. Barrett, 1615), p. 56. See also Henry Maundrell's laconic but detailed account in *A Journey from Aleppo to Jerusalem at Easter 1697* (Oxford: Jonah Bowyer, 1707), pp. 445–6: 'March 27 [1697] – The next morning nothing extraordinary passed, which gave many of the pilgrims leisure to have their arms marked with the usual ensigns of Jerusalem. The artists who undertake the operation do it in this manner. They have stamps in wood of any figure you desire, which they first print off upon your arm with powder of charcoal; then, taking two very fine needles tied close together, and dipping them often, like a pen, in certain ink, compounded, as I was informed, of gunpowder and ox-gall, they make with them small punctures all along the lines of the figure which they have printed, and then, washing the part in wine, conclude the work. These punctures they make with great quickness and dexterity, and with scarce any smart, seldom piercing so deep as to draw blood.' For a set of traditional tattoo patterns, and a careful description of the history of the practice in Jerusalem, see Carswell, *Coptic Tattoo Designs*.

68 In his seventeenth-century account, Melchisedech Thevenot suggests that tattooing is the characteristic practice of both pilgrims and a Christian sect living in Bethlehem: 'Nous emploiames tout le Mardi 29 Avril a nous faire marquer les bras, comme sont ordinairerment tous les Pélerins, ce sont des Chretiens de Bethlehem suivant le rit Latin qui font cela . . . Ils ont une petite canne ou sont deux aiguilles, qu'ils trempent de tems en tems dans l'ancre melée avec du fiel de boeuf, et vous en piquent suivant les lignes marquées par le moule de bois . . . les marques restent bleues, et ne s'effacent jamais, parce que le sang se melant avec cette teinture d'ancre et de fiel de beuf, se marquer encor dedans sous la peau.' Melchisedech Thevenot, *Voyages de Mr de Thevenot* (Paris: Charles Angot, 1689), pp. 638–9.

69 E. Terry, *A Voyage to East India* (London: J. Martin, 1655), Sig E8–E8v.

70 Moryson, *An Itinerary*, p. 237.

71 William Lithgow, *A most delectable, and true discourse, of an admired and painfull peregrination in Europe, Asia, and Africke* (London: N. Oakes, 1614), Sig. R3–R3v.

72 William Lithgow, *The Total Discourse of the Rare Adventures etc.* (a later edition of *A most delectable and true discourse*) (London: J. Oakes, 1640). By Lithgow's own account, the Jerusalem official who saw the tattoo was 'greatly offended with me, that I should have polluted that holy place with the name of such an arch-enemy to the Roman church' (p. 269).

73 Gell, *Wrapping in Images*, p. 10.

74 De Bry, *America I*, Plate 23.

75 Speed, *The Historie of Great Britaine*, p. 182. Simon Forman, *Volumen Primum*. Volume II (1609) (Ashmole 1494) ff 586v–587r. (See Rosecrans, Chapter 5, this volume.)

6 HARRIET GUEST: CURIOUSLY MARKED

1 The title of the islander was Mai, but most eighteenth-century British accounts name him Omai, or Omiah. I have adopted this colonialist form because it is British representations of the islander that I am concerned with. I quote from *The Early Diary of Frances Burney, 1768–1778*, ed., Annie Raine Ellis, 2 vols (London: 1913), I, p. 337.

2 Bernard Smith, *European Vision and the South Pacific* (New Haven, CT, 1985), pp. 80–1.
3 E. H. McCormick, *Omai: Pacific Envoy* (Auckland, 1977), p. 174.
4 *A Voyage round the World*, in *Georg Forster's Werke*, ed. Robert L. Kahn (Berlin, 1968), I, p. 15.
5 O. H. K. Spate, *The Pacific since Magellan, III: Paradise Found and Lost* (Canberra, 1988), p. 256.
6 *The Endeavour Journal of Joseph Banks, 1768–1771*, ed. J. C. Beaglehole, 2 vols (Sydney, 1962), I, pp. 312–13.
7 John Rickman, *Journal of Captain Cook's Last Voyage to the Pacific Ocean* (Amsterdam, 1967), p. 185.
8 See Nicholas Thomas, *Entangled Objects: Exchange, Material Culture and Colonialism in the Pacific* (Cambridge, MA, 1991), ch. 4. The clothing of Reynolds's figure bears some resemblance to that represented in pl. 3 of Sydney Parkinson, *A Journal of a Voyage to the South Seas* (London, 1984), as well as to conceptions of oriental and classical drapery. It may be the kind of clothing Horace Walpole alluded to in his comment that the plates from Cook's published voyages showed men and women 'dressed unbecomingly as if both sexes were ladies of the highest fashion'. Quoted in Michael Alexander, *Omai: Noble Savage* (London, 1977), p. 108.
9 George Hamilton, *Voyage of the H.M.S. 'Pandora'* (London, 1915), p. 127.
10 James Boswell, *Life of Johnson*, ed. R. W. Chapman, rev. J. D. Fleeman (London, 1976), pp. 722–3. On curiosity, see Spate, *The Pacific since Magellan*, 81, and Daniel A. Baugh, 'Seapower and Science: The Motives for Pacific Exploration', in Derek Howse, ed., *Background to Discovery: Pacific Exploration from Dampier to Cook* (Berkeley, CA, 1990).
11 *The Journals of Captain James Cook on his Voyages of Discovery: II: The Voyage of the Resolution and Adventure, 1772–1775*, ed. J. C. Beaglehole, 2nd of 3 vols (Cambridge, 1969), p. 428, n. 2; James Cook, *A Voyage towards the South Pole, and Round the World*, 2 vols (London, 1777), I, p. 169.
12 John Forster, *Observations made during a Voyage round the World* (London, 1778), p. 247.
13 Joshua Reynolds, *Discourses on Art*, ed. Robert R. Wark (New Haven, CT, 1975), p. 58.
14 Letter to the *Gentleman's Magazine*, quoted in McCormick, *Omai: Pacific Envoy*, p. 138, and see 174. The perception of Omai as a potential 'macaroni' clearly alludes to Joseph Banks's reputation for fashionable dress and pursuits. Perhaps the most striking comparison with Omai's pose in Reynolds's portrait is the engraving of 'A Merchant of Java', pl. 31 in Johan Niehof, *Voyages and Travels to the East Indies 1653–1670*, introd. by Anthony Reid (Singapore, 1988). Reid points out that this was 'one of the most influential accounts of the Malay World and South India in English' in the 18th century (p. v).
15 George Colman the Younger, quoted in, for example, Charles Lyte, *Sir Joseph Banks: 18th Century Explorer, Botanist and Entrepreneur* (Newton Abbott, 1980), p. 192.
16 Reynolds, *Discourses*, pp. 136, 135, 137. I discuss this Discourse in more detail in my earlier version of this essay, 'Curiously Marked: Tattooing, Masculinity, and Nationality in Eighteenth-Century British Perceptions of the South Pacific', in John Barrell, ed., *Painting and the Politics of Culture: New Essays on British Art, 1700–1850* (Oxford, 1992). For a fuller reading of Reynolds's argument see John Barrell, *The Political Theory of Painting from Reynolds to Hazlitt: The Body of the Public* (New Haven, CT, 1986), pp. 136–58.
17 Reynolds, *Discourses*, p. 137. Reynolds's portrait of Omai was exhibited at the Academy with a portrait of the same size of Georgiana, Duchess of Devonshire,

in fashionable dress, almost as though in allusion to the juxtaposition of unacceptable fashions in Reynolds's Discourse. See McCormick, *Omai: Pacific Envoy*, pp. 168–9, 174.

18 Reynolds, *Discourses*, 138. On morality, custom, and the constitution of community in these decades see Adam Smith, *The Theory of Moral Sentiments* (1759), pt. 1. ss. 1–2, and pt. v, and John Bender, *Imagining the Penitentiary: Fiction and the Architecture of Mind in Eighteenth-Century England* (Chicago, 1987), pp. 218–28.

19 Banks, *Journals*, II, pp. 330, 332–3.

20 J. Burney, *With Captain James Cook in the Antarctic and Pacific*, ed. Beverley Hooper (Canberra, 1975), p. 96.

21 (? John Marra) *Journal of the Resolution's Voyage* (London, 1775), p. 94. In Burney's account, the European party initially identified what they found as dog's flesh, but in Marra's account they are credited with greater forensic percipience, and the dogs become accomplices in the alien savagery of the islanders.

22 Burney, *With Captain James Cook*, p. 97.

23 The Journal of Charlotte Ann Burney, which reports Charles Burney's comments, also indicates that the discovery of the remains at Grass Cove was not universally regarded as convincing proof of cannibalism, or as an occasion for instinctive horror. David Garrick commented, on hearing of James Burney's whispers: 'Why, what, they didn't eat 'em? . . . we are not sure . . . perhaps they potted 'em!' In Frances Burney, II, p. 283.

24 Furneaux's Narrative, in Cook's *Journals*, II, p. 744.

25 Anderson's Journal, in Cook's *Journals*, III, p. 799.

26 Cook, *Voyage*, I, pp. 127, 245.

27 *Ibid.*, pp. 245–6.

28 *Ibid.*, pp. 245.

29 Parkinson, *Journal of a Voyage*, p. 91. For accounts of the tattooing practices of New Zealand, see Ko Te Riria and David Simmons, *Maori Tattoo* (Auckland, 1989), and Major General Horatio G. Robley, *Moko; or Maori Tattooing* (1896; Auckland, 1987). Robley's account includes drawings and discussions of pieces of tattooed skin from various parts of the anatomy, preserved in his own personal collection. For further discussion of some of these issues and images see Leonard Bell, *The Maori in European Art* (Wellington, 1980), and Margaret Jolly, 'Illnatured Comparisons: Racism and Relativism in European Representations of Ni-Vanuatu from Cook's Second Voyage', *History and Anthropology*, V (1990).

30 Monkhouse's Journal, in Cook's *Journals*, I, p. 586.

31 See Harriet Guest, 'The Great Distinction: Figures of the Exotic in the Work of William Hodges', in Isobel Armstrong, ed., *New Feminist Discourses: Critical Essays on Theories and Texts* (London, 1992), pp. 296–391; and Nicholas Thomas, '"On the Varieties of the Human Species": Forster's Comparative Ethnology', in Johann Reinhold Forster, *Observations made During a Voyage Round the World*, ed. N. Thomas, H. Guest and M. Dettelbach (Honolulu, 1996), pp. xxiii–xl.

32 *John Ledyard's Journey Through Russia and Siberia, 1787–1788: The Journal and Selected Letters*, ed. Stephen D. Watrous (Madison, Wis., 1966), pp. 182–3.

33 See J. C. Beaglehole, 'The Young Banks', in Banks's *Journals*, I, p. 41 and n. 1.

34 *Captain Cook's Second Voyage: The Journals of Lieutenants Elliott and Pickersgill*, ed. Christine Holmes (London, 1984), pp. 20–1.

35 *The Bligh Notebooks, with a Draft List of the Bounty Mutineers*, ed. John Bach (Sydney, 1987), p. 214. James Morrisson, who bore the star and garter tattoo, remained on Tahiti for some time after the mutiny. Writing about his stay, he argued that every

line of the tattoos was significant, dismissing the distinction between public
significance and private whim made by other voyagers.
36 Reynolds, *Discourses*, pp. 137–8.

7 CLARE ANDERSON: GODNA

1 Research for this chapter was carried out in the India Office Library (IOL), with a
grant from the Faculty of Social Sciences, University of Leicester. I inadvertently
found material during a trip to the National Archives of India (NAI), funded by the
Carnegie Trust for the Universities of Scotland. The British Academy generously
supported earlier research in the Mauritius Archives (MA) and Manuscripts Room
of the British Library. I have benefited enormously from discussions with and
comments from David Arnold, Crispin Bates, James Bradley, Jane Caplan, Joanna
de Groot, Roger Jeffery, Patricia Jeffery, Hamish Maxwell-Stewart, Peter Musgrave,
Tamsin O'Connor and Radhika Singha.
2 L. K. Ananthakrishna Iyer, *The Mysore Tribes and Castes*, I (Mysore, 1935), p. 437.
3 R. V. Russell and Hira Lal, *The Tribes and Castes of the Central Provinces of India*, III (New
Delhi, 1975, first published 1919), pp. 123–6. 'Gond' is of course a term used to
describe a vast number of different tribes; quite which group Russell and Lal are
referring to is unclear.
4 J. Forsyth, *The Highlands of Central India; notes on their forests and wild tribes, natural
history, and sports* (London, 1872), p. 148.
5 O. P. Joshi, 'Tattooing and Tattooers: a socio-cultural analysis', in *Marks and
Meaning; Anthropology of Symbols*, ed. O. P. Joshi (Jaipur, 1992), p. 18.
6 Iyer, *Mysore Tribes*, p. 438.
7 '[Burmans] would as soon think of wearing a woman's skirt as of omitting to be
tattooed.' Schway Yoe (pseudonym for J. G. Scott), *The Burman, His Life and Notions*
(London, 1910), p. 39.
8 Russell and Lal, *Tribes and Castes*, p. 308.
9 *Ibid.*, p. 127. There are frequent references to 'burn marks' on the stomach and
limbs in the physical descriptions, recorded in ship indents, of Indian convicts
transported from the subcontinent during the first half of the nineteenth century.
10 Iyer, *Mysore Tribes*, p. 446.
11 Alfred Gell, *Wrapping In Images: Tattooing in Polynesia* (Oxford, 1993), p. 26.
12 J. A. Abbé Du Bois, *Hindu Manners, Customs and Ceremonies* (Oxford, 1943, first
published 1906), p. 271.
13 W. D. Hambly,*The History of Tattooing and Its Significance With Some Account of Other
Forms of Corporal Marking* (London, 1925), pp. 53, 70 ff. Tattoos could also record
religious pilgrimage. Armenians tattooed in Jerusalem used the same word –
mahdesi – for pilgrims and tattoos, marking, literally, the occasion. Likewise,
Muslim pilgrims tattooed in Mecca used the Turkish word *haji* for both. A. T.
Sinclair, 'Tattooing – Oriental and Gypsy', *American Anthropologist*, X/3
(July–September 1908), pp. 362–3.
14 A. David Napier, *Masks, Transformation and Paradox* (Berkeley, 1986), pp. 145–53.
15 Iyer, *Mysore Tribes*, pp. 443–6. In 1908, Risley noted that it was on the decrease
among lower castes in Bengal and had almost died out in some of the districts
around Calcutta. IOL MSS Eur E295/14A Risley Collection: District Reports on
tattooing in Bengal, received by the Superintendent of Census Operations and the
Superintendent of Ethnography, Nov. 1901–Oct. 1908.

16 Joshi, 'Tattooing and Tattooers', pp. 17–18. According to Risley, the exceptions to this were Bihar, Nadia and Dinajpur. This was probably the result of the high number of *adivasis* concentrated in these areas. IOL MSS Eur E295/14A Risley Collection.

17 Risley. A *bindi* is a small dot worn by women on the forehead, symbolizing marriage. Of course, although sometimes tattooed, it may also have been painted, as is most commonly seen today.

18 Joshi, 'Tattooing and Tattooers', p. 21; IOL MSS Eur E295/14A Risley Collection; and Risley, *The Tribes and Castes of Bengal*, I (Calcutta, 1981, first published 1891), p. 291.

19 Iyer, *Mysore Tribes*, pp. 439–40.

20 Forsyth, *Highlands of Central India*, p. 148.

21 The instrument used in Burma was about two feet long. The yat (style part) had a round, sharp point, divided into four by long splits which held the blue coloured dye (lampblack). Yoe, *The Burman*, p. 40.

22 There is a growing literature in this field. A good starting point on orientalist constructions of India is Ronald Inden, 'Orientalist Constructions of India', *Modern Asian Studies*, xx/3 (1986), pp. 401–46 and Ronald Inden, *Imagining India* (Oxford, 1990). Thomas R. Metcalf explores similar themes in *Ideologies of the Raj* (Cambridge, 1994).

23 These marks were not as closely associated to caste as the British believed. As Christopher Pinney states, they were one of a 'set of signs . . . through which British observers sought to order India into a fully legible hierarchy'. 'Anthropology and the Colonial Image', in C. Bayley, ed., *The Raj; India and the British 1600–1947* (London, 1990), p. 289.

24 H. H. Risley, 'Notes on some Indian tatu marks', *Man: a monthly record of anthropological science* (July 1902), pp. 74–5.

25 See, for example, Crispin Bates, 'Race, Caste and Tribe in Central India: The Early Origins of Indian Anthropometry', in P. Robb, ed., *The Concept of Race in South Asia* (New Delhi, 1995), pp. 219–57. The Act was initially applied to the North West Provinces, Oudh and Punjab. It was gradually extended throughout India until, by 1950, thirteen million people were classified under its auspices.

26 Phrenology and anthropometry were of course key in the 'scientific' (racialized) construction of the 'other': see Michael Adas, *Machines as the Measure of Men: Science, Technology, and Ideologies of Western Dominance* (Cornell, 1989), pp. 294–7; and for an illuminating account of the development of phrenology in the Indian context, see Bates, 'Race, Caste and Tribe'. The convergence of 'race' and 'criminality' was particularly exciting for interested observers: see Radhika Singha, *A Despotism of Law: crime and justice in early colonial India* (New Delhi, 1998), p. 208, and Bates, 'Race, Caste and Tribe', p. 233. For other colonial contexts, see: Andrew Bank, 'Of "Native Skulls" and "Noble Caucasians": Phrenology in Colonial South Africa', *Journal of Southern African Studies*, xxII/3 (September 1996), p. 390; Ian Duffield, 'The Life and Death of "Black" John Goff: Aspects of the Black Convict Contribution to Resistance Patterns During the Transportation Era in Eastern Australia', *Australian Journal of Politics and History*, xxxIII/1 (1987), p. 36; and Malcolm D. Prentis, 'The Life and Death of Johnny Campbell', *Aboriginal History*, xv/2 (1991), pp. 149–50.

27 IOL MSS Eur E295/14A–D. Risley Collection.

28 As argued by Gell (in the Polynesian context), *Wrapping in Images*, p. 8.

29 See Gell, *Wrapping in Images*.

30 Anand A. Yang, 'Dangerous Castes and Tribes: the Criminal Tribes Act and the

Magahiya Doms of Northeast India', in Yang, ed., *Crime and Criminality in British India* (Tucson, 1985), pp. 113–14. See also H. H. Risley, *The People of India* (London, 1915).

31 IOL MSS Eur F161/157. Material on the Effective Administration of the Criminal Tribes Act, 1915. Note of D. Gainsford, Inspector of Police, Punjab.

32 Iyer, *Mysore Tribes*, p. 437.

33 C. P. Jones, 'Stigma: Tattooing and Branding in Graeco-Roman Antiquity', *The Journal of Roman Studies*, LXXVII (1987), p. 141; see also his essay in this volume, Chapter 1.

34 Sukla Das, *Crime and Punishment in Ancient India (c. A.D. 300 to A.D. 1100)* (New Delhi, 1977), pp. 64, 75. Singha cites one interpretation which suggests that the forehead was only painted on, not tattooed, as high-caste brahmins could not be wounded. See Radhika Singha, 'The Privilege of Taking Life: some "anomalies" in the law of homicide in the Bengal Presidency', *Indian Economic and Social History Review*, XXX/2 (1993), p. 200.

35 Iyer, *Mysore Tribes*, pp. 437–8.

36 The literal meaning of tattooing – 'chen hua' – was to draw with a needle, prick a pattern. William Woodville Rockhill, *Diary of a Journey through Mongolia and Tibet, in 1891 and 1892* (Washington, DC, 1894), p. 58.

37 As argued by Richard J. Evans, *Tales From the German Underworld: crime and punishment in the nineteenth century* (New Haven, 1998), pp. 20, 98.

38 T. O'Connor, 'Power and Punishment: The limits of Resistance, The Moreton Bay Penal Settlement 1824–1842' (unpublished BA Hons thesis, University of Queensland, 1994), p. 88.

39 Orlando Patterson, *Slavery and Social Death: a comparative study* (Cambridge, MA, 1982), p. 59 and Jones, 'Stigma', p. 142. See also Schrader, Chapter 11, this volume.

40 See Jane Caplan, '"Speaking Scars": The Tattoo in Popular Practice and Medico-Legal Debate in Nineteenth-Century Europe', *History Workshop Journal*, XLIV (1997), p. 115.

41 James Bradley and Hamish Maxwell-Stewart, '"Behold the Man": Power, Observation and the Tattooed Convict', *Australian Studies*, XII/1 (Summer 1997), p. 81. James Bradley has subsequently established that the 'D' was, in fact, *tattooed* on soldiers' bodies.

42 Hilary McD. Beckles, 'Social and political control in the slave society', in Franklin W. Knight, ed., *General History of the Caribbean, III: The Slave Societies of the Caribbean* (London, 1997), p. 201.

43 Maroon slave communities – perceived to pose a serious threat to 'life, limb and property' – emerged shortly after the French colonized Ile de France. Marronage was thus countered with extreme violence. Richard B. Allen, 'Marronage and the Maintenance of Public Order in Mauritius, 1721–1835', *Slavery and Abolition*, IV/3 (April 1993), pp. 214–15.

44 Michael Craton, 'Forms of resistance to slavery', in Knight, ed., *General History of the Caribbean*, vol. III, p. 239.

45 IOL MSS Eur E295/14A Risley Collection.

46 W.S. Seton-Karr, *Selections from Calcutta Gazettes, volume I* (Calcutta, 1864), p. 66.

47 Jorg Fisch, *Cheap Lives and Dear Limbs: The British Transformation of the Bengal Criminal Law, 1769–1817* (Wiesbaden, 1983), pp. 125, 135. See also N. Majumdar, *Justice and Police in Bengal, 1765–1793: A Study of the Nizamat in Decline* (Calcutta, 1960), p. 48, and Tapas Kumar Banerjee, *Background to Indian Criminal Law* (Calcutta, 1990), pp. 58–62.

48 Michel Foucault, *Discipline and Punish: The Birth of the Prison* (London, 1977), p. 109.

49 See Robert Miles, *Capitalism and Unfree Labour. Anomaly or Necessity?* (London, 1987), p. 222.

50 IOL V/8/17. *Regulations passed by the Governor-General in Council, volume II, 1796–1803* (Calcutta, 1803), p. 387.

51 Regulation XVII (1817): a regulation to provide for the more effectual administration of criminal justice in certain cases, 16 September 1817.

52 IOL P/403/19 (21 June 1843). Minute of the Governor, 9 June 1843.

53 IOL V/8/17. *Regulations*, p. 387. Joshi cites a case in contemporary Rajasthan. At a Caste Council of *nath jogis* a runaway girl was discussed. It was said she had a particular tattoo mark on the forehead by which she could be recognized and brought back to the village. Joshi, 'Tattooing and Tattooers', pp. 18–19.

54 Singha, *A Despotism of Law*, pp. 101–2.

55 R.C. Pathak, *Bhargava's Standard Illustrated Dictionary of the Hindi Language* (Varanasi, 1946; 2nd edn 1969), p. 300, and John T. Platts, *A Dictionary of Urdu, Classical Hindi, and English*, vol. II (London, 1959), p. 923.

56 IOL MSS Eur E295/14A Risley Collection.

57 Iyer, *Mysore Tribes*, p. 439.

58 IOL V/8/17. *Regulations*, pp. 35, 72.

59 Duncan Forbes, *A Smaller Hindustani and English Dictionary* (London, 1862), p. 161.

60 See IOL V18979. *Selected Records from the Central Provinces and Berar Secretariat Relating to the Suppression of Thuggee, 1829–1832* (Nagpur, 1939), p. 2, and IOL P/400/65 (13 June 1833). W. Borthwick, Political Agent Narbada and Sagar, to W. H. Wathen, Session Judge Tannah, 6 May 1833. Narbada and Sagar was a 'non-regulation tract', giving it procedural flexibility and making it 'a theatre for experiments of incipient regulation': Singha, *A Despotism of Law*, p. xviii.

61 In Japan, those who were convicted of robbery were marked with a cross. For further crimes, new crosses were added, a visual representation of a criminal record. Seton-Karr, *Selections*, IV, pp. 166, 268.

62 On the construction of the discourse of thuggee, see Metcalf, *Ideologies of the Raj*, pp. 41–2; Radhika Singha, '"Providential" Circumstances: The Thuggee Campaign of the 1830s and Legal Innovation', *Modern Asian Studies*, XXVII/1 (1993), pp. 83–146, and Singha, *A Despotism of Law*, ch. 5.

63 J. F. A. McNair, *Prisoners Their Own Warders; A Record of the Convict Prison at Singapore in the Straits Settlements established 1825, Discontinued 1873, together with a Cursory History of the Convict Establishments at Bencoolen, Penang and Malacca from the Year 1797* (London, 1899), p. 12, and H.L. Adam, *The Indian Criminal* (London, 1909), p. 12.

64 Philip Meadows Taylor, *Confessions of a Thug* (New Delhi, 1985; first published 1839), p. 301. Meadows Taylor wrote *Confessions* while employed in investigating thuggee in 1830s India.

65 On the marking of Cain, see *Genesis* 4:15. I thank James Bradley for bringing this to my attention.

66 IOL P/142/47 (22 April 1846). E. J. Pearson, Officiating Magistrate Sylhet, to A. Turnbull, Under Secretary to Government Bengal, 26 March 1846.

67 IOL P/403/19 (21 June 1843). Circular Orders of the Supreme Court Madras, 20 February 1843.

68 In the *nagri* character: 'ji', spirit, life; 'banna', made; 'boddh', bound, imprisoned; and, 'qaid' imprisonment. Roger Jeffery and Patricia Jeffery kindly supplied this translation.

69 IOL E/4/779 704–6. Judicial Department, 31 July 1844.

70 The system of informing and rewards was extremely common, with rewards routinely offered for the capture of 'wanted men'. In India it was formalized, with professional informers (*goinda*) scooping substantial rewards. Up to 500 rupees

was offered for the capture of a *sirdar dacoit* (chief of a gang of robbers). John R. McLane, 'Bengali Bandits, Police and Landlords After the Permanent Settlement', in *Crime and Criminality*, ed. Yang, pp. 42–3. This has obvious implications for the incorporation of subject populations into the operation of colonial authority.

71 IOL P/403/15 (31 January 1843). S. G. Bonham, Governor of Prince of Wales' Island, Singapore and Malacca, to J. P. Willoughby, Secretary to Government Bombay, 12 November 1842.

72 Convicts were transported to Mauritius from Bengal and Bombay between 1815 and 1837. The practice was then abandoned in favour of the East India Company's new penal settlements along the Malacca Straits.

73 MA Z2A62. W. Staveley, Head of Convict Department, to J. Finniss, Chief of Police, 13 April 1831.

74 MA Z2A108. J. Finniss to G. F. Dick, Colonial Secretary Mauritius, 30 May and 5 June 1838.

75 MA RA1118. W.A. Rawstone, Surveyor General, to C. J. Bayley, Secretary to Government, 10 May 1851.

76 MA Z2A236. Civil Commissary of Plaines Wilhems to A. Wilson, Acting Inspector General of Police, 13 April 1852.

77 IOL P/402/4. (2 August 1837). R. F. Wingrove, Acting Resident Councillor Singapore, 24 February 1837.

78 IOL P/403/15. (31 January 1843). S. G. Bonham to J. P. Willoughby, 12 November 1842.

79 Singha, *A Despotism of Law*, pp. 247–9. The 'he' is correct here; the colonial authorities never sanctioned corporal punishment for women, though some were transported. 'Daghi' also means stained, scarred (with smallpox) or branded.

80 IOL P/403/8 (11 May 1842). List of convicts to Aden *per Zenobia*, 6 May 1842.

81 IOL P/403/47 (13 August 1845). Political Agent Aden, to W. Escombe, Secretary to Government Bombay, 27 June 1845.

82 This corresponds exactly to the description recorded in the indent at IOL P/403/8.

83 IOL P/404/21 (14 July 1847). Resolution on the Honorable Court's Dispatch, 14 July 1847.

84 IOL E/4/792. Legislative Department, 14 July 1847.

85 IOL P/143/30 (28 February 1849). Act II (1849): To abolish the practice of branding and exposing convicts, 27 January 1849.

86 E/4/803. India Legislative Department, 13 March 1850.

87 Rosamund E. Park, *Recollections and Red Letter Days* (private circulation, 1916), p. 52.

88 Mrs Talbot Clifton, *Pilgrims to the Isles of Penance: Orchid gathering in the East* (London, 1911), p. 77.

89 NAI Home (Judicial), original consultations, 3 September 1858, nos 1–2. The proposals are also discussed by M. V. Portman, *A History of our Relations with the Andamanese*, Vol. I (Calcutta, 1899), pp. 262–3.

90 NAI Home (Judicial), original proceedings, 10 December 1870, nos 20–1.

91 Patterson, *Slavery and Social Death*, p. 59.

92 McNair, *Prisoners Their Own Warders*, p. 12, and Adam, *The Indian Criminal*, pp. 12–13.

93 Jones, 'Stigma', p. 143.

94 See also Iyer, *Mysore Tribes*, p. 437.

95 Similarly, in the later context, unmarked convicts in the Andaman Islands were sometimes punished for refusing to wear their numbers around their necks. See, for example, NAI (Home, Port Blair), A Proceedings, August 1872, nos 1–2.

96 Regulation XVII (1817).

97 IOL P/130/17 (8 June 1810). W. A. Clubley, Acting Secretary to Government, to
T. Brown, Chief Secretary to Government Prince of Wales' Island, 10 May 1810.
98 There is a growing literature on the campaigns against sati and female infanticide.
A good starting point is Singha, *A Despotism of Law*.

8 HAMISH MAXWELL-STEWART AND IAN DUFFIELD: SKIN DEEP DEVOTIONS

1 *Hobart Town Gazette*, 4 May 1838.
2 J. Damousi, *Depraved and Disorderly. Female Convicts, Sexuality and Gender in Colonial Australia* (Cambridge, 1997), ch. 4, and R. Evans and B. Thorpe, 'Commanding Men. Masculinities and the Convict System', in *Journal of Australian Studies*, LVI (1998), pp. 17–34.
3 See A. R. Ekirch, *Bound for America. The Transportation of British Convicts to the Colonies, 1718–1775*, (Oxford, 1987), chs 3 and 4; K. Morgan, 'The Organisation of the Convict Trade to Maryland: Stevenson, Randolph and Cheston', *William and Mary Quarterly*, 3rd series, VII (1985), pp. 201–27; A. G. L. Shaw, *Convicts and the Colonies: A Study of Penal Transportation from Great Britain and Ireland to Australia and Other Parts of the British Empire* (London, 1996), ch. 1.
4 P. Coldham, *Emigrants in Chains: A Social History of Forced Emigration to the Americas 1607–1776* (Stroud, 1992), p. 117.
5 J. Reeves, ed., *The Idiom of the People: English Traditional Verse* (London, 1958), p. 217.
6 Authors' emphasis. See Reeves, *Idiom of the People*, p. 218.
7 R. M. Hartwell, *The Economic Development of Van Diemen's Land 1820–1850* (Melbourne, 1954), p. 64.
8 Here we put 'system' in inverted commas, because a perfect mechanism should not be supposed; 'official policy concerning the convicts was never entirely consistent at the top, either among or between metropolitan and colonial policy makers. It also changed over time; was implemented through imperfect instruments, human and technological; and was affected in practice by a complex array of convict agency'. I. Duffield, 'Daylight on Convict Lived Experience', *Tasmanian Historical Studies*, VII (1999).
9 See C. Anderson, 'The Genealogy of the Modern Subject: Indian Convicts in Mauritius 1814–53', in *Representing Convicts: New Perspectives on Convict Forced Labour Migration*, ed. I. Duffield and J. Bradley (London, 1997), pp. 164–82.
10 See H. Maxwell-Stewart and J. Bradley, '"Behold the Man": Power, Observation and the Tattooed Convict', in *Australian Studies*, XII/1 (1997), pp. 71–97, esp. pp. 74–5 and 79–80.
11 Archives Office of Tasmania, Hobart (AOT), Convict Department Records: Con 18, *Description Lists of Male Convicts 1825–53*, 59 vols; Con 19, *Description Lists of Female Convicts 1841–53*, 11 vols; Con 20, *Description Lists of Convicts Arriving on Minor Ships or Convicted Locally, c. 1832–53*, 5 vols; Con 21, *Description Lists of Convicts Arriving from Norfolk Island, July 1845–1851*, 2 vols. Descriptions were also included in the Con 23 and some other record series.
12 Excellent descriptions of the receiving end of this process can be found in William Gates, *Recollections of Life in Van Diemen's Land*, ed. George Mackaness (Sydney, 1961), pp. 39–40; Linus Miller, *Notes of an Exile in Van Diemen's Land* (New York, 1968), p. 285.
13 D. Oxley, *Convict Maids: The Forced Migration of Women to Australia* (Cambridge, 1996), pp. 19–21.

14 Thus, Scottish local prison registers documenting arrest processes at county level exist for the period 1840–1880. See W. J. Forsythe, *The Reform of Prisoners, 1830–1900* (London, 1987), pp. 96–7.

15 See Maxwell-Stewart and Bradley, '"Behold the Man"', p. 73.

16 This alimentary metaphor originates in Evans and Thorpe, 'Power, Punishment and Penal Labour: *Convict Workers* and Moreton Bay', *Australian Historical Studies*, XXV/98 (1992), pp. 90–111.

17 H. Maxwell-Stewart, 'Convict Workers, "Penal Labour" and Sarah Island. Life at Macquarie Harbour', in *Representing Convicts*, ed. Duffield and Bradley (London, 1997), pp. 147–50; I. Brand, *Penal Peninsula. Port Arthur and its Outstations 1827–1898* (Launceston, n.d.), pp. 37, 53, 55, 62, 74 and 157; Thomas J. Lempriere, *The Penal Settlements of Early Van Diemen's Land* (Launceston, 1954), pp. 13, 28, 40–1, 53, 57 and 106. Lempriere served as a civil officer in all three V.D.L. penal stations in the 1820s–30s.

18 For penal work gangs, penal stations and their relationship to the 'system' of managing convicts, see H. Maxwell-Stewart, 'Convict Workers, "Penal Labour" and Sarah Island', pp. 142–62 and Evans and Thorpe, 'Power, Punishment and Penal Labour', *passim*.

19 I. Brand, *The Convict Probation System: Van Diemen's Land 1839–1854* (Hobart, 1990), ch. 2.

20 'Regulations for the Religious and Moral Instruction of Convicts in Van Diemen's Land', Convict Department, 1st December 1843, Correspondence Between the Secretary of State and the Governor of Van Diemen's Land on the Subject of Convict Discipline, Parliamentary Papers (PP), 1845 (78), vol. XXXV, pp. 21–2.

21 'Regulations for the Religious and Moral Instruction of Convicts in Van Diemen's Land', p. 21.

22 Quoted in M. Turner, *Slaves and Missionaries. The Disintegration of Jamaican Slavery, 1787–1834* (Urbana, IL, 1982), pp. 76–7.

23 See *Philemon*, esp. verses 8–19. For an exegesis on this passage, see J. Drane, *Introducing the New Testament* (Littlemore, Oxford, 1986), pp. 342–3 and 388–9. We are grateful to Jill Duffield for drawing our attention to this work.

24 G. Stephens, *Knopwood: A Biography* (Hobart, 1990), p. 123–4.

25 For Schofield at Macquarie Harbour, see H. Maxwell-Stewart and I. Duffield, 'Beyond Hell's Gates: Religion at Macquarie Harbour Penal Station', *Tasmanian Historical Studies*, V/2 (1997), pp. 83–99, esp. pp. 85–9.

26 *Journal of Rev William Schofield*, Mitchell Library, Sydney (hence, ML) A428, entry for 26 September 1830.

27 Very Rev. W. Ullathorne, minutes of evidence, 8 Feb. 1838, Select Committee on the System of Transportation, PP, 1837–38 (669), vol. XXII, pp. 20, 27.

28 AOT, CSO 1/209/4957, Schofield to Butler, 19 Nov. 1828.

29 R. Knopwood, 'A condemned Sermon: Repentance and Conversion Enforced', preached Hobart 27 April 1821, University of Tasmania Archive, K1/5.

30 See M. Field and T. Millett (eds), *Convict Love Tokens: The Leaden Hearts that Convicts Left Behind* (Adelaide, 1998).

31 This point is also made in D. Kent, 'Decorative Bodies: The Significance of Convict Tattoos', *Journal of Australian Studies*, LV (1997), pp. 81–2.

32 For examples see M. and J. Miller (eds), *Miller's Antiques Price Guide*, vol. 4 (London, 1983), p. 34 and H. Felbrigg, 'Teapots', *Antique Collector*, X (1978), p. 81.

33 818 John Bailey, *per Lady East*, AOT, Con 23.

34 525 William Thornton, *per Southworth*, AOT, Con 23.

35 1625 James Henry, *per Stakesby*, AOT, Con 23.

36 T. Millett and P. Lane, 'Known Convict Love Tokens', in *Convict Love Tokens*, ed. Field and Millett, p. 107.

37 145 James Peatfield, *per Juliana*, AOT, Con 23/1.

38 1219 Joseph Summerfield, *per Southworth*, AOT, Con 23/2; 35 Robert Vetch, *per Chapman*, AOT, Con 23/1.

39 16761 Richard Franklin, *per Equestrian* (2), AOT, Con 33.

40 16680 James Banican, *per Equestrian* (2), AOT, Con 33.

41 18420 Duncan Smith, *per Mayda*, AOT, Con 33.

42 Cornelius Hickey, *per Katherine Stewart Forbes*, AOT, Con 23/2.

43 442 William Silvester, *per Prince of Orange*, AOT, Con 23/1; H2543 William Hoyle, *per Westmorland* (4), AOT, Con 33.

44 245 Henry Abrahams, *per Governor Ready*, AOT, Con 23.

45 A. Atkinson, 'Scholarship on the Run: Our Escape from the One Big Gaol', paper given at 'Exiles of Empire: Convict Experience and Penal Policy', University of Tasmania, Centre for Tasmanian Historical Studies, July 1998.

46 340 Robert Dudlow, *per Phoenix II*, AOT, Con 23. This can be read as an unusual variant of the 'I have hope in . . .' type. Obscene tattoos are very rare among Australia's transported convicts; rather one in the eye for adherents of the view that most of them belonged to a morally depraved criminal class, quite separate from the 'virtuous poor'!

47 Damousi, *Depraved and Disorderly*, p. 94.

48 H. Maxwell-Stewart and J. Bradley, 'Convict Tattoos: Tales of Freedom and Coercion', in *Convict Love Tokens*, ed. Field and Millett, p. 48.

49 Damousi, *Depraved and Disorderly*, p. 94.

50 Evans and Thorpe, 'Commanding Men', p. 28.

51 James Ross, 'An Essay on Prison Discipline', in Ross, *The Van Diemen's Land Annual and Hobart Town Almanack for the Year 1833* (Hobart Town, 1833), p. 89. We thank Len Johnson for this reference.

52 Paisley Gaol Register 1841–1847, Scottish Records Office (SRO), HH21/32/1; Ross, 'Essay on Prison Discipline', p. 89.

53 J. Bradley and H. Maxwell-Stewart, 'Embodied Explorations: Investigating Convict Tattoos and the Transportation System', in Duffield and Bradley (eds), *Representing Convicts*, p. 184.

54 Secondary transports (offenders) conveyed to Hobart from Norfolk Island aboard the *Lady Franklin* (1) 6 June 1844; *Lady Franklin* (2) 27 September 1844; *Lady Franklin* (3) 12 October 1845 and *Lady Franklin* (4) 26 November 1845: AOT, Con 33 and Con 39/1–2.

55 2246 William Baker, *per Layton* (4), AOT, Con 33.

56 H. Maxwell-Stewart, 'Collecting By Numbers', *Siglo*, X (1998), pp. 44–9.

57 11688 Aaron Page, *per Anson*, AOT, Con 39/2.

58 See Pippa Brush, 'Metaphors of Inscription: Discipline, Plasticity and the Rhetoric of Choice', *Feminist Review*, 58 (1998), pp. 22–43.

59 27981 Angus Mackay *per St Vincent*, AOT, Con 33.

60 See K. Daniels, *Convict Women* (St Leonards, NSW, 1998), p. 152–3; Damousi, *Depraved and Disorderly*, ch. 3; I. Duffield, '"Billy Blue": Power, Popular Culture and Mimicry in Early Sydney', in press, *Journal of Popular Culture*.

61 J. C. Scott, *Domination and the Arts of Resistance. Hidden Transcripts* (London, 1990), ch. 8.

62 *Ibid.*, p. 205.

63 K. Reid, '"Contumacious, Ungovernable and Incorrigible": Convict Women and Workplace Resistance, Van Diemen's Land, 1820–1839', in *Representing Convicts*, ed.

I. Duffield and J. Bradley, p. 118. See also H. Maxwell-Stewart, 'The Bushrangers and the Convict System of Van Diemen's Land, 1803–1846', Ph.D. thesis, University of Edinburgh (1991), p. 31; Tamsin O'Connor, 'Power and Punishment: The Limits of Resistance. The Moreton Bay Penal Settlement 1824–1842', BA (Hons) thesis, University of Queensland (1994), pp. 15–18.

64 894 William Shemmett, *per William Miles*, AOT, Con 23.

65 451 George Dakin, *per Asia IV*, AOT, Con 23.

66 Ullathorne, minutes of evidence, Questions 271–2, p .27.

67 As in Stephens, *Knopwood*, pp. 123–4.

68 SRO, HH21/32/1, Paisley Gaol Register 1841–1847, entry number 1843 / 361.

69 Kent, 'Decorative Bodies', p. 80.

70 8714 John Green, *per Duchess of Northumberland*, AOT, Con 33.

71 9185 William Poole, *per John Renwick*, AOT, Con 33. He was sentenced to death in January 1846 for his part in an armed convict insurrection in the Westbury district of Northern Van Diemen's Land. This sentence was later commuted to life transportation.

72 *The True Colonist* (Hobart), 15 and 22 March 1844.

73 'Memoranda by Convict Davis Servant to Mr Foster, Superint[enden]t of Convicts, Norfolk Island – 1843 – Relating principally to Macquarie Harbour'. Dixson Library, Sydney, DLMS Q168.

74 J. F. Mortlock, *Experiences of a Convict Transported for Twenty-one Years*, ed. G. A. Wilkes and A. G. Mitchell (Sydney, n.d.), p. 76.

75 Evans and Thorpe, 'Commanding Men', pp. 24–5.

76 Robert Hughes, *The Fatal Shore: A History of the Transportation of Convicts to Australia, 1787–1868* (London, 1987), p. 429.

77 61 Thomas Warwick, *per Morley* (1) to NSW then *Duke of Wellington* to VDL, AOT, Con 31 – 31 March 1828; Schofield, *Journal*, 24 November 1829, Mitchell Library A428.

78 A. J. Raboteau, *Slave Religion: The 'Invisible Institution' in the Antebellum South* (New York, 1976), pp. 301–2.

79 Flogging description, 'Memoranda by Convict Davis Servant to Mr Foster', Dixson Library DLMS Q168; see also 779 John McCarthy *per Mangles* to N.S.W. and *Nereus* to VDL, AOT, Con 31 and Con 23.

80 13042 John Flinn, *per Captain Cook* (to NSW) and *Lady Franklin* (1) (to VDL), AOT, Con 33; 264 Stephen Kelly, *per Parmelia*, AOT, Con 39/1 and 9933; John O' Niell, *per Constant*, AOT, Con 39/2.

81 16639 Christopher Inglesby, *per Marquis of Huntly* (to N.S.W.) and *Lady Franklin* (3) (to VDL), AOT, Con 33.

82 See B. Reece, 'Frank the Poet', in B. Reece, ed., *Exiles from Erin: Convict Lives in Ireland and Australia* (Basingstoke, 1991), pp. 126–30.

83 14141 James Dunn, *per Royal Sovereign*, (to NSW), *Lady Franklin* (2) (to VDL), AOT, Con 33; 9683 John Oldershaw, *per David Lyon* (to V.D.L. 1830), *per Cressy* (to V.D.L. 1843), AOT, Con 39/2.

84 Hughes, *Fatal Shore*, p. 467.

85 Schofield, *Journal*, 29 May 1828. For other references to murder pacts in penal stations see S. Petrow, 'Drawing Lots: Murder at the Port Arthur Penal Settlement in 1835', in *Tasmanian Historical Research Association, Papers and Proceedings*, xvIII/3 (1998), pp. 186–8; Hughes, *Fatal Shore*, pp. 468–9.

86 6542 Joseph Lamb, *per Surrey* (4) AOT, Con 39/2.

87 R. Knopwood, 'A condemned Sermon: Repentance and Conversion Enforced', preached Hobart 27 April 1821;University of Tasmania Archive, K1/5.

88 Parliamentary Select Committee on Transportation, Minutes of Evidence, Evidence of John Barnes Esq., PP XXII (1837–8), p. 43. For other examples of convict agency on the scaffold see: D. Collins, *An Account of the English Colony in New South Wales*, vol. I (Sydney, 1975), pp. 58–9.

9 JAMES BRADLEY: BODY COMMODIFICATION?

Thanks are due to the Wellcome Trust for funding me, and to Clare Anderson, Ian Duffield and Hamish Maxwell-Stewart, for inspiration, ideas and friendship.

1 Anon. (G. L. Craik), *The New Zealanders* (London, 1830), p. 278, describes John Rutherford's experience. For other tattooed 'freaks', see Robert Bogdan, *Freak Show: Presenting Human Oddities for Amusement and Profit* (Chicago, 1988), pp. 241–56; and the essays by Stephan Oettermann and Alan Govenar in this volume (Chapters 12 and 13).
2 Clifford Geertz, 'Deep Play: Notes on a Balinese Cockfight', in *The Interpretation of Cultures*, ed. Clifford Geertz (London, 1993), pp. 432–3.
3 Alfred Gell, *Wrapping in Images: Tattooing in Polynesia* (Oxford, 1993), p. 20.
4 James Bradley and Hamish Maxwell-Stewart, 'Embodied Explorations: Investigating Tattoos and the Transportation System', in *Representing Convicts*, eds Ian Duffield and James Bradley (London, 1997), p. 190–1.
5 *Report of a Committee Appointed by the Secretary of State to Inquire into the Best Means Available for Identifying Habitual Criminals*, Parliamentary Papers, PP.1894 (C.-7263), pp. 68–9.
6 H. Mayhew and J. Binney, *The Criminal Prisons of London and Scenes of Prison Life* (London, 1862), p. 245.
7 See, for example, Robert Fletcher, *Tattooing Among Civilized People* (Washington, DC, 1883), p. 26; Havelock Ellis, *The Criminal* (London, 1890), p. 105.
8 Jane Caplan, '"Speaking Scars": The Tattoo in Popular Practice and Medico-Legal Debate in Nineteenth-Century Europe', *History Workshop Journal*, XLIV (1997), pp. 125–6.
9 Jane Caplan, '"Educating the Eye": The Tattooed Prostitute', in *Sexology in Culture*, eds Lucy Bland and Laura Doan (London, 1998), p. 106.
10 See for example, Rev. W. D. Morrison, *Journal of Mental Science*, XXXV (1889), p. 21.
11 Caplan, '"Educating the Eye"', p. 100.
12 *Ibid.*, p. 103.
13 Ellis, *The Criminal*, p. 103. This is one of the few references to tattooed miners in the literature, although it was commonly known that coal dust infiltrated miners' wounds, leaving a permanent if unintentional tattoo.
14 *Ibid.*, p. 105.
15 Bradley and Maxwell-Stewart, 'Embodied Explorations', p. 184.
16 Stephen Nicholas, ed., *Convict Workers* (Sydney, 1988).
17 Bradley and Maxwell-Stewart, 'Embodied Explorations', pp. 195–6; and Hamish Maxwell-Stewart and James Bradley, '"Behold the Man": Power, Observation and the Tattooed Convict', *Australian Studies*, XII/1 (1997), pp. 85–6.
18 Alfred Swaine Taylor, *The Principles and Practice of Medical Jurisprudence* (London, 1865) contains no references to tattoos; Taylor, *The Principles and Practice of Medical Jurisprudence* (London, 1873), pp. 604; Charles Meymott Tidy, *Legal Medicine* (London, 1883), vol. I, pp. 189–93.

19   See, for example, Frederick Peterson and Walter S. Haines (eds), *Textbook of Legal Medicine* (London, 1903), vol. I, p. 88.

20   M. Anne Crowther and Brenda White, *On Soul and Conscience: the Medical Expert and Crime* (Aberdeen, 1988), p. 38.

21   John Glaister, *A Text-Book of Medical Jurisprudence, Toxicology and Public Health* (Edinburgh, 1902), p. 69.

22   Stephen Jay Gould, *The Mismeasure of Man* (Harmondsworth, 1997), pp. 114–39.

23   George Burchett, *Memoirs of a Tattooist* (London, 1958), p. 98.

24   D.W. Purdy, *Tattooing: How to Tattoo, What to Use, and How to use Them* (London, n.d.), p. vii.

25   Arthur Conan-Doyle, *A Study in Scarlet*, in *The Complete Sherlock Holmes Long Stories* (London, 1929), p. 20.

26   H. Rider Haggard, *Mr Meeson's Will* (London, 1882), pp. 131–9.

27   *Ibid.*, p. 130.

28   Fergus Hume, *Tracked by a Tattoo* (London, n.d. (1894)), p. 237.

29   *Lancet*, II (1851), pp. 309–10.

30   *Second Report of the Commissioners Appointed to Inquire Into the Constitution and Practice of Courts-Martial in the Army Together with the Minutes of Evidence and Appendix*, Parliamentary Papers, PP.1868–9 (4114-I), p. 174, Qu. 4390.

31   *Times*, 13 April 1869, p. 8.

32   See for example, R.W.B. Scutt and Christopher Gotch, *Art, Sex and Symbol: The Mystery of Tattooing* (London, 1986), pp. 21–36, and Stephan Oettermann, 'Introduction' in Stefan Richter, *Tattoo* (London, 1985), pp. 12–14.

33   Ira Dye, 'Early American Seafarers', *Proceedings of the American Philosophical Society*, CXX/5 (1976), p. 354.

34   Burchett, *Memoirs*, pp. 45–7.

35   Burchett, *Memoirs*, p. 70.

36   Prince Albert Victor and Prince George of Wales, *The Cruise of Her Majesty's Ship 'Bacchante' 1879–1882* (London, 1886), II, p. 46.

37   *Sketch*, 23 Jan. 1895, p. 633.

38   J.B. Atlay, *The Tichborne Case* (London, 1917), p. 174.

39   *BMJ*, I (1862), p. 75.

40   This was misreported as a ban among the French services by the *BMJ*, I (1862), p. 257.

41   *BMJ*, II (1882), p. 632.

42   *BMJ*, I (1889), p. 985.

43   *BMJ*, II (1889), p. 601.

44   Account taken from *BMJ*, I (1889), pp. 985–9.

45   *Ibid.*, p. 431.

46   Burchett, *Memoirs*, p. 69.

47   Gambier Bolton, 'A Tattoo Artist', *Pearson's Magazine*, August 1902, p. 175.

48   *Ibid.*, p. 176; also, Burchett, *Memoirs*, pp. 69–70.

49   *Pall Mall Gazette*, 1 May 1889, p. 2.

50   Burchett, *Memoirs*, p. 26.

51   There is no reference to his tattoos in The Dean of Windsor and Hector Bolitho, *A Victorian Dean: A Memoir of Arthur Stanley, Dean of Westminster* (London, 1930), which gives a detailed description of the tour. According to Fletcher, *Tattooing Among Civilized People*, p. 26, knowledge of Edward's tattoos was reported to the British public in an article published by a French magazine, June 1881.

52   Prince Albert Victor et al., *The Cruise of Her Majesty's Ship 'Bacchante'*, p. 41 and p. 46.

53   Harold Nicholson, *George V* (London, 1952), p. 29.

54 Details of Bolton's life taken from the CD-ROM version of *Who Was Who* (Oxford, 1996).
55 Bolton, 'Pictures on the Human Skin', *Strand Magazine*, XIII (1897), pp. 427–34.
56 R.J. Stephen, 'Tattooed Royalty. Queer Stories of a Queer Craze', *Harmsworth's Magazine*, I (1898–9), p. 472.
57 Purdy,*Tattooing*, pp. 9–10.
58 *Ibid.*, p. 12.
59 *Tatler and Bystander*, 25 November 1903, p. 311.
60 Burchett, *Memoirs*, p. 167.
61 Purdy, *Tattooing*, p. vii.
62 Burchett, *Memoirs*, p. 99.
63 See, for example, Bolton, 'A Tattoo Artist', p. 179.
64 James Milne, police no. 532, transported *Eden* 2, tried by Court Martial, Glasgow, 18 Oct. 1841.
65 See Maxwell-Stewart and Bradley, '"Behold the Man"', pp. 85–6.
66 See, for example, Lloyd Robson, *The Convict Settlers of Australia* (Carlton, Victoria, 1965), p. 80; reinterpreted by Maxwell-Stewart and Bradley, '"Behold the Man"', pp. 89–90.
67 Mary Ann Brennan, 906, *Elizabeth and Henry*, Central Criminal Court, 30 Sept. 1847.
68 James Bradley and Hamish Maxwell-Stewart, 'Writing on Oneself – Convict Tattoos and Autobiography', unpublished paper given at 'Lives, Stories, Narratives' Conference, Department of History, Monash University, July 1997.
69 See Michelle Field and Timothy Field (eds), *Convict Love Tokens: The Leaden Hearts the Convicts Left Behind* (Kent Town, South Australia, 1998).
70 Asa Briggs, *Victorian Things* (London, 1990), p. 41.
71 Advertisement in *Medical Directory* (London, 1892), p. 1823.
72 Bolton, 'Pictures on the Human Skin', p. 433.
73 Burchett, *Memoirs*, p. 71.
74 Bolton, 'A Tattoo Artist', p. 175.
75 See N.D. Jewson, 'The Disappearance of the Sick-Man from Medical Cosmology, 1770–1870', *Sociology*, X (1976).
76 Thorstein Veblen, *The Theory of the Leisure Class* (London, 1994), p. 103.
77 *Ibid.*, p. 60.
78 Stephen, 'Tattooed Royalty', pp. 474–5.

10 JANE CAPLAN: 'NATIONAL TATTOOING'

 1 Cesare Lombroso, *L'uomo delinquente* (Milan, 1876), pp. 43–56, and subsequent editions; Alexandre Lacassagne, *Les tatouages. Étude anthropologique et médico-légale* (Paris, 1881). For a fuller enumeration and discussion of their publications, see Jane Caplan, '"One of the Strangest Relics of a Former State": Tattoos and the Discourse of Criminality in Europe 1880–1920', in *The Criminal and His Scientists. Essays on the History of Criminology*, eds Peter Becker and Richard Wetzell (Cambridge, forthcoming).
 2 R. P. Lesson, 'Du tatouage chez les différens peuples de la terre', *Annales maritimes et coloniales*, 1829, Part II, p. 289.
 3 For a profound interpretation of this relationship, see Alfred Gell,*Wrapping in Images. Tattooing in Polynesia* (Cambridge, 1993), ch. 1; and for the place of tattooing in the broader argument that 'European modernism invents itself by inventing primitivism', see Mark Taylor, *Hiding* (Chicago, 1997), pp. 95 ff.

4   See Jane Caplan, '"Speaking Scars": The Tattoo in Popular Practice and Medico-
    Legal Debate in Nineteenth-Century Europe', *History Workshop Journal*, XLIV (1997),
    pp. 107–42.
5   I have explored this in '"One of the Strangest Relics of a Former State"'.
6   For Britain, see Hamish Maxwell-Stewart and Ian Duffield, Chapter 8, this volume.
    The Habitual Criminals Registers issued by the Metropolitan Police after 1869, for
    example, include descriptions of tattoos under the column 'Distinctive marks and
    peculiarities' (Public Record Office, MEPO 6).
7   See the essays by Stephan Oettermann (Chapter 12) and Alan Govenar (Chapter 13)
    in this volume.
8   See the essay by James Bradley (Chapter 9) in this volume; also Jane Caplan,
    '"Educating the Eye": The Tattooed Prostitute', in *Sexology and Culture. Labelling
    Bodies and Desires, 1890–1940*, eds. Lucy Bland and Laura Doan (Cambridge and
    Chicago, 1998) pp. 104–6.
9   Lombroso, *L'uomo delinquente*, pp. 55, 54.
10 *Ibid.*, pp. 47, 56. For the question of tattooing among European prostitute women –
    the only category of women regularly described as tattooed – see Caplan, 'Educating
    the Eye'.
11 Lombroso, *L'uomo delinquente*, pp. 48–50.
12 See e.g. Cesare Lombroso, *L'uomo delinquente*, 5th edn (Turin, 1897), 'Atlante' (i.e.
    'atlas', or volume of tables and illustrations), Plates LXIV–LXIX.
13 Alexandre Lacassaigne (sic), 'Ricerche su 1333 tatuaggi di delinquenti', *Archivio di
    pschiatria*, 1 (1880), pp. 438–43
14 Alexandre Lacassagne, 'Recherches sur les tatouages et principalement du
    tatouage chez les criminels', *Annales d'hygiène publique et de médecine légale*, 3rd. ser.,
    vol. V (1881), pp. 291–2.
15 Lacassagne, *Les tatouages*, and Alexandre Lacassagne and E. Magitot, 'Tatouage', in
    Dictionnaire encyclopédique des sciences médicales, ed. A. Dechambre and L. Lereboulet,
    3rd edn (Paris, 1886), vol. XVI, pp. 95–160, which partially repeats the former
    publication.
16 Lacassagne, *Les tatouages*, p. 115.
17 *Ibid.*, p. 61.
18 Lacassagne, 'Recherches sur les tatouages et principalement du tatouage chez les
    criminels', p. 301.
19 The major collections of tattoos (both Lombroso and Lacassagne assembled
    libraries of several thousand images) were tracings; for descriptions of this method
    see e.g. Lacassagne, *Les tatouages*, p. 20, and Karl Gotthold, 'Vergleichende Unter-
    suchungen über die Tätowierung bei Normalen, Geisteskranken und Kriminellen',
    Klinik für psychische und nervose Krankheiten, IX (1914), pp. 196–7. Tattoos did not
    photograph well with the equipment available in the nineteenth century. Pathology
    clinics might preserve a few examples of tattooed skin, but this was not the standard
    recording method (a technique for doing this is described in L.Stieda, 'Etwas über
    Tätowierung', *Wiener Medizinischer Wochenschrift*, LXI/14 (1 April 1911), pp. 893–8).
20 See e.g. J. Jaeger, 'Tätowierungen von 150 Verbrechern mit Personalangaben', *Archiv
    für Kriminalanthropologie*, XVIII (1904), pp. 141–68, and *ibid.*, XXI (1905), pp. 116–67.
    Régine Plas, 'Tatouages et criminalité', in *Histoire de la criminalité française*, ed.
    Laurent Mucchielli (Patis, 1994), p. 160, also notes this typical pattern for the French
    Archives de l'anthropologie criminelle et des sciences pénales.
21 *Archiv für Kriminalanthropologie*, XXXV (1909), pp. 375–6; Silvio Armando Neri,
    'Tatuaggi osceno in fratelli criminale', *Archivio di psichiatria*, XXIII (1902), pp. 252–3.

22 W. Maschke (military physician in Olmütz), 'Zur Tätowirungsfrage', *Archiv für Kriminalanthropologie*, I (1899), p. 330.

23 Louis Vervaeck, 'Le tatouage en Belgique', *Mémoires de la société d'Anthropologie de Bruxelles*, XXV (1906), p. 16.

24 Abraham Baer, *Der Verbrecher in anthropologischer Beziehung* (Leipzig, 1893), pp. 225–41, translated as 'Tatouage des criminels', *Archives de l'anthropologie criminelle et des sciences pénales*, X (1895), pp. 153–74; Dr. Leppmann, 'Die criminal-psychologische und criminalpraktische Bedeutung des Tätowirens bei Verbrecher', *Vierteljahrsschrift für gerichtliche Medizin*, VIII (1894), pp. 193–218.

25 The pioneer was the important cross-cultural study by Wilhelm Joest, *Tätowiren, Narbenzeichen und Körperbemalen. Ein Beitrag zur vergleichenden Ethnologie* (Berlin, 1887), pp. 99–109 especially; and see e.g. Otto Lauffer, 'Über die Geschichte und den heutigen volkstümlichen Gebrauch der Tätowierung in Deutschland',*Wörter und Sachen. Kulturhistorische Zeitschrift für Sprache und Sachforschung*, VI (1914/5), pp. 1–14, and Erhard Riecke, *Das Tatuierungswesen im heutigen Europa* (Jena, 1925). The outstanding study was the doctoral dissertation by Adolf Spämer, *Die Tätowierung in den deutschen Hafenstädten. Ein Versuch zur Erfassung ihrer Formen und ihres Bildgutes* (Bremen, 1934; reprinted Munich, 1993). For similar research on tattooing among Bosnian Catholic women, see Leopold Glück, 'Die Tätowirung der Haut bei den Katholiken Bosniens und der Hercegovina', *Wissenschaftliche Mittheilungen aus Bosnien und der Hercegovina*, II (1894), 455–62, and Ciro Truhelka, 'Die Tätowirung bei den Katholiken Bosniens und der Hercegovina', *ibid.*, IV (1896), pp. 493–508.

26 Many more Italian contributions seem to have been short research notes rather than longer articles or treatises, though this may reflect the gaps in my own research; an exception is Abele De Blasio, *Il tatuaggio* (Naples, 1905); on Loreto, see Catherina Pigorini-Beri, 'Le tatouage religieux et amoureux au pélérinage de N.-D. de Lorette', *Archives de l'anthropologie criminelle et des sciences pénales*, VI (1891), pp. 5–16.

27 For Spain see below; for Portugal see the brief account by Rocha Peixoto, 'A tatuagem em Portugal', *Revista de Sciencias Naturaes e Sociaes*, II (1893), pp. 97–111 + 5pp. illustrations. The colonial and maritime connection is supported by the evidence from France, Britain, Denmark, and, obviously, by the popularity of tattooing among sailors in most populations.

28 Daniel Pick, *Faces of Degeneration. A European Disorder c. 1848 – c. 1918* (Cambridge, 1989), Part II.

29 Hester Lynch Piozzi, *Observations and Reflections Made in the Course of a Journey through France, Germany, and Italy*, ed. Herbert Barrows (Ann Arbor, 1967), pp. 229–31.

30 Nicolas Minovici, 'Les tatouages en Roumanie', *Archives des sciences médicales*, IV (1899), pp. 51–104 + 31 pp. plates.

31 *Ibid.*, p. 93.

32 Edmond Locard, *Traité de criminalistique*, Part III: Les preuves d'identité (Lyon, 1932), pp. 249, 418.

33 Rafael Salillas, *El tatuage en su evolución histórica, en sus differentes caracterizaciones antiguas y actuale y en los delincuentes franceses, italianos y espanoles* (Madrid, 1908).

34 *Ibid.*, pp. 23–4, 50, 56.

35 *Ibid.*, pp. 146–9, 21–2.

36 *Ibid.*, pp. 192–3.

37 Vervaeck, 'Le tatouage en Belgique', summarized in 'Le tatouage en Belgique', *Archives de l'anthropologie criminelle*, XXII (1909), pp. 333–62. All citations below are from the first and longer version.

38 *Ibid.*, p. 223.

39 *Ibid.*, pp. 175–6. Outside Brussels, recruits were more likely to get tattoos after induction. For the Belgian military conscription system, see Émile Wanty, *Le milieu militaire Belge de 1831 à 1914* (Brussels, 1957), pp. 48–50, 122–6. Tattoos of conscription numbers and matriculation dates were also favoured by soldiers in the Austro-Hungarian army, where regimental insignia were also popular; see Josef Mohl, 'Mitteilungen auf Tätowierungen, aufgenommen an Soldaten der Garnison Temesvàr', *Mitteilungen der anthropologischen Gesellschaft in Wien*, XXXVIII (1908), pp. 312–20.
40 Vervaeck, 'Le tatouage en Belgique', pp. 232, 237.
41 This and the following quotations are from pp. 234–6.
42 This is equivalent to expecting Kafka's convict to set in motion the 'harrow' that carved his sentence into the surface of his body: Franz Kafka, 'In der Strafkolonie', in *idem, Erzählungen* (Berlin, 1963), pp. 199–236.
43 Vervaeck, 'Le tatouage en Belgique', p. 238.

11 ABBY M. SCHRADER: BRANDING THE OTHER/TATTOOING THE SELF

1 Abby M. Schrader, 'Containing the Spectacle of Punishment: The Russian Autocracy and the Abolition of the Knout, 1817–1845', *Slavic Review*, LVI (1997), pp. 613–44.
2 Although officials attempted to distinguish between branding as a form of punishment and the administrative branding of fugitive exiles and vagrants, the two practices were related. Elise Kimerling Wirtschafter, *Social Identity in Imperial Russia* (Dekalb, Illinois, 1997), p. 7.
3 Wirtschafter, *Social Identity*, p. 4; Gregory L. Freeze, 'The *Soslovie* (Estate) Paradigm in Russian Social History', *American Historical Review*, XCI/5 (February 1986), pp. 14–18.
4 Wirtschafter, *Social Identity*, p. 23; Marc Raeff, *The Well-Ordered Police State: Social and Institutional Change through Law in the Germanies and Russia, 1600–1800* (New Haven, 1983).
5 Wirtschafter, *Social Identity*, pp. 42–67, 118–19.
6 N. M. Iadrintsev, *Russkaia obshchina v tiur'me i ssylke* (St Petersburg, 1872), pp. 351, 354–5.
7 Abby M. Schrader, *The Languages of the Lash: Corporal Punishment and the Construction of Identity in Imperial Russia* (Dekalb, IL, forthcoming), ch. 4; Mark Bassin, 'Inventing Siberia: Visions of the Russian East in the Early Nineteenth Century', *American Historical Review*, XCVI/3 (June 1991), pp. 763–94.
8 *Polnoe sobranie zakonov Rossiiskoi Imperii* (PSZ), First Series, #11,166.
9 Iadrintsev, *Russkaia obshchina*, pp. 359–60; Alan D. Wood, 'Crime and Punishment in the House of the Dead', in *Civil Rights in Imperial Russia*, ed. Olga Crisp and Linda Edmondson (Oxford, 1989), pp. 217–21. On the replacement of the death penalty with knouting, see PSZ, First Series, #10,306. On the 1822 institution of exile regulations, see PSZ, First Series, #29,128.
10 S. V. Maksimov, *Sibir' i katorga*, 3rd edn (St Petersburg, 1900), pp. 9–10.
11 Rossiiskii Gosudarstvennyi Istoricheskii Arkhiv (RGIA), f. 1265, op. 1, 1852–9, d. 167, ll. 26ob–27; Maksimov, pp. 7–10.
12 N. M. Korkunov, *Russkoe gosudarstvennoe pravo*, Tom 1, Obshchaia Chast', 8th edn (St Petersburg, 1914), pp. 188–9; *Proekt ulozheniia o nakazaniiakh ugolovnykh i ispravitel'nykh: vnesennyi v 1844 godu v Gosudarstvennyi Sovet* (St Petersburg, 1832), p. v.; Bassin, pp. 766–75; James R. Gibson, 'Paradoxical Perceptions of Siberia: Patrician and Plebian Images up to the Mid-1800s', and Harriet Murav, '"Vo Glubine Sibirskikh

Rud": Siberia and the Myth of Exile', in *Between Heaven and Hell: The Myth of Siberia in Russian Culture*, ed. Galia Diment and Yuri Slezkine (New York, 1993), pp. 67–111.

13   RGIA, f. 1265, op. 1, d. 1, ll. 420b–43.

14   RGIA, f. 1264, op. 1, 1823, d. 392; RGIA, f.1264 op. 1, 1824–30, d. 597; RGIA, f. 1265, op. 2, 1853, d. 127; RGIA, f. 1149, t. 4, 1854, d. 12; RGIA, f. 1149, t. 4, 1854, d. 36.

15   Iadrintsev, *Russkaia obshchina*, p. 360, 378–85.

16   Iadrintsev, *Russkaia obshchina*, pp. 362–85; K. Shreiterfel'd, *Arestantskaia chest* (St Petersburg, 1903), p. 37; Alan D. Wood, 'Russia's "Wild East": Exile, Vagrancy and Crime in Nineteenth–Century Siberia', in *The History of Siberia from Russian Conquest to Revolution*, ed. Alan D. Wood (London, 1991), p. 123; Maksimov, *Sibir' i katorga*, pp. 61, 65.

17   Maksimov, *Sibir' I katorga*, p. 187.

18   Iadrintsev, *Russkaia obshchina*, pp. 357–8, 374; Statute 82, *Uchrezhdenie i ustav o soderzhanii pod strazheiu* and Statutes 802–804, *Ustav o ssylnykh* in *Svod Zakonov Rossiiskoi Imperii*, Volume XIV (St Petersburg, 1832). PSZ, First Series, #10,650, #17,179, #18,978, #20,335, and #21,224; PSZ, Second Series, #3,356, 4,314, and 4,515; RGIA, f. 1286, op. 2, 1817, d. 245, l. 2.

19   Maksimov, *Sibir' i katorga*, pp. 81–2, 86; Dostoevsky, *The House of the Dead*, trans. David McDuff (London, 1985), pp. 220, 342; Iadrintsev, *Russkaia obshchina*, pp. 427–36.

20   Iadrintsev, *Russkaia obshchina*, pp. 432–3.

21   In the 1870s, the Kara prison doctor asserted that, 'all of the Nepomnyashchys at Kara are called Ivan: Ivan Nepomnyashchy, Ivan Without a Name, Ivan without a Surname, Ivan without a Patronymic – all Ivans! There are hundreds . . .' V. Ia. Kokosov, *Rasskazy o Kariiskoi Katorge (iz vospominanii vracha)* (St Petersburg, 1907), p. 120. Also see Iadrintsev, *Russkaia obshchina*, pp. 428–33, Shreiterfel'd, *Arestantskaia chest'* (St Petersburg, 1903), p. 37, and Dostoevsky, *House of the Dead*, pp. 254–5.

22   RGIA, f. 1149, t. 3, 1844, d. 78, ll. 31, 33; RGIA, f. 1149, t. 3, 1845, d. 49, ll. 3–30b, 15–18, 38–9, 42–5; RGIA f. 1160, op. 1, 1845, d. 49, ll. 162–222; RGIA, f. 1261, op. 2, 1852, d. 119a, l. 2; RGIA, f. 1149, t. 4, 1854, d. 54, ll. 2–3.

23   P. Efimenko, 'Iuridicheskie znaki', *Zhurnal ministerstva narodnago prosveshcheniia*, no. 10 (1874), pp. 53–6, 59.

24   P. Efimenko, 'Iuridicheskie znaki', *Zhurnal ministerstva narodnago prosveshcheniia*, no. 11 (1874), pp. 162–5. On standardization, see PSZ, First Series, #27,300.

25   Letter of 20 March 1712 from Peter the Great to Prince Iakov Fedorovich Dolgorukov. Cited in Grigorii Aleksandrov, 'Pechat' Antikhrista', *Russkii Arkhiv*, no. 10 (1873), pp. 2072–3.

26   PSZ, First Series, #2,876. G. Aleksandrov, 'Pechat' Antikhrista', p. 2071.

27   G. Aleksandrov, 'Eshche o pechati Antikhrista', *Russkii Arkhiv*, no. 11 (1873), pp. 2296–7.

28   G. Aleksandrov, 'Pechat' Antikhrista', pp. 2068–72.

29   Cited in Iu. A. Alferov, *Zhargon i tatuirovki u narkomanov v IGU* (Domedovo, 1992), p. 131.

30   PSZ, First Series, #10,305 and #10,306. Branding was reaffirmed in 1818 in PSZ, First Series, #27,300.

31   RGIA, f. 1149, t. 2, 1828, d. 66, ll. 3–30b, 5–50b, 7–8, 100b–11.

32   RGIA, f. 1160, op. 1, 1845, d. 75, l. 187; RGIA, f. 1286, op. 16, 1855, d. 574, ll. 1–3.

33   RGIA, f. 1149, t. 4, 1855, d. 24, l. 345; RGIA, f. 1261, op. 1, 1840, d. 52, ll. 10–11.

34   RGIA, f. 1149, t. 3, 1845, d. 49, ll. 2–3; RGIA, f. 1160, op. 1, 1845, d. 75, ll. 1556.

35   RGIA, f. 1149, t. 3, 1845, d. 49, ll. 30b–4, 5–6, 8, 23–230b, 26–8.

36   RGIA, f. 1149, t. 3, 1845, d. 49, ll. 11, 31–2; RGIA, f. 1160, op. 1, 1845, d. 75, ll. 1620b–163, 1810b.

37 RGIA, f. 1149, t. 3, 1845, d. 49, ll. 18–19; RGIA, f. 1160, op. 1, 1845, d. 75, ll. 203–4.
38 Peter Kolchin, *Unfree Labor: American Slavery and Russian Serfdom* (Cambridge, MA, 1987), pp. 282–3.
39 Thirteen per cent of the 1,832 fugitives apprehended in 1854 and 1855 feigned amnesia. RGIA, f. 1286, op. 16, 1855, d. 574, ll. 5–122.
40 Iadrintsev, *Russkaia obshchina*, pp. 393, 415; Shreiterfel'd, *Arestantskaia chest'*, p. 42.; A. I. Svirskii, *V stenakh tiur'my. Ocherki arestantskaia zhizni.* (Rostov-na-donu, 1894), pp. 38, 47–52; L. Mel'shin (P. F. Iakubovich), *V mire otverzhennykh. Zapiski byvshago katorzhnika.* Volume 1. (St Petersburg, 1911), pp. 11–12.
41 S. Usherbovich, *V tsarskikh zastenkakh* (Kiev, 1925), p. 11.
42 Iadrintsev, *Russkaia obshchina*, p. 400.
43 Svirskii, *V stenakh tiur'my*, p. 4. Also see Usherbovich, *V tsarskikh zastenkakh*, p. 29, S. Ia. Elpat'evskii, *Po Sibirskim tiur'mam i etapam. Otryvki iz vospominanii* (Moscow, 1924), p. 59–60; I. P. Belokonskii (Petrovich), *Po tiur'mam i etapam. Ocherki tiuremnoi zhizni i putevyia zametki ot Moskvy do Krasnoiarska* (Orel, 1887), pp. 159–61; and Iadrintsev, *Russkaia obshchina*, pp. 393–421.
44 Iadrintsev, *Russkaia obshchina*, pp. 364–400; Shreiterfel'd, *Arestantskaia chest'*, pp. 39, 42, 75; Svirskii, *V stenakh tiur'my*, pp. 14–15; and V. Medem, *Po Tsarskim tiur'mam. Tiuremnye vospominanii* (Leningrad-Moscow, 1924), pp. 59–60.
45 Shreiterfel'd, *Arestantskaia chest'*, pp. 40–8, 52, 81–2; V. Aleksandrov, 'Arestantskaia Respublika', *Russkaia Mysl'*, xxv, 9 (Sept. 1904), pp. 73–4, 81–2; Iadrintsev, *Russkaia obshchina*, p. 421.
46 Iadrintsev, *Russkaia obshchina*, p. 395.
47 Shreiterfel'd, *Arestantskaia chest'*, pp. 40–1, 44–7, 71, 87; V. Aleksandrov, 'Arestantskaia Respublika', p. 73; Iadrintsev, *Russkaia obshchina*, pp. 379, 396–9; M. N. Gernet, *V tiur'me. Ocherki tiuremnoi psikhologii* (Moscow, 1925), pp. 49–50, 62.
48 Iadrintsev, *Russkaia obshchina*, p. 396.
49 V. Aleksandrov, 'Arestantskaia Respublika', pp. 69–70; Svirskii, *V stenakh tiur'my*, p. 4; Shreiterfel'd, *Arestantskaia chest'*, pp. 42, 55; Usherbovich, *V tsarskikh zastenkakh*, p. 10.
50 Iadrintsev, *Russkaia obshchina*, p. 403.
51 Usherbovich, *V tsarskikh zastenkakh*, p. 17; Belokonskii, *Po tiur'mam i etapam*, p. 161; Iadrintsev, *Russkaia obshchina*, pp. 235, 421.
52 Shreiterfel'd, *Arestantskaia chest'*, p. 79; Svirskii, *V stenakh tiur'my*, pp. 82–3. Patricia O'Brien notes that that tattooing was one means by which recidivists shaped subcultures and achieved preeminence in French prisons. Patricia O'Brien, *The Promise of Punishment: Prisons in Nineteenth-Century France* (Princeton, 1982), pp. 87–9.
53 Svirskii, *V stenakh tiur'my*, p. 78.
54 *Ibid.*, p. 79. Emphasis added.
55 *Ibid.*, p. 80.
56 Schrader, 'Containing the Spectacle of Punishment', pp. 630–5.
57 Svirskii, *V stenakh tiur'my*, p. 81.
58 A. I. Gurov, *V tiur'me*, pp. 89–90, 102; Varlam Shamalov, 'Such'ia' voina: Ocherki prestupnogo mira.* (Moscow, 1989), pp. 4–5.
59 Iadrintsev, *Russkaia obshchina*, pp. 379–89, 400, 454–61.
60 I. P. Belokonskii, *Po tiur'mam i etapam*, pp. 159–61; Shreiterfel'd, *Arestantskaia chest'*, pp. 38–9, 42, 55, 71–3, 75, 81–2; V. Aleksandrov, 'Arestantskaia Respublika', pp. 69–70; Usherbovich, *V tsarskikh zastenkakh*, p. 10.
61 A. I. Gurov, 'Professional'naia prestupnost', in *Imperiia Strakha*, ed. Edvard Maksimovskii (Moscow, 1992), pp. 84–5, 94–7, 123, 126–32.

62 Dr Ia. M. Kogan, *Tatuirovka sredi prestupnikov* (Odessa, 1928), pp. 11–12; M. N. Gernet, 'Tatuirovka v mestakh zakliucheniia g. Moskvy', in *Prestupnyi mir Moskvy. Sbornik statei*, ed. M. N. Gernet (Moscow, 1924), p. 234.

63 Alferov, *Zhargon i tatuirovki*, pp. 128–35; Shamalov, 'Such'ia' voina, pp. 7, 36; Gurov, 'Professional'naia prestupnost', pp. 96, 132–3.

64 Kogan, *Tatuirovka sredi prestupnikov*, pp. 45–8.

65 *Ibid.*, p. 34.

66 Alferov, *Zhargon i tatuirovki*, p. 135.

67 Gurov, 'Professional'naia prestupnost', p. 95. Vagrants also referred to their comrades as family members and the prison and Siberia as their native homes. Iadrintsev, *Russkaia obshchina*, pp. 412, 418.

68 Alferov, *Zhargon i tatuirovki*, p. 30. Also see Gurov, 'Professional'naia prestupnost', pp. 132–3.

69 Alferov, *Zhargon i tatuirovki*, p. 128.

70 Shamalov, 'Such'ia' voina, p. 36. On pre-revolutionary criminals' *curricula vitae*, see Svirskii, *V stenakh tiur'my*, p. 7.

71 Alferov, *Zhargon i tatuirovki*, p. 129.

72 Kogan, *Tatuirovka sredi prestupnikov*, pp. 45–6, 49, 63.

73 Kogan, *Tatuirovka sredi prestupnikov*, p. 51; Alferov, *Zhargon i tartuirovki*, p. 132; Gurov, 'Tatuirovka v mestakh zakliucheniia g. Moskvy', p. 133; Shamalov, 'Such'ia' voina, p. 8; I. F. Krylov, *V mire kriminalistiki* (Leningrad, 1980), pp. 101–7.

74 Alferov, *Zhargon i tatuirovki*, pp.129, 132, 134.

75 Maksimovskii, *Sibir' i katorga*, p. 21.

76 Kogan, *Tatuirovka sredi prestupnikov*, pp. 28–9, 38.

77 Maksimovskii, *Sibir' i katorga*, p. 45.

78 Gernet, 'Tatuirovka v mestakh zakliucheniia g. Moskvy', pp. 245–6; Alferov, *Zhargon i tartuirovki*, p. 131.

12 STEPHAN OETTERMANN: ON DISPLAY

1 Hugo Ball, *Die Kulisse* (Zürich/Köln, 1971), p.58.

2 *Die XI. Konferenz der deutschen Sittlichkeitsvereine in Nürnberg 1902* (Berlin, 1904), p. 28.

3 W. L. Strauss, *Single-Leaf Woodcut 1550–1600* (New York, 1975), Ill. 201 (see also Ills. 130, 135, 376, 423); and see Hiob Ludolf, *Schaubühne der Welt. Oder Beschreibung der vornehmsten Weltgeschichte des 16. Jahrhunderts* (Frankfurt am Main, 1699–1731), vol. II, p. 536.

4 See William Dampier, *Reystogten rondom de weareldt* (Amsterdam, 1716), pp. 264–73; English translation, ed. John Masefield, *Dampier's Voyages* (London, 1906), p. 540.

5 Their full names were given for the first time in the baptismal ceremony: 'Oak Charinga Tiggvvavv Tubbee Tocholuche inca Navvcheys' and 'Tuskee Stannagee Whothlee Powvovv Micko Istovvlavvleys', in each case the last word indicating their 'nation' or tribe.

6 For the information and quotations in this paragraph, see *Sammlung von Natur- und Medicin- wie auch hierzu gehörigen Kunst- und Literatur-Geschichten* (Breslau, 1722), pp. 310–17; 1724, p. 316; 1725, p. 472; *Kern Dresdnischer Merckwürdigkeiten* (Dresden, 1722), p. 92; 1726, p.106; Iccander, *Sächsisches Kern-Chronicon* (Dresden, 1725), no. 3, pp. 35–8, 559–62, 574; and *Wiener Zeitung* (Wiener Diarium), 1722, no. 40.

7 On Omai, see Guest, Chapter 6, this volume.

8 See *Evangelian Magazine*, London, January 1800; Peter Mortimer, ed., *Geschichte der neuesten evangelischen Anstalten in England* (Leipzig, 1800), vol. 3, pp. 20 ff; and Karl

von der Steinen, *Die Marquesaner und ihre Kunst* (Berlin, 1925), vol. 1, pp. 35, 64–5.

9 D. Langsdorff, *Bemerkungen auf einer Reise um die Welt in den Jahren 1805–07* (Frankfurt am Main, 1812), vol. 1, p. 84.

10 *Ibid.*, p. 163.

11 'M. M.' (i.e. E. T. Oury and J. B. B. Sauvan), *Petite chronique de Paris . . . aux Mémoires de Bachoumont* (Année 1818) (Paris, 1819), p. 221.

12 Von den Steinen, *Die Marquesaner und ihre Kunst*, vol. 1, p. 43.

13 G. L. Craik, *The Great White Chief John Rutherford* (1830) (London, 1847) – identical with *The New Zealanders* (London, 1831), pp. 86–230; German translation *Die Neuseeländer* (Leipzig, 1833). Rutherford's story was exposed by W. L. Williams as a fantasy in 1891, but this did not prevent it from continuing to circulate: see New Zealand Institution, *Transactions*, 23 (1891), pp. 453–61; and Joseph Drummond, *John Rutherford the White Chief* (Christchurch, NZ, 1908).

14 Full title: *A Narrative of Shipwreck Captivity and Suffering of Horace Holden and Benjamin Nute who were cast away in the American ship Mentor, on the Pelew Islands, in the year 1832; and for two years afterwards were subjected to unheard of sufferings among the barbarous inhabitants of Lord North's Islands*, by Horace Holden (Boston, 1836).

15 Alfred Parry, *Tattoo: Secrets of a Strange Art as Practised among the Natives of the U.S.* (New York, 1933), p. 59.

16 W. L. Alden, *Among the Freaks* (London, New York, Bombay, 1896), p. 4.

17 C. W., 'Ein tätowierte Europäer', *Illustrierte Zeitung* (Leipzig), 2 Nov. 1872, pp. 33–6 (with picture).

18 F. Hebra, *Atlas der Hautkrankheiten* (Vienna, 1856), VIII, table 10. For other scientific reports, see e.g. Dr. Kaposi, 'Der Tätowirte von Birma', *Wiener Medizinische Wochenschrift*, 1872, no. 2, pp. 39–45; *British Medical Journal*, Nov. 1871; *Lancet*, 2 Feb. 1872; *Journal of the Royal Anthropological Institute of Great Britain and Ireland*, II, 1872, pp. 228–32; *The Times*, 3 Nov. 1871 and 2 Feb. 1872. From the voluminous popular literature, see e.g. *The true life of Captain Constentenus the tattooed Greek Prince. Written by himself, and translated from the Original Romaic by Prof. Demetri of Athens* (New York, n.d., c. 1881), 24 pp.

19 Parry, *Tattoo*, pp. 65–6.

20 William Sturtevant, 'A Short History of the Strange Custom of Tattooing', in C. H. Fellowes, *The Tattoo Book* (Princeton, 1971), p. 8.

21 Signor Saltarino, *Fahrend Volk. Abnormitäten, Kuriositäten und interessante Vertreter der wandernden Künstlerwelt* (Leipzig, 1895), pp. 137–9.

22 *Allgemeine Zeitung* (Munich), 13 Jan. 1891.

23 *Zeitschrift für Ethnologie*, 18 (1890), Verhandlungen, pp. 304–5.

24 *Ibid.*, p. 305.

25 Parry, *Tattoo*, pp. 65–6.

26 *Ibid.*, p. 67.

27 W. Schönfeld, *Körperbemalen, Brandmarken, Tätowieren. Nach griechischen, römischen Schriftstellern, Dichtern, neuzeitlichen Veröffentlichungen und eigenen Erfahrungen, vorzüglich in Europa* (Heidelberg, 1960), p. 104.

28 *Illustrierte Zeitung*, Leipzig, no. 96 (1891), p. 254; Saltarino, *Fahrend Volk*, p. 138.

29 Hans Scheugl and Felix Adanos, *Showfreaks und Monster* (Cologne, 1974), p. 148.

30 Gerhard Eberstaller, Christian Brandstetter and Bernhard Paul, *Circus* (Vienna, Munich and Zürich, 1977), p. 116.

31 Hugo Ernst Lüdecke, 'Erotische Tätowierungen', *Anthropophyteia*, 4 (1907), p. 80. *Anthropophyteia* was a journal of sexual science that could be obtained only on subscription by professionals.

32 Ibid., p. 78.
33 W. Schönfeld, 'Tätowierte Frauen um und nach der Jahrhundertwende', Der Hautartzt, 6, XI (1955), pp. 487–90; see also 45 postcards in the author's collection.
34 L. Stieda, 'Etwas über Tätowierungen', Wiener Medizinische Wochenschrift, 61 (1911), p. 896.
35 Ball, Die Kulisse, pp. 63–4.
36 Leipziger Rundschau, 5 Feb. 1911.
37 Parry, Tattoo, pp. 67–8.
38 George Burchett, Memoirs of a Tattooist (London, 1958), pp. 164–79.
39 Berliner Tageblatt, 11 Sept. 1932.
40 Alfred Lehmann, Zwischen Schaubuden und Karussells (Frankfurt am Main, 1952), p. 111.
41 8-Uhr-Blatt, 3 Feb. 1938.

13 ALAN GOVENAR: THE CHANGING IMAGE OF TATTOOING IN AMERICAN CULTURE, 1846–1966

1 A.W. Franks, 'Tattooed Man from Burmah', Journal of the Anthropological Institute of Great Britain and Ireland, II (1873), pp. 228–32; A. Lacassagne, Les Tatouages (Paris, 1881); Wilhelm Joest, Tätowiren (Berlin, 1887); R. Fletcher, 'Tattooing Among Civilized People', Transactions of the Anthropological Society of Washington, II (1893), pp. 40–68; G.R. Stetson, 'Tattooing in Tunis', American Anthropologist, VI(1893), p. 282. See also Alan Govenar, 'The Influx of Tattooing into the Western World From Herodotus to O'Reilly', in O. P. Joshi, ed., Anthropology of Symbols (Jaipur, 1992), pp. 72–85.
2 Albert Parry, Tattoo: Secrets of a Strange Art (New York, 1933), pp. 138–40.
3 Tighe Hopkins, 'The Art and Mystery of Tattooing', Leisure Hour, XLIV (1895), pp. 694–8, 774–80; R. J. Stephen 'Tattooed Royalty: Queer Stories of a Queer Craze', Harmsworth's London Magazine, I (1898), pp. 472–5; Gambier Bolton, 'Pictures on the Human Skin', Strand, XIII (1897), p. 425; Oliphant Smeaton, 'Tattooing and Its History', Westminster Review, March 1898, pp. 320–3.
4 T. W. Dodd, 'To Remove Tattooing', Scientific American, 2 May 1891, p. 273.
5 'Tattoo Marks', Scientific American, 26 September 1891, p. 273; 'Removal of Tattoo Marks: Dr. Baillot's Method', Scientific American, 25 January 1896, p. 55; 'Removal of Tattoo Marks', Scientific American, 27 May 1899, p. 344.
6 Ibid., p. 344.
7 'Origin of Tattooing', Scientific American, 19 September 1896, p. 236; 'The Art of Tattooing', Scientific American, 23 April 1898, p. 265; R. I. Geare, 'Tattooing Among Savages', Scientific American, 12 September 1903, pp. 189–90.
8 'Tattooing among Savages', p. 190.
9 Parry, Tattoo, p. 84.
10 Ibid., p. 85.
11 A. Farenholt, 'Some Statistical Observations Concerning Tattooing as Seen by a Recruiting Surgeon', U.S. Naval Bulletin, VII/1 (1913), pp. 21–6.
12 'Tattooing of Soldiers of Empire Division Forbidden,' New York Times, 1918.
13 Farenholt, 'Some Statistical Observations', p. 26.
14 Parry, Tattoo, p. 44.
15 Ibid., p. 45.
16 Newark Tribune (Ohio), 18 December 1902.

17 C.H. Fellowes, *The Tattoo Book* (Princeton, NJ, 1971).
18 *Kansas City Times*, December 1905.
19 For more information on Gus Wagner, see Alan Govenar, *American Tattoo* (San Francisco, 1996).
20 John Michael Vlach, 'American Folk Art, Questions and Quandaries', *Winterthur Portfolio*, xv/4 (1980), pp. 345–55.
21 Alan Govenar, *Flash From the Past: Classic American Tattoo Designs 1890–1965* (Honolulu, 1994), Alan Govenar, 'Continuity and Change in the Aesthetics of Tattooing', in *Pierced Hearts and True Love: A Century of Drawings for Tattoos* (New York, 1995), pp. 80–91, and Alan Govenar, 'The Variable Context of Chicano Tattooing', in *Marks of Civilization*, ed. Arnold Rubin (Los Angeles, 1988).
22 Leonard L. St Clair and Alan B. Govenar, *Stoney Knows How: Life as a Tattoo Artist* (Lexington, Kentucky, 1981), pp. 135–8.
23 Parry, *Tattoo*, p. 48.
24 *Ibid.*, p. 52.
25 *Ibid.*, p. 48.
26 Alan Govenar, interview with Leonard St Clair, 6 February 1976.
27 St Clair and Govenar, *Stoney*, p. xix. For more information, see K. Winkler, 'When Art is a Skin Game: An Interview with Charlie Wagner', *Collier's Magazine*, 13 February 1926, p. 10; 'Old Tattooer Talks Shop', *Science Digest*, March 1945, pp. 21–3.
28 'N.Y. State Assembly Passes Bill Making It Misdemeanor to Tattoo Children Under 16 yrs', *New York Times*, 21 February 1933, p. 13, col. 1.
29 'Prosperity Flourishes Unchecked in the Tattoo Industry', *Literary Digest*, 1 October 1932, pp. 32–3.
30 For more information on Betty Broadbent and the exhibition of women in the circus and carnival, see Margot Mifflin, *Bodies of Subversion: A Secret History of Women and Tattoo* (New York, 1997).
31 Alan Govenar, personal interview with Betty Broadbent, 12 November 1982.
32 *Ibid.*
33 *Ibid.*
34 Judy Aurre, 'Meet Betty Broadbent, *Tattoo Historian*, November 1982, pp. 20–1, 40.
35 *Ibid.*, p. 40.
36 Arthur H. Lewis, *Carnival* (New York, 1970), pp. 155–61.
37 *Ibid.*, p. 157.
38 Alan Govenar, telephone interview with Chappie Fox, 3 January 1981.
39 Marcia Tucker, 'Pssst! Wanna See My Tattoo', *MS*, April 1976, pp. 31–3.
40 Govenar, interview.
41 Hannibal Coons, 'Skin Game Michelangelos', *Collier's Magazine*, 12 December 1942, pp. 24–6.
42 Helen Cumming, 'War Booms the Tattooing Art', *New York Times*, 19 September, 1943, p. 38.
43 St Clair and Govenar, *Stoney*, p. 76.
44 *Ibid.*, pp. 61, 81, 86–8.
45 Alan Govenar and Bruce Lane, 'Stoney Knows How' (film, 1984).
46 Marshall Davenport, 'He Tattoos the Scars Away', *Saturday Evening Post*, 12 January 1946, p. 6.
47 William Kaufman, 'Tattooing Could Save Your Life', *Science Digest*, October 1952, pp. 71–3.
48 'Charlie Wagner Fined for Failure to Sterilize Needles,' *New York Times*, 27 September 1944, p. 23, col. 4.

49 Leonard L. St Clair interview with Alan Govenar, 10 May 1976.
50 *Ibid.*
51 'Poll Shows Decline in Tattooing Among Seamen', *New York Times*, 11 August 1946, sec. 5, p. 6, col. 7.
52 Alan Govenar, telephone interviews with Army, Air Force, and Navy Recruiting Officers, 7 April 1982.
53 Rex Bonesteel, 'Vanishing Tattoo', *Holiday*, June 1953, pp. 29–31.
54 For more information, see Gay Talese, 'Twenty Million Tattooed: Why?', *New York Times Sunday Magazine*, 22 November 1959, pp. 42–9.
55 Leo Burnett, 'The Marlboro Story: How One of America's Most Popular Filter Cigarettes Got That Way', *New Yorker*, 15 November 1958, pp. 41–3; 'PR Man Fones, Adman Burnett Bares Secrets of Modest Marlboro He-man', *Advertising Age*, 29, 17 November 1958, pp. 3, 9.
56 Bruce A. Lohof, 'The Higher Meaning of Marlboro Cigarettes', *Journal of Popular Culture*, III (1969), pp. 442–50.
57 Talese, 'Twenty Million Tattooed', p. 42.
58 'Find Out What Tattooed Man is Really Like', *Science Newsletter*, 31 May 1958, p. 342.
59 R. P. Youniss, *The Relationship of Tattoos to Personal Adjustment* (New London, 1959).
60 R. W. B. Scutt and C. Gotch, *Art, Sex and Symbol: The Mystery of Tattooing* (New York, 1986), p. 116.
61 'Ban on Tattooing', *New York Times*, 10 October 1961, p. 45, col. 4.
62 'N.Y. State Supreme Court Rules Unconstitutional '61 Ban on Tattooing', *New York Times*, 2 July 1963, p. 31, col. 2. 'N.Y. State Appellate Division Overturns '63 Supreme Court Decision', *New York Times*, 2 December 1964, p. 49, col. 2.
63 'ACLU to File Brief in N.Y. State Appeals Court', *NewYork Times*, 20 March 1966, p. 76, col. 6; 'Court Upholds Ban', *New York Times*, 3 June 1966, p. 41, col. 1.
64 Alan Govenar inteview with Leonard L. St Clair, 24 September 1977.
65 Alan Govenar interview with Dave Yurkew, 12 November 1982.
66 St Clair and Govenar, *Stoney*, pp. xxvi, xxix.
67 'Recruits for South Vietnams's New Junk Fleet are Tattooed', *New York Times*, 29 July 1962, p. 14, col. 3.
68 For more information, see Govenar, 'Continuity and Change'.

14 SUSAN BENSON: INSCRIPTIONS OF THE SELF

 1 Michael O'Hanlon, *Reading the Skin: Adornment, Display and Society among the Wahgi* (London, 1989), p. 10.
 2 Terence Turner, 'The Social Skin', in *Not Work Alone: a Cross-Cultural View of Activities Superfluous to Survival*, eds Jeremy Cherfas and Roger Lewin (London, 1980), pp. 112–40.
 3 See, for example, Marilyn Strathern, 'The Self in Self-Decoration', *Oceania*, XLIX (1979), pp. 241–57; Marilyn Strathern, *The Gender of the Gift* (Berkeley, 1988).
 4 Nicole Loraux, 'Therefore, Socrates is Immortal', in *Fragments for a History of the Human Body*, Part II, ed. Michael Feher (New York, 1989), pp. 12–45.
 5 Michel Foucault, *Discipline And Punish: the Birth of the Prison* (Harmondsworth, 1977), p. 25.
 6 Arnold Rubin, 'Tattoo Renaissance', in *Marks of Civilization: Artistic Transformations of the Human Body*, ed. Arnold Rubin (Los Angeles, 1988), pp. 233–62.
 7 C. M. Hurt, interviewed by Body Modification Enzine, (http://www.bme.freeQ.com.people/cmhurt/index.html, August, 1998).

8 Alexandre Lacassagne, quoted in Jane Caplan, '"Speaking Scars": The Tattoo in Popular Practice and Medico-Legal Debate in Nineteenth-Century Europe', *History Workshop Journal*, XLIV, Autumn 1997, pp. 104–42.

9 Alfred Gell, *Wrapping in Images: Tattooing in Polynesia* (Oxford, 1993), pp. 38–9.

10 For a brief general account in English, see Stephan Oettermann, 'An Art as Old as Humanity', in *Tattoo*, ed. Stefan Richter, pp. 11–17; see also his *Zeichen auf der Haut, die Geschichte der Tatowierung in Europa* (Frankfurt, 1979). See also Robin Scutt and Christopher Gotch, *Skin Deep: the Mysteries of Tattooing*, London, 1974).

11 For a brief but suggestive account, see Gell, *Wrapping*, pp. 8–11.

12 I am grateful to Deborah Thom for drawing my attention to the longevity of harsh regimes of corporal punishment in British military and penal institutions. For a discussion of tattooing among women prostitutes in the nineteenth century and how those tattoos were represented see Jane Caplan, 'Educating the Eye: the tattooed prostitute', in *Sexology in Culture*, ed. Lucy Bland and Laura Doan (Cambridge, 1998), pp. 100–15.

13 Jean-Thierry Maertens, *Le Dessein sur la Peau: Essai d'Anthropologie des Inscriptions Tegumentaires* (Paris, 1978).

14 Steve Beard, 'The tattooed Lady: a mythology', in *Tattooed Women*, ed. Chris Wroblewski (London, 1992).

15 Judy Tuttle, 'The Great Omi', in *Modern Primitives: an Investigation of Contemporary Adornment and Ritual*, ed. V. Vale and Andrea Juno (San Francisco, 1989), pp. 119–21.

16 Tattooing was fashionable, for example, among both male and female members of the British and European aristocracy at the end of the nineteenth century; see Scutt and Gotch, *Skin deep*; Oettermann, 'An Art'; and Bradley, Chapter 9 in this volume.

17 See Oettermann, 'An Art'; Oettermann, *Zeichen*; and Oettermann's essay in this volume; also George Burchett, *Memoirs of a Tattooist* (London, 1958); Albert Parry, *Tattoo: Secrets of a Strange Art as Practised among the Natives of the United States* (1933, reprinted 1971, New York); Michael McCabe, *New York City Tattoo: the Oral History of an Urban Art* (Honolulu, 1996); and Bradley, Chapter 9, this volume.

18 Michael McCabe, 'The Moskowitz Brothers', *Tattoo*, 109 (September 1998), pp. 75–9. Reprinted from McCabe, *New York City Tattoo*. For other accounts of twentieth-century practice in the USA, see Clinton Sanders, *Customizing the Body: the Art and Culture of Tattooing* (Philadelphia, 1989); Alan Govenar, 'The Changing Image of Tattooing in American Culture', *Journal of American Culture*, V/2, pp. 30–7, and 'The Variable Context of Chicano Tattooing', in *Marks*, ed. Rubin. There is also valuable material to be found in Lyle Tuttle's series of publications, *Tattoo Historian* (vols i-ii), in the interviews with Don Ed Hardy and Lyle Tuttle in *Modern Primitives*, eds Vale and Juno, as well as in material posted on the Internet: see, for example, Steve Gilbert's interviews with Crazy Eddy Funk, 23 November 1996 (http://tattoos.com.funk/index.htm), or with Lyle Tuttle and Ed Hardy, for *The Tattoo History Source Book* (http://tattoos.com/jane/steve/toc.htm).

19 For a succinct and lucid summary of the American 'tattoo renaissance', see Arnold Rubin, 'The Tattoo Renaissance', in *Marks*, ed. Rubin; see also *Modern Primitives*, ed. Vale and Juno.

20 Historically oriented publications by practitioners and enthusiasts include Lyle and Judy Tuttle's *Tattoo Historian*, and Chuck Eldridge's *The Archive File*. Tuttle's personal collection of books, equipment, 'flash' and other memorabilia forms the basis for his Tattoo Museum in San Fransisco. A similar museum, established by the Dutch artist Hanky Panky (Henk Schiffmacher), exists in Amsterdam.

21 Vale and Juno, interview with Jim Ward, in *Modern Primitives*, ed. Vale and Juno, p.161. For other accounts of the development of the West Coast piercing scene, see Vale and Juno, interview with Fakir Musafar, in *Modern Primitives*, ed. Vale and Juno, pp. 6–24; for the role of Alan Oversby in Britain, see his obituary, by Simon Fraser, in *Tattoo International*, CLXII, p. 18.

22 Quotations from Vale and Juno, interviews with Hanky Panky and with Don Ed Hardy, in *Modern Primitives*, ed. Vale and Juno, pp. 137–8 and 54.

23 Don Ed Hardy, interviewed by Steve Gilbert, *Tattoo History Sourcebook* (http://www.tattoos.com/jane/steve/edhardy.htm, 1997).

24 Don Ed Hardy, *ibid*.

25 Shannon Larratt, interviewed by Raven Rowanchilde (http://www.bme.freeQ.com/people/shannon/index.html, 1998).

26 V. Vale and Andrea Juno, 'Introduction', in *Modern Primitives*, ed. Vale and Juno, p. 5.

27 Vale and Juno, interview with Greg Kulz, in *Modern Primitives*, ed. Vale and Juno, p. 155.

28 Vale and Juno, interview with Don Ed Hardy, in *Modern Primitives*, ed. Vale and Juno, p. 52.

29 The tensions between these assertions of individuality and the recognition of commonality among those who choose to 'step outside' the mainstream is also recognized. The tattoo artist Paul Booth, for example, asserts that while 'some people are just copying others', getting a tattoo also reflects 'a desire to stand out and be unique' – adding, however, 'and then you find other unique people like you and then you form a group' (Paul Booth, interviewed by Damian (http://darkimages.com/newguy.new.htm, 1998). Such contradictions may plausibly be linked to the development of more and more 'extreme' forms of bodily intervention. Steve Hawarth, for example, an American who specializes in metal implants, sees the growing demand for what he offers as linked to 'extreme individualism. Ten years ago if you had a piercing or a tattoo you stood alone, and today, even though piercing and tattooing are still a wonderful form of self-expression, you stand in a group' (interview by Shannon Larratt, hhtp://www.bme.freeQ.com.people/htc.html, August 1998).

30 Adam Bramley, interviewed by Putrid Pete, *Tattoo Savage*, XXIV, September 1998, p. 43.

31 Genesis P-Orridge, quoted in Vale and Juno, interview with G. and P. P-Orridge, in *Modern Primitives*, ed. Vale and Juno, p. 198; Lyle Tuttle, quoted in Vale and Juno, interview with Lyle Tuttle, *ibid*., p. 116.

32 Keith Alexander, *Tattoo Savage*, XXIV, September 1998, p. 21.

33 Vale and Juno, interview with Vyvyn Lazonga, in *Modern Primitives*, pp. 125–6.

34 Ron Salisbury, 'The Protestant Boy Gets Tattooed', *Tattooing International*, CLV, November 1994, p. 11.

35 Fakir Musafar, in *Modern Primitives*, ed. Vale and Juno, p. 8.

36 Tattoo artist Jon Cobb (http://www.bme.freeQ.com.people/jon2/index.html, August 1998).

37 Alex Binnie, in *Skin Shows: The Art of Tattoo*, vol. IV, ed. Chris Wroblewski (London, 1991), p. 7.

38 Debate posted at http://www.ambient.on.ca/bodmod/mutilate.html, August 1998.

39 James Cowan, 'Maori Tattooing Survivals', *Journal of the Polynesian Society*, 30, 1921, p. 242; quoted in Peter Gathercole 'Contexts of Maori Moko', in *Marks*, 1988, pp. 171–7.

40 It is in this light, perhaps, that we should interpret the considerable amount of work tattooists are asked to do to cover up or alter existing designs.

41 Don Ed Hardy, interviewed by Juno and Vale, *Modern Primitives*, p. 51.

42 Jon Cobb (http://www.bme.freeQ.com.people/jon2/index/html, 1998).
43 Vale and Juno, 'Introduction', *Modern Primitives*, p. 5.
44 Ron Salisbury, quoted by Madam Chinchilla, *Tattooing International*, CLIII, June 1994, pp. 10–11.
45 The phrase is from Sonnet 94.
46 Paul Booth, interviewed by Damian (http://darkimages.com/newguy/new.htm, 1998).
47 'Cort's Body Art Page' (http://www.halcyon.com.maelstrm/site/bodyart/index.html, August 1998).
48 Alfred Gell, *Wrapping*, p. 37.
49 Lyrics from 'So Many Tears', from the album *Me Against The World*, Atlantic Records, 1995.

Select Bibliography

Anzieu, D., *The Skin-Ego: A Psychoanalytic Approach to the Self* (New Haven, 1989)

Bolton, G., 'Pictures on the Human Skin', *Strand Magazine*, XIII/76 (1897), pp. 425–34

Bradley, J. and H. Maxwell-Stewart, '"Behold the Man": Power, Observation and the Tattooed Convict', *Australian Studies*, XII/1 (Summer 1997), pp. 71–97

——, 'Embodied Explorations: Investigating Tattoos and the Transportation System', *Representing Convicts*, ed. I. Duffield and J. Bradley (London, 1997), pp. 183–203

——, 'Convict Tattoos: Tales of Freedom and Coercion', *Convict Love Tokens*, ed. M. Field and T. Millett (Adelaide, 1998), pp. 47–52.

Bronnikov, A., 'Telltale Tattoos in Russian Prisons', *Natural History*, XI (1993), pp. 50–59

Brush, P., 'Metaphors of Inscription: Discipline, Plasticity and the Rhetoric of Choice', *Feminist Review*, LVIII (1998), pp. 22–43

Burchett, G., *Memoirs of a Tattooist* (London, 1958)

Caplan, J., '"Speaking Scars": The Tattoo in Popular Practice and Medico-Legal Debate in Nineteenth-Century Europe', *History Workshop Journal*, XLIV (1997), pp. 104–42

——, 'Educating the Eye: The Tattooed Prostitute', in *Sexology in Culture*, ed. L. Bland and L. Doan (Cambridge, 1998), pp. 100–15

——, '"One of the Strangest Relics of a Former State": Tattoos and the Discourse of Criminality in Europe 1880–1920', *The Criminal and His Scientists: Essays on the History of Criminology*, ed. P. Becker and R. Wetzell (Cambridge, forthcoming)

Carswell, J., *Coptic Tattoo Designs* (Beirut, 1958)

Caruchet, W., *Tatouages et tatoués* (Paris, 1976)

Castellani, A., *Ribelle per la pelle: Storia e cultura dei tatuaggi* (Genoa, 1995)

Cowan, J., 'Maori Tattooing Survivals', *Journal of the Polynesian Society*, XXX (1921), pp. 241–5

De Blasio, Abele, *Il tatuaggio* (Naples, 1905)

Delarue, Jacques, and Robert Girard, *Les tatouages du milieu* (Paris, 1950)

Delio, Michelle, *Tattoo. The Exotic Art of Skin Decoration* (London, 1994)

Dye, Ira, 'The Tattoos of Early American Seafarers, 1796-1818', *Proceedings of the American Philosophical Society*, CXXXIII (1989), pp. 520–54

Ebensten, Hanns, *Pierced Hearts and True Love. An Illustrated History of the Origin and Development of European Tattooing and a Survey of its Present State* (London, 1953)

Elm, Susanna, '"Pierced by Bronze Needles": Anti-Montanist Charges of Ritual Stigmatization in their Fourth-Century Context', *Journal of Early Christian Studies*, IV/4 (1996), pp. 409–39

Fellowes, C. H., *The Tattoo Book* (Princeton, NJ, 1971)

Field, H., *Body-Marking in South-Western Asia* (Cambridge, MA, 1958)

Fleming, J., 'The Renaissance Tattoo', *Res*, XXXI (1997), pp. 34–52

Fletcher, R., *Tattooing Among Civilized People* (Washington, DC, 1883)

Franks, A. W., 'Tattooed Man from Burmah', *Journal of the Anthropological Institute of Great Britain and Ireland*, II (1873), pp. 228–32

Gell, A., *Wrapping In Images. Tattooing in Polynesia* (Oxford, 1993)

Gernet, M. N., 'Tatuirovka v mestakh zakliucheniia g. Moskvy', *Prestupnyi mir Moskvy. Sbornik statei*, ed. M. N. Gernet (Moscow, 1924)

Gotthold, K., 'Vergleichende Untersuchungen über die Tätowierung bei Normalen, Geisteskranken und Kriminellen', *Klinik für psychische und nervose Krankheiten*, IX (1914), pp. 193–252

Govenar, A., 'The changing image of tattooing in American culture', *Journal of American Culture*, V/2, pp. 30–7

——, 'The Variable Context of Chicano Tattooing', *Marks of Civilization*, ed. A. Rubin (Los Angeles, 1988)

——, 'The Influx of Tattooing into the Western World from Herodotus to O'Reilly', *Anthropology of Symbols*, ed. O. P. Joshi (Jaipur, 1992), pp. 72–85

——, *Flash From the Past: Classic American Tattoo Designs 1890–1965* (Honolulu, 1994)

——, 'Continuity and Change in the Aesthetics of Tattooing', *Pierced Hearts and True Love: A Century of Drawings for Tattoos* (New York, 1995), pp. 80–91

——, *American Tattoo* (San Francisco, 1996)

Graven, J., *L'argot et le tatouage des criminels* (Neuchâtel, 1962)

Gray, J., *I Love Mom: An Irreverent History of the Tattoo* (Toronto, 1994)

Guest, H., 'Curiously Marked: Tattooing, Masculinity and Nationality in Eighteenth-Century British Perceptions of the South Pacific', *Painting and the Politics of Culture: New Essays on British Art, 1700–1850*, ed. J. Barrell (Oxford, 1992), pp. 101–34

Gustafson, M. T., '*Inscripta in fronte*: Penal Tattooing in Late Antiquity', *Classical Antiquity*, XVI (1997), pp. 79–105

Hambly, W. D., *The History of Tattooing and Its Significance with Some Account of Other Forms of Corporal Marking* (London, 1925)

Hardy, D. E., *Forever Yes: Art of the New Tattoo* (Honolulu, 1992)

——, *Sailor Jerry Collins: American Tattoo Master* (Honolulu, 1994)

Jaguer, J., *The Tattoo: A Pictorial History* (Horndean, Hants., 1990)

Joest, W., *Tätowiren, Narbenzeichen und Körperbemalen: Ein Beitrag zur vergleichenden Ethnologie* (Berlin, 1887)

Jones, C. P., '*Stigma*: Tattooing and Branding in Graeco-Roman Antiquity', *The Journal of Roman Studies*, LXXVII (1987), pp. 139–55

Joshi, O. P., 'Tattooing and Tattooers: A Socio-cultural Analysis', *Marks and Meaning: Anthropology of Symbols*, ed. O. P. Joshi (Jaipur, 1992)

Kent, D., 'Decorative Bodies: The Significance of Convict Tattoos', *Journal of Australian Studies*, LV (1997), pp. 78–88

Kogan, I. M., *Tatuirovka sredi prestupnikov* (Odessa, 1928)

Krakow, A., *The Total Tattoo Book* (New York, 1994)

Lacassagne, A., *Les tatouages: étude anthropologique et médico-légale* (Paris, 1881)

——, 'Recherches sur les tatouages et principalement du tatouage chez les criminels', *Annales d'hygiène publique et de médecine légale*, 3rd. ser., V (1881), pp. 289–304

Lauffer, O., 'Über die Geschichte und den heutigen volkstümlichen Gebrauch der Tätowierung in Deutschland', *Wörter und Sachen. Kulturhistorische Zeitschrift für Sprache und Sachforschung*, VI (1914/15), pp. 1–14

Lesson, R.P., 'Du tatouage chez les différens peuples de la terre', *Annales maritimes et coloniales*, Part II (1820), pp. 280–92

Luedecke, H. E., 'Erotische Tätowierungen', *Anthropophyteia*, IV (1907), pp. 75–83

McCabe, M., *New York City Tattoo: The Oral History of an Urban Art* (Honolulu, 1996)

Maertens, J.-T., *Le dessein sur la peau: Essai d'anthropologie des inscriptions tégumentaires* (Paris, 1978)

Meyer, K., 'Tätowierung bei den Iren', *Zeitschrift für Celtische Philologie*, X (1915), pp. 400–01

Mifflin, M., *Bodies of Subversion: A Secret History of Women and Tattoo* (New York, 1997)

Minovici, N., 'Les tatouages en Roumanie', *Archives des sciences médicales*, IV (1899), pp. 51–104

Mohl, J., 'Mitteilungen auf Tätowierungen, aufgenommen an Soldaten der Garnison Temesvàr', *Mitteilungen der anthropologischen Gesellschaft in Wien*, XXXVIII (1908), pp. 312–20

Napier, A. D., *Masks, Transformation and Paradox* (Berkeley, 1986)

Newman, S., 'Reading the Bodies of Early American Seafarers', *William and Mary Quarterly*, 3rd ser., LV (1998), pp. 59–82

Oettermann, S., 'An Art as Old as Humanity', *Tattoo*, ed. S. Richter (London, 1988), pp. 11–17

——, *Zeichen auf der Haut: Die Geschichte der Tätowierung in Europa* (Frankfurt, 1979; reprinted Hamburg 1994)

O'Hanlon, M., *Reading the Skin: Adornment, Display and Society among the Wahgi* (London, 1989)

Parry, A., *Tattoo: Secrets of a Strange Art as Practised among the Natives of the United States* (1933, reprinted 1971, New York)

Peixoto, R., 'A tatuagem em Portugal', *Revista de Sciencias Naturaes e Sociaes*, II (1893), pp. 97–111

Pick, D., *Faces of Degeneration: A European Disorder c. 1848–c. 1918* (Cambridge, 1989)

Pierced Hearts and True Love: A Century of Drawings for Tattoos, exh. cat., The Drawing Center (New York and Honolulu, 1995)

Plas, R., 'Tatouages et criminalité', *Histoire de la criminalité française*, ed. L. Mucchielli (Paris, 1994), pp. 156–67

Polhemus, T., *The Customized Body* (Baltimore, 1997)

——, *Body Art* (Boston, 1999)

Richie, D. and I. Buruma, *The Japanese Tattoo* (New York and Tokyo, 1980)

Richter, S., *Tattoo* (London, 1988)

Riecke, E., *Das Tatuierungswesen im heutigen Europa* (Jena, 1925)

Riria, K. T. and D. Simmons, *Maori Tattoo* (Auckland, 1989)

Risley, H. H., 'Notes on Some Indian Tatu Marks', *Man: A Monthly Record of Anthropological Science*, 73–82 (July 1902), pp. 74–5

Robley, H. G. *Moko or Maori Tattoing* (London, 1896; reprinted Auckland, 1987)

Rubin, A. ed., *Marks of Civilization: Artistic Transformation of the Human Body* (Los Angeles, 1988)

St Clair, l. L. and A. B. Govenar, *Stoney Knows How: Life as a Tattoo Artist* (Lexington, KY., 1981)

Sallilas, R. *El tatuage en su evolución histórica, en sus differentes caracterizaciones antiguas y actuales y en los delincuentes franceses, italianos y españoles* (Madrid, 1908)

Salisbury, R., 'The Protestant Boy Gets Tattooed', *Tattooing International*, CLV, November 1994

Sanders, C., *Customizing the Body: the Art and Culture of Tattooing* (Philadelphia, 1989)

——, 'Organizational Constraints on Tattoo Images: A Sociological Analysis of Artistic Style', *The Meanings of Things: Material Culture and Symbolic Expression*, ed. I. Hodder (New York, 1989), pp. 232–41

Schiffmacher, H. and B. Riemschneider, eds, *1000 Tattoos* (Cologne, 1996)

Schönfeld, W., 'Tätowierte Frauen um und nach der Jahrhundertwende', *Der Hautartzt*, VI/11 (1955), pp. 487–90

——, *Körperbemalen, Brandmarken, Tätowieren: Nach griechischen, römischen Schriftstellern,*

Dichtern, neuzeitlichen Veröffentlichungen und eigenen Erfahrungen, vorzüglich in Europa (Heidelberg, 1960)

Scutt, R. and C. Gotch, *Skin Deep: The Mysteries of Tattooing* (London, 1974)

——, *Art, Sex and Symbol: The Mystery of Tattooing* (London, New York, 1986)

Sinclair, A.T., 'Tattooing – Oriental and Gypsy', *American Anthropologist*, N.S. x/3 (1908), pp. 361–8

Smeaton, O., 'Tattooing and Its History', *Westminster Review* (March 1898), pp. 320–3

Spämer, A., *Die Tätowierung in den deutschen Hafenstädten: Ein Versuch zur Erfassung ihrer Formen und ihres Bildgutes* (Bremen, 1934; reprinted Munich, 1993)

Sperry, K., 'Tattoos and Tattooing: Part I: History and Methodology', *The American Journal of Forensic Medicine and Pathology*, XII/4 (1991), pp. 313–19

Steinen, K. von der, *Die Marquesaner und ihre Kunst* (Berlin, 1925)

Stephen, R. J., 'Tattooed Royalty: Queer Stories of a Queer Craze', *Harmsworth's London Magazine*, I (1898), pp. 472–5

Stetson, G.R., 'Tattooing in Tunis,' *American Anthropologist*, VI (1893), p. 282

Steward, S. M., *Bad Boys and Tough Tattoos: A Social History of the Tattoo with Gangs, Sailors, and Street-Corner Punks, 1950–1965* (Binghamton, NY, 1990)

Stieda, L., 'Etwas über Tätowierung', *Wiener Medizinischer Wochenschrift*, LXI/14 (1 April 1911), pp. 893–8

Strathern, M., 'The Self in Self-Decoration', *Oceania*, LVIX (1979), pp. 241–57

Tattootime, vols 1– , ed. D. E. Hardy (Honolulu, 1982–)

Thévoz, M., *The Painted Body* (New York, 1984)

Tucker, M., 'Tattoo: the State of the Art' *Artforum* (May 1981), pp. 42–7

Turner, T. S., 'The Social Skin', *Not Work Alone: A Cross-Cultural View of Activities Superfluous to Survival*, ed. J. Cherfas and R. Lewin (London, 1980), pp. 112–40

V. Vale and A. Juno, eds, *Modern Primitives: An Investigation of Contemporary Adornment and Ritual* (San Francisco, 1989)

Van Gulik, W. R., *Irezumi: The Pattern of Dermatography in Japan* (Leiden, 1982)

Vervaeck, L., 'Le tatouage en Belgique', *Archives de l'anthropologie criminelle*, XXII (1909), pp. 333–62

Warlich, C., *Tätowierungen. Vorlagealbum des Königs der Tätowierer*, ed. S. Oettermann (Dortmund, 1981)

Wroblewski, C., *Skin Shows*, 4 vols (London, 1989–95)

Acknowledgements

Putting together this collection of essays has been a matter of serendipity, good luck and generous collaboration. The research from which I derived the original idea was funded by the National Endowment for the Humanities, the John Simon Guggenheim Memorial Foundation and Bryn Mawr College, whose support I acknowledge with thanks. I owe immense gratitude to all the contributors for giving me their advice, introducing me to further contacts and, of course, supplying their essays, and for their patience while the project moved from initiation to completion. I would also like to acknowledge the help of a number of friends and colleagues: in the first place, Bob Moeller, indispensable reader of drafts and source of advice and support; Marilyn Young, Alex Binnie and Jane Lindsay, for contributions of time and ideas; the senior members in the USA, Britain and Germany with whom I have discussed this project in recent years; and Michael Leaman, for his enthusiastic support of publication. Ignacio Gallup-Diaz, James Krippner-Martinez and Ella Schaap kindly helped me with references and Don Juan and Luis Garcia with illustrations. My thanks are also due to Lorraine Kirschner and Anna Canavan, who skillfully induced many recalcitrant PC programs to yield their secrets, and to Karoline Cook, who prepared the bibliography.

Photographic Acknowledgements

The editor and publisher wish to express their thanks to the following sources of illustrative material and/or permission to reproduce it (other than those sources mentioned in captions):

Archives Office of Tasmania, Hobart: 120; Elisa Becker: 188; Tim Brightmore: xxi, 247, 248; British Library Reproductions, reproduced by permission of the Trustees of the British Library, London: x, 96, 97, 103, 109, 111; Photo © British Museum, London, reproduced by permission of the Trustees: 3 (right); Ian Buruma: xiii; Photo Courtauld Institute of Art, reproduced by permission of the Hon. Simon Howard: 84; Folger Shakespeare Library, Washington, DC: 47, 53, 59; Photo reproduced by permission of the Hon. Clive and Mrs Gibson: 89; Glasgow University Library: 145, 147, 154; Photos courtesy of the Alan Govenar and Kaleta Doolin Collection: 216, 218; courtesy of Alan Govenar: 220, 224, 227; photo by Alan Govenar: 221; Museum of Fine Arts, Boston, © 1998: 3 (left); Photos courtesy of the Oettermann collection: 195, 197, 201, 205, 206, 208; University of Pennsylvania Library: 160, 162, 166, 169; The Wellcome Institute Library, London: 149.

Index

308

Nazi Germany 26, 211
tattooed entertainers 193–211
tattoos worn by convicts in Plötzensee
prison, Berlin [166]
Gibbons, Artoria 222, 223–5, [224]
Gibbons, Charlie 'Red' 223, 225
Giolo see Jeoly, Prince
Giton 11–12
Glaister, I. (Glasgow surgeon) 140–1
Glasgow 127
Godna (Indian tattooing) 102–17
    convict responses to 115–16
Golgotha 134
Govenar, Alan xvi, xix, xxii
Graptoi brothers 20, 23, 28, 30
'Great Omi, The' (Horace Ridler) 193, 239
Great White Chief John Rutherford, The 198–9
Greece/Greeks xvi, 1, 2, 4–15, 18, 28, 33, 52, 106, 167,
    172
Green, John 131
Green, William 132
Grimm, Bert 226
Guattari, Félix 66
Guerrero, Gonzalo xvii
Guest, Harriet xv
Gulags, Soviet 30
Gunnoo, Bappoo bin 113–14
Gustafson, Mark xvi, 13
Guys Hospital museum (London) 125, [125], [133]
gypsies 26

Habitual Criminals Act (1869) 138
Hadrian, Pope 36, 79
Haggard, H. Rider 141
Hammam studio, Jermyn Street, London 152
Hammarabi 14
Hance, Gertrude 228
Hanky Panky 243
Happy Hooligan 219
Hardy, Don Ed 63, 64, 233, 243–6
Harley Street, London 152
Harriot, Thomas 71, 73, 77, 82
Hawaiians xix
Hawthorne, Nathaniel 30
Hayes, John 200–1, 203
Hebra, F. 200
Hebrews 125
Hell 134
Hellenistic period 6
Hellespont 7
Henderson, Isabel 34, 39
Henry, James 126
Henry, P. L. 39
Hercules 63
Herodas 8, 24
Herodian 6, 33, 35
Herodotus 4, 6–7, 11, 13, 26

Hiberno-Latin literature 33, 79
Hickey, Cornelius 127
High Security Psychiatric Hospital (St Petersburg)
    [188]
Hilary, bishop of Poitiers 18–19, 21, 23, 28
Hildebrandt, Martin 203, 214
Hill, John 124
Hill, Thomas 92, 97
Hilliard, Nicholas 75
Hindus 102–4, 110
Hippocrates 14
Historie of Great Britaine (Speed) 69
Histories (Herodotus)
Hobart (Tasmania) 121, 123, 127–9
Hodges, William 98, 99, [99], 101
Holden, Horace 199
Holy Land xvi, 13, 146
Honu, chief of Vaitahu 196
Hope (virtue) 126
'Hope and Anchor' (on skin) 125, [125]
Hopkins, Tighe 212
Howard, Annie 203
Howard, Frank 203
Hoyle, William 127
Hughes, Robert 132
Huguenots 71, 75
Hull, Mildred 204
Hulton, Paul 73, 75
Hume, Fergus 141
Hunter, Robert 124
Hurt, C. M. 236
Hutin, M. F. 157

'Ice Man' 2
identification and stigmatization 106–13
identity and escape 113–15
Ile de France (Mauritius) 107
Imperial Russia 174–86
imprimo (imprint) 11
In Search of the Picts (Sutherland) 39
India(ns) 79
    Christian 104
    European practice and colonial expansion
        106–13
    inscribing convicts in the 19th century (godna)
        102–17
    stigmatization and identification 106–13
    uprising (1857) 114
Indian, Ocean 107
Ingeborg, Frøken 210–11
Inhabitant of the Island of Nukahiva (Storer) [x]
inscribo (inscribe) 11
'Integræ Naturæ Artisque imago' (Fludd) [53]
Internet 17
Into You see Binnie, Alex
inuro (brand) 11
Irawadi Valley 102

Ireland/Irish 33, 38–44, 78, 128
Iron Age 39
Isidore of Seville 35, 38, 40
Islam xix, 107
Israelites 2
Italy/Italian tattooing xvii, xviii, 11, 15, 59, 139, 156, 158, 163–9, 171, 173, 194, 213
  criminal tattoos (Lombroso) [160]

Jackson, Kenneth 34, 37
James I of England (James VI of Scotland) 68, 80, 81
Janus xix
Japan/Japanese tattooing xi, [xiii], 30, 61, 142, 146, 153, 196, 213, 242, 244
Java 215, 216
Jenny 203
Jeoly, Prince 194
Jerusalem, cross 80, [80]
  pilgrims xviii, 29, 60, 79–81
Jesus Christ *see* Christ, Jesus
Jews 2, 26, 36
JFK (tattooist) [253]
Joest, W. 212
Jogee, Multhoo Byragee [111]
John of Gaddesden *see* Gaddesden, John of
Johnson, Samuel 15
Jones, Christopher xvi, 17, 24, 25, 32, 33
Joseph Kabris, native of Bordeaux, 'Vice-King and Grand Judge of the Isle of Mendoça' (Steinen) 197
Journal of the Resolution's *Voyage* (Marra) [94]
Judaism 13, 52, 238
Jupiter (sign) 46–7
Justinian 4
'Juvenile Delinquency in Early Ireland' (McCone) 43

Kabris, Joseph *see* Cabris, Jean Baptiste
Kali 109
Kamchatka peninsula 196
Katzenjammer Kids 219
Kaufman, Dr William 228
kauterion (brand) 14, 15
Kelly, Stephen 133
Kent, David 131
Kerala (India) 104, 108
Ketch, Jack 134
Key to Unknowne Knowledge 58
Khan, Murdan [111]
Knopwood, Robert 122–4, 130, 135
Kobel, Bernard 222
Koran 110
Korean War 229, 233
Kosoi (Russian vagrant) 185–6
Krishna 102
Kristeva, Julia 63, 64–5
Krusenstern, Admiral 196

Kulz, Greg 244
Kyumonryu Shishin [xiii]

Lacan, Jacques 61, 65, 69
Lacassagne, Alexandre 139, 156–7, 161, [162], 163, 167–8, 171, 212, 237
Lakshmi 103
Lamb, Joseph 134
Lamen 55
Landseer, Edwin 153
Laos 213
Lapidge, Michael 36
Last Supper (Leonardo) 225
Late Antiquity 13
Laudonniere, René de 71
Lawson, Harry 219, 226
Lazonga, Vyvyn 246
Le Moyne de Morgues, Jacques 71, [72], 72, 73, 74, [74], 75–6, [76], [77], 78
Lebor Gabála Érenn ('The Book of Invasions of Ireland') 39–42
Ledyard, John 99, 100
Lee, Steve 203
lekythos 3
  red-figure *lekythos* showing tattooed Maenad [3]
Leonardo da Vinci 225
Leppmann, Dr 165
Lessing, Gotthold 1
Letter to the Galatians 10, 29, 35–7, 78, 80
Levant 15
Lévi-Strauss, Claude 24
Leviticus 2, 13, 29, 35–6, 78
lex Aelia Sentia (AD 4) 22
Library, Bobby 225
Lichas 11–12
Lilly, William 57
Lindow man III 35
Line, Mr 205
Linnaean system 89
Lister, Joseph 162
Lithgow, William [80], 80–1
Locard, Edmond 167–8
locksmith tattoo (Minovici) [169]
Lohof, Bruce 230
Lombardy 159
Lombroso, Cesare 15, 105, 138–9, 156–9, [160], 161, 163–6, 168, 171–2
Lopo Gonsales, Cape of 49
Loraux, Nicole 235
Loreto, shrine of xvii, [xviii], 159–60, 213
Louis XVIII 198
Lucian 6, 13, 14
Lucifer, bishop of Cagliari 19
Luedecke, Hugo Ernst 205, 207
Luke 130
Lycurgus 3, [3]